Singapore in the New Millennium

The **Institute of Southeast Asian Studies (ISEAS)** was established as an autonomous organization in 1968. It is a regional research centre for scholars and other specialists concerned with modern Southeast Asia, particularly the many-faceted problems of stability and security, economic development, and political and social change.

The Institute's research programmes are the Regional Economic Studies (RES, including ASEAN and APEC), Regional Strategic and Political Studies (RSPS), and Regional Social and Cultural Studies (RSCS).

The Institute is governed by a twenty-two-member Board of Trustees comprising nominees from the Singapore Government, the National University of Singapore, the various Chambers of Commerce, and professional and civic organizations. An Executive Committee oversees day-to-day operations; it is chaired by the Director, the Institute's chief academic and administrative officer.

Singapore in the New Millennium

Challenges Facing the City-State

Edited by
Derek da Cunha

ISEAS

INSTITUTE OF SOUTHEAST ASIAN STUDIES
Singapore

First published in Singapore in 2002 by
Institute of Southeast Asian Studies
30 Heng Mui Keng Terrace
Pasir Panjang
Singapore 119614
Internet e-mail: publish@iseas.edu.sg
World Wide Web: http://www.iseas.edu.sg/pub.html

ISEAS Library Cataloguing-in-Publication Data

Singapore in the new millennium : challenges facing the city-state / edited by Derek da Cunha.

Papers presented to a Conference on Singapore in the New Millennium : Challenges Facing the City-State, Singapore, 25 August 1999, organized by the Institute of Southeast Asian Studies.

1. Singapore—Congresses.
2. Singapore—Politics and government—Congresses.
3. Singapore—Foreign relations—Congresses.
4. Singapore—Economic conditions—Congresses.
5. Singapore—Social conditions—Congresses.

I. Da Cunha, Derek.
II. Institute of Southeast Asian Studies.
III. Conference on Singapore in the New Millennium : Challenges Facing the City-State (1999 : Singapore)

DS599.64 S612 2002 sls2001023169

ISBN 981-230-130-5 (soft cover)
ISBN 981-230-131-3 (hard cover)

Printed in Singapore by Seng Lee Press Pte Ltd.

CONTENTS

PREFACE

The volume of literature on Singapore society, politics, and economics continues to grow at a steady rate. Few other countries of similar size have been so extensively written on. The reason why Singapore continues to come under the microscope of intellectual analysis is that it is unique in many ways. From the way it is governed to the way it conducts its commerce, Singapore has generally charted its own course different from what is generally pursued by most other countries.

Another book on Singapore can only be justified if there are new things to say. In that respect, if this book does reveal to the reader something new, it is a consequence of the impact on Singapore of the significant changes taking place in an increasingly interdependent world, and the equally significant geopolitical changes that have taken place in Singapore's own neighbourhood — Southeast Asia. These changes have occasioned economic, political, intellectual, and societal responses from both the Singaporean state and people, whose defining feature is to keep pace and anticipate change.

This book grew out of a one-day conference of the same name organized by the Institute of Southeast Asian Studies in August 1999. Eight papers were presented at that conference, of which seven were selected, revised in 2001, and now appear as chapters in this book. The editor then commissioned three more chapters, so as to make the book more rounded. The conclusion draws together some of the major themes in the various chapters, highlighting some key challenges that Singapore is likely to face in the years ahead and also reflecting on the significance of the 2001 general election.

The editor would like to thank Mr Jesse Cortes, a graduate student at the University of California, San Diego, for assistance in editing this volume. He would also like to thank the authors of the various chapters for their patience in waiting for the book's publication.

Derek da Cunha

CONTRIBUTORS

Ang Peng Hwa teaches media law and management at the Nanyang Technological University, Singapore, where he is Vice-Dean of the School of Communication Studies. He is a lawyer by training and holds a Ph.D. in the mass media from Michigan State University. His research interest is in legal and policy issues in the media covering areas such as copyright, censorship, and content regulation on the Internet. In Singapore, he has served as the legal adviser to the advertising regulator, the Advertising Standards Authority of Singapore from 1994 till 2000. He has consulted for government and private bodies in Singapore on law and policy regarding the Internet. Internationally, he has consulted for international agencies such as the United Nations Development Programme, and has presented papers to government officials from Asia and the European Union.

Derek da Cunha is a Senior Fellow at the Institute of Southeast Asian Studies, Singapore, where he is Co-ordinator of the Regional Strategic and Political Studies (RSPS) programme and Editor of the journal *Contemporary Southeast Asia*. He has M.Phil. and Ph.D. degrees in the field of International Relations from Cambridge University and the Australian National University respectively. His areas of research specialization include Asia-Pacific defence and security issues, and Singapore society and politics. He is author of the book *The Price of Victory: The 1997 Singapore General Election and Beyond* (Singapore: Institute of Southeast Asian Studies), and editor of *Debating Singapore: Reflective Essays* (Singapore: Institute of Southeast Asian Studies). He is a member of the London-based International Institute for Strategic Studies.

N. Ganesan received his tertiary education in North America, earning a B.A. (Hons.) and an M.A. from McMaster University in Canada and a Ph.D. from Northern Illinois University. He is currently a Senior Lecturer in the Department of Political Science with concurrent responsibilities in the Southeast Asian

Studies Programme at the National University of Singapore. He has also lectured at the Institute of Defence and Strategic Studies, Singapore. His teaching, research, and publication interests are in contemporary Southeast Asian politics and foreign policy. He also lectures regularly for the Singapore Ministry of Defence's Central National Education Office as well as for the Foundation Course for Administrative Service Officers and Induction Course for Senior Officers at the Civil Service College, Singapore.

Kwa Chong Guan is Head of External Programmes at the Institute of Defence and Strategic Studies, Singapore, and Co-Chair of the Singapore National Committee of the Council for Security Co-operation in the Asia-Pacific (CSCAP). He was previously Head of the SAFTI Military Institute's Department of Strategic Studies (which he helped establish) and concurrently Adjunct Associate Professor in the Division of History of the National Institute of Education's School of Arts. He has authored papers on the heuristics of Asian security practice, Singapore historiography, and Southeast Asian art history. He is also co-editor of *Oral History in Southeast Asia, Theory and Method* (Singapore: Institute of Southeast Asian Studies).

Raymond Lim is a Member of Parliament in Singapore, and on 1 December 2001 was appointed a Minister of State (Foreign Affairs and Trade and Industry). He was Managing Director of Temasek Holdings. Prior to that, he was the Chief Executive Officer of DBS Securities and Group Chief Economist of ABN AMRO Asia Securities where he was ranked as one of the best economists in Asia by international fund managers. A Rhodes Scholar, he holds First Class degrees in Economics and Law from the Universities of Adelaide, Oxford, and Cambridge. He is a Board member in the Singapore Broadcasting Authority and Energy Market Authority and Council member of the Economic Society of Singapore.

Linda Low is Associate Professor, Department of Business Policy, National University of Singapore. Her areas of research specialization include public sector economics and public policy, public enterprises and privatization, social security and retirement, health economics, human resource development and manpower policies, international trade and regionalism, development economics, and macroeconomic policies related to the Asia-Pacific and ASEAN economies. She has consulted for various ministries and agencies in Singapore, the United Nations Development Programme (UNDP), the United

Nations Economic and Social Commission for Asia and Pacific (ESCAP), the International Labour Organization (ILO), the Asian Development Bank (ADB), the Asian Secretariat, and the Commonwealth Secretariat. She is a board member of the Central Provident Fund, a Senior Adjunct Fellow at the Institute of Policy Studies, Singapore, a committee member of the Financial Planning Association of Singapore, and a council member of the Singapore Institute of International Affairs.

J. M. Nathan is Assistant Professor in the School of Education, National Institute of Education, Nanyang Technological University, Singapore. He has taught in colleges and universities in Singapore and North America, and was a research scholar in the National University of Singapore before he was awarded a CIDA scholarship to pursue his doctorate in philosophy at Queen's University in Canada. On his return, his interest in the philosophy of psychology, ethics, and values led him to design and write the curriculum for the values-based critical thinking programme for Temasek Polytechnic, where he is now a consultant. He has written articles in a range of journals, including the annual *Southeast Asian Affairs*.

Jason Tan is Assistant Professor in the Policy and Management Studies Academic Group, National Institute of Education, Nanyang Technological University, Singapore. He obtained his doctorate in comparative education at the State University of New York at Buffalo. His research publications focus on the marketization of education, education achievement of the Malay minority in Singapore, and curriculum policy. He is co-editor of *Education in Singapore: A Book of Readings* (Singapore: Prentice Hall) and *Education in Singapore: Issues and Challenges at the Start of the Twenty-First Century* (Singapore: Prentice Hall). He is also Executive Editor of the *Asia Pacific Journal of Education*.

Simon S. C. Tay is Associate Professor in the Faculty of Law, National University of Singapore, where he teaches international and constitutional law. He is a nominated Member of the Singapore Parliament (NMP), and also chairman of the Singapore Institute of International Affairs. His work focuses on the environment, human rights, and civil society in Asia. A Fulbright scholar, he won the Laylin Prize at the Harvard Law School for the best thesis in international law. He is also a prize-winning writer of fiction and poetry. In January 2000, the World Economic Forum at Davos listed him as a "Global Leader of Tomorrow".

C. J. W.-L. Wee teaches literature and cultural theory at the Nanyang Technological University. He was previously a Fellow at the Institute of Southeast Asian Studies, in its Regional Social and Cultural Studies programme, and a Visiting Fellow at the Committee for Cultural Choices and Global Futures, New Delhi. He was also a co-editor of SOJOURN: *Journal of Social Issues in Southeast Asia*, and now is a member of its advisory committee. He is the author of *Culture, Empire, and the Question of Being Modern* (forthcoming) and the editor of *Local Cultures and the New Asia: The State, Culture, and Capitalism in Southeast Asia* (forthcoming), and has published articles in *Positions: East Asia Cultures Critique* and *New Formations*. He did his postgraduate work at the University of Texas, Austin, and the University of Chicago.

1

THE LIMITS OF A CITY-STATE
Or Are There?

Linda Low

1. Introduction

Singapore is *sui generis* as a sovereign city-state. Its very economic success is a bold contradiction of its geographical size. While the title of this chapter suggests some negativism, the subtitle is meant to provoke a revisit of traditional constraints of natural resources and resulting options and strategies. The chapter presents an alternative reassessment, given shifts in capabilities enabled by an internal reorientation of an open society, which has largely been a cause and effect of globalization and technology, especially information technology. The important change in mindset and psychology as a city-state is also moulded and sculpted as a response to the emerging environment. Both spatially and intellectually, the changing regional and international frameworks offer both opportunities and threats to Singapore as a city-state. To what extent and how can Singapore drive itself forward requires an intense scrutiny into the political economy of its viability and survival, and also the perceptions of others.[1]

As Singapore is both a city-state and world city, a conceptual distinction between the two is a necessary preamble. Both geographical constructs exist on the same global extensions and networks, but a world city is perhaps less sensitive politically to how the regional or international hinterland gives it sustenance. A city-state connotes deeper economic, social, security, sovereignty, and political dimensions, and has to deal with them more explicitly, especially if other countries demand that it does. The world city hypothesis, and where Singapore stands, is discussed in Section 2 of the chapter. Singapore as a sovereign city-state, in both the traditional and new thinking, is sorted out in Section 3. The crucial domestic and regional implications of the convergence of both for Singapore are identified and discussed in Section 4. With Hong Kong a Special Administrative Region (SAR) of China, Singapore may well be alone as a city-state in its sovereign status. The issues and strategies of the political economy of a city-state are analysed in Section 5, and some policy suggestions are tendered in the concluding section.

2. Conceptual Distinction of a World City

The etymology of terminology underpinning the world city and city-state has to be tidied up. The driver appears to be spatial geography around which organizations and economic activities revolve, before social and political economy dimensions enter. This evolutionary development has its logic, and is understandable as civilization, and is similarly grounded in geography.

The key word is *globalization*, defined as both the compression of the world and the intensification of the consciousness of the world as a whole.[2] It is the spread of global integration and co-ordination of activities based on the world as a global village driven by centrifugal forces which do not recognize boundaries.[3] It is the growing economic interdependence of countries through trade and technology,[4] or the growing integration into a global economy and global financial system, as transborder production and factor flows are facilitated by communication networks.[5] Put as a paradox, as the world gets bigger spatially and shrinks in connectivity, the more important are the smaller players, from small states to the micro entrepreneurs.[6]

Globalization strategies vary, with global co-ordination and local adaptation as the main drivers. Where a global firm is high on global co-ordination and low on local adaptation, the multinational corporation (MNC) is the reverse as depicted in the matrix shown in Table 1.1. The global firm achieves global efficiency, co-ordinates structure and processes of subsidiaries and aligns with the goals of the firm. The MNC involves special demands on management by the host environment; subsidiaries have to adapt to the environment, and there is little communication between subsidiaries. The international firm has centralized management, and transfers a successful structure and processes from parent to branches. The transnational corporation (TNC) has advantages, from differentiation and co-ordination, to standardization.

TABLE 1.1
Variation of Global Strategies

	Low global co-ordination	**High global co-ordination**
Low local adaptation	International	Global
High local adaptation	Multinational	Transnational

Source: Mirza Hafiz, *Global Competitive Strategies in the New World Economy: Multilateralism, Regionalization and the Transnational Firm* (Cheltenham: Edward Elgar, 1998), p. 35.

The TNC emphasizes strategic decision-making, the co-ordination of production, and the control of operations from more than one country, even if it does not own them.[7] As a strategic centre for control and co-ordination of economic activities — including distribution, marketing and servicing — TNC across nations can exclude portfolio investments, and it does not matter if there are market (like subcontracting) or non-market (like internal transfer) exchanges, so long as strategic decision-making remains within the TNC. Transnationalization need not involve export of financial capital; this is because the TNC exerts control over its foreign operations through other means like technology, and even social and political mechanisms.

The organizational characteristics of these large firms are depicted in Table 1.2.

Regionalization, a process driven by political forces seeking to reduce or eliminate barriers to the movement of goods, capital, and people within a region — involving closer geographical, geopolitical, and cultural linkages, and more economic exchanges and boundaries — can be fuzzy. It is driven by centripetal forces which are antagonistic and is a transitory stage as countries try to reinforce old or build new competitive positions. It can be seen as opposed to the centrifugal forces driving globalization or a stepping stone towards it, as they are driven by the same economic forces. *De jure* political processes and the pooling of sovereignty are implied in regionalization. But regionalization at an international level is more confusing. Regionalism is where interregional pulls are stronger and more realistic; it is a politically-driven process.

One definition has world cities as centres of transnational corporate headquarters, business services, international finance, transnational institutions, telecommunications, and information processing.[8] They are basing points in the spatial organization and articulation of production and markets, and control centres for the interdependent skein of financial and cultural flows. Together, these flows support and sustain the globalization of

TABLE 1.2
Organizational Characteristics of Large Firms

	Assets, Capabilities	Overseas Operations	R&D, Transfer
Multinational	Nationally self-sufficient, decentralized	Discerning, exploit local opportunities	Knowledge developed, retained at national unit
Global	Globally scaled, centralized	Implement parent's strategies	Knowledge developed, HQ retained
International	Source of core competencies centralized, others are decentralized	Adapt, leverage parent's competencies	Knowledge developed at HQ transferred
Transnational	Specialized capabilities, interdependent and dispersed	Differentiated contributions by national units to integrated worldwide operations	Knowledge developed at national unit, best features shared worldwide

Source: Adapted from Christopher A. Bartlett and Sumantra Ghoshal, *Managing Across Borders: The Transnational Solution* (London: Century Business, 1989), Table 4.2, p. 65.

industry. Thus, world cities articulate national, regional, and international economies into a global economy.

The world city hypothesis is about the spatial organization of the new international division of labour and straddles the contradiction of production in an era of global management and the political determinants of territorial interests.[9] A hierarchy of four spatial articulations is in accord with economic power, and for thirty world cities, Singapore — under the multinational articulation — is featured together with Miami, Los Angeles, Frankfurt, and Amsterdam.[10] As a league of their own, the triad of London, New York, and Tokyo are under the global financial articulation. London, New York, and Tokyo also constitute one transterritorial market place, not simply competing with one another but forming a triad. In the 1980s, Tokyo emerged as a centre for the export of capital; London became the main centre for processing capital; and New York became a receiver and centre for investment decisions and production of innovations, maximizing profits. The other two articulations are national (which includes Paris, Zurich, Madrid, Mexico City, Sao Paulo, Seoul, and Sydney) and subnational or regional (which include Osaka-Kobe, San Francisco, Seattle, Houston, Chicago, Boston, Vancouver, Toronto, Montreal, Hong Kong, Milan, Lyon, Barcelona, Munich, and Dusseldorf-Cologne-Essen-Dortmund).

Table 1.3 and Figure 1.1 show the world city hierarchy, with Singapore in the Asian subsystem centred on the Tokyo-Singapore axis; here, Singapore plays a subsidiary role as a regional metropolis in Southeast Asia. Operationalizing the world city hypothesis and finding the quantitative data is compounded by methodological issues. There is also the ever-changing political economy of the globalized system, with an interplay of national political economies and the world system.

A global city may be a reductive and misleading term if it suggests that cities are mere outcomes of a global economic machine.[11] In reality, a complex duality of a spatially dispersed, yet globally integrated, organization of economic activities has a parallel in social structure. Global cities are specific places whose spaces, internal dynamics, and social structure matter. They are not mere nodal points for the co-ordination of processes, but are advanced production sites of specialized services and financial innovations. In turn, sociological and power relations inject themselves in the underlying social structure.

Over time, the dynamics of territorial dispersal of economic activities creates a need for expanded central control and management. Thus, territorial decentralization is accompanied by a corresponding decentralization in ownership and appropriation of profits. But the trend back to density and agglomeration is revived by global connectivity and telecommunications.[12] The relationship between the global city and state becomes problematic as the political dimension of economic changes occurs. Dynamic, high growth in global cities, with a better-educated and skilled workforce, raises issues of

TABLE 1.3
The World City Hierarchy

Core Countries		Semi-Peripheral Countries	
Primary	**Secondary**	**Primary**	**Secondary**
London, Paris, Rotterdam, Frankfurt, Zurich	Brussels, Milan, Vienna, Madrid	—	Johannesburg
New York, Chicago, Los Angeles	Toronto, Miami, Houston, San Francisco	Sao Paulo	Buenos Aires, Rio de Janeiro, Caracas, Mexico City
Tokyo	Sydney	Singapore	Hong Kong, Taipei, Manila, Seoul

Source: John Friedmann, "The World City Hypothesis", in *World Cities in a World-System*, edited by Paul Knox and Peter Taylor (Cambridge: Cambridge University Press, 1995), p.320.

FIGURE 1.1
The Hierarchy of World Cities

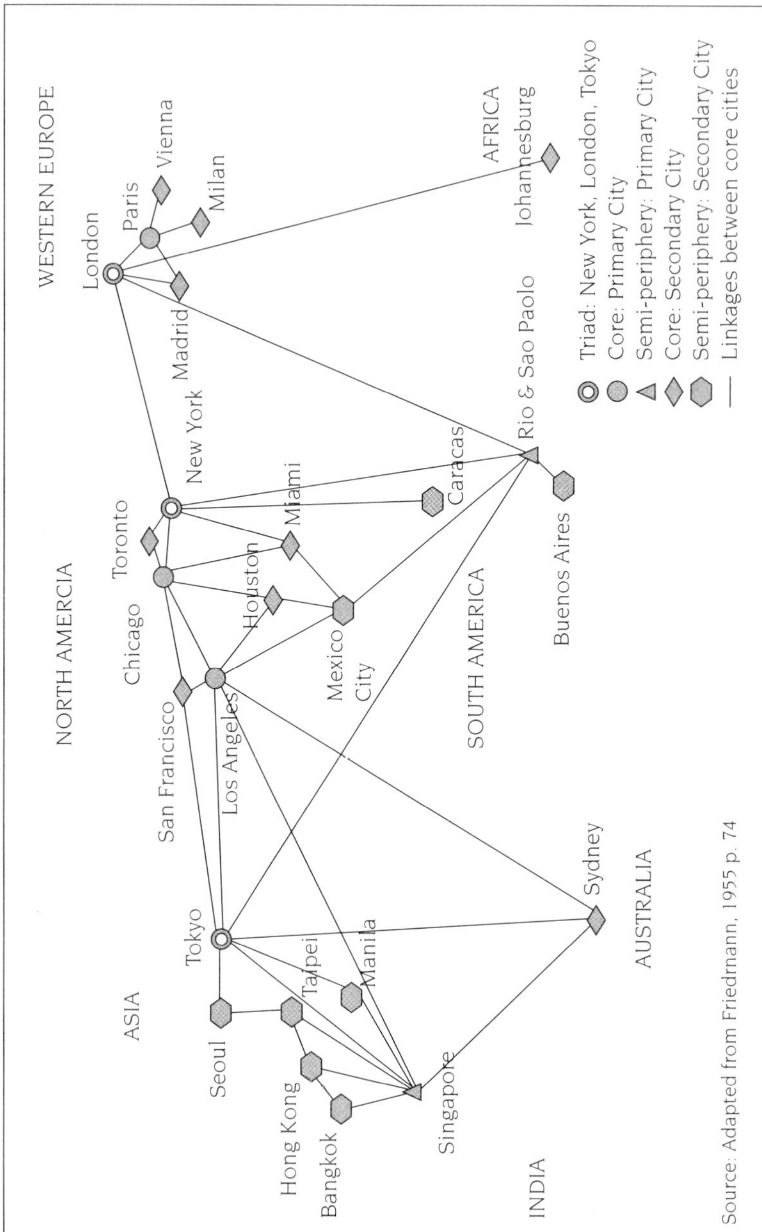

Source: Adapted from Friedrnann, 1955 p. 74

economic and social equity. As much as world cities are involved in the integration with the global economy, linkages in a spatial hierarchy, concentration and accumulation of global capital, and destination of migrants, they also bring into focus the major contradictions of industrial capitalism, including spatial and class polarization.

Rather than an order of nation-states in a global balance of power, an archipelago of technologically highly-developed city-regions or mass consumer technopoles is evolving.[13] An archipelago of world cities within the world economy is intensified by the strategic policies of MNCs. The idea is to achieve commercial supremacy around the triad of core economies in the world system, namely, the United States, Europe, and Japan, which are able to sustain consumer lifestyles. This is what Sony's Akio Morita meant by "global localization". The global-local connection, outward to world city hierarchy and inward to social, economic, and political relations and processes within cities, epitomizes the duality of contemporary world cities.

The premises of this geological metaphor — global-local — include dominant global forces which are economic, penetrating the local level unevenly and even bypassing some institutions, industries, people, and places. These forces are variously embraced, resisted, and exploited. Together with global economic forces, social and political ones also operate at various spatial scales, from global to regional, to urban and neighbourhood. These economic, social, and political scales are relatively autonomous, but they mediate global forces as they penetrate downwards. Where MNCs are more powerful than nation-states, some equilibrium dictating certain behavioural instincts and patterns emerge — best if in a consensual fashion — allowing global-local connections to co-exist.

Asian cities aspire to be world cities as much as they also wish to reflect their own identity with the incipient Asian renaissance just before the 1997 Asian crisis.[14] A case study of the Kuala Lumpur City Centre (KLCC), with its Petronas Twin Towers strictly as a response to globalization of economic activities in the Malaysian capital, has to be balanced with the ambition and vision of Prime Minister Mahathir Mohamad's "Malaysia Boleh" (Malaysia Can) slogan.[15] Such a vision could have conferred upon the KLCC some control over its growth, and not be wholly misled by the bubble economy induced by globalization, as happened in mid-1997.

3. Dimensions of City-State

The city-states of ancient Greece employed a commerce strategy to attain a golden age in culture and politics in the classical world, and which was revived during the period of the Renaissance.[16] Greek merchants commissioned the local manufacture of goods which they sold in bulk in Western markets. And by acting as hubs of trade, Greek ports also became ports for the exchange of ideas between the Near East and Europe. The Greeks innovated the public market, which progressed from barter to monetized trade, reducing transaction costs and enhancing economic freedom, while influencing democracy, as in political individualism.[17]

Among the Italian states, Venice experienced two waves, each was about 300 years in duration — from 1050 to 1350 with the commerce strategy, and from 1350 to 1650 with a conquest strategy.[18] Venice developed the art of commerce to become the most wealthy city in Europe, and at its height — with perhaps 200,000 people, including slaves — the republic held considerable territory in northern Italy along the Dalmatian coast, and along the east and south of the Greek peninsula and Crete. The Venetians sought sea power, not territorial possessions, to draw tribute. Along with the Crusades, which created opportunities for the development of warships, transport, and financial loans, merchant states prospered and gained trading facilities. Venice engineered the fall of Constantinople in 1204 by hijacking the Fourth Crusade, inheriting a quarter of the empire, with the rest forming the Latin empire, to which Venice guaranteed freedom of commerce. The Black Death (1347 to 1349) and war with its chief rival, Genoa, revealed the limits of the commerce strategy, leading to Venice's financial resources being drained.

A search for new strategies led to conquest, not so much for the right to trade but, rather, the right to extract profits and tribute from mainland cities. Competition on the seas from the Spanish and Turks, the English and Dutch sailing freely throughout the Mediterranean, and the regular use of new trade routes around the Cape of Good Hope to India, the East Indies, and China heralded the end of the Mediterranean maritime powers. While Venice was growing wealthy from trading monopolies, north-western Europe had transformed its agricultural and urban bases to provide a firmer-based wealth. When Venice finally and belatedly gave up its conquest strategy to develop agriculture, Europe had moved on to manufacturing. From the heady days of conspicuous wealth, Venice maintained steady growth and prosperity from existing resources, but it was a static, exhaustive strategy. There were no new signs of dynamism, which ultimately led to impending strategic exhaustion. Venice ultimately succumbed to Napoleon Bonaparte in 1797.

Small city-states went out of fashion in the nineteenth century with the reunification of Italy in 1861 and of Germany a decade later. Instead, Britain, France, and the Netherlands assembled empires until decolonization in the twentieth century. While their historical legacies differed somewhat, the development trajectories of Hong Kong and Singapore as commercial hubs serving East Asia and Southeast Asia, respectively, reaffirmed the commerce strategy of ancient city-states. To lock-in their commerce and service sectors, both adopted industrialization as an institutional process to marry the interplay of global economic forces and domestic factors which are socially instituted and historically embedded.[19] But they could not go on to the conquest strategy, except by way of outward direct investment in the region.

The atypicality of city-states need not suggest they fall out of the range in a continuum for comparative analysis, as they do offer some useful insights.[20] Security and a large domestic market are the main benefits of big size, but small city-states may be compensated by an increasing world of liberal trade, globalization, and technology. Small size makes it possible to achieve more rational and intelligent policies when there are fewer interests to reconcile. Development is driven by specialization, with a lack of resources and limited options of development strategy as the logic. Niches are either not attractive to larger countries (but sufficient for smaller ones) or they are, in areas where smaller countries can and do compete more effectively. It makes more sense for relatively small countries to join trade blocs and enjoy the luxury of specialization so as to exemplify efficiency. There are, however, potential vulnerabilities and benefits even from such economic integration and reliance on new communications and information technology. Yet, the fastest growing modern economies are those in "weightless" financial services, software, and data processing, and others where distance is relatively unimportant and cyberspace matters more. Governments are forced to play a larger role in supporting industry because of the imperatives of size. In domestic politics, there is an acute awareness of the fragility of small states, their open economies and dependence on overseas markets, which in turn shape the democratic corporatist structure. They rely heavily and participate actively in regional and international organizations.

The lessons for Singapore from Venice — as the most successful case of a "pure commerce" society — are patently clear. Like Venice, poverty of resources was turned into a major asset as a lesson in survival. Unlike Venice, Singapore realized that a sustainable base for wealth and prosperity cannot be premised on commerce entirely and, even if it did, it must have an edge over others. Venice faced tremendous competition from the Dutch, English, and French. Belatedly, Venice turned to its agricultural and manufacturing sectors and, while Singapore has only industries, the lesson is the same: that Singapore needs to diversify and develop niches. Conquest is out of the question in modern times, and economic conquest has its limitations, as seen in industrial parks and townships such as in Suzhou, China, which, for Singapore, has proven a great disappointment.[21] The lessons learnt from the Suzhou experiment were more in terms of how Singapore failed to engage the Chinese to complete the project as originally mooted, and how the Singapore development model could not be so easily cloned elsewhere, as political economy factors became more fractious. But the most damaging implication was that, if Singapore could not handle the Chinese, how can it support its claim to help others invest and do business in China and the region?

Talents and skills build city-states, as seen in the Venetian merchants, though they fossilized following the advent of innovating trading hubs and monetized markets. The lesson from Amsterdam and the Dutch was that, despite being under sea level and having to spend fortunes to build and maintain dykes, their tolerance of religion and their being the most "open society" attracted talents, innovations in financial arrangements, and entrepreneurship. The Americans of European stock upheld their open-door policy to immigrants, with the promise of the American dream, as the bastion of dynamism and creativity. With the possible exception of Japan, which is singular in its cultural drive, immigrants and foreign talents were part of the success in other parts of Europe (from Milan to Antwerp), Canada, Australia, Hong Kong, and Singapore. They benefited from countries which, after investing in their human capital, failed to create the environmental incentives for the educated and talented to use their minds to make them stay. Prosperity comes with the commercialization of ideas.

Additionally, Singapore initiated a policy to nurture "technopreneurs" (or technology entrepreneurs) in areas of creativity and innovation. The Government has been willing to share the risks of high technology and research and development (R&D) through incentives and the easing of prohibitive bankruptcy laws, rules, and regulations. Singapore's local population is too small, and any educational reform would take time. Thus, talent infusion has been necessary to engender the commercializing and patenting of ideas. Creative and innovative talents at the professional and skilled range is a progression from a policy on foreign workers as foreign talents since the 1980s. Singapore aspires to be a knowledge-based economy where creative, innovative, and problem-solving skills are applied to all economic spheres and facilitated by information technology. The most basic ingredient remains people, thinking, and working productively and intelligently, with a positive work attitude to match.

4. Regional and International Order

It is a simplistic untested hypothesis or perception that the contemporary regional and international order — riding on globalization, technology, foreign direct investment (FDI), and MNCs — is more conducive to the concept of world city. Moreover, there is a convergence in income and consumption trends, with growing affluence and a closing of the disparity between industrialized/developed states and the developing world, especially the newly industrializing economies (NIEs) and dynamic Asian economies (DAEs) before the Asian crisis of 1997–98. The city-state, premised on a commerce strategy, implying some hegemony as a regional hub, is probably more antiquated, unless modern information technology, cyberspace, and electronic highways generate another virtual concept for it. But electronic commerce and the associated disintermediation may mean less middlemen functions for Singapore, unless new value-added services are designed and offered. Moreover, information technology, information infrastructure, hardware, and software can be purchased and acquired. Malaysia's multimedia super corridor (MSC), a new administrative capital at Putrajaya, and the KLCC, are testimony to the shortened, telescoped pace of such technological leap-frogging. The human element and productivity remain more evolutionary and not easily purchased, no matter what amount of management and training may be expended, if mindset change is not present. Singapore's challenge to management and labour, given contestable markets and potential competition, is how to combat complacency and to instill a spirit of keeping ahead.

But whatever Singapore does is inevitably conditioned by the regional and international environment. Structural competitiveness is a systemic attribute of the strength and efficiency of the productive structure of a national economy, dependent on the governance and management of the interaction of different components in aggregate.[22] But there are externalities which also affect the internal factors to make the national economy's industrial structure proficient and flexible. The global efficiency of the national system depends more on systemic and environmental features which are external. To go beyond organic externalities — as the Asian business system is built on social capital and trust[23] — structural competitiveness may become a more important component of externalities in Asia than in North America. Even the role of the Government in technocratic–corporate partnering in a strategic alliance, as in R&D, has both an externality and welfare perspective.

As the immediate constraints for a city-state hark back to traditional scarcity and resulting dependence on neighbouring countries for the most worrisome resource, namely, water, the regional context may dictate the global.

Malaysia asked Singapore to look elsewhere for water after Singapore refused to budge from its demand that Johor double its supply under a new 100-year agreement ending 2161. Johor currently supplies 350 million gallons a day (mgd) of raw water under two agreements expiring in 2011 and 2061, respectively; and Singapore wants 750 mgd from Johor, though it really needs 950 mgd. But, with its own interests to consider, Malaysia cannot commit itself to such a quantum increase. There was bickering over Singapore's projected seven million population by year X (translated into 134 gallons per person) when Malaysia queried both the projected population size and how a mega-city like London used only 76 gallons per person a day, and Malaysia, only 112 gallons per person a day. A related issue is the profit derived by Singapore, as Singapore pays Johor three Malaysian cents per 1,000 gallons of raw water. Its revenue from 250 mgd is about RM1.09 billion, with profits of RM630 million, giving a profit margin of 230 times the price Singapore pays for raw water. Johor's revenue and profits are RM460 million and RM85 million, respectively.

With the right policies, Singapore may be able to handle land and labour shortages better, as well as the need to import raw materials, fuel, food, and other necessities. In the case of water supply, it has no bargaining power, and the only long-term solution is desalination, expensive though it might be. Even here, the traditional concept of desalination — as distilling water from the sea, which is energy intensive — may be replaced by a newer, cheaper technology or reverse osmosis, such as getting reconstituted water from industrial waste, repugnant as the idea might be. But, like the Dutch battling with below sea-level topography, or the Japanese with potential earthquakes, lack of water is Singapore's Achilles' heel, and it has to continually source the right technology to make desalinated or reconstituted water viable. This challenge can be turned into a technological asset and free the city-state from such a life-threatening and politically sensitive liability. It is a matter of paying the financial costs and changing mindsets to battle the odds.

The Asian economic crisis of 1997 should have taught Singapore a lesson, insofar as difficult economic and social conditions can cause strains in relations with neighbouring countries. These may take the form of externalizing domestic issues into the regional arena, by putting the blame on others, to deflect criticism over domestic shortcomings. These may also be translated into more competitive strategies which may subvert or constrain the rival's capabilities, as in water, airspace, and other territorial issues between Singapore and Malaysia. Because of political sensitivities, even the expropriation of minority shareholders' rights, such as Malaysia's capital controls — resulting in the freezing of shares of Singaporeans in the Central

Limit Order Book (CLOB) system, which Malaysia claimed never to have recognized as legal — cannot be taken as a sovereign issue.

Indonesia poses another concern for Singapore, even if there is less historical baggage relative to that of Malaysia. Indonesia is definitely on a threshold, hopefully a forward trajectory. While the prospects of a stable, democratic, and prosperous Indonesia is unquestionably desirable, two issues remain. One issue is how Indonesia's democratic election of 1999 is effectively translated into a stable democratic political culture with the right institutions and structures. A second issue is how Indonesia's foreign policy and relations with neighbours in the Association of Southeast Asian Nations (ASEAN) and the wider region would work out, and whether this may be likened to China's awakening two decades ago, even if the scale is not the same. Soeharto's foreign policy had steered Indonesia away from intrusive regional involvement and projected a generally benign image. Any change, or a more active Indonesia (given its size and "big brother" mentality), might be problematical and induce some rearrangement of both ASEAN and bilateral relations with Indonesia itself.

A couple of incidents between Indonesia and Singapore has soured bilateral relations somewhat. When President Soeharto named B. J. Habibie as his vice-president in February 1998, Senior Minister Lee Kuan Yew remarked that the financial markets were "disturbed" that the choice had been based on the appointee's expertise in science and technology and a known propensity for high-spending on such projects. Habibie, who subsequently became president, probably neither forgot nor forgave Singapore for that remark. He later commented in an interview that he did not see Singapore as falling in the category of "a friend in need is a friend indeed".[24] To him, Singapore was just a "red dot" in his office map amidst the enormous green of Indonesia.

To Indonesia, particularly President Habibie, humanitarian assistance to Indonesia in its hour of need, as provided by Singapore, is charity, and Singapore was deemed merely a fair-weather friend. As citizens of the fourth most populous country in the world, Indonesians are proud and nationalistic. Since Singapore sees itself as a reputable international financial centre, its help to Indonesia could more appropriately be to get that country investments and provide assistance in its external debt financing. The inter-ethnic problems in Indonesia should also alert Singapore, as a large Chinese enclave, of the inextricable link it shares with ethnic Chinese in Indonesia. Perhaps, because of resentment towards a small city-state's success (despite the fact that success is not a zero-sum game), a "big brother" mentality arises which cannot be ignored. In such circumstances, both Malaysia and Indonesia can easily accuse Singapore of being rule- and efficiency-driven, thinking strictly in efficiency and functional terms, rather than in building relations from the heart. Incidentally, when Malaysia withdrew its US$1 billion loan offer made in October 1997 to Indonesia in view of its own economic problems, Indonesia made no comment.

A more grievous misunderstanding between Singapore and Indonesia was Habibie's mistaken notion that there were no Malay officers in the Singapore Armed Forces (once similarly suggested by Malaysia), calling Singaporeans "racists".[25] This showed not just a "big brother" mentality but also dangerous connotations of intolerance of Singapore's success based on meritocracy. Thus, while Singapore may have no domestic Chinese problems, its Chinese characteristics, as perceived externally by others (i.e., as a Chinese enclave and centre for capital), do pose potential problems for it in its interactions with other states.

Despite its efficiency — which is based on international competitiveness, rule of law, good governance, and relative absence of corruption — Singapore cannot overcome its limitations as a small and open city-state. It needs the political goodwill of its much larger neighbours to give it both physical sustenance and economic space. As a virtual capital of overseas Chinese, Singapore may not be so easily forgiven for being a safe haven whenever there is capital flight due to political instability in nearby Malaysia or Indonesia, even if it did nothing to offer such refuge.[26] Indonesians want a people's economy with equal opportunity for small- and medium-sized enterprises (SMEs) and not capital flight to Singapore, seen as aiding and abetting the rich and huge Chinese conglomerates.

Senior Minster Lee Kuan Yew has noted that Asian countries with large reserves have not been tight-fisted in helping floundering neighbours recover from the Asian economic crisis.[27] However, he cannot see how any Asian government can impose conditions on financial assistance it receives — assistance best channelled through organizations like the International Monetary Fund (IMF) with the capacity to confront governments. He warned Singaporeans "to prepare for more heat" as leaders in the region come under stress, making more accusations and threats.[28] On relations with Indonesia, Lee cautioned patience and suggested that, until political uncertainties are resolved, Singapore's only involvement would be humanitarian relief. An Indonesian adviser to Habibie, Dewi Fortuna Anwar, viewed Lee's warning as paranoid because Indonesia does not view Singapore as a threat.[29] Prime Minister Goh Chok Tong has also anticipated retorts from Indonesia and reiterated Singapore will say little in response to Indonesia's verbal onslaught, minimizing provocation and avoiding becoming a party to Indonesia's domestic politics.[30] This non-confrontational approach by Singapore, juxtaposed against the need to assert its sovereignty, epitomizes the dilemma of a city-state.

Another source of contention with Indonesia could come from the seasonal haze originating from forest fires in Sumatra and Kalimantan. The fires tend to raze land more than fifty times the size of Singapore. Sensitive to being viewed as a rich victim, Singapore has chosen to go under the ASEAN umbrella in urging Indonesia to control the fires. However, Indonesia has been strapped for funds and resources and has put the blame for the fires on farmers (for their "slash and burn" method of clearing forests) and logging companies.

These incidents point out both vulnerabilities in resource- and service-based activities which depend on the region and the resolve on Singapore's part to strategize and look harder for options. Singapore's obsession with scenario-planning has earned both its leaders and people a reputation of being constant worriers, often ahead of time. Because success in regional co-operation is based on buoyant economic growth and full employment all round, neighbourliness, and economic diplomacy — based on ASEAN and the Asia-Pacific Economic Co-operation (APEC) frameworks — become important. The question of whether relying on the region or on the global economy is the better option for Singapore makes the concept of world cities and city-states quite stark, although the choice need not be mutually exclusive.

As ASEAN is the inevitable forum in matters of political economy, at some point, when all members have recovered adequately from the Asian crisis, ASEAN's leadership will have to be reasserted. ASEAN has to finish the agenda it had set in putting in place the ASEAN Free Trade Area (AFTA), integrating the new Indochinese members, and finally get on with extending regionalism to the multilateral World Trade Organization (WTO) framework. The mantle of leadership and vision would fall on Indonesia because of its sheer size and potential, or at least it should be consulted, as ASEAN's politics and economics are still based on a hierarchy. On the other hand, if Indonesia remains mired in a messy socio-political transition, younger and more dynamic statesmen from elsewhere in ASEAN may emerge, as happened when more democratic Thailand and the Philippines tried to suggest that member states become more engaged in each other's internal affairs, instead of preserving the long-standing principle of non-interference. Whether more "constructive engagement" will evolve together with greater democratization all round (as democrats and the *Reformasi* movement begin to outnumber or prevail upon older autocrats in all of ASEAN) is an interesting question to ponder.

Singapore's trade in manufactures is, however, geared towards the industrialized economies of the Organization for Economic Co-operation and

Development (OECD). Notwithstanding the geographical distance, working with the OECD countries may turn out to be more dependable, stable, and technologically superior than working with the region. Singapore is rule-based like the OECD countries, respecting the rule of law, transparency, and corporate governance, and is also used to dealings with MNCs. Singapore is in the OECD league in terms of broad economic development indicators, and, while not aspiring to be a member as yet, it has observer status in some OECD committees such as finance, telecommunications, and technology.

Singapore straddles both the regional and international economy, and the ideal situation for it is to become a "megalopolis" or mega-city liberated from traditional constraints by the technological strategy which it is presently pursuing. Apart from natural resource dependence, the technological strategy allows Singapore to be less vulnerable to political competition from the region, on which it may have no choice. Through technology, having the global economy at Singapore's doorstep becomes a more practical and logical ambition. Macroeconomic co-operation between the United States and Europe has surged on the strength of strategic alliances in technology, R&D, and the building of complementarities, in areas such as entrepreneurial innovation and discovery. Singapore should not miss out on similar opportunities with the advanced OECD economies. In the same vein as structural competitiveness, structural complementarities and impediments require some policy co-ordination and collective management if Singapore is to tap the mega-markets in the United States and Europe.

5. Issues and Prospects for Singapore's Duality

One thread to be picked out from above is how Singapore has to balance between regional and international environments to survive both as a world city and a city-state. On the water problem, desalination is on track and the cost simply has to be paid, while conservation and the more efficient use of water are matters of national policy. On traditional physical constraints as related to security and defence matters, Singapore is not altogether helpless. With hardware in military equipment and technology, and software and heartware as in the people's support and loyalty to defend the city-state, Singapore may even play the role of a small, soft superpower in intermediating among the ASEAN "big brothers". Joseph Nye has commented that, for a small state, Singapore has embarked on a "sensible" strategy of maximizing its "soft power", rather than trying to overwhelm its neighbours with "hard power".[31] Embracing information technology and making itself into a learning hub is one dimension of Singapore's "soft power", which also includes influence and goodwill to make itself attractive to others. In politics, recognition, reputation, and credibility can be enhanced by information technology, and used to Singapore's advantage in furthering its survival as a city-state. Governance in the information age has a levelling effect among states, and this is a boon to small ones like Singapore. Apart from existing squabbles with neighbours, the Malay and Islamic world is a growing force to contend with.

Another issue has to do with Singapore's emerging status as a developed country and how that identity might affect relations with the other ASEAN states, on the one hand, and the OECD countries, on the other. By most counts, Singapore appears to have attained developed country status except in two areas.[32] One is in science and technology and R&D, which is related to its size and lack of critical mass. Singapore's Science Park, generous government funding and support for R&D, and a "technopreneurship" programme (and everything that policy can do to nurture this dimension) have to evince a mindset change beyond science and technology indicators. The second area is stickier, namely, that Singapore is perceived to be a laggard in democratization and politics.[33] As Singapore grows prosperous and progressive in technology, there is this one worrying domestic factor which may spell a Venetian demise. During the seventeenth and eighteenth centuries, Venice's political structure became increasingly inflexible and oppressive as the landed gentry clung to its existing assets in the absence of a viable dynamic strategy. Political institutions stagnated and apathy about political matters had the Government falling into the hands of a minority of nobles. In Singapore, what seems like a castrated opposition and the artificial injection of Nominated Members of Parliament (despite calls for a civil society), may become its own version of an inward-looking political city-state.

Despite the People's Action Party's (PAP) incredible staying power as the Government since 1959, its success has not quite imparted the confidence and gracefulness as a mature party and government, with respect to criticism and comments made about certain policies and mechanisms. This "thin skin" also applies to top civil servants, because of their long association with politicians. A functional rationale may be that they perceive both the economy and society too fragile to withstand strident dissent, and forces must pull together in the same direction to engender the correct environment for sustained growth. The challenge is that the civil society — the creative, innovative society — which Singapore desires can thrive only with a certain amount of unrestrained experimentation in thought and ideas. An ordered and sanitized milieu tailor-made by campaigns and socialized by consultative practices, however defined, and generally not catering to anything unprecedented and untried, especially when nothing is broken and in need of fixing, is inconsistent with declarations of welcoming change.

A third issue alluded to earlier is the economic philosophy and management style of the state, synonymous with the PAP, in having such a heavy hand in the economy. Unlike Japanese *keiretsu* and Korean *chaebol* which remain privately owned, even if by families, Singapore's versions of big local conglomerates are the government-linked corporations (GLCs). Two clear strategies may be discerned with respect to GLCs. One is that they will lead the way to high-technology industries and the next wave of Singapore's industrial growth. The other is a fine tuning of Temasek Holdings with its stable of GLCs[34] to stress good corporate governance and a bid to become world-class companies,[35] which can be taken to imply two trends. One, is that the Government is sensitive of the usual distrust of government in business, or political business, which caused plenty of woes in the Asian crisis partly caused by cronyism and corruption. Two, is a reaffirmation of the Singapore Incorporated model which the Government is not giving up so easily. In fact, the hands-off approach in management is taking a more proactive but not intrusive mode.[36] This may prove a strategy to develop internal dynamism, entrepreneurship, and technopreneurship. But, that it is deemed a technology strategy, with GLCs blazing the trail, is a more critical issue, as it implies continuation and reinforcement of the "Singapore Inc." model. Taken to its ultimate conclusion, with indigenous entrepreneurs and enterprises, somewhat sheltered, and top-down thinking by fiat, even the promise of a consultative and participatory approach may be very difficult to engender. Like everyone else, Singapore needs change, not continuity.

A fourth issue is that Singapore's identity is at the crossroads. Singapore has geared itself through the Committee for Singapore's Competitiveness which concluded in 1998; the Singapore 21 committee which reported in 1999 on the values and thinking of Singaporeans faced with regionalization and globalization challenges; and the financial liberalization package over the next five years, which was announced in 1999. These efforts represent forward and dynamic strategies to ensure survival and prepare various sections of the population for the necessary restructuring.

A fifth issue is about becoming a world city, whether Singapore can aspire to become a political "basing point" and/or "centre for co-ordination and control" beyond the new international division of labour. Singapore could move into a higher order of functions and activities as a headquarters of international social and political institutions, and not merely business. Singapore was justifiably proud that Caltex decided to shift its global headquarters from Texas to Singapore, which can be read as an endorsement of Singapore's credentials as a world city. Becoming a global headquarters to established and well-known institutions could be a source of legitimacy and insurance for the city-state. As a sovereign state, Singapore can also play this role more effectively than Hong Kong, given some of its unchallenged capabilities.

A sixth issue is that the city-state will eventually graduate to attain a developed country status. The technology criterion may be remedied by the policy on foreign talent, while the democracy element may lead to further loosening of socio-political debate. With a younger, better-educated generation (many of whom are graduates of foreign universities and institutions), and with half the population travelling, studying, and working abroad, this faster pace of political liberalization and democratization is unavoidable.

Seventh, there is a strategy of twinning with other city-states equally anxious about sustaining dynamism and growth. What Singapore can do together with Hong Kong, for instance, may be a natural alliance starting with the lowest common denominator.

Quantitatively, there may be more state intervention in Singapore, though the SAR Government appears to have moved into the market aggressively, too, as in propping up the Hong Kong stock market in August 1998. But the debate or comparison may be misplaced, as the contrast lies in the role of the state in both cities, directing industry with different forms of intervention. Singapore might have its statutory boards and GLCs as more direct instruments, but state intervention in Hong Kong is more subtle and implicit. Both are goal-driven to provide the right environment and forge social cohesion with social expectations under constrained maximization.[37] Like Singapore, Hong Kong was said to have only one natural advantage, its harbour.[38] Historically, that was true, but by modern contemporary notions, with the right technology and mindset change, both have achieved a place as a virtual headquarters of production activities dispersed in the region. They would benefit from a co-operative and friendly hinterland in ASEAN and China, respectively. Made *by* Hong Kong, rather than made *in* Hong Kong, is suggestive that production based on geography has been superseded by ownership and management by Hong Kong firms through international chains of networked production.[39]

It is critical for both Singapore and Hong Kong to become regional and global hubs by exploiting information technology, and they can learn from each other with respect to information technology policy and infrastructure.[40] Singapore has long admired Hong Kong's enterprise and entrepreneurship. That there may be more Singaporeans living in the SAR, learning and doing business with China through Hong Kong, than there are foreign talents coming to Singapore is testimony of this virtue which more closeted Singaporeans lack. On the other hand, Hong Kong may need to twin with Singapore in areas of information technology and other areas of high-technology R&D. The government-led model in Singapore is more suited to such long-term activities because of externalities which need state support. In this respect, Hong Kong is a latecomer, but synergies between the two cities would be more advantageous in sharing costs and knowledge. Media hype and misguided thinking may view them as competing with each other in regional and international financial services. But Singapore has acknowledged that Hong Kong was better at certain fund packaging activities, probably because the SAR's fiscal and regulatory framework was more liberal and will be so until Singapore's liberalization package takes effect over the next five years. But with the right mindset, complementarities between the two cities can be maximized.

Finally, in regional and international diplomacy, the city-state has to balance its sovereignty with inescapable dependence on its neighbours for goodwill and continued supply of crucial resources and materials, including labour, airspace, seaspace, and water. Singapore cannot afford to be stepped on by bigger states, but others might readily impute a sense of arrogance to its affluence and stage of development. What would assist Singapore is if it projected its image and legitimacy in the international arena and used information technology to level up its size with its capability, credibility, and reputation as an efficient economy and effective polity. As already noted, a small state could at best influence and trust the logic and good sense of an international community which would afford some assistance and support when needed. The more outward-looking the ASEAN region becomes, the better it is for Singapore in handling international relations, especially when the bigger fora — APEC, the Asia-Europe Meeting (ASEM), and the ASEAN Regional Forum (ARF) — are engaged as well. Singapore's bid for free trade arrangements with the Pacific Five (involving the United States, Australia, New Zealand, Chile, and Singapore) and its initiation of the East Asia-Latin America Forum (EALAF) are illustrative of its continued efforts to take a higher international profile in order to balance its status as world city and city-state.

Conclusion and Policy Implications

While not yet empirically tested, the perception seems to be that Singapore as a world city may be easier to achieve and sustain than as a city-state. The concept of city-state conventionally allows for some hinterland from which the world city draws its sustenance, as widely connoted as the triad of New York, London, and Tokyo, based simply on competitiveness and technological capability. When borders and national sovereignty impinge upon a city-state, it is clearly faced with more politically constrained and sensitive choices. However, through lessons of ancient city-states, particularly Venice, Singapore as a city-state need not always fall into the pessimistic trap of dependency on water and other natural resources from the region. Venice had been most successful in its commerce strategy and moved to the conquest strategy to shore up its wealth accumulation. As it did nothing to plan ahead to deal with emerging competition from others in Europe, it declined into an exhausting strategy before petering out and meeting its end under Napoleon's conquest.

Singapore has done better in buttressing the commerce strategy of the city-state with the technology strategy afforded by information and communication technology. It has put in the programmes, funds, and incentives to institutionalize the technology process. The dynamic pathway of the modern world is linear rather than circular, and institutions never re-emerge in the same forms but develop in entirely new and strikingly different ways. While mindset change is at best slow and belaboured with socio-political sensitivities, some progress may be discerned, even in the way the Singapore Government is prepared to share risks with technopreneurs and to probe issues, such as through the Singapore 21 project.

Other dynamic strategies can include twinning with Hong Kong (as the last pair of successful city-states) for mutual benefit and synergy. Such economic co-operation may be easier to engender with a richer, more developed, mature, and pragmatic economy as is Hong Kong than with the ASEAN member-states. Regional and ASEAN politics remain a function of size rather than capability. Some scope, however, may exist for Singapore as a soft, small superpower to bridge the developing ASEAN and wider APEC regions with industrialized countries' groupings. This is slippery and would benefit from support in the larger East Asian and international community, however postured.

The pending developed country status which Singapore will achieve by 2030 or 2040 is congruous with the concepts of world city and city-state. With its acquired and strategic policy with respect to FDI and MNCs, Singapore has emerged as a hub network in both manufacturing and services. It aims to be a city of life and a good place to live and work in. It merely has to work harder, with respect to attainment in science and technology, as well as in overall quality of life, to attain the cultural vibrancy of cities in developed countries.

In the final analysis, two fundamental factors, internal and external, shape the next phase of Singapore's survival as a world city and city-state. The domestic strategy is well within its reach and policy manipulation by tapping the new technology in information and communication with a vengeance, to become wired and on a par with other OECD countries. But the technology policy has to go beyond the hard infrastructure to get Singaporeans to manage the next millennium's way of conducting business and networks. Singaporeans are sheltered and not as hardy and nimble as Hong Kong entrepreneurs who have become what they are precisely because there is no state safety net. Singapore GLCs may be a solution to catalyze and groom a more dynamic, less risk-averse lot of companies and chief executive officers (CEOs) with infusion of foreign expertise and experience. But the GLC-led strategy would perpetuate the Singapore Inc. model and its interventionist culture. Maybe, there is no better alternative at the moment but to reinforce and strengthen that model. This, however, creates a path dependency, in which having the state play the role of nanny might become mutually addictive for both the state and the entrepreneur.

The external factor is more problematic and worrisome. First, with respect to its nearest neighbours and the issue of water supply, it is reckoned that Singapore has to tap technology (expensive as it is to invest in desalination), which may remind more natural suppliers that business, rather than politics, would be better for all parties concerned. Second, with technology and the right connectivity, Singapore has to widen and reinforce its bearings, with the OECD countries as the source of superior technology, expertise, experience, and markets. It needs more creative, rather than technical, skills from these advanced industrial countries. Working with more mature political systems and cultures may be less competitive and stressful as efficiency, functionality, and business prevail, rather than petty and short-sighted rivalry. Also, if Singapore can credibly lock itself into partnership with the developed world, MNCs and FDI located in Singapore will afford it some insurance and protection through the presence of foreign interests here. Most would recognize that all Singapore wants is to make a decent, righteous living and play a role suited to its resources and capabilities on the world stage. In this respect, its size should not strictly pose a threat to larger economies, and all it needs is some space in the region, rather than feel that it is crowded out.

Notes

1. See Linda Low, *The Political Economy of a City-State: Government-Made Singapore* (Singapore: Oxford University Press, 1999).

2. See R. Robertson, *Globalisation: Social Theory and Global Culture* (London: Sage, 1992).
3. See Marjan Svetlicic and H. H. Singer, eds., *The World Economy: Challenges of Globalisation and Regionalisation* (London: Macmillan Press, 1996).
4. See Mirza Hafiz, *Global Competitive Strategies in the New World Economy: Multilateralism, Regionalization and the Transnational Firm* (Cheltenham: Edward Elgar, 1998).
5. See Peter Dicken, *Global Shift* (London: Harper & Row, 1992).
6. See John Naisbitt, *Megatrends Asia* (New York: Simon & Schuster, 1996).
7. See Henry Wai-chung Yeung, *Transnational Corporations and Business Networks: Hong Kong Firms in the ASEAN Region* (New York & London: Routledge, 1998), pp. 7–9.
8. See Paul Knox and Peter Taylor, eds., *World Cities in a World-System* (Cambridge: Cambridge University Press, 1995), p. 6.
9. See John Friedmann, "The World City Hypothesis", in ibid., pp. 317–31; also John Friedmann, "The World City Hypothesis", *Development and Change* 17 (1986): 69–83.
10. John Friedmann, "Where We Stand: A Decade of World City Research", *in World Cities in a World-System*, edited by Knox and Taylor, p. 24.
11. Saskia Sassen, *The Global City: New York, London, Tokyo* (Princeton, N.J.: Princeton University Press, 1991), p. 4.
12. Ibid., p. 5.
13. See R. Petrella, "World City-States of the Future", *New Perspectives Quarterly* 8 (1991): 59–64.
14. See Fu-chen Lo and Yue-man Yeung, eds., *Globalization and the World of Large Cities* (Tokyo and New York: UN University Press, 1998); and Yeung, *Transnational Corporations and Business Networks*.
15. See Morshidi Sirat and Suriati Ghazali, *Globalisation of Economic Activity and Third World Cities: A Case Study of Kuala Lumpur*, (Kuala Lumpur: Utusan Publications & Distributors, 1999).
16. See John J. Norwich, *Venice: The Greatness and the Fall* (London: Allen Lane, 1981).
17. See Graeme D. Snooks, *The Dynamic Society: Exploring the Sources of Global Change* (New York and London: Routledge, 1996) and Graeme D. Snooks, *The Ephemeral Civilization: Exploding the Myth of Social Evolution* (New York and London: Routledge, 1998).
18. See Snooks, *Ephemeral Civilization*.
19. See Stephen Wing-kau Chiu, K. C. Ho, and Tai-lok Lui, *City-States in the Global Economy: Industrial Restructuring in Hong Kong and Singapore* (Boulder, Col.: Westview Press, 1997), p. 9.
20. See P. Saul, "The Economic Development of Small Nations: The Experience of North West Europe in the Nineteenth Century", in *Economies in the Long View*, Vol. 2, edited by Charles P. Kindleberger and Guido di Tella (London: Macmillan, 1985), pp. 111–31; and Peter J. Katzenstein, *Small States in World Markets* (Ithaca, N.Y.: Cornell University Press, 1985).
21. See *Straits Times* and *Business Times*, 10, 11, and 30 June 1999, and *Far Eastern Economic Review*, 8 July 1999.

22. See John de la Mothe and Gilles Paquet, "Structural Competitiveness and Interdependence: Regional Patterns", in *Structural Change and Co-operation in the Global Economy*, edited by Gavin Boyd and John H. Dunning (Cheltenham: Edward Elgar, 1999), pp. 82–112.
23. Robert D. Putnam, *Making Democracy Work* (Princeton, N.J.: Princeton University Press, 1993); and Francis Fukuyama, *Trust: The Social Virtues and the Creation of Prosperity* (New York: Free Press, 1995).
24. See *Asian Wall Street Journal*, 4 September 1998.
25. See *Straits Times*, 10 February 1999.
26. Even this may be subtle, as the Ministry of Manpower (MOM) launched a graduated new work pass system for all foreign talents and workers in three categories starting on 1 September 1998: P category for professional, managers, administrators, investors, entrepreneurs, and others; Q category for skilled workers, technicians, and those with specialized skills; and R category for the semi-skilled and unskilled (*Straits Times*, 25 July 1998). For the P category, long-term dependants' passes extend to parents and parents-in-law (the timing is uncanny, considering the racial riots in Indonesia which culminated in Suharto's downfall in May 1998).
27. See *Sunday Times*, 31 January 1999.
28. See *Straits Times*, 21 February 1999.
29. See *Straits Times*, 24 February 1999.
30. See *Straits Times*, 5 March 1999.
31. See *Straits Times*, 8 January 1999 and *Business Times*, 9 January 1999.
32. Linda Low, ed., *Singapore: Towards a Developed Status* (Singapore: Oxford University Press, 1998).
33. Stephan Haggard, "An External View of Singapore's Development Status", in ibid., pp. 345–75.
34. They include Singapore Telecommunications, Singapore Power, Singapore Airlines, Keppel Corporation, Development Bank of Singapore, Singapore Technologies, Neptune Orient Lines, and Port of Singapore Authority Corporation. Temasek companies account for 10 per cent of Singapore's economic output and about 25 per cent of the local market capitalization, with Temasek's strategic stake in its listed companies amounting to $47 billion. But, transparency of information and statistics is not a strong feature of GLCs.
35. See *Business Times* and *Straits Times*, 25 June 1999.
36. Changes include closer monitoring of diversification plans of Temasek companies, performance benchmarks, terms of chairmen and directors, attracting foreign talents, and helping smaller companies expand overseas by sharing risks.
37. See Geoffrey Murray and Audrey Perera, *Singapore: The Global City-State* (Folkstone, Kent: China Library, 1995).
38. See Warren I. Cohen and Zhao Li, eds., *Hong Kong Under Chinese Rule: The Economic and Political Implications of Reversion* (Cambridge: Cambridge University Press, 1997), p. 8.

39. See Susan Berger and Richard K. Lester, eds., *Made by Hong Kong* (Hong Kong: Oxford University Press, 1997).
40. See Janice M. Burn and Maris G. Martinsons, eds., *Information Technology and the Challenge for Hong Kong* (Hong Kong: Hong Kong University Press, 1997).

2

EXTERNAL CHALLENGES FACING THE ECONOMY

Raymond Lim

Introduction

Though economists may disagree about whether globalization today is unprecedented compared with an earlier period a hundred years ago, there is broad consensus that the trend in the new millennium is towards greater integration of national economies across factor and product markets, fuelled by the rapid developments in information and communication technologies.[1]

Globalization and the information and communications revolution, and their effects on Singapore and the city-state's responses to them, dominate discussions on the country's economic future. They are the key external challenges. This chapter examines three aspects of this debate — financial liberalization, attracting foreign talent, and the role of government intervention in the Singapore economy.

Financial Liberalization

Global Casino

> Speculators may do no harm as bubbles on the steady stream of enterprise. But the position is serious when enterprise becomes the bubble on a whirlpool of speculation. When the capital development of a country becomes a by-product of the activities of a casino, the job is likely to be ill-done.[2]

> Lenin was right. There is no subtler, no surer means of overturning the existing basis of society than to debauch the currency. The process engages all the hidden forces of economic law on the side of destruction, and does it in a manner which not one man in a million is able to diagnose.[3]

These two quotes exemplify the two worries on the globalization of capital markets for national economies — the capriciousness of capital and its capacity to wreak havoc with national currencies and domestic stability. Malaysian Prime Minister Mahathir Mohamad has, for instance, denounced the volatility of capital as a Western conspiracy to destroy the country's economy. He has likened foreign speculators to "rogues" and "scoundrels". The Soeharto government in Indonesia at the height of the Asian crisis had accused foreign speculators of subversion, a crime that it pointedly confirmed was a capital offence. This sentiment was also shared by the Chavalit government in Thailand, although, unlike Indonesia, it did not make clear that speculators ought to be hanged.

Conspiracy theories and subversion charges typically rear their heads when an economy is under severe stress. Thus, in 1992, the French Government felt that the exchange-rate mechanism (ERM) crisis was an Anglo-Saxon conspiracy. There is thus a certain emotional fluidity in economic thought that must be kept in mind when assessing economic issues to get the right perspective. It is the case with the debate on the globalization of capital. Prior to the crisis, for instance, Malaysia, Thailand, and Indonesia opened their doors — in retrospect, too widely — to foreign capital. Kuala Lumpur and Bangkok had even harboured hopes of displacing Singapore as Southeast Asia's regional financial centre.

Foreign capital and its free flow was seen as a good thing in improving resource allocation and in allowing developing countries to grow faster. The financial sector was seen as the other major engine of economic growth, in addition to manufacturing. No Malaysian, Thai, or Indonesian politician raised any reservation that, by facilitating this flood of Western capital into Asia, their financial sectors and — given the official encouragement to these efforts — their governments may be parties to a Western conspiracy to subvert the rapid ascendancy of Asia in the global economic arena.

Small boats and ocean liners

In the good times many forgot it remains true that when the United States, the European Union (EU), or Japan sneezes, Thailand might contract pneumonia. It does not end there, as this virus — capital flight — is highly contagious. It was not just Thailand that went down in 1997 and 1998, but the whole region caught a chill of varying severity. The disparity in size between the industrialized and Asian economies forms part of the problem, which affected the magnitude of the adjustment in Asia. We can see the disparity by looking at Asia's market capitalization as a percentage of the combined market capitalization of Microsoft and General Electric. From mid-1996, at no time was the entire market capitalization of the Singapore stock market more than that of these two U.S. stocks. See Figure 2.1. It shows us that a slight shift in financial asset allocation out of the United States and other developed countries can translate into a massive inflow of capital into Asia. Private capital inflows into emerging markets went up fivefold from 1990 to 1997 — US$42 billion in 1990 to US$256 billion in 1997. See Figure 2.2.

But what comes in can go out and, because of advances in computer and telecommunication technologies, it can go out swiftly. It has been estimated that close to US$100 billion at a net level exited Asia's crisis economies in 1996 and 1997. Net capital outflow in 1998 for Indonesia, Malaysia, and Thailand was 4.8 per cent, 3.6 per cent and 9.3 per cent of gross domestic

FIGURE 2.1
Singapore Market Capitalization

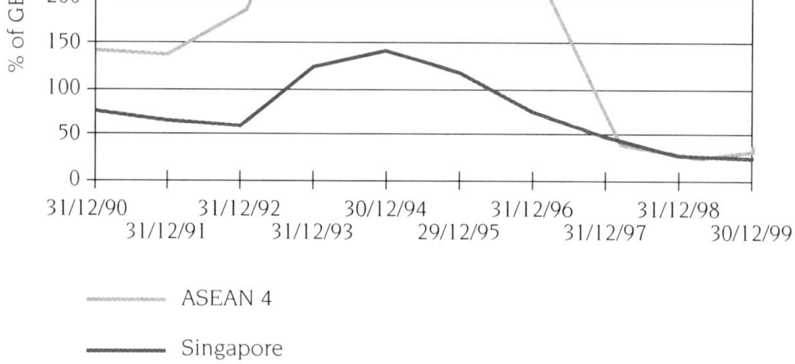

* GE: General Electric, MS: Microsoft
Source: CEIC & Datastream.

FIGURE 2.2
Short-term Commercial Credit and Portfolio Flows

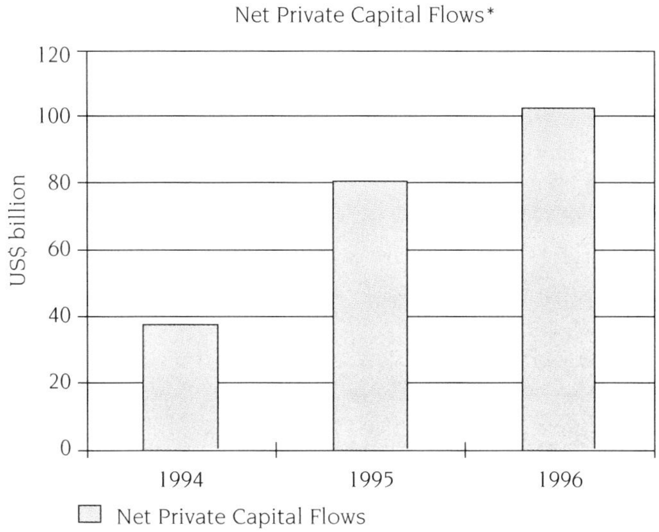

* Indonesia, Malaysia, South Korea, Philippines, and Thailand.
Source: IIF.

product (GDP), respectively. As capital flew out, currencies took a battering and economies contracted sharply. The opinion pendulum on capital account liberalization has thus started swinging to the negative end. China and India have been cited as examples of countries that have been spared the worst of the financial crisis as they have closed capital accounts. In the face of the crisis, Malaysia shut down its capital account in September 1998 and terminated its aspirations to be a rival regional financial centre to Singapore.

Where Angels Fear to Tread

Singapore, however, responded to the Asian financial crisis by actually stepping up the pace of financial liberalization. Other Asian economies have also done so — Thailand, South Korea, and Indonesia are all opening up their financial sectors to greater foreign ownership and competition. But Singapore stands out, as it is doing so out of voluntary choice; whereas the other countries were dragged into it by the International Monetary Fund (IMF). Singapore is not being foolhardy but sensible in moving towards financial liberalization:

- Singapore is a tiny economy. By its very nature it cannot rely heavily on domestic demand as a sustainable engine of growth, unlike its larger neighbours in the Association of Southeast Asian Nations (ASEAN). See Figure 2.3. Singapore thus operates a very open economic system to allow it to benefit from global trade and services. It is a trend-taker rather than trendsetter in the global economy. A key element of its economic strategy must be to identify larger global trends early and position itself to best benefit from them.
- Significantly for Singapore, the Asian crisis has not led to greater protection of national capital markets. Given that investors are less discerning than the Singapore authorities may wish, and given its position as a regional financial hub, any retreat into economic nationalism by countries in Southeast Asia would have adversely affected it, as foreign capital might have shun the region as a whole. Instead, crisis economies under IMF supervision have opted for further liberalization of their domestic capital markets.
- The exception is Malaysia because it had a choice, as it did not seek IMF assistance. But even in Malaysia, there has been a gradual relaxation of capital controls, the most notable being the lifting of the exit tax on portfolio investments in May 2001. Clearly, this shows that the Malaysian

FIGURE 2.3
Domestic Demand of Southeast Asian Countries

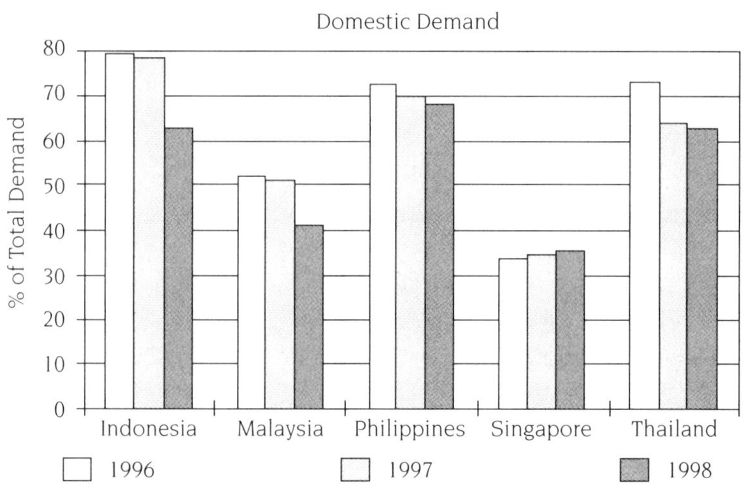

Source: ABN AMRO & CEIC.

Government, despite its anti-Western rhetoric, recognizes that the country is better off having access to foreign capital, and that the problem is really the size and quality of capital inflows, rather than outflows. Capital can only flow out after it has come in. And if capital cannot flow out easily, it will not come in.

- The larger trend towards financial liberalization in Asia remains intact and, in fact, has been accelerated in the aftermath of the crisis. With that, Singapore should and has, indeed, seized the opportunity of the present lull in regional financial services competition to position its financial sector for the next wave of regional growth. In doing so, it has sought to reposition itself not as a regional centre but as an international financial centre in the global capital markets network.
- To this end, Singapore has sought to put strategic distance between itself and its regional competitors, by improving disclosure standards, boosting the fund management industry, deepening the local bond market, and relaxing restrictions on the use of the Singapore dollar by non-residents.
- The most decisive factor in securing Singapore's position as a global financial hub is that Singapore had shown that in the crisis it reacts in a predictable, rational, and progressive manner, in contrast to the other Asian financial authorities. The reputational advantages of a financial centre that is stable, reliable, and well managed by level-headed policy-makers give Singapore a huge edge over its competitors.
- Regulatory, industrial, and fiscal incentives can be easily copied by other countries. In fact, there has been such a convergence across countries prior to the crisis. But, building up a reputation as a financial centre and — even harder — repairing a reputation that has been damaged are much more long-term processes.

Don't Run before You Can Walk

Are there dangers here? To get a perspective on the risks, one needs first to debunk the view that the Asian crisis was due to financial liberalization. It was not financial liberalization *per se*, but the speed at which capital markets were opened up — before proper regulatory and supervisory mechanisms were put in place in Asian economies — that was a major cause of the crisis. In the absence of these institutional structures, financial liberalization will magnify underlying economic weaknesses.

Second, this suggests that proper sequencing of financial liberalization is important. Notably, the recent financial liberalization package in Singapore was conceived not as a "Big Bang" but as a series of "small bangs". This serves to put gradual but rising pressure on local banks to upgrade to international standards. This is necessary, as, increasingly, location is not the deciding factor in winning and retaining the share in the domestic banking market. A vast array of complex hybrid financial products and the new information and communication technologies make location an ineffective barrier to external competition. Unless Singapore wants to be hostage to the different priorities of foreign global banks, there must be sizeable local banks with first-class service and product levels. The only effective way is to increase the competitive pressures on local banks and force them to move up the value curve.

Third, is the issue of whether, even with proper sequencing in opening up the financial markets, greater integration would lead to greater instability in the Singapore economy. Jeffrey Frankel, a member of the Council of Economic Advisers to the United States President, gave an instructive anology:[4]

> Today's financial markets are like superhighways. They get you where you want to go fast. By this I mean that they are useful: they help countries finance investment and therefore growth, and they smooth and diversify away fluctuations. But accidents do occur, and they tend to be big ones — bigger than they used to be when people were not able to drive so fast. The lesson is not that superhighways are bad. But drivers need to drive carefully, society needs speed limits or speed bumps, and cars need air bags.

Good Boy in a Neighbourhood of Rowdies

As the Asian crisis has shown, even with proper regulatory and supervisory mechanisms in place, Singapore was not spared the contractionary effect of volatile capital outflows. On its own, Singapore can reduce its vulnerability by monitoring its short-term and foreign debt positions, as currency and liquidity mismatches were other proximate causes of the crisis. But it is not immune to contagion, in which economic difficulties in one country with superficial similarities to Singapore lead to capital flight from Singapore, because investors place the two countries in the same class of risk — Southeast Asian or emerging markets risks. The problem is compounded by the herd instinct of investors. See Table 2.1 for a comparison of short-term debt coverage of emerging economies during 1997–98.

Singapore, therefore, cannot insulate itself completely from short-term capital volatility. Chile, for instance, has been cited as an example where a tax on short-term capital inflows has affected the maturity structure of capital

TABLE 2.1
Emerging Economies: Short-Term Debt Coverage

	June 97			June 98		
	ST Debt	Reserves	ST Debt/ Reserves	ST Debt	Reserves	ST Debt/ Reserves
Argentina	23,891	19,740	1.210	34,570	22,769	1.518
Brazil	44,223	55,849	0.792	52,978	69,615	0.761
Chile	7,615	17,017	0.447	10,056	15,135	0.664
Colombia	6,698	9,940	0.674	6,810	8,690	0.784
India	7,745	25,702	0.301	6,948	24,297	0.286
Indonesia	34,661	20,336	1.704	27,658	17,950	1.541
Jordan	582	1,624	0.358	577	2,122	0.272
Korea	70,612	34,070	2.073	33,161	40,835	0.812
Malaysia	16,268	26,588	0.612	11,199	19,702	0.568
Mexico	28,226	23,775	1.187	28,209	30,646	0.920
Pakistan	3,047	1,249	2.440	2,529	844	2.996
Peru	5,368	10,665	0.503	8,889	1,119	7.944
Philippines	8,293	9,781	0.848	10,170	9,024	1.127
Russia	38,308	20,396	1.878	34,650	11,161	3.105
South Africa	13,247	4,241	3.124	13,746	4,610	2.982
Sri Lanka	414	1,770	0.234	380	1,864	0.204
Taiwan	21,966	90,025	0.244	18,590	83,286	0.223
Thailand	45,567	31,361	1.453	27,767	25,785	1.077
Turkey	13,067	16,055	0.814	20,315	26,456	0.768
Venezuela	3,629	13,215	0.275	4,794	12,556	0.382
Zimbabwe	731	447	1.635	839	154	5.448

Source: S. Radelet & J. Sachs (1998)

towards the longer end. But, over time, economic agents always find ways to circumvent these taxes. Studies have shown that periodic increased tightening of controls on capital inflows in Chile have led to a pattern of migration from covered to uncovered inflows.[5] In the case of Singapore, any tax on short-term capital inflows would affect its status as a financial centre; unless there is a global move towards such a tax, capital would bypass it for a friendlier jurisdiction. Even if there were global co-ordination on regulating short-term capital inflows, the odds are that some countries would opt out.

Economists love trade-offs. The trade-off for Singapore, then, are the benefits of free global capital flows and its positioning as a global financial hub against that of the potential destabilizing effects of these flows. Singapore's response should be and has been to reduce the extent of these destabilizing flows, not by shutting the door on capital inflows, but by strengthening its financial system and adopting sound domestic economic policies. That Singapore has weathered the Asian financial crisis relatively well bears testimony to the efficacy of this approach.

Whither National Currencies

A related but separate issue is whether a small open economy like Singapore should have its own national currency. The argument is that the size of global capital flows today are in the order of US$1.25 trillion a day, which is more than the combined reserves of all the ASEAN economies put together. Most of these flows are in the nature of hot money which seeks quick returns rather than reflecting trade and investment flows. Small open economies like Singapore are in no position to fight off a full-scale speculative attack and should either adopt a currency board exchange rate system or dollarize the economy.

In a currency board system, a country only issues local currency which is fully backed by a foreign currency, typically a hard currency like the U.S. dollar, at a fixed rate. Dollarization takes the arrangement further, with the country giving up its own national currency and adopting the U.S. dollar instead.

The currency board system does not eliminate speculative attacks on the currency. The Hong Kong dollar, for instance, suffered heavy speculative pressure during the Asian crisis. The key determinant is not just whether the size of reserves is sufficient to cover monetary obligations under the currency board system, but the Government's commitment to the Hong Kong dollar peg. This commitment is what the market was testing as it assessed the competing demands faced by the Government. The market realized that it was not just the peg that mattered to the Government's survival, but also that the sharp hike in interest rates necessitated by its defence of the peg would lead, if sustained, to rising unemployment, corporate failures, banking distress, and collapsing asset prices. These were strongly competing government objectives, and the market was aware of them. Britain, for instance, in 1992, despite having sufficient reserves to defend the pound parity position in the European Monetary System, allowed the pound to float because the British Government was reluctant to let interest rates rise, as home mortgages were linked to market interest rates.[6]

Quite clearly then, adopting a currency board does not eliminate speculative attacks. When there is a significant external shock, as happened recently, it may encourage speculative attacks, as it is a one-way bet on the currency's value. The cost of the bet is the price of the position taken to sell the Hong Kong dollar. There is no currency risk, as the value of the currency remains.

Since a currency board gives no guarantee against the destabilizing effects of speculative attacks on a national currency, some economists have suggested that dollarization is the best option for small open economies or those prone to government failure. By adopting the dollar, there is no currency to speculate against. Argentina has been looking closely at taking such a route from its present currency board system.[7] This only means that speculation against the Argentine peso is eliminated. But currency volatility remains, except Argentina will go on the U.S. dollar roller-coaster. The sharp gyrations of the dollar-yen rate in the past twenty years highlights this point (see Figure 2.4).

FIGURE 2.4
Gyrations of the Dollar-Yen Rate

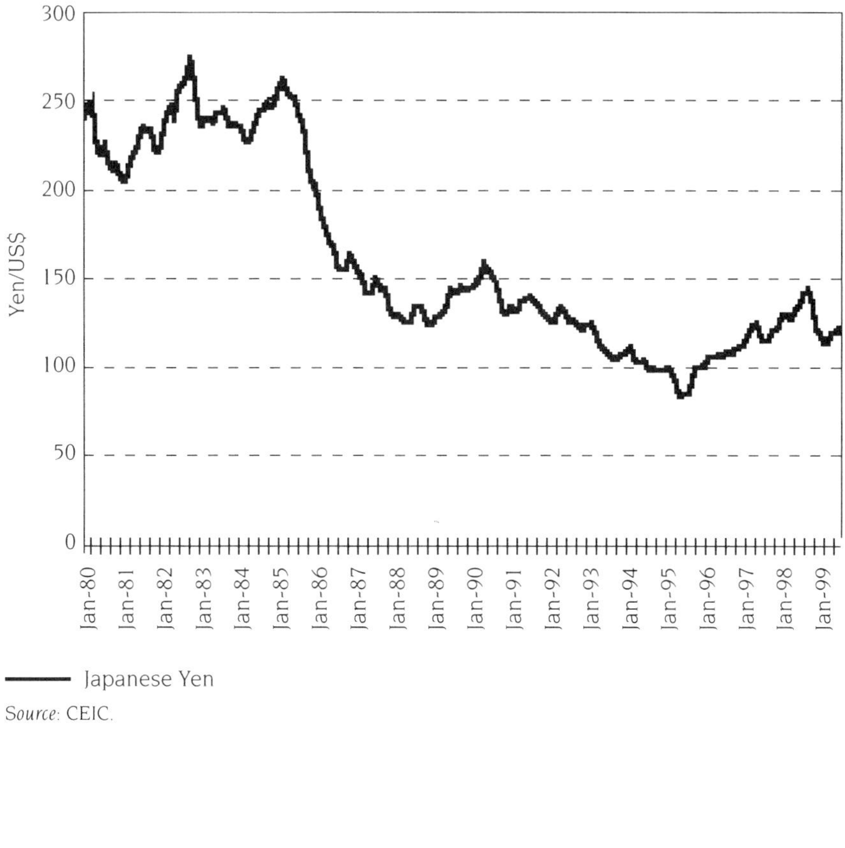

Source: CEIC.

Financial Disarmament

Should Singapore dollarize, or take the currency board route? There are compelling reasons against both. In both the dollarized model and the currency board system, the economy can only adjust to an external shock by domestic price deflation. It is easier and quicker to let the currency take part of the adjustment of an external shock, than for the multitude of wages and prices in the domestic economy to fall. There is also a socio-political dimension to wages that makes its adjustment downwards stickier than the depreciation of a currency. Further, in both systems the absence of a lender of last resort in the form of central bank liquidity intervention means that a balance of payment crisis can be turned into a banking crisis, as happened in Argentina in 1994. This is so, as capital flight will lead to a contraction of the monetary base, causing interest rates to rise and putting pressure on financial markets and the banking system.

Currency boards and dollarization remove monetary policy from the national authorities. This financial disarmament may be sensible for countries such as Italy, where it is said that when the Banc d'Italia practices independent monetary policy, investors cannot run fast enough, and inflation-prone Latin American countries which have a history of the monetization of their fiscal deficits. But Singapore does not fall into these categories.

Often, countries which give up the ability to conduct their own monetary policy do so because their central banks have given them nothing but grief. The Monetary Authority of Singapore does not have this credibility problem. Central bank policy can be good as well as bad. To give up this policy option is to remove the central bank's ability to do good when needed to stabilize and facilitate economic recovery. This monetary straitjacket, therefore, cuts both ways.

Significantly, a currency board system or dollarization would mean substituting the United States' monetary policy for that of Singapore's. It thus assumes that these two economies are on the same economic cycle. This is not the case, as recent events have clearly shown. The United States grew strongly in 1997 and 1998, but Singapore went downhill. Even though the United States is Singapore's major trading partner, the latter's fortunes are increasingly tied through trade and investment to the ASEAN region, which in those two years did very badly. Figure 2.5 illustrates the desynchronization between Singapore and U.S. economic growth in 1997–99.

This question must be answered before Singapore gives up its monetary policy, as some have suggested: Is there any assurance that by tying the

FIGURE 2.5
Desynchronization between Singapore and U.S. Economic Growth

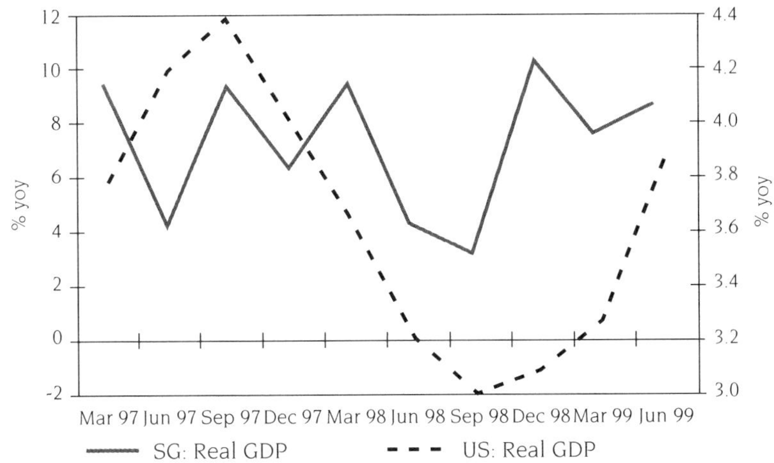

Source: CEIC.

Singapore dollar to that of the United States in a currency board system, or giving it up for the U.S. dollar, Singapore's interests would be taken into account when U.S. monetary policy is being formulated? There is none.

There have also been suggestions that there should be an ASEAN common currency. It took Europe forty years before convergence. It went from a free trade area to customs union before going into a single market and currency union. It took a long time, as it involved political will. At the height of the crisis in Asia, there was a proposal from the Thai and Philippine foreign ministers that ASEAN should be more actively involved in the affairs of individual member states. This view was not carried through, as members were against what they perceived as interference in their domestic affairs. ASEAN is not a band of brothers. It is precisely because of that that it was set up to manage differences in the region. These differences in politics and economics remain and would be a major obstacle towards a common ASEAN currency. As Malaysian Prime Minister Mahathir said, he rejected IMF aid, as the IMF not only wanted to help the economy but also to take control. And once it has economic control, it will have political control. An ASEAN central bank or an ASEAN common currency is simply unacceptable to many member countries at this stage of political and economic co-operation, as it impinges unacceptably on national sovereignty.

Foreigners Welcome

Why the knowledge-based economy? Together with financial liberalization, knowledge-based economy are the buzzwords of the new millennium. Whereas resistance to liberalization has been confined to the local banks, resistance to the knowledge-based economy is greater, since one aspect of it involves the government policy to attract foreign talent. In the wake of the crisis, foreigners were perceived as taking jobs away from Singaporeans.

It makes sense for Singapore to move into a knowledge-based economy from a capital-intensive one because global trends are moving that way. From the early 1980s, technological changes have been biased towards skilled rather than unskilled workers. Evidence of this in the United States stems from the sharp rise in wages of skilled workers relative to unskilled workers.

As Paul Krugman has pointed out, in 1979 a college graduate with five years experience earned only 30 per cent more than a high school graduate with similar experience.[8] Ten years later, the premium had gone up to 74 per cent. Technological changes in the economy are increasingly biased towards skilled workers, otherwise employers would have substituted less skilled workers for the more expensive skilled workers. The evidence suggests that increasing emphasis is being placed on *how* goods and services are produced, and not just on *what* are produced. Lester Thurow, for instance, had cited that, when the Japanese Ministry of International Trade and Industry speculated in 1990 on the new growth industries in the future, it identified knowledge-intensive industries such as microelectronics, biotechnology, telecommunications, robots, and computers.[9]

In Singapore, the bulk of foreign direct investment (FDI) since the 1980s has been in the services, rather than the manufacturing, sector (see Figure 2.6). The significance of this is that the services sector requires a higher level of skills and competence than the manufacturing sector. Reflecting this, all services sub-sectors, except commerce, have higher average wages than the manufacturing sector (see Figure 2.7). Further, many manufacturing jobs are really services jobs, such as design, packaging, and marketing.

The trend, therefore, is for future economic growth to be powered by human capital — skills and knowledge residing in individuals and systems — rather than the traditional factors of production, capital, and labour. Again, Singapore takes the evolving global economic environment as a given and positions itself to benefit from it. To do this, it can rely on its own talent pool, which would restrict or, at the very least, slow down the growth of knowledge-intensive industries such as computer software, where not that many

FIGURE 2.6
FDI into Singapore by Industry

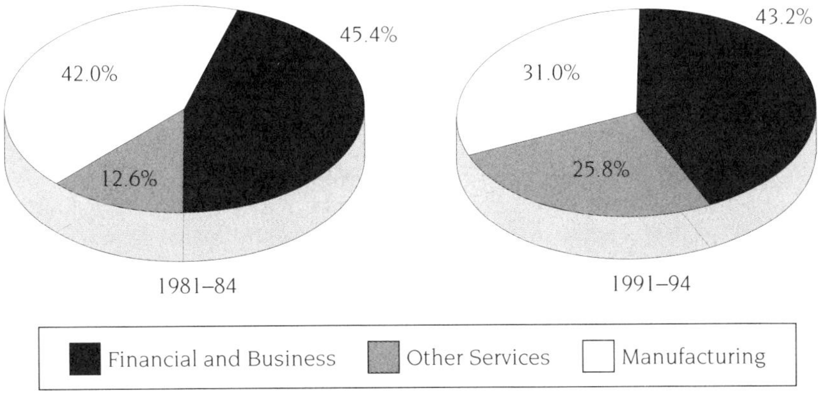

FIGURE 2.7
Average Monthly Earnings

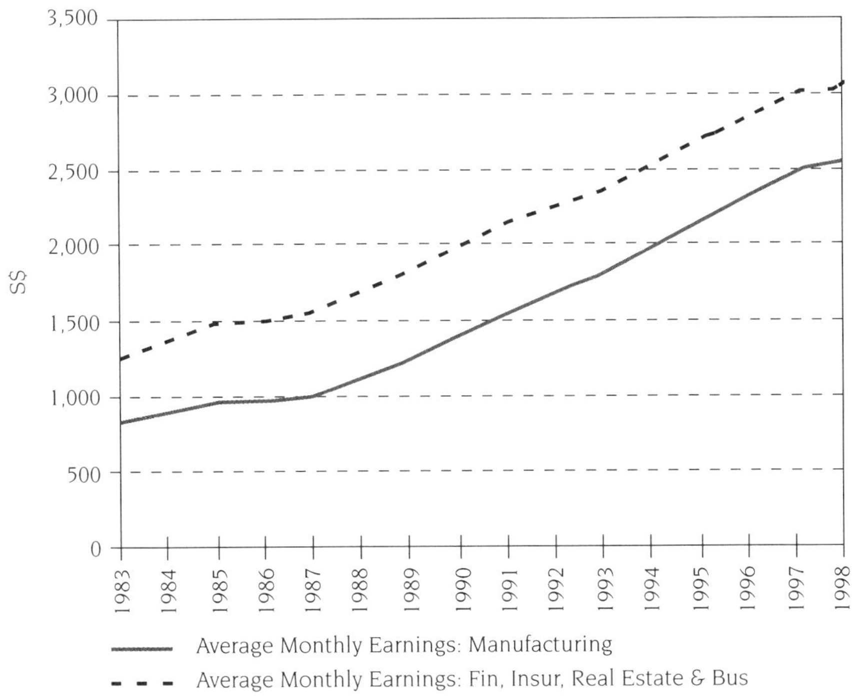

Source: CEIC.

Singaporeans have the requisite skills, or it could encourage software experts around the world to set up business or work in Singapore. Even in areas where local talent is available, such as in the financial industry, the number of skilled locals might not be enough to create a critical mass.

Foreign talent is thus vital for Singapore to make the successful transition to a knowledge-based economy. This is similar to Singapore's earlier industrialization policy, where it welcomed foreign firms to invest in Singapore and build up its export manufacturing capability. Again, the same reasoning underlies Singapore's opening of its financial markets to foreign financial institutions in the 1970s in wholesale, treasury, capital markets, and offshore banking activities. Simply put: Singapore will welcome and attract to its shores foreign capital, businesses, and expertise that are either absent in the country or not sufficient to achieve its development objectives.

Foreign does not always equal talent. Some have suggested that Singapore's foreign talent policy should be more restrictive in that, foreigners should be excluded if there is a local with a better or commensurate skill. It is only when a case has been put up by the prospective employer that no local can do the job, that a foreigner be given an employment pass. Politically, this makes sense. In terms of economics, however, it assumes that the government body that approves or vets these applications has the capacity to assess these skill levels. In practice then, these criteria may be difficult to assess. The onus of proof may be on the employer, so forms are filled up justifying the employment of the foreigner, advertisements placed, but what then? Should the approving agency second-guess the assessment of the firm on its needs? As a rule, it is inefficient to substitute an administrative decision for a market decision.

Singapore has always had a liberal employment policy. This was a complement to its policy of welcoming multinational manufacturing firms and foreign financial institutions. It was a critical complement, as an important factor in the decisions of these firms to locate and invest in Singapore was that they could easily transfer staff or skilled foreigners to Singapore. So the foreign talent policy is not new. The renewed emphasis is not so much a shift in government policy but, rather, an effort to take a more proactive approach in attracting global talent to Singapore. From being a complement to help attract foreign investments, it is now a central plank of policy as the engine of growth shifts from capital to talent. But in raising the decibel on this policy, it entails political costs. No economic policy can be fully effective if it does not have political support. In the midst of the crisis, some have pressed for the foreign talent policy to be slowed down. If a country's strategy is to attract foreign expertise, the credibility of the policy is compromised if it depends on the economic winds that are prevailing at a given time. Economic nationalism is understandable in times of crisis, but the costs, unfortunately, are borne long after the crisis is over. It is no different from Malaysia shutting down its capital account. Such policy flip-flops will be negatively factored in by foreign firms deciding to invest in Malaysia, even if capital controls were removed completely tomorrow.

However, there is a political dimension to the foreign talent policy that must be handled sensitively. The risk is that the administrative machinery goes overboard in implementing the policy. In what is still very much a top-down society, this is a real risk. In the early 1990s, for instance, the Government issued a call to Singapore firms to go forth and invest in China. A rush followed, but very few Singapore firms have yet to strike gold. The Government's flagship project in China, the Suzhou Industrial Park, has now been written off as an expensive tutorial lesson on how not to do business in China.

In the foreign talent policy drive, the risk is that domestic firms swing from reluctance to the other extreme of seeking foreign talent first to fill higher-skilled positions, rather than to scout for the best available talent, foreign or local. The signals must be clear. The policy should be one that encourages domestic firms to recruit locally for unskilled workers and the best globally for higher-skilled positions. As expected, government-linked corporations (GLCs) are taking the lead here. Yet the way to increased efficiency in the GLCs, and domestic firms in general, lies not just in recruiting foreign talent but increased competition. Increasing the competitive pressures on domestic firms — in particular, opening up the non-traded sector to international competition — will force these firms to recruit the best available talent, foreign and local, to survive and prosper. What should not happen is for local firms to recruit foreigners because it is now the politically correct decision to make, rather than on business grounds. Unintended reverse discrimination by an overzealous implementation of this policy by government agencies and firms must be guarded against, as it will affect the political support necessary for this policy to be successful. The foreign talent policy is to maximize Singapore's talent pool — foreign and local. It might have been better politically to have called it a "global talent" policy rather than a "foreign talent" policy. By putting "foreign" ahead of "talent", the policy may have been unnecessarily laden with an emotional dimension, clouding its actual aim: to attract the best talent from anywhere in the world to work in Singapore and, just as importantly, to retain, nurture, and develop local talent to world class standards. This sense of balance must not be lost in its implementation.

Government Intervention

The Visible Hand

The analysis so far has assumed that government intervention can influence the economy. It is, however, worth examining whether the effectiveness of government intervention is affected by globalization. To begin with, we should make a distinction between macroeconomic and microeconomic intervention. Government intervention at the macro level comes through monetary and fiscal policies.

A country which has an open capital market regime and an exchange rate peg cannot use monetary policy to influence the domestic economy through changes in interest rates. If it chooses to use monetary policy to affect the domestic economy, then it needs to let its exchange rate float. This is the basic constraint on the effectiveness of monetary policy: that one policy instrument cannot be used to achieve two targets — the exchange rate and the domestic economy. Globalization has neither affected the effectiveness of monetary policy, when it is aimed at a single target, nor its ineffectiveness when it is aimed at multiple targets. Thus, in the case of Singapore, its monetary policy is to target the exchange rate to maintain price stability, given that it imports most of what it consumes. Interest rates are thus left to the market. Contrary to suggestions made by some commentators, the recent Asian crisis has not shown that the increasing globalization of capital markets has affected the effectiveness of Singapore's monetary policy. The Singapore dollar did relatively well in the crisis (see Figure 2.8).

At the height of the Asian crisis in January 1998, the Singapore dollar depreciated by only 1.1 per cent on a real effective exchange rate basis, compared to 54.8 per cent for Indonesia, 36.2 per cent for Malaysia, 35.7 per cent for Korea, 34.2 per cent for Thailand, and 29.9 per cent for the Philippines (see Table 2.2). The Singapore economy was also not as volatile as in the other countries. Inflation in Singapore peaked at 2.5 per cent year-on-year in October 1997, compared to Malaysia at 6.2 per cent, Indonesia at 82.4 per cent, Thailand at 10.7 per cent, and the Philippines at 11.5 per cent. Singapore's exchange rate policy was indeed doing its job of keeping price stability.

Fiscal policies are more problematic. Governments have no problems spending, at least few suffer unduly from such restraints. The difficulty is in raising the money to finance this spending. Of course, a government can borrow in the capital markets. But, ultimately, this will be constrained by the revenue that it can raise to service the debt incurred. So the ability to spend turns on the ability to tax. The rapid growth of the Internet and telecomm-

FIGURE 2.8
The Volatility Rate of Regional Currencies

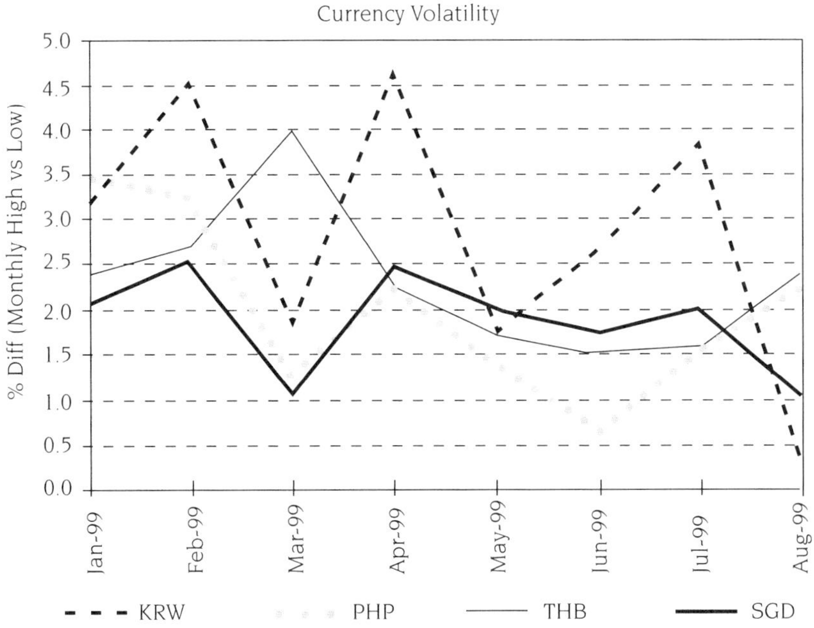

Source: ABN AMRO & CEIC.

unication technologies will complicate tax efforts. The Singapore Government, like many other governments, has been moving away from direct to indirect taxation, principally through a value added tax.

As a general rule, it is easier to tax physical goods than services. In line with the experience in other industrialized economies, the service sector in Singapore has been growing in importance since the mid-1990s.[10] In 1980, manufacturing was 28.8 per cent of real GDP, and services 60.8 per cent. In 1995, services had gone up to 64.9 per cent, whilst manufacturing had slipped to 26.3 per cent.

Services can be easily transmitted across the Internet. As electronic commerce and cross-border transactions grow, it will be harder to levy indirect taxes. A transaction effected in Singapore can be disguised as originating from an account outside the country. Besides tax evasion, there are jurisdictional issues such as the exact location of the transaction — the supplier or the recipient country. Even direct taxes may be under threat in a web world, as it is easier for companies to set up and people to work anywhere

TABLE 2.2
The Singapore Dollar Weathered the Storm Well

	Purchasing Power Parity		Real Effective Exchange Rate	
	% chg (Jun 97 vs Latest)	% chg (Jun 97 vs Jan 98)	% chg (Jun 97 vs Latest)	% chg (Jun 97 vs Jan 98)
China	(5.7)	(0.2)	2.1	7.6
Hong Kong	(1.2)	3.3	5.2	5.8
Indonesia	(14.6)	(59.3)	(7.6)	(54.8)
South Korea	(17.5)	(39.5)	(12.4)	(35.7)
Malaysia	(28.4)	(42.6)	(21.6)	(36.2)
Philippines	(19.8)	(35.1)	(15.0)	(29.9)
Singapore	(16.9)	(17.8)	(5.3)	(1.1)
Taiwan	(18.2)	(12.4)	(13.6)	(6.8)
Thailand	(23.3)	(43.4)	(9.4)	(34.2)

Note: () means undervaluation or gain in competitiveness.
Source: ABN AMRO.

in the world. However, the mobility of companies and people may be overstated. When companies invest in Singapore, when they actually commit physical capital, it is much harder to shift out. Take for instance petrochemical and wafer fabrication plants. These cost massive amounts of money, and the physical capital cannot be easily moved out of Singapore. In fact, part of Singapore's investment strategy in attracting capital intensive industries to locate in the country is precisely that mobility is limited once physical capital is sunk. It also ensures a flow-on of investment from these firms, as they need to upgrade the existing plants to stay competitive in the global market place. Further, what is overlooked is that, when firms locate in Singapore, it is not just fiscal considerations that matter but the totality of doing business in the country — among others, first-class infrastructure and, according to *Time* magazine, being an increasingly "funky" place in Asia.[11] Similarly, people choose to work in Singapore because of the better quality of life and perhaps particularly for its citizens — culture, family, and language ties. In short, a sense of belonging to the country.

The picture then on fiscal policy is problematic but not bleak. Just as technology creates avenues for illegal tax evasion and legal avoidance, it will enable governments to think of new ways to tax. Singapore's electronic road pricing system is, of course, a case in point. Thus, the United States, the leading country in this information age, has not, for instance, suffered any significant fall in its tax revenue since the early 1990s (see Figure 2.9). In fact, taxes have risen from 9.8 per cent of GDP in 1990 to 12.0 per cent in 1998 — a reflection, no doubt, of strong economic growth, but also that information and communication technologies have not had a discernible impact on the country's ability to tax.

This is important as, even though Singapore's open economy makes fiscal policy a less effective demand management tool, the generation of tax revenue gives the Government the capacity to have economic growth with equity. Redistributive policies, such as the upgrading of Housing and Development Board (HDB) flats and other measures to effect a sense of shared prosperity, is a key factor for political stability. These policies of social inclusion are all the more crucial, as globalization and technological changes have and will lead to rising income inequality in the country. In the United States, for instance, income inequality has been rising, from having a Gini coefficient of 0.428 in 1990 to 0.459 in 1997, where 0 suggests perfectly equal income distribution to 1 for wholly unequal distribution. In Singapore, over that same

FIGURE 2.9
United States Income Tax Revenue

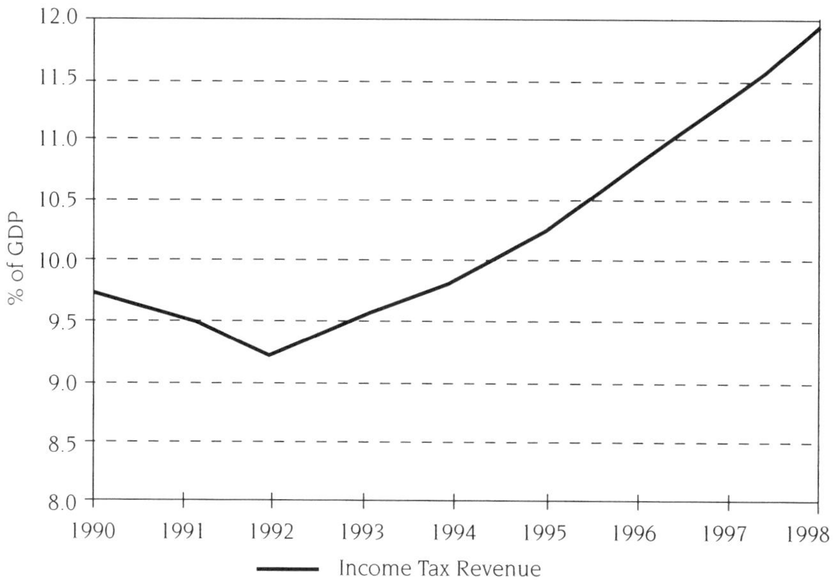

Source: CEIC.

period, the coefficient was relatively stable at 0.444 in 1997 compared with 0.428 in 1990. But if we take the United States as setting global trends, then, as Singapore's Department of Statistics has warned, household income distribution may become more unequal, as the demand for less skilled workers falls due to on-going economic restructuring. Shared growth to foster social and political stability will thus remain an important element of economic management.

Entrepreneurial State

Economists are schizophrenic when it comes to government intervention. Whilst more would accept intervention at the macro level, many more would frown at micro level intervention, often referred to as industrial policy.

Singapore actively practices industrial policy. Oil refining, ship repairing, and the electronics industries are just some past examples. A more recent example would be the promotion of non-electronic industries, such as chemicals, to diversify the export base. More recently, there has been a concerted push to promote the financial industry, which is seen as a major engine of growth. It is regarded as the vanguard which will pull up the other service sectors, such as information technology, accounting, and legal services. Concurrent with the emphasis on the financial sector, there is also a drive to create more "technopreneurs" — a fancy name for entrepreneurs in the information and telecommunication industries.

Notwithstanding undeniable past successes, are such efforts misplaced in the new global economy? There is a curiosity here. Economists do recognize that governments can at times create comparative advantages in certain industries through subsidies and other support. Strategic trade theory, as it is called, argues that comparative advantage is often the product of history and chance, and not differences in natural resources and workers' skills. This, then, leads to the question of whether governments should create this comparative advantage. European governments did precisely that, with the aerospace European Consortium, Airbus, taking on Boeing's dominance of the passenger airliner market.

So governments can make a positive difference at the micro level. But some economists disagree, as they say that governments are not in a position to pick winners. Krugman, for instance, doubts whether governments are sophisticated enough and objective enough to do the job right.[12] Framed this way, the issue is not whether industrial policy can make a positive difference but the government capacity to effect it. The fact that good governance is a highly normative term does not detract from the fact that governmental capability is a key determinant of the success or failure of industrial policies. Expectations on the government's institutional ability to effectively implement policies contribute to the success of these policies, as it generates confidence and co-operation from private sector players.

Given its past successes, the issue in Singapore is not whether the Government should intervene, but rather how. Past successful intervention — such as in oil refining, ship repair and disk drives — through fiscal incentives, infrastructure support, and direct intervention may be less appropriate, as the country has virtually caught up on the development cycle. This method of the entrepreneurial state — of leading from the front — may also not be very effective because domestic firms have grown in size and have greater independence from the Government. A case in point is that, despite the clear intent of the Government that the local financial industry should consolidate, the response from local banks and stockbrokers to this has been decidedly lukewarm. Globalization of trade, investment, and capital also means that the leverage which the Government has on local industry has lessened and will continue to weaken as such international economic linkages grow in strength. Further, an economy driven by technology and innovation growth is quite different from one that relies on capital investment to move ahead.

The modalities of intervention will thus have to change. Technological innovation-driven growth suggests that fostering a venture capital culture may be more crucial for success than picking winners. Rapid changes in technology support Krugman's view that governments might not be sophisticated enough to pick winners. But providing the capital for entrepreneurs to give effect to their ideas, and testing them in the markets, may well facilitate such technological-driven growth.

In a broad sense, it involves a mindset change in the whole economy. Credit providers need to move from a collateral-based credit culture, typically property, to that which values an asset that is intangible — an idea or a concept that resides in the head of the entrepreneur. The business culture also needs to change from one that sees the goal of business, not as an accumulation of assets, but as the generation of revenues and the maximization of shareholders' value. The social culture also needs to change to one that sees success, not as avoiding failures, but taking risks to achieve goals, and where failures are regarded as setbacks, rather than dark blots on one's copybook. The political culture also needs to change from one that is top-down to one that is more horizontal. Paternalism may have been necessary in the past to engender shared purpose and trust between the government and the governed, but into the future, its consequence — that of a petitioning society — sits uneasily with the "get-up-and-go" attitude that is at the heart of an entrepreneurial culture. The pragmatism that underlies government intervention in Singapore is what suggests that such a mindset change is being set in motion by the Government. Singapore 21, which looks at the heartware or the software aspect of the country's development, is a manifestation of the Government's intention to effect such a change. Its aim should not just be an aspirational mission statement of Singapore, but a concrete attempt to foster a more textured, multi-layered society which will help the country transit successfully from the industrial economy to the information age.

Conclusion

In conclusion, this quote from financial consultant Henry Kaufman best sums up the way ahead for the Singapore economy. Writing in *Interest Rates, the Markets and the New Financial World*, he said:

> At the dawn of history, life was dominated by huge dinosaurs, fifty foot crocodiles, and the seas swarmed with twenty-foot lizards. The mammals, small and shrewlike in form, hid in thickets and grasses during the day and ventured out only at twilight or in the dark. Undoubtedly, a modern day rating agency would have accorded the dinosaurs the highest credit rating and given no rating at all to the frightened mammals. Today the dinosaurs are extinct and mammals are the dominant life form.[13]

And so it is, that even as globalization throws up challenges for city-states like Singapore which have to take the global environment as a given, yet the trends that are developing — rapid, unpredictable changes fuelled by information and technological innovation — are moving in its favour. It may well be that in the information technology age, the city-state may be the best sized economic unit to adapt, survive, and prosper in the stormy global seas. In the electronic economy, the slow, as they say, die first.

Notes

1. D. Michael Bordo, Barry Eichengeen, and Irwin A. Douglas, "Is Globalization Today Really Different from Globalization a Hundred Years Ago?", NBER Working Paper No. W7195 (June 1999), p. 1–73.
2. John Maynard Keynes, *General Theory of Employment, Interest and Money* (London: Macmillan, 1936), p. 159.
3. John Maynard Keynes, *Economic Consequences of the Peace* (London: Macmillan, 1924), p. 220–21.

4. A. Jeffrey Frankel in the keynote speech on "The Asian Model, The Miracle, The Crisis and the Fund", delivered at the U.S. International Trade Commission, 1998.
5. Bernard Laurens, Jaime Cardoso, and Monetary and Exchange Affairs Department, "Managing Capital Flows: Lessons from the Experience of Chile", Working Paper WP/98/168, p. 11–15.
6. Maurice Obstfeld and Kenneth Rogoff, "The Mirage of Fixed Exchange Rates", *Journal of Economic Perspectives* 9, no. 4 (1998): 78.
7. A. Guillermo Calvo in the keynote speech before a "Joint Hearing of Subcommittees on Economic Policy and International Trade and Finance on Testimony on Full Dollarization: Economic Policy and International Trade and Finance", Washington, D.C., University of Maryland, College Park, 1999.
8. Paul Krugman, *Pop Internationalism* (Cambridge, Mass.: MIT Press, 1996), p. 197.
9. Lester Thurow, *The Future of Capitalism: How Today's Economic Forces Will Shape Tomorrow's World* (London: Nicholas Brealey Publishing Limited, 1996), p. 67.
10. Monetary Authority of Singapore, "Singapore's Services Sector in Perspective: Trends and Outlook", Occasional Paper, No. 5, 1998, p. 5.
11. "Singapore Swings", *Time*, 19 July 1999, p. 16.
12. Paul Krugman, *Peddling Prosperity: Economic Sense and Nonsense in the Age of Diminished Expectations* (New York: W.W. Norton & Company, 1994), p. 241–43.
13. Henry Kaufman, *Interest Rates, the Markets and the New Financial Word* (London: I.B. Tauris & Co. Ltd, 1986), p. 236–37.

3

GOVERNANCE
Its Complexity and Evolution

N. Ganesan

Introduction

Governance, or the art of government, traditionally evolved along with contractual or consensual government in Western political thought. Accordingly, together with the democratic belief that state sovereignty is ultimately vested in citizens, governance has conceptually focused on the twin pillars of accountability and responsibility. Accountability is typically a reference to the conduct of public officials and the policies that they implement. Both of these must serve the public good or interest. A narrower focus on fiduciary matters is commonplace in many countries, since public officials are entrusted with public resources in the fashioning and discharge of policies.[1] Responsibility, on the other hand, is typically a reference to public officials undertaking policies to meet, within permissible limits of legality and morality, the demands of the citizenry. Hence, the traditionally articulated twin pillars of governance — centred on responding to public demands in a transparent and acceptable manner.

More recently, the literature on governance has tended in the direction of what has come to be called capacity-building. This newer notion of governance entails elements of a proactive approach while preserving the spirit of accountability and responsibility. Capacity-building, in turn, may be in one of two forms. The first is a structural-functional understanding of the term and is a reference to vertical or horizontal organizational growth to better cater to citizen demands. The second, which is sometimes termed empowerment, is a reference to human resource development — the introduction or facilitation of higher-order skills. Over and above capacity-building, the literature on governance has also encompassed strategic planning, which is essentially a reference to proactive forecast planning to meet public needs in a variety of areas, from the provision of utilities to health and educational opportunities for future generations. In this regard, governance has increasingly gravitated in the direction of pre-emptive planning.

Finally, governance has also increasingly appropriated market principles to achieve a certain efficiency and seamlessness. Whereas this is not a new development since public choice theory has been in existence for almost half a century, the enthusiasm and rapid spread of this approach is only some two decades old.[2] In the past, writers and practitioners of governance acknowledged fundamental differences between the private and public sector. However, increasingly, governance is being conceptualized and rationalized in terms of market principles. Among other things, the adoption of market principles will weaken the compact achieved between citizens and the public sector, especially since citizens were previously accustomed to the public sector performing a guardian or trusteeship function. Secondly, such an approach has the potential for governments to preclude the provision of services that drain the public purse. Worse, since market principles are driven by profit motives, governments have the ability to profit from the provision of services.

This chapter examines the theme of governance in Singapore. The theme itself naturally twins politics with administration. Accordingly, the term governance is interpreted broadly, rather than in a narrow sense. The chapter is divided into five major sections. The first section examines the state's political ideology and rationale, while the second looks at evolving political and administrative structures. The third section identifies major political issues for the Government, while the fourth details the tensions between regulation on the one hand and liberalization on the other. The fifth and final section is an attempt to plot future issue areas for governance.

State Ideology and Rationale

The historical developments that led to Singapore's separation from the Malaysian Federation and eventual independence in August 1965 had a definitive impact on state ideology and its rationalization. The uneasy membership in the Malaysian Federation from 1963 to 1965 eventually led to Singapore's expulsion from the former. Up until then, the People's Action Party (PAP) Government had conceded that independent statehood for Singapore was quite simply absurd and unsustainable.[3] In fact, even at the time when independence was thrust upon Singapore, the PAP leadership was anxious and uncertain about the developmental possibilities that lay ahead. Nonetheless, the situation was a *fait accompli*, and appropriate policies had to be undertaken to ensure political survival.

For the first two to three years of political independence, survival was truly an issue.[4] After all, historically and geographically, Singapore had developed alongside the Malay Peninsula in what appeared to be a complementary socio-economic and political relationship. This twinning of destinies was established as early as 1826 when Singapore, together with Malacca and Penang, became part of the Straits Settlements. This seeming indivisibility guided British colonial policy towards Singapore up until the time of Singapore's inclusion in the Malaysian Federation.

Apart from the bonds of history and geography, the early PAP élites were concerned about political survival on a number of counts. On the basis of historical precedence deriving from the Greek city-states, the early élites were initially convinced that independent city-states were incapable of extended political survival.[5] This precedent was compounded by domestic political turbulence between the PAP and the Barisan Sosialis up to the time of the 1968 election when the former secured a parliamentary monopoly as a result of the Barisan's boycott of those elections. Labour and student agitation considerably worsened the situation.

External developments were equally unfavourable. The separation from the Malaysian Federation led to significant bilateral tensions with Singapore's immediate northern neighbour.[6] Especially contentious was the dissolution of joint-stock companies like Malaysia-Singapore Airlines, and the introduction of a separate currency for Singapore. Indonesia, which had launched a policy of military confrontation against the Malaysian Federation since the time of its formation in 1963, continued its hostilities against Singapore until 1966.[7] Singapore's decision to hang two Indonesian marines for sabotage that led to the loss of civilian lives in 1968 marked another low point in bilateral relations with Jakarta, even after the Confrontation was formally concluded in July 1967 in Bangkok and the formation of ASEAN a month later in August.[8] Finally, the British announcement of the policy of withdrawal in areas "East of the Suez" significantly exaggerated the vulnerabilities of independent statehood, although external security continued to be guaranteed under the terms of the Anglo-Malayan Defence Agreements (AMDA) until 1971.[9] Apart from its political significance, the British withdrawal was to hollow out some 25 per cent of Singapore's domestic economic revenues. Hence, all in all, the theme of political survival became deeply etched in the minds of both the political élite and policy formulators in the early years of independence.

Deriving from this survivalist phase in domestic politics was a strong compact which the PAP achieved with the domestic population — a compact which would allow it to retain a parliamentary monopoly until 1981. By highlighting the vagaries of independent political existence and the insurmountable odds against which development and prosperity had been achieved, the PAP was able to combine its fortunes and destiny with those of Singapore in the first two decades of independence. Together with an efficient and honest civil service that promptly attended to the needs of its citizens, particularly in the areas of housing, health, and education, the PAP secured easy victories in the first two decades. This development in turn allowed for the eventual evolution of a dominant party system. Over time, together with the isolation of performance criteria to enhance political legitimacy, the PAP's political success became interactive with the entrenchment of the dominant party system.

There were a number of other developments, particularly in the area of public policies, that derived from the PAP's historical interactions with the Malaysian Federation. Given that one of the areas of disagreement between the PAP and the Alliance Government (led by the United Malays National Organization) pertained to ascriptive policies that favoured ethnic Malays in land, education, and occupational allocations, post-independent Singapore chartered an ethnically neutral course. Accordingly, the state espoused multiethnicity and multiculturalism as processes and targets in policy-making. Meritocracy was emphasized as the fundamental avenue for occupational and upward social mobility. However, in recognition of its historical association and geographical location in the Malay Archipelago, the national anthem is in Malay. Additionally, Malay was identified as the national language, although English eventually evolved to become the main working language (of business and administration).

During Singapore's early years of statehood, the PAP Government took decisive action against Malay and Chinese chauvinism, since these had the potential to challenge and fissure society. Communalism and communism were identified as the two threats that the state had to overcome. The Barisan's leftist political leanings, for example, would lead to the detention of many of its leaders.[10] By incorporating all the ethnic groups within its ranks, the PAP demonstrated that politics and development did not need to be ethnically defined. As part of its crackdown against chauvinism, the Government clamped down on the two major ethnically inspired newspapers — *Utusan Melayu* and the *Nanyang Siang Pau* in 1970 and 1971, respectively.

The PAP Government disqualified both class and ethnicity as rationalizations for political mobilization and contestation. As a result, politics in post-independent Singapore evolved differently from the Federation experience. Until today, the Pertubuhan Kebangsaan Melayu Singapura (PKMS) remains as the only ethnically inspired political party in Singapore and has been unable to make any inroads in political contestation. The PAP's inclusion of minority candidates, to numbers that approximate the percentage of their representation in the electorate, has further pre-empted the need for ethnic minority mobilization.

Other aspects of governance that have a historical rooting are an interventionist approach and proactive strategic planning. Right from the outset, the PAP Government has identified both systemic coherence and successful development as issues that cannot be taken for granted. Additionally, since survival and prosperity were crafted against overwhelming odds, it has appropriated a certain legitimacy, as well as an interventionist style. As a result, observers of the domestic political scene are often surprised at some of the prescriptive and proscriptive policies of the Government — from when citizens should get married and how many children they should have, to the banning of chewing gum. In a sense, the Government does not typically distinguish between public and private realms of action, especially if actions are thought to impinge on broad social well-being and alter the fabric of society negatively.

Proactive strategic planning is meant to anticipate the demands of the citizen body. These may range from housing and educational needs, to the vigorous push for trade enhancement, financial liberalization, and plans for the construction of desalination plants. Although the Government recognizes market-style efficiency and appropriates it whenever and wherever possible, there is also an attempt to intervene and create conditions necessary for the fulfilment of certain broad objectives. Whereas the demands of the market and central planning may in some instances be irreconcilable or conflictual, the situation has generally been managed quite well. The PAP's record on governance, interventionism, and strategic planning are all interactive. In this regard, it has traditionally emphasized good government over specific regime types or forms of government. Increasingly, in its discourse on governance, the Government has emphasized qualitative performance over structural forms. In view of its record to date, the argument quite ingeniously rationalizes existing structures and practices as inherently good and certainly worthy of retention.

Evolving Political and Administrative Structures

From the time when the British colonial authorities granted Singapore internal self-government in 1959, the country has functioned well within the framework of a Westminster-styled unicameral parliamentary structure. The civil service and statutory boards have typically complemented the elected Government in the discharge of its functions. Beginning with decentralized administrative structures that usurped the functions of the statutory boards, especially in the area of public housing, the Government has introduced a number of organizations to facilitate governance. More importantly perhaps, from the mid-1980s, the Government has introduced a number of structural changes to the parliamentary system of government inherited from the United Kingdom. Many of these changes have fundamentally altered the rules of political contestation and representation in Parliament. Over and above these changes, Singapore also introduced a directly elected presidency in 1993, with a six-year term of office. The primary responsibilities of the Elected President are, in the first instance, to ensure fiscal prudence and responsible appointments to higher-level administrative positions.

The most important structural change for political contestation introduced in Singapore was the Group Representation Constituency (GRC) scheme.[11] This scheme, which was initially introduced in the 1988 general election, welded together a number of individual electoral constituencies into larger units. It was originally rationalized by the Government as incorporating a broader voter base and initially comprised three Members of Parliament (MPs) per GRC (which included at least one ethnic minority candidate — Eurasian, Indian, or Malay), alongside constituencies with single MPs. A subsequent refinement to the scheme in 1991 stipulated that each GRC comprise a total of four MPs. The PAP rationalized that the GRC scheme would ensure minority representation in Parliament. The Government argued that it was committed and had a desire to protect the interests of the ethnic minorities, in order to be consistent with its promotion of multiethnicity as being in the national interest. The political opposition, however, charged that the GRCs communalized the political process and reduced its chances of winning seats in larger multiple-MP constituencies. Such rationalizations and charges notwithstanding, the introduction of GRCs significantly altered the political system.

At the time when the general election was called in January 1997, Parliament comprised a total of eighty-one MPs — sixty drawn from fifteen GRCs, with four MPs from each, and the remaining twenty-one from single-member wards. Prior to the election, in October 1996, additional changes were made to the scheme such that GRCs could comprise a total of up to six MPs. Additionally, the 75 per cent ceiling on the total number of seats held by MPs from GRCs was also lifted in favour of a minimum of eight single-member wards. Accordingly, arising from these changes and the outcome of political contestation during the 1997 election, Parliament subsequently had four 6-member GRCs, six 5-member GRCs, five 4-member GRCs, and nine single-member wards for a total of eighty-three MPs. Two of the single-member wards, Potong Pasir and Nee Soon Central, are held by members of the political opposition.

In order to deflect criticism that the changes made to the GRC scheme in 1997 diluted minority representation in Parliament, the Government assured the electorate that the previous number of minority candidates in Parliament (seventeen out of seventy-seven) would be retained. The Government also deflected opposition charges of gerrymandering electoral boundaries by stating that it planned to fight opposition candidates squarely at the polls, rather than by co-opting opposition constituencies into GRCs. The *ex post facto* nature of the subsequent announcements, however, led to some measure of public disquiet.

Another significant structural change to the practice of democracy in Singapore is the Non-Constituency Member of Parliament (NCMP) scheme. Following the outcome of the 1984 general election, the PAP made provisions for Parliament to include three opposition candidates who had polled the highest number of votes despite having lost the election, in the event that less than three opposition candidates failed to secure election. The scheme was meant to invigorate debate in Parliament, in view of the marginal presence of the opposition (two out of a total of eighty-one MPs). Unfortunately, the NCMP scheme proved to be unpopular, since opposition political candidates were generally not keen on what was regarded as a back-door entry into Parliament by the grace of the Government.

Owing its origins to and deriving from the NCMP scheme is the Nominated Member of Parliament (NMP) scheme, which was introduced in 1990. The PAP's rationalization for the NMP scheme was that the interests and aspirations of credible and distinguished private citizens without political affiliations should be represented. Additionally, it was argued that such persons would be able to sharpen the oratorical skills of elected MPs. The opposition, on the other hand, charged that the PAP was drawing on a limited talent pool that was subject to its approval, and that such a scheme would deteriorate into sectoral and gender representation. The NMP scheme, when it was initially launched, made provisions for up to six 2-year term appointments to Parliament. The scheme was subsequently enlarged to accommodate up to nine NMPs in 1997. The enlargement of the NMP scheme is laudable in that it allows for a larger sampling of the views of competent private citizens to be heard. Such a development is well in line with the PAP's view that the Westminster-style parliamentary system of government inherited from the British is inherently combative in nature and ill-geared towards achieving the sort of consensus on issues that it desires. Whereas the plurality of views offered by the NMPs in the past had helped to stimulate parliamentary debates, it was also true that the NMPs who were ideally meant to offer coherent and divergent views on public policies increasingly began to represent sectoral and gender interests. In this regard, the scheme had deteriorated to some extent. On the other hand, if there was such a natural gravitation, then the enlargement of the scheme is an entirely appropriate strategy to achieve the originally intended goals. After all, a broadening of the scheme would allow for a greater representation of specific sectoral issues that, in the process, will weave a national agenda. Nonetheless, it must be noted that the enlargement of the scheme is meant, at least partly, to deal with the deterioration, or at least the detraction, from the originally intended purpose of the scheme. Finally, a broadening of the scheme would lead to the evolution of an indigenous political institution with the capacity to preserve the dominant party system of Singapore.

The last and most recent structural adjustment to parliamentary democracy is the establishment of an Elected Presidency (EP) in 1993.[12] The office of the EP, which was to co-habit with the Prime Minister in Parliament, was meant, in the first instance, to safeguard Singapore's substantial financial reserves accumulated by previous governments and exercise a discretionary veto to key appointments in the public sector. It was, as the PAP put it, meant to be the "second key" to prevent the unlocking of previously accumulated surpluses by irresponsible incumbent governments in order to retain popularity. The institution of the EP significantly altered the structure of government and dispersion of power within it. Technically, the EP, since he or she is elected into an executive office, has a far greater democratic mandate than the Prime Minister, who is the chief executive officer of the Government on the basis of leading the majority party that forms the government. Additionally, a veto by the EP on the drawing of previously accumulated surpluses and key appointments in the public sector diminishes the Prime Minister's authority, quite simply because there is the possibility of an executive override on a decision. Although the Prime Minister can overcome the veto of an EP by calling for a referendum, the fact remains that an additional check has been installed on his decision-making capacity.

The office of the EP, which was meant to function in Singapore's national interest, was crafted for an individual without affiliation to a political party. Over time, this non-partisan quality became codified as a necessary condition for eligibility, over and above a minimum age requirement of forty-five years and demonstrated ability in the management of a company with a paid-up capital of at least S$100 million, among others. In other words, the incumbent was to be a mature person in good standing with a demonstrated capacity for fiscal management.

Singapore's first EP, Ong Teng Cheong, polled some 58 per cent of the popular vote against Chua Kim Yeow, a one-time senior public servant who was relatively unknown in the political arena. Ong, who stepped down from the Deputy Prime Ministership, was a veteran PAP second generation politician who had risen to political prominence in the labour movement. His rather poor performance at the presidential polls, at least by PAP standards, was probably attributable to general unhappiness at the nomination of a senior PAP politician for what was to be a non-partisan executive office. Ong, whose six-year term expired in August 1999, was replaced by S. R. Nathan, a senior civil servant, without contest. The change of office-holders did not attract much debate, given the rigorous nature of the screening process for potential candidates. However, what attracted much attention were the remarks made by Ong during a press conference before stepping down, where he noted that he found "no compelling reason" to continue as the EP.[13] He subsequently recalled some of the difficulties he encountered in discharging his functions, in particular, the cataloguing and verification of the country's national reserves, and went on to note how he was sometimes regarded as a nuisance. He ended by urging elected politicians and public officials to fulfil their constitutional duty in co-operating with the EP. The episode revealed a number of things. Firstly, Ong obviously took his office and the duties associated with it seriously. Secondly, and perhaps more importantly, the EP requires the co-operation of the incumbent government and the civil service to discharge his duties. Thirdly, the terms of the EP's office may require the adoption of a position contrary to or in conflict with that of an incumbent government, for which there may be little recourse within existing structures and provisions. Finally, it may be noted that structural adjustments to an existing system may yield latent repercussions that may have been previously ignored.

Alongside structural changes to the political system, the Singapore Government has, over the years, introduced a number of grassroots organizations, in order to decentralize some of its administrative services and invoke citizen participation in the formulation and discharge of public policies.[14] Whereas some of these organizations are relatively mature and owe their origins to the introduction and expansion of the public housing programme in the 1960s and 1970s, some of them are of more recent vintage. The objective of administering to the needs and demands of the citizens, as well as the dissemination of information regarding public policies, however, remain the major rationalization for administrative decentralization. In other words, it is meant to invoke governance from below, with direction from above.

The earliest of such organizations is the Citizens' Consultative Committees (CCCs), which were formed in 1965. In order to supplement the function of the CCCs and to help citizens better accommodate each other, given differences in culture, ethnicity, and religion, Residents' Committees (RCs) were introduced in public housing estates. For many of the same reasons, as well as to make MPs perform a representative function that was interactive with their constituency, the Government established Town Councils (TCs) in 1988. Over time, the TCs appropriated many of the functions that were previously performed by the Housing and Development Board (HDB), such as the general maintenance and landscaping of public housing estates, refuse disposal, and the collection of monthly conservancy charges.

The most recent administrative structure designed to facilitate decentralized governance are Community Development Councils (CDCs), which were introduced in 1997 and described as "grassroots organizations, given the task of building community bonds among the residents in the district".[15] The terms of reference include a significant financial component — the Government would provide a grant of S$1 per resident each year, as well as a S$4 top-up for every dollar raised in the district. Whereas the CDCs are well in line with the Government's attempts at involving greater participation in administrative decision-making affecting residents of a locality, the new organization will have to evolve a discrete mandate, different from that already held by RCs and TCs. The Government's announcement that only PAP MPs will be assigned the role of mayors to head the CDCs further complicates matters. Government funds disbursed to PAP MPs in opposition-held wards are likely to create some problems in terms of the opposition MPs' legitimate needs to serve their constituents and the erosion of their administrative scope, if the CDCs replace some of the functions currently executed by the TCs.

The growing trend of administrative decentralization and the reduction in the role of statutory boards that are increasingly performing a regulatory function augurs the potential for dysfunctions created by politicizing administration.[16] Whereas there is some legitimate concern that existing grassroots organizations are increasingly alienated from, and incapable of attending to, their constituents, the politicization of new structures with an enlarged scope may not address the present situation. The reason for this observation is that the budget and agenda of the CDCs, on the basis of politically partisan appointees, will derive from a political mandate, rather than the administrative one which the process of decentralization is meant to serve.

Major Political Issues

The major political issues in Singapore essentially derive from the interactions between the Government and its various agencies and the general public. It may, from time to time, also be the function of a specific policy initiative or unhappiness with what is perceived as an inadequate or insufficient response to a situation. In terms of the origins or identification of the problem, the initiative may derive from the state or, alternatively, from the ground upwards, through the various feedback mechanisms available. Specifically, four issue-areas may be identified as constitutive of the present situation. They are the Government's perceived lack of bonding with the citizenry, pressures deriving from the importation of foreign talent and class stratification, pressures for greater participation and consultation from the ground, and the inherent tensions resident in the relationship between governance on the one hand and freedom and empowerment on the other.

The issue of bonding with the Government is a more serious problem than it is acknowledged to be. This problem derives partly from the PAP's own success and partly from technological advances and the growing demands of daily living. The simple fact is that the Singapore Government is quite far removed from regular interactions with the citizenry, compared to a few decades ago. Part of the reason for this development is the PAP's firm belief that the art of governance should be entrusted to a highly-qualified and skilled technocratic élite. Demands may derive from the ground, but the tools associated with the formulation and discharge of public policies is the concern of the Government alone. This observation is not to suggest that the Government has been unsuccessful in the formulation of policies. Rather, it has been very successful. Its stunning success and firm conviction that policy formulation is its own exclusive domain have led to some measure of frustration and resulting apathy; the average citizen is generally unconvinced that he or she has a substantive impact on public policies.

Singapore's history of successful governance has also created a general mood of complacency among its people. When policies are generally efficient and pre-emptive in nature, citizens feel the need to do little beyond observing the rules and complying with them. The inherently legalistic nature of governance in Singapore only requires clearly identifiable responses. Consequently, the average person in Singapore expects the Government to be honest and efficient, and is generally unable to function well in situations where this cannot be taken for granted. Today, for the most part, interactions with the Government occur quite simply in the form of an electronic deduction in a person's bank account, to pay, for example, income taxes or water and electricity bills. Whereas such transactions may make for efficient governance, valuable interaction with the public is lost. Accordingly, interaction with the Government has been reduced to life's defining moments — marriage, birth, death, and perhaps the acquisition of property. Everything else can, quite simply, be dealt with electronically.

The second issue of foreign talent and class stratification is perhaps a more serious issue than bonding, at least in so far as it has the potential to unravel the fabric of social harmony if it is not managed carefully. Foreign talent has always been attracted to Singapore, and the state has generally been supportive of the infusion of highly-skilled foreign talent. As a young state with roots in migrants from the Asian region, it is arguable that the work attitudes, thrift, and commitment of migrants has always been appreciated, especially by the Government. However, beginning from 1997, the Singapore Government has become especially aggressive in sourcing for foreign talent with technical, research, and managerial skills, to transform the nature of the economy and to ensure Singapore remains relevant as a global metropolis in a number of tertiary and research sectors. To make Singapore attractive to such talent, subsidized housing and other expatriate benefits are often made available. The provision of such facilities and the Government's constant call for the needs of such talent to be recognized have led to some measure of unhappiness from a segment of Singaporean society that regards such foreigners as exercising privileges that are unavailable to locals. Additionally, such foreign talent is exempted from the compulsory military service that all able-bodied male Singapore citizens perform. Such grievances have in the past received widespread attention.

Class stratification, which is an invariable by-product of socio-economic development, exists in Singapore and is interactive with skill and educational levels and, indirectly, foreign talent. The rough and ready rule of thumb that is often employed is the distinction between "cosmopolitans" and "heartlanders," as identified by Prime Minister Goh Chok Tong in his National Day Rally Speech in August 1999. This distinction, which derives from and overlaps with the population breakdown in public and private housing estates, is often thought to distinguish the cosmopolitan from the heartlander. Strict government regulation on income levels as part of the eligibility criteria for public housing reinforces the divide. The Singapore Government, which has traditionally been conscious of class cleavages, has attempted some amount of redistributive justice through progressive income and property taxes and sizeable annual offsets to rent and conservancy charges to those living in public housing estates. National educational and medical endowments have also been created to alleviate the burden of those unable to afford basic services. Nonetheless, as the demand for higher order skills grows, it is to be expected that class stratification will become even more clearly defined.

Participatory and consultative pressures are an issue that is attendant on all democratic governments. Rising literacy levels and regular exposure to lifestyles in other countries have made educated citizens much more vocal in their demands for recognition and participation.[17] A variety of regulatory measures governing the mass media and the formation of interest groups previously helped the Government deal with what was perceived as negative demands. Alongside these restrictions, greater attempts were also made to accommodate public opinion. Accordingly, beginning from the 1980s, the Singapore Government has convened open public debates on policy matters, has regularly issued White Papers on such deliberations, and established the Institute for Policy Studies in 1987 and a Feedback Unit in 1985 that is co-ordinated by the Ministry of Community Development. Nonetheless, the pressures for participation and the availability of alternative views have continued to mount. The establishment of two non-governmental discussion groups, The Roundtable and the Socratic Circle in the 1990s, is also probably indicative of the trend of future developments.

The final issue of the tension between governance and freedom is also a generic one. Western liberal conceptions of government resolved the problem by distinguishing, within limits, between the realms of public and private actions. Government, which administered in the realm of public decision-making, was expected to regulate transactions which had a collective impact. Since much of Western society originated with theistic, ecclesiastical, and monarchical claims to power, contractual government, which drew its inspiration from the Enlightenment, sought to minimize and regulate the role of government. Both the classical and neoliberal scholars believed in the intrinsic ability of aggregate demand and supply to achieve an equilibrium in most aspects of life. Accordingly, the general thrust of governance in recent times has been to trim the role and scope of governance, since individuals are assumed to be rational utility maximizers. This general drift in global governance is clearly at odds with the interventionist and legalistic nature of governance in Singapore. As the next century unfolds, the contradictions arising from these two opposing trends will become more manifest.[18]

Regulation versus Liberalization

Together with administrative decentralization, the Singapore Government has embarked on an aggressive policy of liberalization. This policy, which is of relatively recent origin, is most apparent in the telecommunications and financial sectors. There are numerous motivations for this initiative. The initial overriding consideration was government divestment from a number of sectors in order to derive the benefits of a market-centred private sector approach to the delivery of services. In other words, it was, in the first instance, meant to transform the nature of the Government's involvement in certain sectors from enforcement to regulation. Apart from opening up consumer choices and stimulating private enterprise, the policy was also meant to divest peripheral areas of governance. An additional reason, especially pertaining to reform in the financial sector, is meant to position Singapore as a global financial hub in the Asia-Pacific region. Hence, there is an element of strategic planning associated with these initiatives as well.

Divestment from non-core areas of governance provided the most compelling reason for liberalization at the outset. The state-led model of economic development that Singapore implemented in the 1970s and 1980s had led to excessive state involvement in the domestic economy. This development was a natural consequence of investments being dominated by foreign-owned multinational corporations and the relative scarcity of domestic investment capital. The pressures of competition and higher levels of socio-economic development also took its toll on small domestic entrepreneurs. Government investments in strategic industries like defence, micro-electronic chip manufacture, and the establishment of the wafer fabrication industry compounded the lopsided nature of economic developments in favour of the public sector. The need by the Government to invest sizeable financial surpluses that were steadily accumulated into productive activity was another consideration.

The convergence of these developments and the general global trend of governments divesting their economic portfolios made the task much more urgent. The public listing of government monopolies like Singapore Telecoms and the planned listing of Singapore Power should be seen in such light. Citizens are allowed to subscribe to shares in such corporations at discounted prices. The ensuing capitalization significantly deepened the domestic stock market and allowed the Government to set up regulatory agencies that performed a simpler overseer function, such as the Telecommunications Authority of Singapore.

The initiatives undertaken for financial liberalization, however, have significantly different motivations. Although they are generally within the spirit of divestment from governance and regulation, rather than enforcement, they are directed at two different constituencies. Domestically, the new regulations, especially those pertaining to the banking sector, are meant to introduce foreign competition into what is regarded as an overprotected and lethargic local banking sector. Naturally, increased competition will also yield significant benefits to local consumers. The second and perhaps more important reason is to establish Singapore's presence as a global financial market. In this regard, the reforms are to be viewed alongside attempts to attract significant foreign fund managers to maintain a presence and operate out of Singapore, incentives to the creation of an active bond market, and the deregulation of the insurance industry. Collectively, these efforts are meant to significantly deepen and widen Singapore's tertiary sector, which is natural, given the absence of a primary sector and a secondary sector pegged at some 25 per cent of domestic production. The changes are also well in line with Singapore's growing emphasis on high value-added manufactures and services. Therefore, liberalization of the financial sector goes well beyond divestment and is an aspect of strategic planning.

Collectively, many of these changes which transform the role of governance from a guard dog to a watchdog function are well in line with international norms. However, the aggressive nature of the policy thrust is likely to create some measure of unhappiness with indigenous providers of such services who had previously benefited from protectionist policies. The increased reliance on technology and information will also require some amount of management and complicate the Government's ability to monitor and censor all information flows. Finally, the financial liberalization package will enhance "cosmopolitanism" and lead to some measure of dissatisfaction from the "heartland" communities. Older citizens who are considerably less savvy in technology-related matters may also become anxious at the forced and rapid pace of change. These constituencies of citizens have the potential to register their unhappiness with the PAP at election time.

Future Issue Areas

On the basis of the discussion thus far and given the present trajectory of developments, a number of issues will arise for the future governance of Singapore. Some of the issues, like increased pressures for participation and challenges deriving from the information revolution and globalization, have already been identified as existing issues. Over time, their relevance for governance will also rise in importance. Two other issues — leadership generational change and the demonstration effect of regional political developments — will evolve in importance over time.

Increased pressures for political participation and input into the policy formulation process are demands that the future political élite of Singapore will face. Such pressures will derive from individuals as well as groups. Higher literacy rates and increased educational qualifications have traditionally been a source of empowerment and upward socio-economic mobility. Accordingly, as institutions and processes mature in Singapore, the nature of challenges for governance will be different from those of yesteryears. It may be noted here that, with the exception of sudden cyclical downturns in the global economy and regional political and economic turbulence, governance in Singapore essentially involves system maintenance and incremental changes, rather than an entire overhaul of the system. Such incremental changes may be insufficiently responsive to future demands for participation. Accordingly, a change in the assumptions and attitudes regarding the governance of Singapore is essential. A paternalistic unidirectional top-down approach to governance will prove to be unpopular. The governance of rising expectations, rather than concrete demands, will also prove to be problematic. Finally, the nature of the clamour for consideration and involvement in government will not only be demanding, but also divisive. As a result, the nature of the change will be both quantitative and qualitative. Policies will, over time, require the utilization of a range of instruments to satisfy the demands of more discrete and smaller constituencies.

Challenges to governance will also come at a time of unprecedented technological advances, with corresponding spillover into information systems and globalization. Countries like Singapore, which have expressed a desire to be at the forefront of the information revolution, will have significantly less lead time to cope with the situation. A number of challenges derive from this single source of change. Firstly, the Singapore Government is accustomed to being able to control sources of information and, if necessary, censor them or insist on the right of robust reply. Such "rules of the game" will become irrelevant over time. Not only will the Government be unable to control information flows, it will also be unable to pinpoint or take action against a source of information — a private website in the United States, for example. This monopoly on information is an important aspect of governance in Singapore

Secondly, and perhaps more importantly, information flows will become more complex and global over time. What this means is that attempts to censor information will become unsuccessful, and the nature of the information, global in its reach. As a result of such interconnectedness and complex interdependence, the forces of globalization will exert great pressures on governance. Globalization and its attendant impact on consumer culture and values will assault many Asian values that are regarded as intrinsically good, like the family as the basic unit of society, filial piety, and society above self. Such drastic changes in value systems which have previously been taken for granted, will lead to challenges in the realm of public policy-making. The rapid entrenchment of global "cosmopolitan" values will exert further pressures on social stratification in Singapore and significantly exaggerate future generation gaps.

Finally, as a young nation, Singapore is just now slowly beginning to fashion elements of nation and nationhood. The Government has begun raising the profile of a "national education" curriculum to instill greater awareness and a sense of belonging in the younger generation. Under the circumstances, it is very easy to imagine how some of the lessons of national education will quite simply be dismissed as state-sponsored propaganda. After all, Western-styled rational utility-maximizing consumption patterns know no boundaries or attachments that would be regarded as emotional or irrational. In other words, globalization truly has the potential to seriously disrupt nationhood in Singapore. Well-educated cosmopolitan types, with their highly mobile skills, will have much greater opportunities for relocation outside of Singapore if they view governance as unresponsive to their demands. Over time and into the next millennium, if the well-educated cosmopolitan types exert pressure on the Government, so will those who have been left behind in the structural transformation. Low-skilled workers will find the demand for their labour shrinking.[19] Similarly, the elderly, of which there will be a significantly larger proportion in forthcoming decades, will also exert pressure on the Government for services. Collectively, such pressures will require some minimal welfare provisions for continued social cohesion.

At the turn of the millennium, as Singapore braces itself for the challenges that will arise from governance in the future, the PAP already has a third generation leadership in place to replace the current generation of leaders. However, it is also increasingly clear that the Government continues to encounter significant difficulties in recruiting new talent. The rigours of public office and the loss of private time and space are often cited as reasons why citizens prefer to abstain from holding public office. This difficulty in leadership rejuvenation will become amplified over time, and the Government may be forced to rely more and more on returning scholars from the civil service and statutory boards for induction into government. This process, which has already begun, is likely to become more entrenched over time, in the absence of direct recruitment. In fact, as everyday life becomes more complex and demanding, the Government will also encounter difficulties in recruiting members for its numerous grassroots organizations. On the issue of leadership renewal, it should also be noted that Singapore should prepare itself for a post-Lee Kuan Yew era. After all, since internal self-government in 1959, the Singapore electorate has become accustomed to the overwhelming influence of Lee in politics and policy. Given his larger-than-life achievements and close association with Singapore's independence and progress, Lee commands moral authority in the country that is rarely disputed. As a result, his successors in senior governmental positions will have significantly less accomplishments and corresponding legitimacy and authority in governance. Challenges to politics and governance will, therefore, become more likely and pronounced over time.

The final issue in Singapore's future governance has to do with the demonstration effect of regional developments. Despite being significantly different from its immediate neighbours in terms of size, population composition, and levels of socio-economic development, Singapore is very much located in the heart of Southeast Asia. As a result, regional political developments, both positive and negative, will have a profound influence on Singapore. Especially important will be developments that pertain to democratization, like those that swept the Philippines in 1986 and Thailand in 1992. Both Indonesia and Malaysia, Singapore's immediately adjacent neighbours, are presently undergoing significant political change and contestation. If, over time, the situation is resolved in favour of higher levels of democratization, Singapore can ill-afford to ignore such a trend. This is especially so, since socio-economic development has traditionally yielded political liberalization.

Notes

1. Financial accountability has traditionally been highly prized in Singapore's public sector. However, there were recent revelations of discrepancies in financial records as reported by the Auditor-General. See *Straits Times*, 8 September 1999.
2. See, for example, Vincent Ostrom, "Some Developments in the Study of Market-Choice, Public Choice, and Institutional Choice," in *Handbook of Public Administration*, edited by Jack Rabin et al. (New York: Marcel Dekker, 1998).
3. The most recent work that examines the turbulent period of Singapore's membership in the Malayan Federation is Albert Lau, *A Moment of Anguish: Singapore in Malaysia and the Politics of Disengagement* (Singapore: Times Academic Press, 1998).
4. See Chan Heng Chee, *Singapore: The Politics of Survival, 1965-67* (Singapore: Oxford University Press, 1971).

5. Leszek Buszynski, "Singapore: A Foreign Policy of Survival", *Asian Thought and Society* 29 (July 1985): 128–36.
6. Lau Teik Soon, "Malaysia-Singapore Relations: Crisis of Adjustment, 1965-68", *Journal of Southeast Asian History* X (March 1969): 155–76; and R. S. Milne, "Singapore's Exit from Malaysia: The Consequences of Ambiguity," *Asian Survey* VI, No. 3 (March 1966): 175–84.
7. See Donald Hindley, "Indonesia's Confrontation with Malaysia: A Search for Motives", *Asian Survey* IV, No. 6 (June 1964): 904–13.
8. Singapore's difficulties in its bilateral relations with Indonesia is documented in Lee Khoon Choy, *An Ambassador's Journey* (Singapore: Times Books International, 1983).
9. See Chin Kin Wah, *Five Power Defence Arrangements and* AMDA (Singapore: Institute of Southeast Asian Studies, 1974).
10. See Shee Poon Kim, "The Evolution of the Political System", in *Government and Politics of Singapore*, edited by Jon S.T. Quah et al. (Singapore: Oxford University Press, 1985).
11. The structural changes described in this section are examined in N. Ganesan, "Democracy in Singapore", *Asian Journal of Political Science* 4, No.:2 (December 1996): 63–79
12. See Hussin Mutalib, *Singapore's Elected Presidency and the Quest for Regime Dominance*, (Working Paper No. 9, National University of Singapore, Department of Political Science, 1994; Linda Low and Toh Mun Heng, *The Elected Presidency as a Safeguard for Official Reserves: What is at Stake?* (Singapore: Times Academic Press for the Institute of Policy Studies, 1989).
13. Andrea Hamilton, "The President Speaks Out", *Asiaweek*, 30 July 1999, p. 25.
14. A recent survey of grassroots organizations can be found in M. Shamsul Haque, "A Grassroots Approach to Decentralization in Singapore", *Asian Journal of Political Science* 4, No. 1 (June 1996): 64–84.
15. *Sunday Times*, 3 August 1997.
16. See N. Ganesan, "Singapore: Entrenching a City-State's Dominant Party System", in *Southeast Asian Affairs* 1998 (Singapore: Institute of Southeast Asian Studies, 1998), pp. 232–33.
17. See Garry Rodan, "Class transformations and political tensions in Singapore's development", in *The New Rich in Asia: Mobile Phones, McDonald's and Middle-Class Revolution*, edited by Richard Robison and David S. G. Goodman (London: Routledge, 1996).
18. For a recent treatment of this tension, see Lam Peng Er, "Singapore: Rich State, Illiberal Regime," in *Driven by Growth: Political Change in the Asia-Pacific Region* (Revised Ed.), edited by James W. Morley (New York: M. E. Sharpe, 1999).
19. In 1998 alone, there were 29,000 low-skilled workers retrenched, while the figure is expected to total some 15,000 in 1999. See *Straits Times*, 2 September 1999. In anticipation of the need for skills upgrading, the Government has announced a $200 million fund to provide retraining. See *Straits Times*, 1 September 1999.

4

THE FUTURE OF CIVIL SOCIETY
What Next?

Simon S. C. Tay

> *Civil society groups are okay for committee meetings and issuing statements and press conferences.*
>
> — Senior Minister Lee Kuan Yew,
> *Straits Times*, 11 August 1999

There is a problem in thinking about the future of politics and civil society. This is so both generally in much of the world, and specifically in Singapore. Intellectual thought in the late twentieth century has lost the polarity that characterized the decades after World War II, between democracy and capitalism on the one hand, and socialism and totalitarian systems on the other. The end of the Cold War has not been the end of history, as Francis Fukuyama suggested in his *End of History and the Last Man*. But the neoliberal programme of democracy and free markets has become the dominant set of arrangements in most thinking about politics.

The dominance of the idea of democracy and free markets has been resisted by some, not only in Asia but also in the United States and Europe, among both conservatives and progressives. There has been talk of a "third way", both in Europe and the United States. Some, such as Etzioni, Sandel, and Putnam, have also suggested the need for communitarian democracies. Much of this, however, seems a rearguard defence of socialist democracy, and a nostalgia for community. Thinking about political futures has, in this context, fallen prey to new forms of determinism and fatalism. This is especially the case in most political predictions about Asia's future.

In the late 1980s and after, some suggested that the new rich in Asia would necessarily bring democracy. South Korea and Taiwan were seen as examples of this trend, moving away from "soft authoritarianism" to true democracy. There were some who predicted the same would inevitably come to pass in Singapore and other countries that resisted this trend. This set the context for the "Asian values" debate that seemed, in the mouths of some, to argue for essentialized differences in perpetuity.

The economic crisis and the "new" poverty in much of Asia that arose from mid-1997 have bred another form of deterministic thinking about the rise of democracy in Asia. Indonesia, Thailand and, further afield, South Korea are seen as demonstrating that aspect of the crisis; with the fall of Soeharto and the first free election for forty years in Indonesia, the consolidation of a "people's democracy" and a new Constitution in Thailand, and the election as President of once-dissident Kim Dae-Jung in South Korea. To others, however, the crisis is a cause to emphasize good governance and strong leadership, so long as it is clean and has concern for the public good. They warn that what transpires in Indonesia may not result in democracy but chaos. They express concern that democracy in Thailand, South Korea, and other societies may disguise vested interests and prevent necessary but painful structural reforms to national industries, domestic élites, and labour unions. In both sides of such debates, whether before the crisis or presently, the common element in our thinking about the future in politics and civil society has been deterministic, especially in their application to Asia. We are deterministic about the rise of democracy, whether from new wealth or new poverty. Or we are deterministic in our arguments of resistance, citing culture, and developmental needs.

Asian scholars and leaders have largely either been nativist collaborators or nationalistic resistance-fighters to democracy and civil society. The nativist collaborator took concepts of democracy, human rights, and civil society from their original roots in Western thinking and (often elaborately) argued for native foundations for the same or substantively similar ideas. So, for example, Hinduism or Islam is examined and found to have a concept of human dignity, and is therefore a suitable base for democracy, human rights, and civil society. Much of the cross-cultural work in human rights is predicated on such premises. The nationalistic resistance-fighter is the mirror image; the same but wholly different. This leads many to think of change in societies around the world in stark terms, as a choice between, in Barber's neat phrase, the "McWorld" of globalized homogeneity and the "*Jihad*" of radicalized differences and stark separations. It is then a short step to predicting the clash of civilizations, as Huntington has done.

In seeking to think about the future of civil society, democracy, and human rights in Asia and, particularly, in Singapore, this chapter is written against much of these forms of thinking. The ideas that characterize the chapter are guided by human agency, not determinism, and therefore the future is contingent. In seeking out evidence of possible changes and trends, this chapter examines the open text of public statements and acts of everyday resistance, as much as it looks to overt opposition and revolutionary action. In suggesting what may (or may not) come, this essay seeks institutional innovation and experimentalism, rather than institutional fetishism. In this regard, it takes international influence as breeding hybridity, rather than a stark dichotomy between conformity and absolute rejection. Determinism has the danger of breeding fatalism and a sense that individuals need do nothing to either fight or foster change. Dichotomy has the danger of demanding both too much and too little of the future; we will either remain as we are today, or we will tomorrow copy what someone already has today.

The three central ways of thinking proposed in this chapter — contingency and human agency, acts of everyday resistance, and hybridity — of course have their own dangers. They can be accused of vague idealism and romanticism, of overambition and overly specific analysis, and of assuming easy half-way houses between conflicting positions. There is perhaps one critical difference between the two sets of ideas and their different difficulties in trying to look at the future. The first set of ideas — deterministic and dichotomous — tries to answer what will be. The second set of ideas — contingency and agency, acts of everyday resistance, and hybridity — suggests instead what might be, if some want to try to achieve something. In taking up the second set of ideas, the chapter will proceed in three steps. The first is to sketch the recent renaissance of interest in civil society and some of the contested concepts in the renewed discourse. The second is to trace the case of Singapore so far, from pre-independence days, but with a closer examination of quite current events from 1997 onwards. The third section will suggest possible experiments that can arise in the Singapore case and probable outcomes.

The Contested Concepts of Civil Society

After a century of neglect,[1] the contemporary discussion of civil society was revived first and foremost in the struggles against authoritarian socialist states in Eastern Europe.[2] "Civil society", although an elastic term that differed in use from one East European situation to another, emerged as a "shining emblem" of resistance.[3] In this context, it seems mainly a code word to ask for what the Western "liberal" democracies already have, and a means to delegitimize non-liberal regimes.[4] In this conception, civil society is posed against the state, or at least seeks to impose limits to an authoritarian and seemingly omnipresent state apparatus. Civil society opposes the state or seeks to make it irrelevant to the ordinary life of citizens.

But while this East European context was the root of recent interest in the concept and role of civil society, it is not the only interpretation. Civil society has become a contested concept. Its meaning has become entangled with different political debates, such as the differences between Asia and the West; the defence of the welfare state against neo-conservative anti-statism; rights-oriented liberalism against communitarianism; and élite versus participatory democracy.[5] These debates have added to, and sometimes deviated from, the original East European idea of a civil society opposed to the state. Broadly speaking, two additional conceptions of civil society can be discerned as emerging, which may be of particular relevance to Singapore.

The first of these views civil society as the means of trimming back the state. The argument is that, as civil society grows, it should unburden the state of social and cultural duties, such as the protection and promotion of religion, arts, families, and education. Civil society lends itself for use as the vehicle to take up the roles that the state abandons. It helps buttress the neo-conservative notion that rejects the social welfare model of democracy and argues the state should do less. "Civil society", then, becomes an argument for a minimal state. This "minimal state" civil society largely equates the concept with middle-class, bourgeois community.[6]

Another strand of the concept of civil society is quite different. This emphasizes the role of civil society in furthering democracy and keeping democratic culture alive. Proponents of this view — of which de Tocqueville was perhaps the first major theorist[7] — see that civil society should be the lifeblood of political culture, essential to the socialization of the citizen. It is the best safeguard for a stable democracy and the prevention of domination by any one group over others. It is also what best brings individual rights-holders together for the common cause. This "democratic" civil society concept does not seek primarily to cut back the state or to oppose it; rather, it seeks to make the state more democratically accountable to the citizenry and to better enable the widest possible participation in governance. Present proponents of this concept of "civil society" reject the notion that civil society should be equated with or dominated by the bourgeois middle class. They call for civil society to be a pluralist entity, with participation that cuts across race, age, gender, and economic status, such that it is more fully representative of the society.

The three concepts outlined — a civil society opposed to the state; a civil society assisting a minimal state; and a pluralist civil society — are, of course, not merely academic conceptions. The discourse of civil society has been contested and shaped by different political agendas. The way we define "civil society", then, affects our expectations of what it means to be in favour of its establishment, or in opposition to it.

The Regional Context

Civil society in Asia is very much a received concept. There are, of course, native, indigenous substitutes that correspond to the broad idea of community representation, self-organization and action. After all, society preceded the state in pre-colonial Asia. Each society and sub-group has its *banjar*, *kampung*, *kapitan*, or other unit of community. Yet, the place of civil society on the agenda relates not so much to indigenous antecedents, but to intellectual fashion, especially post-Eastern Europe.

Nevertheless, there has been a growing interest in, and literature on, civil society in Asia. This can be briefly reviewed to sketch the regional context for Singapore. State–civil society relations in Asia have been broadly characterized by Riker as three differing "waves".[8] First, by the mid-1980s, civil society and non-governmental organizations (NGOs) were seen as having a complementary role in promoting development.[9] Civil society groups were seen to enable the process of privatization. The main tasks given to civil society in this minimal state conception were to: promote production and market activities; deliver services to communities and groups beyond the reach of the state; and foster participation in the development process.

Towards the start of the 1990s, the second wave of civil society was seen as being an autonomous and countervailing power to the state. This concept, drawing its roots from Western liberal thought and events in Eastern Europe, witnessed NGOs and civil society more generally play a greater role in calling Asian governments to account for a wide range of issues, such as the environment, poverty alleviation, women's rights, and human rights. The second wave of civil society has, in some countries, fostered new arrangements and forms of political organization upon the existing political parties. This was often marked by cross-cutting alliances among different sectors of civil society, such as students, the media, the middle class, and even business interests. A stark example of this was seen in events in Thailand following the aftermath of the May 1992 protests, and the push for democratic reforms.

The third wave in Asia has been characterized as a reaction by governments to moderate the growing pressures from civil society groups and to incorporate them as an instrument of state.[10] Observers have noted the trend for governments in Asia to place legal controls on NGO activities and to make efforts to co-opt civil society and demobilize the more political policy advocacy groups.[11]

The three waves identified by Riker correspond (at least partially) to the different conceptions of civil society outlined earlier. The first wave follows from the minimal state concept of "civil society". The concept of civil society as a pluralist platform for democracy is embedded, but seems not to be the essence of, the second wave identified by Riker. Rather, the second wave seems to correspond more to the conception of a civil society opposed to the state. So does the third wave, in which the state seeks to control or co-opt civil society. The second and third waves share the concept of a civil society opposed to the state. The main differences between them is which of the opposing entities — state or civil society — is in the ascendant.

Present and unfolding developments since the advent of the economic crisis in Asia in 1997 have revitalized the interest in civil society. In Southeast Asia, the changes have been dramatic, especially in Thailand, Indonesia, and Malaysia. Some observers see the final vindication of their thesis that democracy and civil society will come to the region. They see events in Thailand, the Philippines and, further afield, South Korea as consolidating democracy.[12] Others, to the contrary, are concerned with the failure of governance and a rising tide of anarchy, especially in Indonesia. They may also not be so sanguine about the strength and capacity of these democrats to govern effectively and, therefore, to deal with possible backlash. How might these trends in other parts of the Asia-Pacific apply in Singapore?

The Case of Singapore, So Far

1. Pre-Independence to the Mid-1990s: Accidents and Actors

In June 1997, Prime Minister Goh Chok Tong called for the promotion of civil society in Singapore.[13] The call came in a major speech in Parliament, newly constituted after the triumph of the People's Action Party (PAP) in the general election of 2 January that year. The election had seen the PAP sweep all but two seats, reverse its decline in the popular vote and, perhaps most significantly, retake two seats from the opposition.[14] The reassertive and triumphant PAP may have been expected to read the results as a vindication of its concept of good, strong government. Indeed, in a post-election statement, Goh asserted the election evinced a rejection of "liberal democracy" as seen in the West.[15] The victory might then have provided a mandate for the continuation of the PAP's existing style, with a minimum of democratic consultation and participation.

Prime Minister Goh's call in 1997 for a civil society did not come in a complete vacuum. The relationship between state and civil society in Singapore may be broadly traced through four periods. These correspond to the social and political developments of the times. The first stage relates to pre-independence Singapore.[16] At that time, civil society was indigenous and strong, given the propensity of ethnic groups to organize self-help organizations, such as the Chinese clan associations, and the equal propensity of the colonial government to provide little in the way of social services and welfare. The second stage of Singapore civil society may be characterized by the movement towards independence in the 1950s and 1960s. The call for "Merdeka" (independence) awoke not only political society, but also quickened the pulse of civic associations, such as trade unions and student groups.[17] The women's movement in this period was active and led a successful campaign for steps towards equality, such as the abolition of polygamy and the passing of the Women's Charter in 1961.[18] The third stage for Singapore civil society corresponds to the dominance of the PAP in the 1970s and 1980s. The PAP Government, as part of a then prevailing socialist-democratic ethos, began to provide housing, welfare, and a range of other services well beyond what the colonial government had provided. It thereby reduced the scope of needs met previously by self-organized civil society groups. The focus of the time, moreover, was the politics of economic survival and progress.[19] Civil society organizations such as trade unions and the professions were to form co-operative relationships with the PAP Government. Others were co-opted, curtailed, or legally circumscribed. The space for civil society shrunk. Politics in this period of economic survival and progress cooled down. The dominant political analysis in this period and its aftermath suggested that politics in Singapore was not to be found in the contest between political parties, but had been submerged in the bureaucracy.[20]

The fourth stage of state–civil society relations in Singapore is present and still unfolding. It can be said to have started in the late 1980s, with the pending accession of a second generation leadership and the politics of consultation. In 1990, then Deputy Prime Minister Goh Chok Tong promised, as one of three goals for the 1990s, to "practise a more constructive, participatory-style democracy".[21] On assuming the office of prime minister, he pledged to expand intellectual and creative space by fostering intellectual discussion.[22] Institutions for consultation and participation were set up, both in the run-up to Goh's succession to the office of prime minister, and in the early years of his tenure. These included Town Councils, which devolved local administration of public housing areas to allow for more participation by residents. Institutions established specifically for consultation were the Feedback Unit and Institute of Policy Studies. While the term civil society was not specifically mentioned, it was clearly implied as part of the politics of consultation. The Government would consult people either as individuals or, more often, as organized associations or sectors; that is to say, civil society groups.

In 1991, Minister for Information and the Arts, Brigadier-General (NS) George Yeo gave a speech specifically on civil society.[23] Although preferring the term, "civic society", Minister Yeo clearly identified the strata of institutions between the state and the individual.[24] Most significantly, perhaps, his speech identified the PAP Government as a "banyan tree" which did not allow other civil (or civic) institutions to grow in its imposing shade and had therefore to be pruned.[25] The Minister recognized:[26]

> For our civic institutions to grow, the state must withdraw a little and provide more space for local initiative. If the state is overpowering and intrudes into every sphere of community life, the result will be disastrous. ... The problem now is that under a banyan tree very little else can grow. When state institutions are too pervasive, civic institutions cannot thrive. Therefore it is necessary to prune the banyan tree so that other plants can also grow.

In this period, activities by civil society groups, such as the Nature Society of Singapore (NSS) and the Association of Women for Action and Research (AWARE) became more evident. The NSS, an environmental NGO, lobbied the Government to adopt a Green Plan to conserve nature areas in the run-up to the 1992 Earth Summit at Rio (United Nations Conference on Environment and Development).[27] The NSS also publicly and successfully opposed plans by a government body to develop a golf course in a nature area.[28] AWARE petitioned the Government on a number of issues relating to gender equality, including the better protection of women from domestic violence. Their president, Dr Kanwaljit Soin, was appointed a Nominated Member of Parliament (NMP) and succeeded in highlighting gender issues in the House.[29]

She introduced a private member's Bill on domestic violence and, while this was not passed, many of its provisions informed the government Bill that followed.[30] These two brief examples demonstrate the growing strength of civil society in Singapore to influence the political sphere. They were not, however, without exception.

The fourth stage in civil society has also witnessed setbacks and changes by which the Government reasserted control over civil society and set limits to socio-political engagement. The setbacks relate chiefly to the 1991 General Election. The PAP were returned to government with a vast majority and a considerable share of the popular vote.[31] However, four opposition members were returned, the highest number since the PAP established its dominance in the 1970s. The PAP's own analysis of the results was that they showed that the politics of consultation did not have a pay-off in votes. These initiatives were accordingly de-emphasized by Goh's Government in the post-election period. Some observers believed that the 1991 results signalled that Singapore was joining in what they saw as a worldwide movement towards democracy, tagged the "Third Wave" by Huntington.[32]

Perhaps the event that most clearly demonstrated the change of policy towards civil society was what may be called the Catherine Lim controversy in 1994. The controversy related to an article in the *Straits Times* by Dr Catherine Lim, better known for her short stories and novels.[33] Dr Lim's comments suggested that the PAP Government suffered from a confusion of governing styles, alternating between a hard style, associated with Senior Minister Lee Kuan Yew, and the more consultative style of Goh.[34] Government reaction to this comment was swift and strong, with the Prime Minister's press secretary countering the allegations and, moreover, calling on Dr Lim to join an opposition political party or to cease public commentary. The Government warned that those who "want to set the political agenda" would be treated, "as though you have entered the political arena".[35] Clearly, such a policy did not promote the engagement of a civil society with public issues. The space for civil society under the politics of consultation was perceived as having shrunk.

Going into the 1997 General Election, the politics of consultation did not feature prominently on the PAP platform. Rather, the PAP Government strategy relied on linking votes to the provision of upgrading work on public housing. It was only to emerge, as already outlined, in the aftermath of the PAP's victory. As such, Prime Minister Goh's call for civil society in Singapore came after a pause in progress and notable instances of the Government reasserting control over the space available to civil society. Not surprisingly, therefore, the call did not illicit strong and immediate public support and enthusiasm, with the exception of some public commentary.[36] The relatively cool response may be contrasted with the more positive public reaction to the initial introduction of the politics of consultation. This cool public reaction to PM Goh's call for civil society may be attributed to several factors. The first of these are the setbacks in the politics of consultation, some of which have already been noted. The second, and perhaps most immediate, factor in 1997 was the barrage of contemporaneous defamation actions filed by the PAP leaders in their personal capacities against two opposition candidates, Tang Liang Hong and J. B. Jeyaretnam.[37] Yet, even in the face of these political events, civil society in Singapore proceeded with more public notice and at a greater pace after Prime Minister Goh's call of 1997. Much of this, moreover, was at the instigation of the Government, as a managed project of civil society.

2. From 1997 on: The Civil Society Project

In endorsing civil society in 1997, Prime Minister Goh tied it to a wider-ranging "new vision" for the nation, called Singapore 21. Civil society was one of five elements identified as supporting such a vision. The idea of Singapore 21 was explained by the Prime Minister:

> We need a new vision for Singapore, an ideal, a fresh mindset. We need to move beyond material progress, to a society which places people at its very centre. Singapore 21 is my team's vision for the future of Singapore, a Singapore where people make the difference, where each citizen is valued, a Singapore which is Our Best Home, an ideal home which we all help to build... The Government can provide the conditions for security and economic growth. But in the end, it is people who give feeling, a human touch, a sense of pride and achievement, the warmth. So beyond developing physical infrastructure and hardware, we need to develop our social infrastructure and software. ... We need to go beyond economic and material needs, and reorient society to meet the intellectual, emotional, spiritual, cultural and social needs of our people.

Similarly, in his 1991 speech, Information Minister George Yeo also argued that civil society would have the function of enhancing citizens' "emotional attachment" to Singapore, fostering a "soul" and thereby making the nation-state more attractive and competitive.[38]

From these broader statements, a number of different reasons for the Government to promote civil society can be identified or inferred as follows:

(i) Singapore as Home

The PAP Government has identified the outward emigration of Singaporeans as a potential problem.[39] In response, it has sought to make them think of Singapore as their home, instead of a "hotel". As part of this, civil society can play a part in allowing greater participation, ownership and, therefore, sense of affiliation. This was emphasized by Minister George Yeo in his 1991 speech.[40] He recognized that participation in civic or civil society institutions would help develop "the affections and traditions that make a hotel a home".[41] Prime Minister Goh recognized that: "When people participate actively and become involved in community and national issues, they build ties among themselves and bond to the country."[42]

(ii) To Assist Decentralization and Self-Governance in Local Government

The PAP Government has decentralized certain functions of the state, first to Town Councils and then to Community Development Councils (CDCs), which are to function under a mayor, like a municipal township.[43] To support this move towards decentralization, a more active and participatory civil society may be required.[44] A related reason is to allow a greater sense of self-governance and responsibility. In calling for civil society, Prime Minister Goh emphasized: "All Singaporeans must feel a responsibility for solving local issues and shaping their own communities. ... One good way to do this is for concerned citizens to get involved in voluntary work or in the running of their own local communities, through the Town Councils, CDCs or RCs."[45]

(iii) To Assist in the Delivery of Welfare, Education and Other Services

By the 1980s and certainly in the 1990s, the PAP Government had clearly rejected the ideal of a welfare state, in preference for a state that provides a minimal safety net in terms of welfare, medical care, and other services. As the state retreated from these sectors, voluntary welfare associations — civil society, in short — were welcomed. This has been called the "many helping hands" policy.[46] Similarly, in the privatization of schools, there has been an emphasis on seeking citizens to make greater contributions to education, especially in terms of funding.

The above reasons reveal the concept of civil society that the PAP political leadership holds. This can be compared to the different concepts earlier identified: the civil society opposed to the state; civil society supplementing the minimal state; and a pluralist civil society. In making this comparison, the concept the PAP leaders seem to see is the second, supplementary role. The supplementary work of civil society is seen to be, first, to take over selected functions that the state chooses to retreat from (e.g., welfare, education) and, secondly, to supply the "emotional attachment" of citizens to the state. Such a concept of "civil society" would be nationalistic. It might also be expected to be relatively conservative, socially and politically, and largely middle class.

The reasons of government leaders do not point to any acceptance of the concept of a civil society opposed to the state. Nor do they suggest the role of civil society in enriching democracy. These other reasons can instead be discerned from statements by participants in civil society and NGOs. These are, briefly:

(i) To Respond to a More Educated and Demanding Citizenry

There is a degree of recognition that during the 1990s the Singapore citizenry has become more educated and demanding. The politics of consultation and the newer call for civil society can, therefore, be seen as an adjustment within the existing political system.[47] The adjustment, moreover, is meant to allow the continuation of a PAP Government.

(ii) To Foster Participation and Strengthen Democracy

Civil society is seen by some as supporting democracy, not just for the élite, but for all citizens.[48] It is also seen as an experiment in creating relationships between citizens, thus rejuvenating the word "community".[49] The potential of civil society to contribute ideas and policy proposals is less emphasized by the Government, although it has been acknowledged.[50] Non-governmental spokesmen have suggested that the Government holds no monopoly on wisdom and, as such, policies would benefit from greater participation by civil society.[51] Other observers, however, have suggested that civil society might be a way of weakening the political opposition, especially such "non-partisan" institutions as the Nominated Member of Parliament.[52]

From this brief summary, we can clearly discern differences between the reasons for civil society given by government leaders and those put forward by civil society participants and commentators. The latter seem to emphasize the potential of helping Singapore develop a more mature democratic culture, with greater participation by citizens, greater consultation by the Government prior to taking decisions, and correspondingly, a greater legitimacy of the process of governance. On the other hand, government leaders can be seen to emphasize civil society as part of a second stage of nation-building in which citizens take on more self-responsibility in local settings and the provision of welfare services. A premise of the government vision of civil society is that the central decisions on the remaining policies of state remain much as they have been. Notably, even in Minister George Yeo's 1991 speech, a strong centre for the Government was still envisaged.

In mid-1998, Singapore held its first civil society conference that gathered many of the major groups and individuals involved in both the theory and practice of civil society. The conference chairman concluded that a new stage in Singapore's development of civil society was signalled. This was confirmed by the keynote speech, given by Minister George Yeo. In 1991, he had called for the "pruning of the banyan tree" as an allegory of the trimming back of the state. Seven years on, in 1998, he recognized that civil society would rise in parallel to government, as its equal.[53] He saw this as inevitable and unchangeable, given technology and other changes:

> [S]tate-society relations in Singapore ... [are] also going through a major transformation. In the old paradigm, the state was hard while society was soft. In the web world, the state and society exist in parallel. The organization of Singapore is becoming less hierarchical.[54]

Moreover, Minister Yeo welcomed the development as there were many things that he recognized civil society could do better than the Government, such as making decisions on censorship. Another younger minister also encouraged civil society in 1998. This was Rear-Admiral (NS) Teo Chee Hean, the Minister for Education and Second Minister for Defence. Minister Teo was appointed by Prime Minister Goh to head a government committee to consider changes in attitudes and "heartware" that were necessary for Singapore in the twenty-first century. In the context of this "Singapore 21" (S21) committee, Teo commissioned five committees on specific subjects, including one to study the processes of decision-making and participation and their relation to state power and efficiency. This was framed as the dilemma, "consultation and consensus versus decisiveness and quick action", to recognize the tensions in policy.[55] The committee on this issue was co-chaired by a union leader and by a nominated (non-party) Member of Parliament.[56] A few months into the study, Minister Teo issued a call for Singapore to develop a "people sector". He contrasted this to the public sector of government and the private sector of business. As such, while avoiding the term "civil society" or the more conservative connotations of "civic society", the minister endorsed greater activity and say from citizens.

The S21 committee as a whole held a conference on 21 November 1998 to publicly share some of its draft recommendations for change to government policies. The committee's report was published as, *Together, We Make the Difference*.[57] This report was debated in Parliament and endorsed, albeit with some reservations.

A third minister added his voice for civil society in late 1998. This was Minister for Community Development, Abdullah Tarmugi. The minister voiced the need for a centre for volunteerism, and expressed willingness to start such a centre in partnership with civil society. He suggested that such a centre might serve as a clearing house for ideas, as well as a training centre for skills and know-how needed for the management of non-profit organizations.

The response of civil society groups to these government initiatives was generally receptive. There were, however, some doubts expressed whether the state would seek to control or make civil society more conservative. What seems clearer is the increase in public advocacy in Singapore by civil society groups and individuals. This was demonstrated in a number of different areas of interest, including the environment and international issues of concern, and was reported widely by the media. Some examples follow.

Reacting to reports of riots and rapes in Indonesia, in June 1998, the Singapore women's rights group, AWARE, launched a public petition and organized an exhibition. It issued public statements condemning the gross violations of human rights and called for full investigations by the Indonesian authorities and the United Nations.

In Singapore, civil society concerns increased over a number of environmental issues, such as the haze caused by Indonesian fires, infrastructure development in Singapore itself that intruded on declared nature reserves, and urban development that compromised mangroves and other habitats for animal and plant species. In the case of the haze, the Singapore Environment Council, the umbrella organization for green groups, held its first international dialogue involving regional and international NGOs, and issued a statement calling for action by the Indonesian Government and other actors.[58] These events are of interest in that both environmental issues and criticism of Indonesia had previously been sensitive areas for the Singapore Government. To date, however, no action has been taken to silence or control these emerging expressions of civil society concerns.

Civil society in Singapore in 1998 also saw the emergence of a fledgling coalition or umbrella organization for different groups: the working committee on civil society ("TWC"). This is a loose and nascent coalition formed by groups such as the Necessary Stage, The Roundtable, Project Access, as well as individuals interested in and involved with civil society groups. It pointedly excludes groups initiated and appointed by the Government. The function and significance of the TWC is yet to be understood. It could grow or it could fade. However, it is noted as one of the earliest attempts in Singapore to form cross-issue and cross-sectoral alliances in civil society, outside of government.

Another phenomenon of note was the performance of Nominated Members of Parliament (NMPs). Some commentators have suggested that the NMPs are co-opted by the Government and do not possess the independence that is characteristic of civil society. Events from 1998 have tended to question this aspersion. In a number of cases, NMPs have voted against government Bills. One example related to a government move to ban the making of "political films". Most recently, one NMP has supported a motion by the Opposition, to review the defamation laws of Singapore. Again, to date, no action has been taken to limit these actions by NMPs.

While these have been encouraging signs of an evolving civil society in Singapore, there are other signals of reservation. Senior Minister Lee Kuan Yew perhaps exemplified this in his remarks in a parliamentary debate on the Singapore 21 report.[59] He suggested that achieving even half of the Singapore 21 report, including its recommended principles that "Every Singaporean Matters" and for "Active Citizens", would take twenty years and "that is a tremendous achievement".[60]

Imagining Civil Society in Singapore

Given the dominance of the PAP Government from the 1970s onwards, there has been a tendency to consider that it is omnipotent within the sphere of Singapore's domestic politics. This continues to be so in view of the setbacks for the political opposition in the 1997 General Election.[61] From such a view, the answer to the future of civil society — like other issues — is simple indeed: civil society will conform to the PAP Government's policies, or there will be no civil society at all. The Government, analysts say, has the veto of power. The corollary of this view is that civil society cannot honestly co-operate with the Government in such a setting; it is doomed to be co-opted. In this view, powers of appointment, of setting agendas, and of patrolling the limits of discussion and action are deterministic. They breed a form of fatalism, without the recognition of human agency and subtler resistance seen in everyday acts.[62] More broadly, this is also true of most attempts to imagine Singapore's future. The government imprint on the economic and social landscape, as much as the physical landscape of the city-state, is taken to be primary. An example of this is the book, *Singapore: Re-engineering Success*, whose editors say, in the introduction, is a book "about the future".[63] The book has nine chapters written by members of the Government, senior civil service, judiciary or Parliament — a full half of the book.[64] This example illustrates the heavy, non-invisible hand that Singaporeans see and (many) accept in guiding society into the future. There is a mindset that the future is largely a governmental creation. If civil society has a part in that future, it will be government policy that allows it.

Possible Experiments and Probable Outcomes

Laws may be shaped to conservatively control and limit civil society to the requirements of the state, or to progressively encourage and strengthen it as a sector separate from the state.

1. Law: Limiting Factor or Enabling Element?

The existence of civil society depends on basic human rights or fundamental liberties.[65] The Singapore Constitution, the supreme law of the nation, promises many of the fundamental liberties, or rights, that are necessary for civil society groups. Primary among these are the rights of free speech, assembly, and association, found in Article 14 of the Constitution.[66] These correspond, in part, to international human rights (see Table 4.1).

TABLE 4.1
Singapore Constitution and Universal Declaration of Human Rights

Type of Right	Singapore Constitution	Universal Declaration
Liberty of person and the prohibition of slavery and forced labour	Articles 9 (liberty) and 10 (against slavery)	Articles 3 (life, liberty, and security) and 4 (against slavery)
Equality, or the freedom from discrimination	Article 12	Article 7
Freedom of movement and the right to remain in Singapore	Article 13	Article 13
Freedom of speech, assembly and association	Article 14	Articles 19 (speech and opinion) and 20 (assembly and association)
Freedom of religion	Article 15	Article 18

Singapore was not present at the adoption of the 1948 Universal Declaration; it was not then a nation.[67] Nor has it ratified any of the international human rights conventions on civil and political rights.[68] The correspondence between the Constitution and the Universal Declaration, however, suggests that Singapore might have — like the United States or the United Kingdom — a basic similarity in approach to civil and political rights with countries that uphold the idea of rights and allow civil society, whether from universal human rights or their respective constitutions. Instead, present public discourse in Singapore emphasizes duties instead of rights, and community in place of individuals. This has been enshrined in the "national values", promulgated in 1990.[69]

The Singaporean imagination presents no strong vision of individual freedom as a cornerstone of society. It does not recognize individual rights as the "trump" — to use Dworkin's phrase[70] — that the individual holds over collective or majoritarian demands. How, in the face of the Constitution's promise of fundamental liberties, did this shift of imagination come about? It is notable that the Constitution, in the act of creating these fundamental liberties, also qualifies them.[71] At the same time that law promises the basis for civil society, law also limits the existence and activity of civil society. Many of these limits are for the common good, for reasons such as public order and security. Indeed, these exceptions can be expressly found in the very Constitution that makes the promise of freedom. For example, express limits in the Singapore Constitution to free speech are: friendly relations with states; security; public order; morality; contempt of Court and of Parliament; and defamation.[72] A brief survey of the specific laws that limit free speech in Singapore demonstrates the exceptions.[73]

(i) Security

The Internal Security Act (Chapter 143) allows for detention without trial on the basis that the person is acting in any manner prejudicial to the security of Singapore or the maintenance of public order or essential services. Such acts could include speech. There are also wide powers against "subversive" publications and against "entertainment or exhibition" that is detrimental to the "national interest". The Official Secrets Act (Chapter 213) creates an offence to obtain, publish, or communicate any document or information for a purpose that is prejudicial to the safety or interests of Singapore. Under the Sedition Act (Chapter 290), it is an offence if statements or actions have a "seditious tendency", which is defined to include bringing into "hatred or contempt or to excite disaffection against the Government".

Singapore's laws on security are not uniquely constraining. Each has counterparts in many democracies, such as the United Kingdom. Perhaps the significant differences lie in the circumstances in which such laws are invoked. The powers of detention under the Internal Security Act, for example, are not limited to periods when a national emergency is declared, as is the exception recognized by universal human rights and practised in some other democracies. Such wide powers are, instead, available to the Government at any time, to be exercised at their judgment.

(ii) Public Order

Speech can be taken to include symbolic action, such as the staging of protest marches or assemblies. In countries such as the United States, this can be done without government permission, especially in areas that are deemed to be public fora. The position in Singapore differs. The Miscellaneous Offences (Public Order and Nuisance) Act (Chapter 184) provides that any assembly or procession in a public place may be prohibited or restricted if the authorities are satisfied that it might result in public disorder, property damage, or disruption to community life. It also provides that public processions and demonstrations must be licensed. The Penal Code (Chapter 224) creates a similar offence for unauthorized public demonstrations.

One aspect of public order that has received considerable attention is that relating to ethnic and religious differences. The Maintenance of Religious Harmony Act (Chapter 167A), enacted in 1990, allows for orders to be made restraining an official or member of a religious group, or any other person, acting in such a way that might cause feelings of enmity between different religious groups. Similarly, carrying out activities to promote "a political cause", under the guise of propagating or practising religious belief, can also be restrained. The Penal Code also has provisions on religion, including speech that deliberately intends to wound the religious feelings of any person (Article 298).

(iii) Morality

Perhaps surprisingly, there is little legislation that allows for restrictions specifically on the grounds of morality. By and large, questions of morality are dealt with by the application of licensing provisions that are general and do not explicitly set out morality as a basis for their exercise (see below). The exception is mass media: films and television. For films,[74] the censorship board acts along the lines set by a practice code, which incorporates criteria for classification of films on the basis of morality. In respect of broadcast media, the reference to morality is explicit, even if its scope may be unclear. The Singapore Broadcasting Authority Act (Chapter 297) gives the authority the duty of ensuring that no broadcast is "against public interest or order, national harmony or which offends *good taste and decency*" (emphasis added).

(iv) Contempt of Court and Defamation

The Courts have powers to institute proceedings for speech that scandalizes the Court and might undermine public confidence in the administration of justice. In Singapore, a considerable number of cases have been brought on allegations of executive bias among the judiciary. The most recent of these involved American academic, Christopher Lingle, while those previously prosecuted include an opposition candidate and a journalist for a foreign publication.[75] The legal restraints in the United Kingdom are similar, if far more seldom invoked. The common law of defamation in Singapore[76] provides civil recourse against those who cause damage to the reputations of another. Similar to the United Kingdom but unlike the United States, it affords equal protection to public officials and figures as it does to private individuals. Government leaders (in their private capacity) have successfully brought suits against opposition politicians for considerable sums in damages. There is, additionally, criminal liability for defamation under the Penal Code[77] if there is intent to harm the reputation of the person. There are relatively few criminal prosecutions. An exception, however, involves an opposition politician who made allegations against then Prime Minister Lee Kuan Yew.[78]

(v) General Licensing

In addition to these laws invoking specific exceptions to free speech, there are further restrictions on general grounds. The Undesirable Publications Act (Chapter 338) allows the prohibition of publications on the grounds that it is against "the public interest"; this can be interpreted quite broadly to relate to morality, security, or other exceptions. Another general restriction on freedom of speech is created by government licensing. This includes the licensing of newspapers under the Newspaper and Printing Presses Act (Chapter 206) and the licensing of public performance (including political speech) under the Public Entertainments Act (Chapter 257).

These differ from the laws previously mentioned in that licensing is apparently content-neutral; there is no explicit connection to any of the stated exceptions to freedom of speech, such as security or morality. In practice, however, the Public Entertainments Act is also used to censor public performances on both moral and political grounds. The licensing officer may, moreover, place whatever restrictions on the venue and timing, number of speakers and use of amplification, "as he thinks fit", so long as it is not an arbitrary decision wholly without justification.[79] Similarly, the yearly licence to newspapers may be revoked under the Newspaper and Printing Presses Act. The Act also requires ministerial approval for those who wish to hold a special class of "management shares" that are necessary for the ownership and control of the newspaper company. While these provisions do not create prior restraint or censorship, the macro controls over management and the possibility of post-publication penalties tend to pressure free speech. Owners and editors may self-censor, rather than risk incurring government disapproval. They need little reminder how two newspapers, the *Singapore Herald* and the *Eastern Sun*, were closed in 1971. Their licence or right to own management shares can also be revoked, perhaps as a sanction for publishing articles found objectionable.

From this brief survey, it is apparent that the list of exceptions to free speech is already formidable and still increasing. Each exception to the freedom of speech may have its justification; indeed, many of these laws have their counterparts in Western democracies.[80] But the net effect of these formal limitations is to circumscribe how we imagine the sphere of freedom for speech and, more broadly, for civil society. This is especially so as, unlike other countries, many of the listed laws are not "dead" laws, which are seldom invoked. They have been actively exercised in the courts.

Other Constitutions, such as America's, differ in that they do not expressly state their exceptions. The freedoms in such Constitutions are worded near absolutely. Yet, even if exceptions are not expressly stated, they may be implied. In this way, all societies limit the freedom of citizens to some degree and allow general exceptions such as security and morality. For example, the U.S. courts do prohibit defamation of normal citizens, but only allow public officials to sue if there has been actual malice.[81] Singapore law differs by refusing to limit the rights of politicians to sue for defamation, on par with normal citizens.[82] As such, the difference between the two countries, although considerable, is not on the broad principle of whether free speech should be limited by concerns with defamation. Rather, it is more finely ratcheted on the question of the specific application of those rights to public figures and the effect of allowing them to sue or not to sue. Differences — although very real — are most often of degree, rather than broad principle. In recognizing this, we move away from abstract questions of values (especially between

"Western" and "Asian"), to differences that relate to the institutions and instruments which establish and interpret such limits to freedom, and the discretionary or objective nature of such limits. There are three basic dimensions of difference in Singapore

(i) Institutions

In some countries, it is the courts that are the primary institution to interpret limits, rather than the executive or bureaucracy. Yet, even where it is the same institution — the courts — that construe the limits to freedom, the attitude and approach of the courts may differ from country to country or even, over time, in the same country. In some democracies, the approach of the courts is that fundamental freedoms are to be construed generously, and the laws that limit such freedoms must, therefore, be strictly scrutinized.

The Singapore case of Ong Ah Chuan advocated this approach.[83] The Court considered that: "a constitution ... particularly that part of it that purports to assure to all individual citizens the continued enjoyment of fundamental liberties or rights ... refer(s) to a system of law which incorporates those fundamental rules of natural justice that had formed part and parcel of the common law of England ..." The Court therefore called for a "generous interpretation" and a "full measure" of fundamental liberties for individuals. Some commentators have suggested that generosity towards fundamental liberties has, however, been tempered in more recent cases, with the courts showing greater deference to national security and other concerns that limit freedoms.

(ii) Instruments

In some countries, many limits of behaviour are enforced not so much through laws and penalties, but by conventions or codes of social behaviour. In contrast, in Singapore, there is a reliance on an array of state-imposed laws. These regulate individual behaviour across a wide spectrum of activities. Such laws differ from codes and norms of social behaviour. They are externally imposed, made without a necessary basis in majority public opinion, and can exact legal sanctions. As such, these laws are perceived to intrude more on the individual and on civil society than any substantively similar rules of social conduct. Additionally, when social norms and codes do arise to condition social behaviour, it is not always the case that they arise from society. Rather, codes in Singapore often result from the political leadership. If laws in Singapore are formal or "hard" regulations, these codes may be seen as a form of "soft" or informal regulation.

The prime example of "soft" regulation of speech and activity in civil society is what has become known as "OB markers". The idea borrows golfing parlance to suggest what is and is not within the limits of public discussion. This marking of limits is above and beyond the legal regulations earlier surveyed, although they are backed by the powers of sanction given by licensing and other laws. Under the rubric of "OB markers", the Government has welcomed "constructive" feedback, while warning that those who take on the Government should expect "robust" arguments. Prime Minister Goh was quoted[84] as saying: "Well-meaning people who put forth their views in a very well-meaning way will receive a very gentle and very well-meaning reply." In contrast, those who used snide remarks and mockery must expect a "very very hard blow from the Government in return". The government response is, therefore, very much a question of the tone and motive of someone exercising free speech. As tone and motive are often subjective, such differentiation creates uncertainty about the government response at the point of time when the speech is exercised. This is admitted in Prime Minister Goh's comment that: "You will know *when the blow lands on you* whether it's gentle or robust" (emphasis added). In this way, "OB markers" are not prior restraints to speech, censoring the speaker before the right is exercised, but act retroactively. In so doing, they pressure or "chill" free speech and tend towards self-censorship. The analogy of "OB markers" in this sense may be misleading. What is out of bounds is not marked out by clear-cut and objective criteria known beforehand; it is, rather, a subjective judgement made after the fact.

A further parameter in deciding how the Government will treat those who exercise free speech is whether they are seen to be engaging in politics. In the late 1980s, the Law Society under the leadership of Francis Seow was deemed to be thus engaged when it commented on proposed legislation concerning press control. Called before the Parliamentary Select Committee considering the Bill, members of the society were accused of "taking on" the Government and arduously questioned in respect of their past personal history.

A connected idea is that of the hierarchy between the speaker and the political figure commented upon. Minister for Information and the Arts, Brigadier-General (NS) George Yeo, explained that before Singaporeans engaged in political debate about elected politicians and institutions such as the judiciary, they were advised to "remember your place in society" and "make distinctions — what is high, what is low, what is above, what is below (in hierarchy)".[85] This was reiterated by the Feedback Unit chairman, Dr Ow Chin Hock, who saw three questions that shaped the government response to criticism: "What is the motivation? What is the manner of criticism? What is the tone?"[86] Again, the differences in how we see "manner" and "tone" may be vague. The differences in treatment by the Government, the rebukes meted out and the "blow that lands on you" are, however, sharp.

(iii) Discretionary Powers and Permits

Another significant difference relates to the ease of citizens in practising these rights of speech, association, and assembly in public. Singapore law, as surveyed above, is marked by a fairly large number of permissions and permits that need to be obtained before exercising these rights.[87] For example, the Public Entertainments Act regulates speech at public gatherings by requiring speakers to have permits in advance. The Societies Act also requires citizens' groups to register. Failure to have the proper permit is an offence, regardless of the constitutional liberties that are promised.[88]

Other countries often have similar requirements for licensing for certain activities. However, in many democracies these licences are almost automatically given, upon the applicant furnishing certain particulars and paying any relevant fees, much as a television licence is automatically given. They are not, as such, considerable impediments to civil life. In Singapore and some other countries, however, licences are not automatically given but are, rather, subject to considerable discretion.[89] The difference between these two approaches can be seen in Singapore by comparing the procedures for registering a private company for business,[90] as opposed to the registration of a society.[91] The former is a near automatic process, upon paying of certain fees and the filing of required forms. The time needed to do so is minimal. The situation of societies is quite different, in that the Registrar of Societies has the discretionary power to refuse registration if he is of the opinion that such a society may be contrary to certain concerns, such as security and public order.[92]

While no society gives free licence to speech and other activity by individual citizens or civil society groups, it is clear that some societies have laws that are more conducive or enabling for such activities. The differences in Singapore are not just the limits to freedom themselves, but the strong role of the Executive in construing those limits, and the general dependence on laws, with attendant penalties, for control by the Government. The elements that, on the other hand, contribute to a more enabling climate for civil society include:

(a) judicial approaches which give more generous interpretation to fundamental liberties and more scrutiny to laws that seek to limit them;

(b) increased regulation of social behaviour by social norm or by civic groups, rather than state-imposed regulation; and
(c) automatic permits to exercise fundamental liberties of speech, association, and assembly, or strict supervision of any discretion in granting such permits.

While the content of laws may be more or less conducive to civil society, process is equally important. Another important factor in the connection between law and civil society is the process by which laws are derived, and the participation (or non-participation) of civil society groups in making law.

2. Law-Making as Civil Society Process

Laws are not merely end products on paper. Law-making is a process that responds to social impulses and the needs of people. In representative democracies, the Parliament, as the representative of the people's will, is the primary law-making institution. While this is the case in Singapore,[93] there may be differences in the concept of the role and duty of elected representatives. At one extreme, the representative may be conceived as being accountable to people only at election time. In between, the representative need not take in and represent the views of constituents. At the other end of the spectrum, a more participatory process may be envisaged in which citizens make their views and opinions known directly to the Parliament and government, or through their elected representatives. As such, individual citizens and civil society groups have a more direct part in the law-making process, in addition to and beyond the election of their representatives. In many democracies, there are a variety of avenues for political participation by civil society groups, allowing them to advocate laws or give feedback on laws that the government seeks to implement.

This is done to some degree in Singapore through diverse means, whether at the grassroots level, from institutions such as meet-the-people's sessions by MPs and the Feedback Unit, to more élite mechanisms such as the Institute of Policy Studies and Parliamentary Select Committees. While Singapore has mechanisms for citizens and civil society groups to participate in the making of laws and policies, there are also limits. They relate to concerns that those giving feedback could constitute "lobby groups" who would be disruptive or ignorant of national considerations and interests. There is also some perception that efforts for wider consultation would undermine the ability of the Government to take quick and decisive action, including those which may be unpopular with a majority of people but are seen by the Government to be in the national interest.[94] The disutility of increasing citizens' participation is a concern for the Government. Neither is the utility of such participation always accepted. There may be perceptions that the Government and bureaucracy are more than able to reach the best decision, without assistance. Even where there is some recognition of the value of participation by citizens, there are often limits imposed by the Government. This has led some to recognize that government policies towards greater participation and openness may aim to achieve a better balance in policy-making and participation, but not democratization.[95]

Against this background, it is not surprising that the existing avenues for participation are less than might be expected. There are a number of criticisms of the existing avenues for feedback and participation and possible recommendations for improvement. Some of the most common perceptions are summarized in the Table 4.2.

Beyond giving feedback through consultative institutions and mechanisms, there are other avenues for more civil society participation in the law-making process. The first is to support the work of NMPs who may be allied to or supportive of the cause(s) espoused by particular civil society views. By their nature, NMPs do not operate under the control of a political party. They are able to participate in almost all aspects of law-making, however, including the introduction of motions and of private members' Bills. These powers could be used to allow greater access of civil society groups to the

TABLE 4.2
Limits on Feedback and Recommendations for Improvement

Existing Limit	Possible Prescription
Feedback given is often ignored[96]	Government to respond to comments and criticisms
Actions against political opponents or critics, by civil or criminal suit[97]	Greater acceptance of criticisms and diversity of opinions
Feedback sought after a policy has been decided; limited to tinkering on details	Seek feedback at early stage of concept and identification of problems and issues
Insufficient information is given for citizens to form alternative points of view	Greater public access to information
Atomized feedback, allows individual but not group participation	Allow civil society groups to make views known

law-making process. The NMP position can thereby serve as a bridge between political society and civil society. The second avenue for greater participation is through the use of public petition. This procedure, which already exists, allows civil society to directly present petitions to Parliament for its consideration.

In sum, there a number of ways in which the existing systems can be improved. There are also additional avenues which could be added (for example, an ombudsman). The difficulty is not the prescription of improvements or new institutions. Rather, the difficulty is to address the underlying reasons for reluctance on the part of the state, as briefly outlined. In part, the Government signalled this change when Prime Minister Goh called for a challenge to existing mindsets; for acceptance of ideas from all; and for greater civil society. It remains an open question, however, whether the appropriate policy and legal reforms will follow these statements of political intent and, if so, to what extent they will allow for greater participation by civil society groups in the making of laws and policy.[98]

The Past Imperfect and the Future Tense

It is easy enough to generate recipes for a future with a stronger, more independent civil society. For example, some suggest the ingredients as:

(1) lesser legal constraints and fewer "OB markers";
(2) a concept of having both a strong state and a strong society;
(3) allowing for non-partisan civic voices;
(4) recognizing the media's role in a two-way communication between the state and society; and
(5) increasing the capacity and professionalism of civil society groups.[99]

The S21 report's chapter on "active citizens" also suggests principles:

(1) for citizens to participate and feel an ownership in existing channels of consultation and participation, and be willing to self-organize for common cause;
(2) for the state to welcome suggestions and participation by citizens, and to share more information with them;
(3) for the state and citizens to share differences of opinion in a fair and rational, open-minded civic discussion;
(4) to recognize suggestions by citizens that are adopted and actions which are of assistance; and
(5) to spell out OB markers more clearly.[100]

More specific suggestions were made by the S21 committee on the issue, which were submitted to the main S21 committee and published as a "summary of the deliberations of the subject committee". These suggestions aimed at increasing the quantity and quality of consultation by:

(1) giving recognition and ownership to citizens;
(2) fostering tolerance towards a diversity of ideas and views;
(3) defining "OB markers" more clearly and limiting them to matters of national security;
(4) formalizing consultation between the state and civil society organizations and recognizing the latter as "stakeholders" on issues;
(5) expanding the role of government parliamentary committees to act as a more active feedback channel on key national issues;
(6) increasing the number of active and capable civil society groups and reviewing government policies and rules to facilitate the formation and running of such groups;
(7) restricting government intervention in the mass media;
(8) re-positioning grassroots organizations to address the existing perception that they are only mouthpieces of the Government;
(9) re-inventing the Government's Feedback Unit to be a civil society or "people sector" organization;
(10) organizing "peaks of consultation" around the Budget and National Day rally;
(11) increasing consultation with citizens to include stages before a policy is formulated;
(12) granting fuller access to information for civil society groups;
(13) balancing the interests of civil society organizations so they are not blinded by narrow, sectoral interests, to the neglect of the broader national concerns; and
(14) building up a set of conventions or principles to facilitate the engagement between the state and society.

Doubtless, any, many, and all of these prescriptions (and others that have been elsewhere suggested) would assist the growth of civil society. But the central question of civil society that has yet to be fully answered is not how to do it, or even why.[101] It would be easy enough to let civil society develop if the state would willingly take up these measures and the citizens responded to encouragement. But state allowance and encouragement is measured out, circumscribed, and managed as a government project.

It is more difficult (although still possible), on the other hand, to imagine how civil society might develop in spite of the state. One could imagine a civil society arising in spite of the state in limited circumstances, for instance, if there was a prolonged economic crisis or if there were external impulses of knowledge, ambition, and other global forces that were unmet in Singapore. Ironically, one could even suggest that a civil society in Singapore might also arise in spite of the state if the state were to take stronger, more martial attempts to stop it, rather than its present policies of management.

But the realities of Singapore would seem to be that civil society is not likely to arise in full form, either because or in spite of the state government policy to manage a civil society project. The present situation denies civil society proponents both the liberty of full acceptance, on the one hand, and the energy of overt opposition against authoritarian rule, on the other.

Accordingly, one needs to return explicitly to the central methods of this chapter in order to sketch the future of civil society. One has to think in terms of human agency, of acts of everyday resistance, and of hybridity and institutional experimentalism. Brief notes on some aspects of these methods follow:

1. Human Agency

Whatever the recipes for civil society in the future, one should consider who will undertake the work of seeing that recommendations are made, considered and undertaken, and how this work will be achieved. The question of what is to be done cannot, in this real sense, be divorced from the question of who is to do it. In this, human agency and contingency become guiding ideas for a future that is being made up along the way and by very human people. Within this framework, at least three key ideas can be suggested:

(i) Political Activity

A greater level of political activity is necessary. In the Singapore of today, politics — at the national and community or local level — are all at relatively low levels of interest and activity. This may suit many of those in power, or who otherwise subscribe to forms of élite domination, but it should not be taken for granted by those who wish to foster civil society. For the latter, there is a need to find and use occasions of heightened interest and activity in politics, to broaden the concern and involvement of citizens.

Passion and a sense of political occasion are therefore key attributes if civil society is to grow. "Arm chair" criticism and cynical inertness are negatives (although they may selectively be useful as acts of everyday resistance).

(ii) Independence and Self-Organization

Whether it is co-operative or in conflict with the state, a key attribute of civil society must be its independence. Only with independence is true co-operation possible. Those who wish civil society to prosper should envision an independent and self-organizing civil society. It should preferably be one that cuts across different and narrower areas of interest. In so doing, an umbrella coalition of civil society would be essential.

Moreover, it should represent and, indeed, experiment in its own structures to develop an example of a different and more democratic politics of organization. The key product is not policies or projects, although this is what they may produce and do. The essential thing for civil society organizations and alliances is to produce a greater level of trust and co-operation among citizens.

Such civil society would also need to have relationships with a more independent private sector, and with more generous and broad-minded foundations. State-controlled companies that dominate private economic activity, and state boards that monopolize public giving, would be elements that would limit support for civil society.

(iii) Actors

In the present day, the state often directly selects leaders in many civic organizations. Organizations may also feel the pressure to choose those who may be acceptable to the Government. A change is necessary for the future of civil society. The actors of civil society can and should constitute an open list. Civil society leaders should ideally arise from the heightened political activity within their organizations, as both builders and beneficiaries of the trust and networks that civil society can engender. Such civic leadership can be a significant contrast to the state, where leadership often conforms to academic or other criteria and is more a matter of anointment.

There will, of course, be a need for honest brokers and bridge builders, as there are in any community and in all transactions between communities. The situation in which all civil society actors must be brokers or must be led by brokers is, however, to be avoided.

In looking at the actors and leaders of civil society, one must also avoid neglecting the contingency of activity and occasion (previously sketched). It is clear from the history of social movements that such actors and leaders can sometimes emerge quickly in the crucible of important political events and turning points. Conversely, those who practise a more incremental form of civil society leadership, often working within the governmental boundaries, face a danger of being overtaken by events. Advocates of moderate change are often undermined by revolutions, as much as the old authoritarian regime itself. An unfolding and uncertain future may, therefore, give the occasion for new civic leadership, provided that such potential leaders are alive to the possibilities.

2. Acts of Everyday Resistance

Scott's thinking on "acts of everyday resistance" has been much applied (and misapplied) in many areas. Trying to locate and depend on such acts can be subject to romanticism and over-analysis of what are, in the longer-term view, trivial events. There is considerable evidence that acts of everyday resistance exist and help the oppressed in a society cope and live through that oppression. There is far less evidence that acts of everyday resistance lead to significant challenges to those systems of oppression.

The validity and potential strength of the idea should not be over-argued. However, it would seem that acts of everyday resistance do have at least three potential lessons for an emergent civil society in Singapore.

(i) Beyond Overt Opposition

Looking at acts of everyday resistance allows and encourages us to look beyond acts of overt opposition, which are few and far between in many cases. The approach gives one a more sensitive barometer by which to gauge political and social change.

This is especially important in Singapore of the present day, where there are meaningful opportunities to co-operate with the government project of civil society. Reading the public record in a more sensitive way allows one to better understand who is co-operating and who is co-opted, or rather when an entity is co-operating and when another action of the same entity is essentially a co-opted enterprise.

(ii) Dealing with Management

Secondly, acts of everyday resistance lends one the tools to deal with the state management of civil society. If the PAP Government appears to have the veto of power, the fledgling civil society has the veto of non-co-operation. Actors in civil society can be open to take part in certain government initiatives, but may be cautioned against always being so engaged. Understanding acts of everyday resistance, then, opens up a field of alternatives to participation. Non-participation and cynicism, and silence and humour, must be recognized as forms of resistance to the Government's management of civil society. Strategic decisions should be open to "lend" or "deny" co-operation. This would depend on the reading of the civil society entity (or individual), whether it would further the growth of civil society in a meaningful way.

(iii) Indirection and "Tricksters"

The sociological writing on acts of everyday resistance can be interestingly read against the trickster figure in literature. The trickster figure, such as the Monkey King featured in many Asian classics, represents a different form of leadership. It is schooled in indirection and subtlety, rather than the bold and direct statements we often associate with leaders. This is because, among other reasons, the trickster is never the most powerful figure or the anointed leader. For example, in the Ramayana, the leader and epitome of manly qualities is Rama, in contrast to Hanuman, the trickster.[102] Reading acts of everyday resistance in this manner can then change one's view of actors and actions that may have leadership or significance in state–society relations. The act of political satire or political cartoons, for example, are, therefore, not merely a small diversion. What happens in our arts too has a greater significance. (This must be seen by civil society, although we may have to claim that it is not, in order to trick the censor.)

Hybridity and Institutional Experimentalism

Hybridity and institutional experimentalism[103] should be embraced by a fledgling civil society. This view rejects both Western democracy and Asian democracy, and human rights as propounded by some governments and as wholesale models. In this way, civil society rejects both dichotomy and wholesale copying of institutions, whether imported or nativist. What is required, instead, is to begin the imagination and elaboration of another set of arrangements and institutions, with aspects borrowed from various sources.

The relationship of civil society to the state is, therefore, not to blindly follow past patterns. Nor is it fated to differ from the Americans because our history and "culture" differ. The relationship of democracy to the market is not fixed. The meaning of democracy itself, and of civil society within democracy, is not fixed. Institutional experimentalism holds that these can be defined and combined in different ways. It also holds that such different ways can be realized, not by a massive, all-or-nothing change, but by smaller yet significant experiments. For example, by a change in property or labour laws.

In this sense, while a civil society must be built, we have a very different perspective on the process of building. The approach of a government-managed project of civil society is to have a blueprint, budget, performance specifications, and other set criteria. There is a Master Architect. The approach that embraces hybridity and institutional experimentalism is quite different. It is more akin to construction in peasant cultures. In this tradition, material is often found or appropriated from other uses (or pilfered from other owners); there is no building approval; there is a proximate sense of proportion, methods, and purpose, but no Master Architect's blueprint; there is a tradition and many hands at work that subtly change the tradition in the act of work; there is a freedom to add rooms or change them as the project goes on.

Conclusion: Fatalism and Action

What do we talk about when we talk about the future? In some settings, it is our hopes. In others, our fears. In many instances, when we talk about the future of Singapore, it is, however, someone else's hopes and fears. The imagination of alternatives in Asia, and in Singapore especially, is twice captured. First, it is captured by Western thought. Second, it is captured by the rational and often overwhelming thinking of the PAP Government. The imposition of other people's hopes and fears on us, and these captured imaginations, breeds fatalism. The future is what someone else will decide and bring about. We cannot, then, meaningfully imagine alternatives. We describe the Master Plan. Some may elaborate or be elaborate in our disagreement to the Master Plan, but it remains central and whole.

This chapter has worked from different premises towards different ends. The ideas of contingency and agency, acts of everyday resistance, and hybridity suggest, instead, what might be, if some want to try to achieve something. The chapter, in this sense, does not predict or even prescribe, but imagines possibilities. In imagining these possibilities for civil society, there are several possible starting points, but no certain or detailed map. What comes next? Much depends, as should be the case, on what people want and are willing to do. We may rescue the future from fatalism, and prescribe action. But when we do, there is no real certainty of what can be done or who will do it, other than what each of us, individually and in different collectives, is certain about and is willing to do.

Notes

1. Civil society was much discussed at the end of the eighteenth century, before disappearing into obscurity in the second half of the nineteenth century. Most scholars trace the term back to the work of Hobbes and Locke in England. Others suggest a starting point in the work of the Scottish Enlightenment and the work of Adam Ferguson. See Adam Seligman, *The Idea of Civil Society* (New York: Free Press, 1992). For an overview of the history of the term, see Seligman, *The Idea of Civil Society*, or John Keane, "Despotism and Democracy: The Origins and Development of the Distinction between Civil Society and the State 1750-1850", in *Civil Society and the State*, edited by John Keane (London: Verso, 1988), pp. 35–72.
2. On the East European experience, see Vladimir Tismaneanu, *Reinventing Politics: Eastern Europe from Stalin to Havel* (New York: Free Press, 1992). On the movement in Poland, see Z. A. Pelczynski, "Solidarity and the Rebirth of Civil Society in Poland, 1976–81", in *Civil Society and the State*, edited by Keane.
3. See Chris Hann and Elizabeth Dunn, eds., *Civil Society: Challenging Western Models* (London: Routledge, 1996).
4. A more "radical" tendency that questioned the sufficiency of Western-style democracy can, however, be detected in the writings of such activists as Vaclav Havel. See Havel, "Anti-Political Politics", in *Civil Society and the State*, edited by Keane.
5. See Jean Cohen and Andrew Arato, *Civil Society and Political Theory* (Cambridge, Massachusetts: MIT Press, 1997).
6. This seems to be the position in much of "communitarian" thinking today in the United States. See, for example, Amitai Etzioni, ed., *New Communitarian Thinking: Persons, Virtues, Institutions and Communities* (Charlottesville: Univ. Press of Virginia, 1995); Amitai Etzioni, ed., *The Spirit of Community: Rights, Responsibilities and the Communitarian Agenda* (New York: NY Crown Publishing, 1993); and Michael Walzer, ed., *Towards a Global Civil Society* (Providence: Bergahn Books, 1995).
7. Alexis de Tocqueville, *Democracy in America*, especially Vol. II, Ch. V, at para. 245. For a survey of Tocqueville in perspective with earlier conceptions of civil society, see Laurence Whitehead, "Bowling in the Bronx: The Uncivil Interstices between Civil and Political Society", in *Civil Society: Democratic Perspectives*, edited by Fine and Rai, 1997.
8. James V. Riker, "Reflections on Government–NGO Relations in Asia: Prospects and Challenges for People-Centred Development", in *Government–NGO Relations in Asia: Prospects and Challenges for People-Centred Development*, edited by Noeleen Heyzer, James V. Riker, and Antonio B. Quizon (Hampshire: MacMillan, 1995), pp.194–96.
9. Chandra de Fonseka, "Challenges and Future Direction for Asian NGOs", in *Government–NGO Relations in Asia*, edited by Heyzer, Riker, and Quizon.
10. Riker, "Reflections on Government–NGO Relations", in *Government–NGO Relations in Asia*, edited by Heyzer, Riker, and Quizon.

11. Riker, "From Co-optation to Co-operation and Collaboration", in *Government–NGO Relations in Asia*, edited by Heyzer, Riker, and Quizon.
12. Similarly, they read the rise of President Estrada in the Philippines as being a demonstration of mass-based democracy, vindicating the belief in the "people's revolution" in that country (which they already consider democratic). They interpret Estrada's victory as further progress from the oligarchic limits under the Ramos and Aquino administrations and the preceding Marcos dictatorship.
13. *Singapore Parliamentary Reports*, 5 June 1997, pp. 401–11, especially at pp. 409–10.
14. For contemporary accounts of the election, see "Why voters swung to the PAP", *Straits Times*, 4 January 1998; and "PAP must go be package politics to win the people's hearts and minds", by The Roundtable, a non-partisan policy discussion group, *Straits Times*, 10 January 1998. For a fuller and later commentary on the elections, see Derek da Cunha, *The Price of Victory: The 1997 Singapore General Election and Beyond* (Singapore: Institute of Southeast Asian Studies, 1997).
15. "PM Goh on reasons for large swing to party: PAP's concrete programmes the key", *Straits Times*, 3 January 1998.
16. Singapore, founded as a British possession in 1819, was granted independence as part of the Federation of Malaya in 1963, and then seceded from the federation in 1965.
17. For an account of the history of this period, see Constance Mary Turnbull, *A History of Singapore: 1819-1988*, 2nd Ed. (Singapore: Oxford University Press, 1989); and Ernest Chew and Edwin Lee, eds., *A History of Singapore* (Singapore: Oxford University Press, 1991).
18. See Chan Heng Chee, *Notes on the Mobilization of Women into the Economy and Politics* (Singapore: Department of Political Science, University of Singapore, 1975); Constance Singham, "Introductory Remarks", in *The Future of Civil Society in Singapore*, Association of Muslim Professionals Occasional Paper Series, Paper 4-97, 1997, p. 5; Phyllis Chew, *The Singapore Council of Women and the Women's Movement* (Singapore: Singapore University Press, 1999), pp. 2, 10–12, and 18–27.
19. For an overview of policies of this period, and into the 1980s, see, Kernial Singh Sandhu and Paul Wheatley, eds., *The Management of Success: The Moulding of Modern Singapore* (Singapore: Institute of Southeast Asian Studies, 1989).
20. Chan Heng Chee, "Politics in an Administrative State: Where has the Politics Gone?", in *Understanding Singapore Society*, edited by Ong Jin Hui, Tong Chee Kiong, and Tan Ern Ser (Singapore: Times Academic Press, 1997).
21. "Chok Tong's three goals for the '90s", *Straits Times*, 7 January 1990.
22. "Govt to disclose info used in formulating policies"; "Let me know which rules stifle"; "PM: Let's Make this the Finest Nation", *Straits Times*, 30 April 1991.
23. George Yeo, "Civic Society — Between the Family and the State", *Speeches* 15, no. 3.
24. Ibid., p. 80.
25. Ibid., p. 82.
26. Ibid., from p. 82.

27. For an overview of the Green Plan as finally adopted, see Ministry of the Environment, *Annual Report* 1993 (Singapore: Ministry of the Environment, 1993), p. 11.
28. The Nature Society (Singapore), *Proposed Golf Course at Lower Peirce Reservoir: An Environmental Impact Assessment* (Singapore: NSS, 1992).
29. The post of Nominated Member of Parliament (NMP) was created by Constitutional Amendment in the late 1980s to provide a wider range of views to be represented in Parliament. NMPs are meant to be non-partisan. It has been suggested by some observers, however, that NMPs serve the PAP Government's idea that an opposition is unnecessary and has been "co-opted"; see Garry Rodan, "State-Society Relations and Political Opposition in Singapore", in *Political Oppositions in Industrialising Asia* , edited by Garry Rodan, (London and New York: Routledge, 1996).
30. See "Women's Charter changes to give wider protection", *Straits Times*, 27 October 1995; and "Debate on the Family Violence Bill", *Straits Times*, 2 November 1995.
31. For an analysis of the 1991 General Election, see Garry Rodan, "The Growth of Singapore's Middle Class and its Political Significance", in *Singapore Changes Guard: Social, Political and Economic Directions in the 1990s*, edited by Garry Rodan (Melbourne: Longman Chesire, 1993).
32. Samuel P. Huntington, *The Third Wave: Democratization in the Late Twentieth Century* (Norman: University of Oklahoma Press, 1991).
33. For example, *The Bondmaid* (London: Orion Press, 1997), and *O Singapore!* (Singapore: Times Books International, 1989).
34. "One Government, Two Styles", *Sunday Times*, 20 November 1994.
35. "PM: Debate welcomed but Govt will rebut malicious arguments", *Straits Times*, 24 January 1995.
36. For example, Simon Tay, "Is Prime Minister's Call for Civil Society A Second Step Forward?", *Straits Times*, 12 June 1997.
37. See Simon Tay, "Domestic Politics 1997", in IPS *Year in Review*, 1997 (forthcoming).
38. Yeo, "Civic Society", especially p. 79 and 86.
39. See "Minimizing the Outflow", *Straits Times*, 7 March 1991, or, more generally, *The Next Lap* (Singapore government, 1991), at p. 29.
40. Yeo, "Civic Society", at p. 79: "The problem is how to make Singapore more than just a nice hotel to stay in, how to make it a home worth living and caring for."
41. Yeo, "Civic Society", at p. 86.
42. *Singapore Parliamentary Reports*, 5 June 1997, p. 409.
43. "Enlarged GRC will have 'GE' effect", *Straits Times*, 30 October 1996.
44. Yeo, "Civic Society", at p. 82.
45. *Singapore Parliamentary Reports*, 5 June 1997, p. 409. On CDCs in particular, and on government-initiated institutions generally, see Ooi Giok Ling and Gillian Koh, "State-Society Synergies: New Stakes, New Partnerships", in *Singapore: Re-engineering Success*, edited by Arun Mahizhnan and Lee Tsao Yuan (Singapore:

Institute of Policy Studies and Oxford University Press, 1998), p. 98, especially pp. 101–3.

46. See *The Next Lap*, pp. 117–28. The Government believes the policy "is better than increasing taxes and leaving the Government to be the sole provider for the welfare of the people" (p.128).
47. Garry Rodan, for example, sees many of the changes in the 1990s as stemming from the PAP's efforts to deal with middle class disaffection with its policies and style. See Rodan, "The Growth of Singapore's Middle Class", in *Singapore Changes Guard*, edited by Rodan.
48. Constance Singham, "Introductory Remarks", in *Future of Civil Society in Singapore*, p. 7.
49. Simon Tay, "Introductory remarks", in *Future of Civil Society in Singapore*, p. 13.
50. *Singapore Parliamentary Reports*, 5 June 1997, p. 409. PM Goh said, "We must change the mindset that only a few leaders at the top of the system need to think and take responsibility for social and national issues, while the rest of society can simply mind their own business and go about their daily lives".
51. Kwok Kian Woon, "Introductory Remarks", in *Future of Civil Society in Singapore*, p. 18.
52. Garry Rodan, "State-Society Relations and Political Opposition in Singapore", in *Political Oppositions in Industrialising Asia*, edited by Rodan.
53. Speech at the Institute of Policy Studies Conference on Civil Society, 6 May 1998. The full text of the speech is pending publication by the IPS. Excerpts of Minister Yeo's speech were released in "Worldwide Web: Strengthening the Singapore Idea", *Speeches* 1998, MITA, May-June 1998. In his 1991 speech, Minister Yeo preferred the term, "civic society". In 1998, he used the term, "civil society".
54. Yeo, ibid., pp. 50–53: "In discussing the role of civil society, we need first to look at the way the world is going for we do not exist in isolation.... The world is going through a major transformation brought about by the revolution in information technology. The current Asian crisis, which is both economic and political, is part of it. Old structures are being undermined, while new structures have yet to crystallize....We are moving from a hierarchical world to a web world.... The power of the state is weakening."
55. Although framed as dilemmas, Minister Teo publicly acknowledged that these issues could be resolved and were, therefore, not true dilemmas.
56. The union leader is Lim Swee Say, who is also an MP for the PAP. The Nominated MP is Simon S. C. Tay.
57. Singapore 21 Committee, *Singapore 21: Together, We Make the Difference* (Singapore: Singapore 21 Committee, 1999).
58. The SEC conference was held on 4-5 June 1998, and included international NGOs such as World Wide Fund for Nature (WWF) and Conservancy International.
59. *Singapore Parliamentary Debates*, 6 May 1999, col. 1646-1655.
60. Ibid., col. 1655.

61. The opposition lost two seats, and the Singapore Democratic Party, which held three seats in the previous Parliament, failed to win any in the 1997 General Election. See da Cunha, *The Price of Victory*.
62. Much of Rodan's writing on this point seems to be based on such thinking. It seems a structural argument, reducing politics to a mechanistic arbitration of outcomes.
63. Mahizhnan and Lee, eds., *Singapore: Re-engineering Success*. See "Introduction", p. vi.
64. Of the remaining nine chapters, two are contributed by non-Singaporean scholars, two by IPS staff, and one by an academic who also serves as a high-level consultant to a Ministry. Only four chapters are written by those who may be said to be academics or private sector representatives.
65. Human rights and constitutional liberties differ in concept, as the former are held to be universal, while the latter are promises made by a particular state to its citizens or others over whom it has jurisdiction. They also differ in their means of implementation, with human rights promising international scrutiny and redress beyond the national sphere. There is, however, a substantive overlap. The 1948 Universal Declaration of Human Rights sets out civil and political rights that are enshrined in many Constitutions, including Singapore's. There are also social, economic and cultural rights, akin in many Constitutional promises of socialist states and in newer Constitutions, such as that of South Africa.
66. "Fundamental Liberties" are set out in Part IV of the Constitution, from Article 9 to 16.
67. Notwithstanding this, there are considerable legal arguments that human rights have become part of customary international law, binding even on countries that have not acceded to the Declaration and other covenants.
68. It has, however, ratified Human Rights Conventions against Genocide, to Eliminate All Forms of Discrimination against Women (CEDAW) and on the rights of the child. See Simon Tay, ed., "Singapore and International Law", in *Singapore Journal of International and Comparative Law*, January 1997.
69. See Jon Quah, ed., *In Search of National Values* (Singapore: Times Academic Press, 1990).
70. Ronald Dworkin, *Taking Rights Seriously* (Cambridge: Harvard University Press, 1977).
71. An exception is Article 10(1) against slavery, which is unqualified.
72. Exceptions to the right of association are: public order, public health, and morality. Exceptions to the right of assembly are: public order and security.
73. Of these, no laws specifically restrict speech regarding relations with foreign nations. Practically, however, the generality of laws under the other exceptions would avail themselves to this purpose, if need be.
74. Films Act (Chapter 107).

75. Attorney-General v. Wong Hong Toy [1983] 1 MLJ 370; and Attorney-General v. Pang Cheng Lian [1975] 1 MLJ 69.
76. The Defamation Act (Chapter 75) does not create a right of action in defamation. It assumes that right under common law, similar to the English law. The Act, then, deals specifically with certain aspects of defamation law, such as the defences of justification and fair comment.
77. Chapter 75, sections 499–502.
78. Harbans Singh Sidhu v. Public Prosecutor [1973] 1 MLJ 41. Mr Sidhu was the leader of the United Peoples Front.
79. J. B. Jeyaretnam v. Public Prosecutor [1990] 1 MLJ 129.
80. Britain, for example, has similar defamation laws, as well as laws relating to seditious libel, contempt of court, obscenity, blasphemy. and treason that regulate free speech.
81. Established in the landmark case of New York Times v. Sullivan.
82. The Sullivan case was considered by the Singapore courts in the cases of Lee Kuan Yew and J. B. Jeyaretnam, and was rejected.
83. [1981] 1 MLJ 64, 68 (Privy Council, on appeal from Singapore).
84. "PM: Debate welcomed but Govt will rebut malicious arguments", *Straits Times*, 24 January 1995.
85. "Debate yes, but do not take on those in authority as 'equals'", *Straits Times*, 20 February 1995.
86. "Respect: Hierarchy of Positions must be maintained, says Dr Ow", *Straits Times*, 4 March 1995.
87. Among the laws that potentially concern civil society organizations are: the Societies Act, the Charities Act, Public Entertainments Act, Public Lotteries Act (raising of public moneys), Newspaper and Printing Presses Act (licensing of newsletters), and Penal Code (relating to unlawful assembly, obscene or other speech subject to criminal sanction).
88. In the case of Public Prosecutor v. J. B. Jeyaretnam, the defendant was refused a permit under the Public Entertainments Act. He felt that the refusal was unjustified and spoke without a permit in reliance on his constitutional rights. The Court held that if the bureaucracy refused a permit without good reason, it would quash that decision and it would be open for the Court to take such measures to enforce the rights of citizens. However, the Court also held that, in the absence of such a court decision, Jeyaretnam could not speak without a permit.
89. The difference, in terms of public law, is between ministerial authority and discretionary authority.
90. Under the Companies Act.
91. Under the Societies Act.
92. See section 4 of the Societies Act.
93. This is notwithstanding non-elected MPs and the increasing role of law-making by the executive in the form of subsidiary legislation.

94. This concern is addressed by the committee under the Singapore 21 main committee, "Consultation & Consensus v. Decisiveness and Quick Action". The author is co-chairman of the committee.
95. See, for example, Chua Beng Huat, *Communitarian Ideology and Democracy in Singapore* (London and New York: Routledge, 1995), and, also, "State and Society: Ambling Towards Greater Balance in Singapore", in *Re-Engineering Success*, edited by Mahizhnan and Lee.
96. In the work of the S21 committee, this has been called the "Black Hole" syndrome, indicating that no one knows what becomes of the feedback given.
97. The other perception that limits wider citizen participation is the "Black Book", the perception that those with dissenting views may be punished.
98. There is a tension between the wish for a flourishing civil society and continuing government control. This may make civil society the crucible for politics in Singapore. See Simon Tay, "Towards a Singaporean Civil Society", in *Southeast Asian Affairs* 1998, (Singapore: Institute of Southeast Asian Studies, 1998), pp. 244–61
99. Ooi and Koh, "State-Society Synergies: New Stakes, New Partnerships", in *Singapore: Re-Engineering Success*, edited by Mahizhnan and Lee, pp. 106–8.
100. *Together, We Make the Difference*, pp. 52–54.
101. The main reasons for civil society, put forward by both the Government and by civil society practitioners and advocates, are set out above, at pp. 79–80 of this chapter.
102. Paula Richman, ed., *Many Ramayanas* is a good source for the different discourses and versions of the Ramayana. For a good read of the Ramayana in English, and in non-traditional form, see R. K. Narayan's version, 1987.
103. The term "institutional experimentalism" and the ideas behind it have been developed by R. M. Unger in many of his writings, especially *False Necessity*.

5

RELATING TO THE WORLD
Images, Metaphors, and Analogies

Kwa Chong Guan

Oh, we have been described as aspiring to be various things: Athens, Venice, Switzerland, Israel, Cuba, Red City *and* Third China ... *But, having considered all things, it would perhaps be better if* Singapore *contented itself with being the* Singapore *of* Southeast Asia. *Not aiming high perhaps, but then we would be ourselves and that is not a bad thing.*

– S. Rajaratnam (1985)[1]

Self-Image and Others

The policy options for how a small state like Singapore relates to its neighbours and the wider world are fairly well defined.[2] They are based on the assumption that a small state is constrained and vulnerable *vis-à-vis* its larger neighbours and major powers.[3] Its susceptibility to risks and threats are set at a much lower threshold than its larger neighbours. The small state is disadvantaged and weak in a self-help world. The challenge for a small state is how to offset its vulnerability by increasing its national capacity and international presence.[4] This challenge of being a small state was thrust upon Singapore on August 1965.

Prior to 9 August 1965, Singapore had always been part of a larger entity and related to the world as part of that entity. In 1824, Dr John Crawfurd made Singapore a territory of the East India Company when, as the Company's second Resident Administrator succeeding Colonel William Farquhar, he persuaded Sultan Hussain and his Temenggong to jointly sign away Singapore to the Honourable Company.[5] Before that, Singapore was a part of the Johor-Riau sultanate based in Tanjong Pinang and, earlier, up the Johor River. Even earlier, in the fourteenth century, the Majapahit Empire, from its centre in east Java, claimed Singapore. Singapore became part of the Straits Settlement, together with Pinang and Melaka, starting in 1826, following the dissolution of the East India Company — the nucleus of a British Malaya in an expanding British Empire. In 1942, Lieutenant-General Tomoyuki Yamashita renamed Singapore *Syonan*, or "Light of the South", in Japan's Greater East Asian Co-prosperity Sphere. The British eventually reclaimed Singapore as one of its crown colonies and excluded it from the Malayan Union which was to succeed the old British Malaya.

This separation of Singapore from the Malayan Union, and the ensuing Federation of Malaya, undermined the historic role of Singapore as the entrepôt and capital of British Malaya.[6] Singapore had grown as an integral part of a developing Malayan peninsula, and the concept of it as an independent entity, separate from its Malayan peninsula hinterland, was inconceivable. In 1948, this dense network of economic, political, and kinship relations linking Singapore to the peninsula (which was its *raison d'être*) was perceived to be threatened by the proposal to federate the peninsula states without Singapore. Political parties and groups that saw this separation of Singapore from the peninsula as creating a historical discontinuity that undermined Singapore's existence emerged to argue for some form of unification of Singapore with the peninsula. The drive to reunite Singapore with Malaya became a fundamental theme of the politics for independence in both Singapore and Malaya in the 1950s, culminating in the creation of Malaysia in 1963, from which Singapore was, in the words of Mr Lee Kuan Yew, "ejected" in 1965.[7]

Singapore has always related to others as part of a larger entity. The vision that Singapore can relate to the world as an independent entity is absent. For what is Singapore as an entity separate from a larger whole? The answer to this fundamental issue defines how Singapore relates to others, especially to its two most immediate neighbours. This chapter explores the phases of how Singapore has related to the rest of the world *vis-à-vis* the evolution of how Singapore has defined and identified itself.

Defining the Premises and Principles

The world of August 1965 into which Singapore was born was a rough-and-tumble world. Indonesian *Konfrontasi* with Malaysia was still ongoing. The attempted coup and counter-coup that would decimate the Indonesian Communist Party and topple President Soekarno was seven weeks in the future. In Vietnam, the war was escalating with the dispatch of two U.S. Marine Corps battalions to Danang in March and their deployment in combat in June. In China, Mao was plotting and planning the launch of his Cultural Revolution, which would engulf China for the next decade. Mr Lee Kuan Yew, at a press conference at noon on 9 August 1965, was asked how Singapore intended to relate to this threatening world. This was the press conference at which Mr Lee was overcome by his emotions when narrating the sequence of events leading to Singapore's proclamation of independence earlier that morning.

Asked how he intended to conduct relations with Indonesia, Mr Lee stated that he wanted "to be friends with Indonesia", but on equal terms. Jakarta, Mr Lee stressed, must recognize Singapore's "right to survive" and its independence. Jakarta will have to acknowledge that Singapore is not a "neo-colonialist nation", but a "sovereign nation with a will and capacity of its own". This capacity, Mr Lee admitted, "is rather limited. But, nevertheless, within that capacity, and with help of all friends, Commonwealth friends who would help our survival, we intend to survive".[8]

In a telling metaphor, Mr Lee, during an interview with Independent Television News on 11 August 1965, compared Singapore to:

> [A] suburban house with fruit trees: apples, pears ... And I [Mr Lee] have got a table laden with peaches and television sets, refrigerators ... I have got a very fragile fence, and outside — this is in a tenement area — a very hungry people, hungry, and therefore angry and worked up. ... And if they come into my compound and with knives and knuckle-dusters beat me up and take the apples and pears and the suits and the television set and the radio and the refrigerator and the furniture and I have got the right to get help from whoever I can and that includes the British.[9]

This metaphor is repeated in another interview on the same day with Malay journalists. In this interview, Mr Lee went on to point out that:

> [A]lthough our house is small, in our house, how we arrange the tables and the chairs, and the beds is our own affair. Not our friends' or our neighbours' affair. No one has the right to say that the bed should be moved over there, the chair should be moved over here.

> This is our house. Although it is small, it is our property. It is the right of the people of Singapore to manage Singapore as the people of Singapore want it to be.[10]

Mr Lee hoped that "in the end we will convince our Indonesian neighbours that they have to live in peace with us because it is the best thing for them and for us. We do not intend to be swallowed up by anybody". Mr Lee emphasized that he would be prepared to meet his Indonesian counterparts "anywhere in the world" once they recognized that Singapore was "a separate entity, an international person" and he, Mr Lee, "is not the voice of Mr Harold Wilson or Mr Menzies or Mr Holyoake...".[11]

Likewise with the Malaysians, Mr Lee wanted "to co-operate with them, on the most fair and equal basis. The emphasis is co-operate. We need them to survive. Our water supply comes from Johore".[12] This need for continuing co-operation with Malaysia was reiterated on 9 August and in interviews over the next three days.[13] Mr Lee revealed that he was relieved when Tunku Abdul Rahman assured him that "co-operation between our two countries was most necessary if either of us is to survive the pressures from common enemies".[14] Mr Lee noted that "there is an inexorable nexus between security and commerce and industry",[15] and co-operation must, therefore, include economic and defence co-operation. One could not do without the other. Mr Lee reminded his various audiences that it was this logic of co-operation with Malaysia that drove the imperative for merger, and, Mr Lee envisaged, would lead to the eventual re-unification of Singapore with Malaysia.[16] It was this interdependence that appeared to underlie Mr Lee's belief in his right to comment on Malaysian affairs that could affect Singapore.

Trade was a major component of economic co-operation with Malaysia that Mr Lee hoped would continue. However, it was not only with Malaysia that Mr Lee hoped trade would continue, but also with Indonesia and the rest of the world. Mr Lee, in the interviews he gave on the first days of Singapore's independence, stressed that Singapore "welcome[s] trade with everybody", even with China and the Soviet Union, so long as it was *bona fide* trade and not a conduit for the subversion of Singapore.[17] "We trade", said Mr Lee, "so long as you leave my furniture and my family alone".[18]

Mr Lee was clear that his priority was the continued economic development of Singapore through co-operation with the rest of the world. Singapore's survival, security, and continued prosperity, in Mr Lee's view, depended upon economic development. The challenge for Mr Lee was how to ensure co-operation in a turbulent and potentially irrational world. Singapore's ejection from Malaysia, in Mr Lee's view, was because of the irrationality of "just six men, six wild men" whom the Tunku should have "smacked down".[19] Mr Lee argued that Singapore in Malaysia would have been like "a three-legged stool: firm, stable". But Singapore's ejection from Malaysia left Mr Lee with only one leg, "like a shooting-stick. We are resting on a shooting stick".[20] Mr Lee conceded that "it may not be as comfortable as the stool, but it will stand". Like the metaphor of the villa in a tenement area, this metaphor of Singapore sitting on a shooting stick recurred in Mr Lee's interviews. Mr Lee declared that he "intends to sit on that shooting stick …[and] will jolly well make it a strong shooting stick … made of steel".[21]

For Mr Lee, this shooting-stick he was sitting on was positioned in the centre of Southeast Asia, the cockpit of big power conflicts. In another interview with foreign correspondents on 14 August, Mr Lee rhetorically asked his interviewers:

> Singapore is the heart of Southeast Asia; it is the linchpin, isn't it? You take out this linchpin and you tell me what sense you make of Vietnam and all the American commitments and all the dangerous escalation going on is worth. The linchpin is gone, do you send Marines to Vietnam?[22]

Within this geopolitical framework, Mr Lee argued the need for British bases in Singapore to continue — for the security, not only of Singapore, but also of Malaysia. Mr Lee agreed with a Malaysian journalist, in an interview on 11 August, that "we get rid of British bases … for the sake of friendliness with Indonesia".[23] But, after that, could Singapore be assured that Indonesian troops will not enter Singapore like the Japanese did in 1942?

In these interviews he gave in the first week of Singapore's independence, Mr Lee virtually laid out the fundamentals of Singapore's foreign policy, which have since become its policy bedrock.[24] The fundamental issue was that Singapore's status as a sovereign nation-state was not only uncertain but, more significantly, contested and challenged by others. Singapore's claim to nationhood could not, therefore, be taken for granted, and must be reiterated, assertively if necessary. Mr Lee made it quite clear that, having been "ejected" from Malaysia, he saw his responsibility was to ensure the political and economic survival of Singapore as an independent nation, free from external subversion and interference. In undertaking this responsibility, Mr Lee and his colleagues were setting out to disprove several hundred years of history in which Singapore had always been part of a larger entity and had no identity of its own, the corollary of which was that Singapore was incapable of surviving on its own. To the extent that then Malaysian Prime Minister Tunku Abdul Rahman and his colleagues also shared this historical vision that Singapore could not survive apart from a larger entity and would continue to be dependent upon Malaysia, then the basis for an enduring rivalry was laid on the morning of 9 August 1965, when Mr Lee virtually declared his intention to show up any expectations which the Tunku may have had, of Singapore sooner or later reapplying for membership with Malaysia.[25]

In the concluding two paragraphs of his first volume of memoirs, Mr Lee confirms this perception of Malaysian intentions and his response:

> The Tunku and Razak thought they could station troops in Singapore, squat on us and if necessary close the Causeway and cut off our water supply. They believed, not without foundation, that Singapore could not exist on its own — what better authority than the speeches of the PAP leaders themselves, myself included, and the reasons we had given for it? As Ghazali bin Shafie, the permanent secretary, external affairs ministry, said soon after separation, after a few years out on a limb, Singapore would be in severe straits and would come crawling back — this time on Malaysia's terms. ... No, not if I could help it. People in Singapore were in no mood to crawl back after what they had been through for two years in Malaysia, the communal bullying and intimidation. Certainly Keng Swee and I, the two directly responsible for accepting this separation from our hinterland, were not about to give up. The people shared our feelings and were prepared to do whatever was needed to make an independent Singapore work. I did not know I was to spend the rest of my life getting Singapore not just to work but to prosper and flourish.[26]

The goal Mr Lee and his colleagues set for themselves was to meld Singapore into a "steel shooting stick" that would sit, albeit uneasily, in the centre of a turbulent Southeast Asia. Mr Lee envisaged that this could be achieved through economic development and co-operation, especially through trade with anybody and everybody who was prepared to trade with Singapore, without attempting to subvert it. Having friends like the British, who were prepared to help defend Singapore as the linchpin of Southeast Asia, also counted. These imperatives of how Singapore related to a rough-and-tumble world has, in turn, fundamentally shaped its self-image.

A Rugged Society in a Self-Help World

To survive in this anarchic world, Singapore turned to old friends in the Non-Aligned Movement, primarily because their philosophy of anti-colonialism and neutrality in the Cold War appealed to Mr Lee and his colleagues when they founded the People's Action Party in 1955. The Party's publication, *Petir*, carried fulsome reports on Nasser's Egypt, on Soekarno's shaping of Indonesian politics in the late 1950s and especially on Nehru's socialist policies in India. Consequently, it is not surprising that among the first to be notified of Singapore's independence were Cambodia's Sihanouk, Egypt's Nasser, India's Shastri, and Burma's Ne Win. Indeed, Mr Lee's initial role model for foreign policy was Cambodia. Mr Lee declared at his 9 August interview that:

> There is no difference basically in attitudes between Prince Sihanouk and myself. He wants to survive; he wants Cambodia to survive. I want my own people to survive. He has got bigger neighbours; I have got bigger neighbours. I think we understand each other. Within this Non-Aligned Movement ideology, Singapore adopted a rather anti-American stance.

But the contradictions of combining a foreign policy of neutrality with the desire for British military bases, as guarantor of Singapore's security, eventually moved Singapore more and more towards the United States, especially when Britain announced its intention to withdraw from east of Suez. By late 1966, Mr Lee recognized that Singapore's survival was probably better insured by ensuring that the major powers had a stake and interest in Singapore's independence, and this would be achieved by modernizing Singapore society so that the major powers could identify with and commit to, perhaps even respect, it.[27]

The problem was that Mr Lee and his lieutenants inherited from the British a plural society in which the different ethnic groups met only in the market place,[28] and, as such, lacked the "social glue"[29] to meld these groups into a nation. A nation, according to Harvard Professor of Government Rupert Emerson, "is a community of people who feel that they belong together in the double sense that they share deeply significant elements of a common heritage and that they have a common destiny for the future". By this definition, which Mr Lee and his colleagues had quoted, Singapore would not qualify to be a nation, especially with the additional criteria that a nation "is also a community which, in contrast to others such as family, caste, or religious body, is characteristically associated with a particular territory to which it lays claim as the traditional national homeland".[30]

The quest was how to build — out of the disparate immigrant groups in Singapore — a community that would be rooted to the island where it resided. Israel became an analogy for Singapore. Israel, like Singapore, comprised recent immigrant groups that had successfully integrated into a new whole.

Israel's Histadrout labour movement was strong, but responsible and co-operative. Moreover, Israel had responded to Singapore's appeal for help and advice in building up a national service (conscript) army that could defend the island against the larger armies of more populous potential adversaries, as the Israeli Defence Force had successfully done. Israel was a tightly organized society driven by an ideology of survival in a hostile environment. Mr Lee appeared to have Israel in mind when he declared that:

> [S]ocieties like ours have no fat to spare. They are either lean and healthy or they die. We have calculated backwards and forwards for eleven months, on an independence we never sought, that our best changes lie in a very tightly organized society.[31]

The battle cry that went forth was to build a "rugged society" to ensure Singapore's survival.[32] The core of this tightly organized "rugged society" identity that Singapore adopted was a classical realist perception of an anarchic society of nation-states challenging, if not threatening, each other in furtherance of their national interests. As a small state in the centre of a turbulent region in which the major powers were contending for influence, Singapore was exceptionally vulnerable. How to overcome the threats to Singapore's survival and independence as a small state had been the fundamental preoccupation of Mr Lee and his colleagues. The answer that Mr Lee and his colleagues came to was that, ultimately, while Singapore had to be eternally vigilant in the cockpit of contending powers balancing each other, it had to depend upon itself for its survival and to develop the wherewithal to do so. As in Israel, an armed force capable of — in the words of the mission of the Ministry of Defence — "securing a swift and decisive victory" over any aggressor, in the event of a breakdown of diplomacy and failure of deterrence, was and continues to be the final guarantee of Singapore's independence.[33]

The circumstances of Singapore's birth led it to adopt what is best described as a Kautilyan perspective of the region around it.[34] Central to this perspective of the world formulated by the third century BC Indian statesman is the assumption that threats to one's state emanates from neighbours, the corollary of which is that states adjacent to one's neighbours, and hostile to it, are one's natural allies.[35] Such a view of the region led Singapore in the first decade of independence to be sceptical of regionalism and the Association of Southeast Asian Nations (ASEAN), of which it was a founding member in 1967. Coupled with its pragmatism, which measured projects and proposals in terms of what was possible and practical, Singapore assessed ASEAN to be more rhetoric than substance in those early years.[36] The Association's 1971 proposal for a Zone of Peace, Freedom, and Neutrality (ZOPFAN) received only nominal support from Singapore and most of its ASEAN partners who, based on their essentially realist perspective of the world, were sceptical of the value of the Association and its schemes.[37] It was only after the fall of Vietnam in March 1975 that ASEAN assumed a new-found significance for Singapore, as the platform to reach out to the Vietnamese, with whom ASEAN now had to live. ASEAN assumed even greater significance for Singapore and its partners in the Association when it became the platform on which a joint plan of action was created to challenge the Vietnamese takeover and occupation of Cambodia in 1979.[38]

This self-image of Singapore as a "rugged society" preoccupied with its survival may have been a justifiable response to ejection from Malaysia into a rough-and-tumble neighbourhood. But it was an image designed not to endear Singapore to its neighbours and friends. Australian Prime Minister Gough Whitlam thought Singapore the odd man out in the region, with its "thoroughly selfish attitude".[39] Malaysians perceived Singapore's construction of a "rugged society" to be in contradistinction to their society and were both irritated and alarmed by it.[40] Indonesia's New Order Lieutenant-General Soeharto was deeply offended when Singapore rebuffed his personal appeal for the lives of two Indonesian Marines who had been sentenced to death for infiltrating the island during *Konfrontasi* in order to plant a time bomb in front of Mcdonald House on Orchard Road. The trauma of that incident did not heal until 1972 when Mr Lee visited Indonesia and was persuaded to sprinkle flowers on the graves of the two Marines executed by Singapore.[41] Even the Americans were not spared when Mr Lee chose to expose a Central Intelligence Agency effort to recruit a senior Singapore government security official.[42]

By the early 1970s, the Singapore leadership was beginning to recognize the cost of comparing the country to Israel. Singapore could not afford to be in a state of tension with its neighbours like Israel was, for, unlike Israel, Singapore was a trading state. Singapore could not afford to antagonize its neighbours and friends if it wanted to trade with them. Moreover, unlike Israel, Singapore could not be assured of United States backing in any conflict it got into.[43] Singapore looked further and deeper into history for other small countries that had survived and could be an analogy for it.

A City-State in Search of a Hinterland

The search for analogies zeroed in on the historical city-state, which antedated the nation-state by at least two and a half millennia. Athens and Venice[44] became the preferred analogies for Singapore. Both were similar to Singapore — geographically small, maritime, and confined entities, with little resources.

How did Athens and Venice — both of which began with territories smaller than Singapore's — create an aeonian imprint on the historical landscape? One analogy that Singapore appears to have drawn is that both Athens and Venice survived because they had political systems that were ahead of their times. The Athenian solution to political problems is today held up virtually unchallenged as the solution to our own political problems. This Athenian solution was resurrected by the Italian city-republics in the twelve century, among which was Venice, which managed to sustain this Athenian approach to government and politics for the next five centuries. So, like Athens and Venice, Singapore had to have a government that was better and ahead of its neighbours and immediate world, if it was to survive. More importantly, both Athens and Venice survived, not through control of territory, but through trade. In the case of Venice in its heyday, it controlled much of the trade from Asia to Europe. Together with Quanzhou, Melaka, Cambray, Baghdad, Cairo, and Bruges, Venice formed a network of cities that controlled global trade in the thirteenth century. To aspire to be like Venice meant that Singapore aspired to global status, to become a hub of global trade, like Venice had been.[45]

Singapore grew as an entrepôt for the redistribution of imported manufactures, foodstuffs, and local raw materials.[46] In the years after 1965, external trade represented, on average, more than three times Singapore's gross national product (GNP). As a city-state dependent upon trade, like Venice, Singapore's foreign policies have to a large extent been driven by its foreign trade policies. Singapore has been a leading advocate for freer trade among the ASEAN member countries. This has taken time, with the first modest step forward having been taken only in 1977 when a "Preferential Trading Agreement" was approved, providing for tariff preferences for trade among ASEAN states. Singapore then had to wait fifteen years before the next major step could be taken, which was an agreement to form an ASEAN Free Trade Area (AFTA). Concurrently, Singapore has expanded its trading hinterland to the Organization for Economic Co-operation and Development (OECD) countries, in particular the United States, followed by Japan. Singapore has also been working to establish trade niches with China as it opens up. Globally, Singapore has actively participated in the old General Agreement on Tariffs and Trade (GATT) and its successor, the World Trade Organization (WTO).

But Singapore's free-port status and its advocacy of intra-regional trade have set it against the more protectionist policies of its neighbours, such as ASEAN import-substituting schemes, whether these be ASEAN industrial projects or customs unions. More importantly, Singapore's function as an entrepôt, like that of Venice, has been envied and challenged by others who perceive entrepôt activities to be parasitic, profiteering from the movement of goods and products from one country to another. Singapore's Chinese demographic profile has accentuated its image as the "Jew of the Orient" and has led its two immediate and larger trading partners to reduce, if not break, their dependence upon Singapore's entrepôt facilities.[47] Singapore's response to the substitution policies of its two neighbours has been to further develop and maintain its competitive edge, not only as a regional, but also a global, port. Like Venice, Singapore decided that its survival lay in being one, if not two, steps ahead of its competitors. Would Singapore, like Venice, find itself envied and respected but never liked?

Singapore was not the first to look to Venice as a model of a global city it could learn from.[48] A century earlier, British Prime Minister Benjamin Disraeli spoke in the House of Commons about the "considerable similarity between the conditions of Great Britain and the Republic of Venice". Like Singapore, the British at the end of the last century were searching for analogies of their future, because Britain, like Venice earlier, had a global commercial empire at its disposal and was governed by an aristocratic oligarchy headed by a titular monarch. Was the fate of Venice a premonition of the future of Britain? The lessons drawn depended very much on British perceptions of the Venetian past. Was Venice's collapse in 1797 the consequence of a "suspicious and tyrannical oligarchy", as Disraeli had analysed, and — given its liberal parliamentary system — would Britain, therefore, be spared the same fate? Or, was Venice a victim of the stress of empire in the aggressive *weltpolitik* of European states. Venice's decision to confront the new territorial monarchies of Europe in the early sixteenth century (in the wars of the League of Cambria) was — according to the nineteenth century historiography of Venice — the turning point of Venetian history, when Venice turned away from the sea to try to become a continental power. If this was the lesson to be drawn, then Britain should not be drawn into the *weltpolitik* of Europe, but, rather, build itself up on the strength of its naval power and colonial empire. The empire need not drag Britain down, in the way empire brought down Rome, as Edward Gibbon had argued. These analogies of Venice helped transform what was Britain's "low imperialism" of mid-Victorian merchants and missionaries, into the "high imperialism" of proconsuls and viceroys.[49]

How Venetian history is interpreted[50] will likewise shape the kinds of lessons Singapore elects to learn from identifying Venice as an analogy for itself. Is the lesson that Venice declined when it turned away from the sea to become a territorial power relevant to Singapore? Are Venice's relations with Ottoman Turkey and Islam another relevant lesson? Venice needed the Islamic world and was more dependent upon Muslim trade than the Islamic world needed Venice and its trade. This made Venetian relations with Islam equivocal and problematic. Venice continued to maintain its trading stations in Egypt and Syria while participating in more than one crusade. It continued to trade with Turkey while alternately fighting it and appeasing it. Venice projected itself as a champion of Christianity to Christendom, but also as a neutral service centre to *Darul Islam*. Will Singapore be like Venice, dependent upon its global network, on the quality and expertise of its services and on its market competitiveness as an entrepôt to determine whether it survives and prospers, or declines?

The critical issue, however, is the long-term viability of the city-state. Compared to the later nation-states, city-states — from Carthage to Venice and the Hanseatic League — may have had a greater influence on the shape of the historical landscape and, *ipso facto*, may have been the catalyst for the emergence of states in Europe.[51] In the last two centuries, the nation-state has overshadowed and incorporated the city-state. However, we may be witnessing the rebirth of city-states in the form of today's megacities. Their sheer size gives them a life of their own, separate from the nation-states in which they are located. These reconstituted city-states are redefining the landscape of the nation-state; they are the generators of wealth and growth, creators of hinterlands.[52] In the United States, a new set of megacities — such as Dallas, Seattle, and Phoenix — is emerging, serving as new foci for economic activity, governance, and social organization, and functioning as city-states in all but name.[53]

The Foreign Relations of a Global City

It was this potential of Singapore to become a new-generation city-state that then Foreign Minister S. Rajaratnam argued for in 1972, in a speech that was ahead of its time.[54] Mr Rajaratnam pointed out that Singapore was confounding critics who had expected it to collapse when it was separated from Malaysia in 1965. He argued that this was because Singapore was transforming itself into a global city. Mr Rajaratnam derived this concept of a "global city" from Arnold Toynbee[55] who, in 1970, envisaged the megacities or "megalopolises on all the continents ... merging to form Ecumenopolis, a new type of city that can be represented by one specimen, since Ecumenopolis is going, as its name proclaims, to encompass the land-surface of the globe with a single conurbation".[56] Toynbee termed this Ecumenopolis "the coming World-City".

A global city, Mr Rajaratnam outlined, is no longer dependent upon its immediate hinterland and the surplus it creates for its survival (and on which traditional entrepôts depend). Mr Rajaratnam envisioned Singapore the global city to be linked via sea-lanes, air routes, and telecommunications to other global cities, moving commodities from regions where they are produced and plentiful to where there was a market demand for them. The world becomes the hinterland for a global city. Singapore's survival, Mr Rajaratnam contended, would depend upon its ability to establish a niche in the rapidly expanding global economic system.

In his 1972 speech, Mr Rajaratnam was fashioning a new identity for Singapore. The underlying thrust of his argument was that Singapore could have a life apart from Malaysia. As a global city, Singapore would not be dependent upon the Malaysian hinterland for its survival, as it had been as an entrepôt. The world would now be its hinterland. In 1972, this vision — like Toynbee's vision of "the coming World City" emerging out of the "present urban explosion"[57] — was prophetic, because the information technology which today links us with the world had yet to be conceived, and few economists then could conceive of a global economy linked by a series of world cities in the midst of the bipolar Cold War.

The 1973 oil price adjustment by the Organization of Petroleum Exporting Countries (OPEC) undermined the global economy, which, until that point in time, had enabled Singapore to achieve double-digit growth and provided the underlying rationale for Mr Rajaratnam's optimistic vision. During the decade 1973–84, Singapore's growth rate was reduced to single digits. Rising protectionism in many industrialized countries reduced Singapore's market access. Singapore was forced to review the export-oriented industrialization strategy that had served it well. Rising domestic costs and a labour shortage added to the pressure to revise economic strategies. Starting in 1979, Singapore decided to compete in the new international division of labour by moving into high-technology and knowledge and information industries. The 1985 recession drove home the need to restructure and consolidate Singapore's economy into an international service, financial, and high-technology centre. In its benchmark 1986 report entitled, *The Singapore Economy: New Directions*, the Economic Committee — chaired by Brigadier-General (Reservist) Lee Hsien Loong — identified offshore activities as the future direction for the Singapore economy. A series of plans was launched to internationalize the Singapore economy and shift it from GDP- to GNP-driven growth. This need to change mindsets, to think globally, was in large part driven by the shift in the 1980s from an international economy still dominated by the nation-state, to a more global economy driven by the market and technology, and based on a network of global cities. Functioning as part of a network, the global city differs considerably from the capital cities of old empires or modern nation-states.[58]

Singapore as a global city has now become the dominant self-image of the city-state.[59] As an aspiring global city, Singapore has to be seen and accepted as comparable — if not to London, New York, and Tokyo — then to second-rank articulations, such as Miami (relative to the Caribbean), Los Angeles (relative to the western Pacific Rim), or Frankfurt and Amsterdam (relative to Western Europe).[60] Singapore must show that, in spite of its small size, it has comparable capabilities. Singapore's survival should be defined in terms of its competitiveness[61] *vis-à-vis* these cities.[62] The consequence of this self-image, for Singapore's foreign relations, is that Singapore now wants to lever itself beyond the region to the same level as other aspiring global cities. Relating to neighbours and the region becomes a part of the wider global framework in which Singapore aspires to operate.

Singapore's success as a global city will in large part depend upon its success in articulating global capital and transnational corporations with local and regional markets. So, as Singapore moves into a post-industrial "world city" status, it finds, paradoxically, that it has to interact even more with its surrounding neighbourhood than as a city-state growing on export-oriented industrialization. As an aspiring global city, Singapore has to look beyond the metaphorical city walls of its former status as a city-state. If it wants to establish its claim as a global city, Singapore has to look into creating an extended metropolitan region that will penetrate the Strait of Malacca, and link up with the region's cities and towns into a mega-urban corridor.[63] The mid-1980s economic depression and threat of increased protectionism further impressed upon Singapore that there are limits to its global aspirations[64] and that, ultimately, it has to come to terms with the local region. In December 1989, Singapore launched a "Growth Triangle" that links it with Johor and the islands of Batam and Bintan, in order to more effectively exploit the different factor endowments and comparative advantages among these areas and to form an extended metropolitan region driven by market dynamics.[65] If it wants to succeed as a global city, Singapore must engage the region more proactively and, perhaps, even drive it.[66]

The cosmopolitanism of a global city also threatens the social cohesion and identity of a plural society in a small state. Like other small states with multiethnic, multicultural, and multireligious societies, Singapore's carefully managed social stability can be destabilized by the different lifestyles and values flowing through today's "borderless" world. The values and lifestyles of a global city pose challenges to the identity of Singapore as a cohesive and disciplined city-state. Singapore's response has been to fashion and maintain a set of shared "National Values" which it hopes will distinguish it from others in the global community. This exercise in promulgating a set of shared values, which has widened into a debate about "Asian values", is an attempt to establish a "communitarian" future for Singapore that differs from the liberal individualism stereotypically identified with the West and often seen as the source of its social problems. The desire to enforce these shared values led Singapore to charge and punish American teenager Michael Fay for vandalism. Singapore's action ran counter to its liberal economic and realist security interests, and threw Singapore–U.S. relations into a crisis.[67]

Conflicting Self-Images

Two images have defined Singapore's perception of itself and shaped its identity. The first is Singapore as a twenty-first century version of the old city-states exemplified by Athens and Venice. The other more recent image is of Singapore as an emerging world city, like Rotterdam, Houston, or Boston. These two self-images and identities are recognized as responses to external circumstances, especially those surrounding its attainment of nationhood in 1965. These two images have a broadly similar domestic policy impact, but rather different foreign policy implications. The domestic impact is that, as with Athens and Venice, Singapore's survival as a city-state and its ability to achieve world city status will be a consequence of the quality of government and policy decisions. Domestically, the state and its government assume centre-stage in either self-image of Singapore.[68]

This state-centric identity leads to and drives realist foreign policies dedicated to ensuring and preserving Singapore's sovereignty as a city-state. Given that this sovereignty was contested and continues to be periodically questioned, then the security of Singapore's sovereignty is best ensured through a deterrent capability that matches potential threats to the city-state. However, the sovereignty of Singapore — as a small state with no natural resources and dependent upon international trade and foreign investments for its survival — can also be challenged via its economy. This external challenge to Singapore's comparative advantage, especially in the form of tariffs and protectionism against free trade, shapes Singapore's foreign policies. The central role of government in the economic development and security of Singapore was premised on an essentially neo-classical economics paradigm complemented by public choice theory, which is preoccupied with the issue of why governments fail. The policy import of the preceding is: how, then, to ensure good governance that can regulate the market — the central institution in classical and neo-classical economics — and prevent market failure.

But the assumptions and concepts defining a global city are perceived to run contrary to those of a city-state, especially a state-centric city-state. The global city is shaped by the transnational and multinational corporations which challenge the sovereignty of the city-state and the autonomy of its government.[69] The multinationalization of production, the integration of financial markets for global capital flows, and the search for competitive — rather than comparative — advantage in international trade blur,[70] if not render irrelevant, the old distinction between the domestic and international economy. Singapore's decision to go global and join the league of global/world cities was, as this chapter has argued, fundamentally a strategic response to its birth as a small city-state. Going global was perceived to be the way to break out of the vulnerabilities and constraints of a small city-state dependent upon its neighbours for survival.[71] Singapore rapidly discarded its old function as entrepôt for the products of its historical hinterland in Malaya and Indonesia, and moved from an import-substitution to an increasingly high-technology and higher value-added export-oriented economy, and now into information and knowledge industries. Singapore geared itself up to become the transport and communications hub of the region. It put in place the infrastructure to become an international financial, investment, and service centre. In short, Singapore banked on achieving a competitive global advantage to offset its comparative advantage as a small city-state.

Is the policy choice regarding how Singapore relates to the world in the twenty-first century dependent upon how it perceives its external environment? The political fallout from the Asian economic crisis of 1997–98 is a reminder to Singapore that it is ultimately a very small city-state — a "little red dot", in President B. J. Habibie's now infamous description — seated on a "shooting stick" — as Mr Lee Kuan Yew described it — in the centre of Southeast Asia. Singapore may have no choice but to enter the twenty-first century as a city-state surviving in a predatory world by having a deadly sting, like the poison shrimp, or by being nimble, like the proverbial mouse deer of Malay folklore. Whether Singapore can transform into a global city will depend upon whether the forces of more open and free international trade and technology — especially information technology — balance out the primordial tribalism, such as that which caused the disintegration of the old Yugoslavia and currently challenges Indonesia. As more than one Singapore leader has reiterated, Singapore as a city-state cannot shape but only respond to the course of events. So, whether Singapore relates to the world as a city-state or a global city will depend on its external environment.

The underlying argument of this chapter, however, has been that the self-images and identities that shape Singapore's relations with the world are not entirely dependent upon its environment.[72] On the contrary, these self-images and identities are endogenous to Singapore's relations with its world. Singapore may not be the helpless actor it often makes itself out to be. Singapore may have wittingly or unwittingly shaped its world and its self-images. Singapore's strategic location in the region — as the region's "linchpin", as Mr Lee Kuan Yew has described it — was not self-evident. The sultans of Johor-Riau did not perceive Singapore's location to be strategic, and one even offered to give Singapore as a gift to an English trader. The image of Singapore as strategically located arose out of Stamford Raffles' attempt to justify his plans for an East India Company factory on the island. This image was then reinforced by Britain's decision in the 1920s to hinge the defence of its Eastern Empire on a great naval base to be located on the island. It was this image of Singapore's strategic location that Mr Lee seized upon in justifying Singapore's place in the region as the anchor of its relations with the rest of the world. Singapore's claim to global city status is partly a rational economic response to an evolving international economic environment; in greater part, it is an attempt to construct an image and identity that would reposition the island in Southeast Asia and the wider Asia-Pacific.

These attempts by Singapore to define itself in the region as a city-state, and now as a global city, have not gone uncontested. Former Indonesian President B. J. Habibie's labelling of Singapore as a "little red dot" on the map may have been a visceral reaction to the diminution of Indonesia's status by the Asian financial crisis. But it could equally have been an expression of his perception of Singapore as an assertive and expansive city-state that needed to be put down. In part, Singapore's assertiveness in its relations with Indonesia and Malaysia may have been due to its belief that its sovereignty and survival continue to be questioned and probed. Singapore's relations with Malaysia have been and will continue to be problematic because, more than Indonesia, Singapore defines itself against Malaysia. Singapore's leaders have stressed that Singapore is what Malaysia is not. Malaysia's response to what it perceives as gratuitous comments from Singapore on its political and economic systems, and Singaporean counter-responses, ensure that relations between the two countries will continue to be problematic.[73]

As this chapter has argued, a number of analogies and metaphors have helped fashion Singapore's image of its place and role in the world. These began in the traumatic days of August 1965, when Singapore's leaders had to create metaphors, such as that of Singapore sitting on a shooting stick, to help them think about Singapore's place in the world. These metaphors and analogies were cognitively necessary, as there were no historical precedents to draw upon. On the contrary, the historiography implied that Singapore might not survive on its own. Analogies disproving this had to be sought. These metaphors of Singapore — as a poison shrimp, as a city-state like Athens or Venice, as a global city like Hong Kong or, more recently, as a renaissance city or cosmopolis — appear to have served Singapore well, in that they have helped define and shape its policy options and project its image to its own people and to the wider world. How Singapore relates to the world in the twenty-first century will continue to be shaped by how Singapore sorts out its different images. Will Singapore continue to think of itself as a poison shrimp or nimble mouse deer in a predatory world? A Singapore that relates to the world as a poison shrimp or mouse deer will be different from one that thinks of itself as a dolphin swimming among the sharks.

Notes

1. Interviewed by Chan Heng Chee and Obaid ul Haq in their *The Prophetic & the Political: Selected Speeches and Writings of S. Rajaratnam* (Singapore: Graham Brash, 1987), p. 540.
2. See, for example, David Vital, *The Inequality of States: A Study of the Small Power in International Relations* (Oxford: Clarendon, 1967) and his later *The Survival of Small States: Studies in Small Power/Great Power Conflict* (London: Oxford University Press, 1971); August Schou and A. O. Brundtland, eds., *Small States in International Relations* (Stockholm: Almquist & Wiksell, 1971); Marshall R. Singer, *Weak States in a World of Powers* (New York: Free Press, 1972); Michael I. Handel, *Weak States in the International System* (London: Frank Casss, 1981/1990 ed.); Commonwealth Advisory Group, *A Future for Small States: Overcoming Vulnerability* (London: Commonwealth Secretariat, 1997), revising and updating their 1985 report, *Vulnerability: Small States in the Global Society*. Brigadier-General (NS) Lee Hsien Loong attempted a summary of these options in an often-quoted address to the Singapore Institute of International Affairs on "Security Options for Small States," on 16 October 1984, when he was leaving the Singapore Armed Forces to enter politics (address reported in the *Straits Times*, 6 November 1984).
3. The definition of what constitutes a small state ranges from large countries with small populations to small countries with large populations, and small countries with small populations. The Commonwealth Secretariat study, *A Future for Small States: Overcoming Vulnerability*, defines a small state as a country with a population of 1.5 million or less. On this criteria, there are thirty-one small states in the Commonwealth. Within Asia, only Brunei qualifies as a "small state"; Singapore does not.
4. The primary focus of the Commonwealth Advisory Group report, *A Future for Small States: Overcoming Vulnerability*.

5. This 1824 British treaty with Sultan Hussain (reproduced in J. de V. Allen, A. J. Stockwell, and L. R. Wright, eds., *A Collection of Treaties and Other Documents Affecting the States of Malaysia*, 1761-1963 (London: Oceana Publs. Inc., 1981), p. 37) defined in international law Singapore's boundaries as a small state up to today. A 1927 "Boundary Treaty", signed with the Sultan of Johore, refined and extended the 1824 demarcation. A third stage in the demarcation of Singapore's boundaries is contained in the 25 May 1973 agreement with Indonesia on the boundary in the Main Straits and the Singapore Straits.
6. The place of Singapore in Malayan historiography was first defined by Sir Frank Swettenham in his *British Malaya: An Account of the Origin and Progress of British Influence in Malaya* (London: Bodley Head, 1906, subsequent editions by Allen & Unwin). Sir Frank not only made history as a long-serving member of the colonial administration (retiring as Governor-General of the Straits Settlement and High Commissioner for the Federated Malay States), but lived long enough to write of his role in history and reiterate it in several editions of his text, which was still in print in 1955. For better or worse, Sir Frank's text has defined the historical framework within which the history of Malaya and Singapore are interpreted. Sir Frank's description of the Straits Settlements as "the Clapham Junction of the Eastern Seas" (p. 342) has been adopted by C. M. Turnbull as the title of a chapter in her *A History of Singapore*, 1819-1988 (Singapore: Oxford University Press, 1989).
7. Documented and analysed by Noordin Sopiee, *From Malayan Union to Singapore Separation: Political Unification in the Malaysian Region*, 1945-65 (Kuala Lumpur: University of Malaya, 1974).
8. Transcript of a press conference given by the Prime Minister of Singapore, Mr Lee Kuan Yew, at Broadcasting House, Singapore, at 1200 hours on Monday, 9 August 1965, (hereafter referred to as "Transcript of 9 August 1965 press conference"), p. 4, deposited in National Archives of Singapore.
9. Transcript of an interview given by the Prime Minister, Mr Lee Kuan Yew, to Mr Gerry Seymour, Resident Correspondent of Independent Television News (ITN), on 11 August 1965 and recorded at the studios of Television Singapura, (hereafter referred to as "Transcript of 11 August 1965 interview given to Mr Gerry Seymour"), p.6, deposited in National Archives of Singapore.
10. Press conference of the Singapore Prime Minister, Mr Lee Kuan Yew, with Malay journalists at the studio of TV Singapura on Wednesday, 11 August 1965, (hereafter referred to as "Press conference of 11 August 1965 with Malay journalists"), pp. 6–7, deposited in the National Archives of Singapore.
11. Transcript of the "Proceedings when Singapore and Malaysian PAP leaders met followed by a press conference at Cabinet Office, City Hall, on 12 August 1965", pp. 12–13, deposited in National Archives of Singapore.
12. Mr Lee Kuan Yew's reply to the first question put to him on his attitude towards Indonesia and his view of relations with Indonesia, in Transcript of 9 August 1965 press conference, p. 2.

13. It is recalled in Lee's memoirs, *The Singapore Story* (Singapore: Times Editions, 1998), p. 649.
14. Transcript of 9 August 1965 press conference, p. 12.
15. Ibid., p. 16.
16. At another press conference on 12 August 1965, Mr Devan Nair — representing the PAP members left in Malaysia — also expressed this hope of re-unification. Mr Nair stated that "the PAP in Malaysia cannot accept the ejection of Singapore ... we think it supremely illogical that such a situation should have been brought about. ... and it will be part of our [PAP in Malaysia] responsibility ... to bring about a political climate suitable to the ultimate re-unification of Singapore with Malaysia". See Lau Teik Soon, "Malaysia-Singapore relations: crisis of adjustment, 1965-68", *Journal of Southeast Asian Studies* 10, No. 1 (1969): 155–76.
17. Transcript of 9 August 1965 press conference, p. 6.
18. Transcript of 11 August 1965 interview given to Mr Gerry Seymour, p. 7.
19. Transcript of an interview given by the Prime Minister, Mr Lee Kuan Yew, to Mr Neville Peterson of the Australian Broadcasting Commission, on 12 August 1965, recorded at the studios of Television Singapore, p. 2, National Archives of Singapore. These references to Syed Ja'afar Albar are also in the Transcript of an interview given by the Prime Minister, Mr Lee Kuan Yew, to four foreign correspondents on 14 August 1965, at the studios of Television Singapura (hereafter referred to as "Transcript of 14 August 1965 interview given to four foreign correspondents"), p. 7; and Transcript of 11 August 1965 interview given to Mr Gerry Seymour, p. 2.
20. Transcript of 14 August 1965 interview given to four foreign correspondents, p. 20.
21. Transcript of 11 August 1965 interview given to Mr Gerry Seymour, p. 4.
22. Transcript of 14 August 1965 interview given to four foreign correspondents, p. 21.
23. Press conference of 11 August 1965 with Malay journalists, pp. 4–5 of translation.
24. Summarized in Kawin Wilairat, *Singapore's Foreign Policy: The First Decade*, Field Report Series No. 10 (Singapore: Institute of Southeast Asian Studies, 1975), pp. 29–51; also Bilveer Singh, *Singapore: Foreign Policy Imperatives of a Small State*, Occasional Paper, Centre for Advanced Studies (Singapore: National University Faculty of Arts and Social Science, 1988), pp. 11–21.
25. Three decades later Mr Lee himself raised the issue of remerger with Malaysia and sparked off another acrimonious debate between Singapore and Malaysia — on which, see Shamira Bhanu Abdul Azeez, *The Singapore-Malaysia "Remerger" Debate of* 1966 (Hull: Centre of Southeast Asian Studies, University of Hull, 1998). See N. Ganesan's stress on the factor of political leadership in his "Factors affecting Singapore's foreign policy towards Malaysia", *Australian Journal of International Affairs* 45, No. 2 (1991): 182–95.
26. Lee, *The Singapore Story*, p. 663.

27. See Chan Heng Chee's analysis, "Singapore's Foreign Policy, 1965-1968", *Journal of Southeast Asian Studies* 10, No. 1 (1969): 177–91.
28. As defined by the British colonial civil servant, J. S. Furnival, in his 1939 *Netherlands India: A Study of Plural Economy* (reprinted ed., Cambridge: University Press, 1967), esp. pp. 446–69, and *Colonial Policy and Practice: A Comparative Study of Burma and Netherlands India* (Cambridge: University Press, 1948). Furnival offers his model of a "plural society" as an alternative to Dutch descriptions of their colony as a "dual society", juxtaposing a Western colonial capitalist society on an underdeveloped "Eastern society". Furnival's model was perceived to be a better description of colonial societies, not only in Southeast Asia, but also the West Indies and Africa. The key features of this model of a plural society have since become part of the policy assumptions of nation-building leaders.
29. See Chua Beng Huat's explanation of why and how capitalist economic development and modernization became the "social glue" to holding Singapore together in "Racial-Singaporeans: Absence after the hyphen," in *Southeast Asian Identities: Culture and the Politics of Representation in Indonesia, Malaysia, Singapore and Thailand*, edited by Joel S. Kahn (Singapore: Institute of Southeast Asian Studies, 1998), pp. 28–50.
30. Rupert Emerson, *From Empire to Nation: The Rise to Self-Assertion of Asian and African Peoples* (1960; reprinted ed., Boston: Beacon Press, 1966), pp. 95 and 105. For students of Malayan politics and history, Emerson established his reputation in 1937 when he published *Malaysia: A Study in Direct and Indirect Rule*, which has since become a classic and has been reprinted a number of times.
31. *The Mirror*, 25 July 1966, p. 1.
32. Chan Heng Chee's analysis of this politics of "survival" in her *Singapore: The Politics of Survival*, 1965-1967 (Singapore: Oxford University Press, 1971) is still relevant.
33. Willard A. Hanna describes the then "New Singapore Armed Forces", AUFS *Reports: Southeast Asia Series* 21, No. 1 (1973).
34. C. E. Morrison and A. Suhrke, *Strategies of Survival: The Foreign Policy Dilemmas of Smaller Asian States* (St. Lucia, Australia: University Queensland, 1978), p. 187, make this comparison in relation to Singapore's perception of its threats.
35. This doctrine of inter-state relations described in books 6-14 of the *Arthashastra* is referred to as a *mandala* or circle of states, prescribed as twelve, around a state that is either threatened or preparing to expand and therefore needs allies.
36. See, e.g., Lee Kuan Yew's inventory of ASEAN recommendations implemented in his address to the fifth ASEAN Ministerial Meeting in April 1972: in its first year ASEAN committees drafted 102 recommendations, of which none were implemented. In their second year, ASEAN committees drafted 161 recommendations, of which ten were implemented, or 6.2 per cent. This percentage of recommendations implemented slowly climbed over the next two years from 6.2 per cent to 10.6, then 22.3 per cent. Singapore's regional policy and contributions to regional co-operation is reviewed in Wilairat, *Singapore's Foreign Policy*, pp. 74–103; also Lau Teik Soon, "Singapore's perceptions of ASEAN's role", in *Political*

and Social Change in Singapore, edited by Wu The-yao (Singapore: Institute of Southeast Asian Studies, 1975), pp. 155–70.

37. See Heiner Hanggi, ASEAN *and the* ZOPFAN *Concept*, Pacific Strategic Papers No. 4 (Singapore: Institute of Southeast Asian Studies, 1991), for an assessment of the ZOPFAN proposal.
38. Lau Teik Soon, "Singapore and ASEAN," in *Singapore: Development Policies and Trends*, edited by P.S.J. Chen, (Singapore: Oxford University Press, 1983), pp. 285–300.
39. Reported in *Straits Times*, 14 August 1973, and quoted in Kawin Wilairat, *Singapore's foreign policy: a study of the foreign policy system of a city-state*, Ph.D. dissertation, Georgetown University, 1975 (Ann Arbor: Xerox University Microfilm), p. 470.
40. Abdullah Ahmad, *Tengku Abdul Rahman and Malaysia's Foreign Policy*, 1963-1970 (Kuala Lumpur: Berita Publishing Sdn Bhd, 1985), p. 90. Chan Heng Chee also notes this in her 1971 *Singapore: Politics of Survival*, p. 54.
41. Then Singapore Ambassador to Indonesia, Mr Lee Khoon Choy, describes this scene in his *An Ambassador's Journey* (S'pore: Times Books International, 1983), p. 218 and his role in persuading Mr Lee Kuan Yew to sprinkle these flowers in the preceding chapter of his book.
42. This event is discussed by Chan Heng Chee in her "Singapore's Foreign Policy, 1965-1968", pp. 181–82.
43. See Yuan-li Wu's argument that the United States may not want to be in the region if uninvited, in his *Strategic Significance of Singapore: A Study in Balance of Power* (Washington, D.C.: American Enterprise Institute, 1973), p. 28.
44. See, for example, Brigadier General (NS) George Yeo's elaboration of Venice as an analogy for Singapore, in his farewell speech on leaving the Armed Forces to enter politics, "Venice — an inspiration to Singapore; How limitations of size can be overcome", reproduced in *Straits Times*, 19 August 1988, p. 27. See also Michael Leifer's foreword to the English translation of Philippe Regnier's *Singapore: City-State in South-East Asia* (London: C. Hurst & Co), where he writes that Dr Regnier "regards Singapore as a latter-day Venice of Southeast Asia, and expects it, unlike its historical forebear, to survive as a prosperous independent state".
45. Thinking analogically about Singapore and Venice or Athens is more than just searching for similarities between Singapore and Venice or Athens. The search for similarities is driven by our purpose in looking for similarities and, in this search, what differences we obscure or ignore are crucial, because these differences may undermine the analogy-based inferences we are drawing. What kind of similarities we are making between Singapore and Venice, and how they are made, also frames the inferences we draw. See Keith J. Holyoak and Paul Thagard, *Mental Leaps: Analogy in Creative Thought* (Cambridge, Massachusetts: MIT Press, 1995), on the invaluable insights than can be gained from, and also dangerous errors of, analogical thinking.
46. This entrepôt trade is analysed by Joe McCellan, "Entrepôt trade", in *The Singapore Economy*, edited by You Poh Seng and Lim Chong Yah (Singapore: Eastern Universities Press, 1971), pp. 180–88 and Wong Lin Ken, "Singapore: Its growth

as an entrepot port, 1819-1941", *Journal of Southeast Asian Studies* 9, No. 1 (1978): 50–84.

47. Regnier, *Singapore: City-State in South-East Asia* , pp. 39ff.
48. See John Pemble, *Venice Rediscovered* (Oxford: University Press, 1996), on how the European and American image of Venice has evolved since its political extinction two centuries ago and how this has helped frame the development of Western sensibility.
49. Pemble, *Venice Rediscovered*, pp. 101ff, on what Britain chose to learn from its version of Venetian history.
50. J. Grubb, "When Myths Lose Power: Four Decades of Venetian Historiography", *Journal of Modern History* 58 (1986): 43–94, on how Italy's changing views of Venetian history informed its political development to fascism in the first half of this century.
51. Charles Tilly and W. P. Blockmans, eds., *Cities & The Rise of States in Europe*, AD 1000 *to* 1800 (Boulder, Colorado: Westview Press, 1994).
52. Brilliantly argued by Jane Jacobs in her *Cities and the Wealth of Nations: The Principles of Economic Life* (New York: Random House, 1984); also her earlier *The Economy of Cities* (New York: Random House, 1969). This argument is also noted by Goh Keng Swee in a 1967 address on "City as modernizers" reprinted in his *The Economics of Modernization and Other Essays* (Singapore: Asia Pacific Press, 1972), pp. 19ff.
53. N. R. Peirce, et al., *Citistates: How Urban America Can Prosper in a Competitive World* (Washington, D. C.: Seven Locks Press, 1993).
54. Text of S. Rajaratnam's 16 February 1972 speech to the Singapore Press Club is in Wee Teong Boon, ed., *The Future of Singapore — The Global City* (Singapore: University Education Press for Democratic Socialist Club, n.d.), pp. 15–32, and slightly abbreviated in Chan Heng Chee and Obaid ul-Haq, eds., *The Prophetic and the Political: Selected Speeches and Writings of* S. *Rajaratnam* (Singapore: Graham Brash, 1987), 223–31.
55. Toynbee noted that "in the World of 1969 the most important sovereign independent city-state is Singapore", but he was pessimistic of its future because city-states are an earlier milestone in the journey of *Cities on the Move* (London: Oxford University Press, 1970), pp. 54–55. Toynbee thought that, as an independent city-state, Singapore would be at the mercy of Malaysia, just as Gibraltar would be at the mercy of Spain if it opted for independence, and Hong Kong would be at the mercy of China should it opt for independence.
56. Toynbee, *Cities on the Move*, p.196.
57. T. G. McGee reviews how the urbanization that Toynbee envisaged and globalization of the economy is today producing a series of global and sub-global systems of highly linked cities in his "Globalization, urbanization and the Emergence of Sub-Global Regions: A Case Study of the Asia-Pacific Region", in *Asia-Pacific: New Geographies of the Pacific Rim*, edited by R. F. Watters and T. G. McGee (London: Hurst & Co., 1997), pp. 29–45.

58. P. J. Taylor outlines the differences in his "World Cities and Territorial States: The Rise and Fall of their Mutuality", in *World Cities in a World-System*, edited by P. L. Knox and P. J. Taylor (Cambridge: University Press, 1995), pp. 48–61.
59. John Friedmann, author of the seminal 1986 essay, "The World City Hypothesis", in *Development & Change* 17, No. 1 (1986): 69–83, recalls being invited to Singapore to advise on how the city-state might achieve a "world city" status in "Where We Stand: A Decade of World City Research", in *World Cities in a World-System*, edited by Knox and Taylor, p. 36.
60. P. L. Knox, "World cities in a world system", in *World Cities in a World-System*, edited by Knox and Taylor, pp. 3–20, reviews the nature of world cities within global networks of economic flows. Also, John Friedmann's review of his seminal 1986 essay on "The World City Hypothesis" in "Where We Stand: A Decade of World City Research", pp. 21–47 and Linda Low's chapter in this volume.
61. Toh Mun Heng and Tan Kong Yam, eds., *Competitiveness of the Singapore Economy: A Strategic Perspective* (Singapore: Singapore University Press and World Scientific, 1998), discuss the options for Singapore to retain a competitive edge as a regional transportation hub, international finance centre, and regional centre for technology and education.
62. See Saskia Sassen on "Servicing the Global Economy: Reconfigured States and Private Agents," in *Globalization and the Asia-Pacific: Contested Territories*, edited by Kris Olds et al. (London: Routledge, 1999), pp.149–62.
63. Hong Kong, whom Singapore considers its twin city, is forming another mega-urban corridor with Guangzhou, the Zhujiang river delta, Taibei, and Xiamen. Osaka, Tokyo, Seoul, Shanghai, Tianjin, and Beijing are being networked to form a Bhai rim region; see Yue-man Yeung and Fu-chen Lo, "Global restructuring and emerging urban corridors in Pacific Asia", in *Emerging World Cities in Pacific Asia*, edited by Yue-man Yeung and Fu-chen Lo (Tokyo: United Nations University Press, 1996), pp. 17–47.
64. How to balance between globalism and regionalism is explored by Amitav Acharya and M. Ramesh, "Economic Foundations of Singapore's Security: From Globalism to Regionalism?" in *Singapore Changes Guard: Social, Political and Economic Directions in the 1990s*, edited by G. Rodan (Melbourne: Longman Cheshire, 1993), pp. 134–52.
65. Scott Macleod and T. G. McGee, "The Singapore-Johore-Riau Growth Triangle: An Emerging Extended Metropolitan Region," in *Emerging World Cities*, edited by Yeung and Lo, pp. 417–64.
66. Noted by Michael Leifer, "Singapore in Regional and Global Context: Sustaining Exceptionalism," in *Singapore: Re-engineering Success*, edited by Arun Mahizhnan and Lee Tsao Yuan (Singapore: Institute of Policy Studies and Oxford University Press, 1998), pp. 23ff and Chapter 5 of his *Singapore's Foreign Policy: Coping with Vulnerability* (London: Routledge, 2000), which is entitled: "Driving and Suffering the Region?". Also J-L. Margolin, "Singapore: New Regional Influence, New World Outlook?", *Contemporary Southeast Asia* 20, No. 3 (1998): 319–36.

67. See Leonard C. Sebastian's discussion of these issues and implications for foreign policy in his "Values and Governance Issues in the Foreign Policy of Singapore", in *Changing Values in Asia: Their Impact on Governance and Development*, edited by Han Sung Joo (Singapore: Institute of Southeast Asian Studies; Tokyo: Japan Center for International Exchange, 1999), pp. 219–50.
68. Linda Low has documented how the Government made Singapore in her *The Political Economy of a City-State: Government-Made Singapore* (Singapore: Oxford University Press, 1998). A decade earlier, Lim Chong Yah and his colleagues argued that Singapore's fate is consequent to its governance policies in their *Policy Options for the Singapore Economy* (Singapore: McGraw-Hill, 1988).
69. J. Stopford and S. Strange, *Rival States, Rival Firms: Competition for World Markets* (Cambridge: University Press, 1991) and S. Strange, *The Retreat of the State: The Diffusion of Power in the World Economy* (Cambridge: Cambridge University Press, 1996).
70. See M. E. Porter, *The Competitive Advantage of Nations* (New York: Free Press, 1990), on the distinction between comparative and competitive advantages.
71. See Narayanan Ganesan, "Singapore: Realist Cum Trading State", in *Asian Security Practice: Material and Ideational Influences*, edited by M. Alagappa (Stanford: University Press, 1998), pp. 579–607, on the tensions inherent in Singapore as a realist city-state and as a neoliberal trading state.
72. This argument draws on the theoretical framework constructed by Alexander Wendt in his benchmark "Anarchy is What States Make of It", *International Organization* 46, No. 2 (1992): 391–421. Also Jonathan Mercer, "Anarchy and Identity", *International Organization* 4, No. 2 (1995): 229–52.
73. Leifer makes a similar point in his "Singapore in Regional and Global Context: Sustaining Exceptionalism", in *Singapore: Re-engineering Success*, edited by Mahizhnan and Lee, p. 24.

6

DEFENCE AND SECURITY
Evolving Threat Perceptions

Derek da Cunha

Introduction

A small country has a natural and inherent sense of insecurity, as the historical record of nation-states in both the modern and classical worlds has attested. And so it has similarly proven to be the case with the state of Singapore since it was expelled from the Federation of Malaysia on 9 August 1965. Since that time, against all odds, Singapore has succeeded in not just surviving but prospering in Southeast Asia — a region with a myriad of geopolitical cleavages that have not infrequently erupted into conflict of one form or another, both intra-state and inter-state. How has Singapore survived and prospered within that environment and despite an acute sense of insecurity and vulnerability, is one of the questions this chapter will address. How Singapore will continue to survive and prosper in the new millennium, as its threat perceptions evolve and changes occur in the Southeast Asian geopolitical environment, is another question that will be addressed.

Singapore's security can be examined at three systemic levels. The first of these levels is the domestic, in terms of general regime and state (or internal) security. The second is the external level, in terms of threats to national security emanating from the external environment. And the third and final level is that of the region, in terms of the region's (or ASEAN's) security being indivisible from that of Singapore's. In the current absence of identifiable threats to internal security (which were pervasive in the past — especially the 1960s — but are now no longer apparent), this chapter will examine the second and third levels of security. It will also ascertain how Singapore's threat perceptions will likely evolve in the first two decades of the new millennium. But before all that, it is important to set out the sources of Singapore's sense of insecurity and how the city-state has attempted to minimize that insecurity.

Sources of Singapore's Sense of Insecurity

The sources of Singapore's sense of insecurity derive from two separate categories that are related. One category constitutes structural sources of insecurity; they are sources that are ingrained in the body-politic and physical nature of the nation-state. The other category constitutes sources of insecurity which are cyclical and/or events-driven in nature; they derive largely from changes that might occur to the geopolitical environment of which Singapore is a part, and which might impact negatively on the city-state.

Structural Elements

Being small in size — in both land area and population — is the first and obvious variable that contributes to Singapore's sense of insecurity. This is compounded by the fact that Singapore's smallness comes into sharp focus when seen against the backdrop of its two far larger neighbours, Malaysia and Indonesia. Smallness of size necessarily means that there is a natural asymmetry between Singapore and its two neighbours. Put very simply, the policies and attitudes of the Governments of Singapore's two larger neighbours can affect Singapore far more than can the Singapore Government's policies and attitudes affect those two neighbours. The issue here is one of relativity — a relativity that is a function of the asymmetrical size of countries in proximity to each other.

The ethnic composition of the city-state in relation to that of its two larger neighbours also contributes to feelings of Singapore's insecurity. Singapore is essentially an ethnic Chinese city-state (78 per cent of the population is ethnic Chinese) amidst a Malay sea. (Indonesians, especially from the main island of Java, might view it differently, preferring to view themselves as predominantly Javanese — and therefore of a different lineage than Malay.[1]) Ethnic primordial impulses cannot be understated. Within the Southeast Asian context, such impulses may have been generally dormant — or quiescent — in Malaysia, Singapore, and Indonesia during much of the 1970s, 1980s, and part of the 1990s, but now they have risen significantly to the fore of individual, community, and national consciousness. The volatility of such impulses is legion; they are impulses that are not easily given to rationality. This is especially so when ethnicity is mixed with religion, language, and culture to make a potent brew.

The lack of natural resources and near-complete reliance on the import of food, fuel, and a large part of water constitutes another source of Singapore's insecurity. An overwhelming reliance on outside sources for such basic needs highlights a major vulnerability — that, due to some reason or other, those sources might be disrupted. Singapore's independence on calm and predictable externalities is therefore all too obvious. However, its ability to ensure that externalities remain calm and predictable is not entirely apparent.

The three immediately identifiable aspects of Singapore's insecurity, outlined above, are structural in nature. That is to say, barring geopolitical or technological changes of a cataclysmic or revolutionary nature, these sources of insecurity will remain with Singapore indefinitely. As such, any attempt to enhance Singapore's sense of security must spring initially from mitigating or minimizing these ingrained sources of insecurity. We will return to an examination of this point later.

Cyclical and/or Events-Driven Aspects of Insecurity

If the structural elements of insecurity remain an abiding concern for Singapore, cyclical and/or events-driven aspects of insecurity occasionally throw up new challenges for the city-state. Such insecurity can derive from a host of factors, and might include some of the following:

- Changes in the political complexion of governments in neighbouring states, which governments might then not be as well disposed towards Singapore relative to previous governments. An example would be the entrenchment of kinds of democratically-elected governments that are susceptible to popular pressure, and which, out of political expediency, initiate a type of foreign policy that proves inimical to Singapore's interests.
- The changing nature of middle-power relationships in Southeast Asia and great-power relationships in the wider Asia-Pacific region, which might have adverse consequences for both the region and Singapore. A possible example could be a significant deterioration of Sino–American relations, and the effect that that might have on Singapore's ties with China, in view of the city-state's burgeoning defence relationship with the United States.
- The "second order" effect of regional flashpoints impacting on Singapore. An example here would be the simmering dispute over the Spratly Islands and the possibility of extended military conflict over those islands.

Although Singapore is not a claimant to the Spratlys, any major military action by one of the claimants to enforce rights of national sovereignty over the islands will have what is known as a "second order" effect on Singapore.[2] Extended military conflict over the Spratlys could affect shipping traffic in the South China Sea, and which would naturally impact Singapore, as it is heavily dependent on maritime commerce as its lifeblood.

Approaches to Minimizing Singapore's Insecurity

Singapore has adopted a multi-pronged approach to minimize its sense of insecurity in Southeast Asia; or viewed another way, it has attempted to enhance its security through a range of approaches. Six approaches, among others, come immediately to mind:

- Employing economics in the service of national security.
- Enhancing social and national cohesion to project a unified front by the population in facing potential external security threats.
- Cultivating Southeast Asian élites, or those identified as future leaders.
- Engaging in regional and international diplomacy of a wide-ranging nature.
- Establishing and enhancing defence ties with a number of countries.
- Building up robust and formidable armed forces.

This multiple and layered approach to security highlights the extent to which Singapore's political leadership views soberly and seriously the potential challenge to Singapore's security from a range of sources. No effort is spared — in terms of money, time, and talent — in relentlessly improving the effectiveness of each of these approaches. It would be appropriate to examine briefly these six approaches and to analyse their effectiveness.

Economics

There are few countries in the world which have employed economics in the service of national security in the way and extent Singapore has. With a recognition that Singapore's economic success has been partly and significantly a consequence of its economic interactions with its neighbours, attempting to ensure that those same neighbours have a stake in Singapore's continued prosperity has been a conscious policy of the Singapore Government. Enhancing trade and investment linkages between Singapore and its neighbours was very much a priority goal in the 1970s and 1980s. In the 1990s, that goal was elevated to a higher plane and made less ad hoc and more formalized. This was seen via the rubric of the growth triangle project that was to link Singapore with the Malaysian state of Johor and the Indonesian island of Batam and the wider Riau Archipelago. SIJORI, as that growth triangle is called, had enormous economic potential.[3] It would combine Singapore capital, and managerial and organizational expertise with relatively low-cost inputs of land and labour in both Johor and Riau. With sizeable Singapore investments funnelled into both Johor and Riau, the logic ran that both Malaysia and Indonesia would have a substantial stake in the success of the project. In other words, both Malaysia and Indonesia would not take any measures harmful to Singapore's interests as that would impact adversely on the growing, and mutually beneficial, economic ties amongst the growth triangle partners. Singapore's economic interests would therefore be indivisible from those of Malaysia and Indonesia, so it seemed to be the implicit theory.

In reality, however, SIJORI has had a mixed record and impact. An objective analysis might conclude that Singapore has benefited far more from the project than have Malaysia and Indonesia. Malaysia, in particular, might feel that the amount and nature (significantly in real estate) of Singapore-originated investments in Johor, though substantial, is not substantial enough to have any sizeable effect on the economic fortunes of Malaysia as a whole. Indeed by the late 1990s, Malaysia appeared to have lost much interest in SIJORI, not least because it was perceived that much of the Singapore focus was on the development of Batam and Bintan.

The outbreak of inter-ethnic violence in Batam between the Bataks and Flores during the Asian economic crisis of 1998–99 also highlighted the extent to which threats to security and to a peaceful environment can suddenly arise right at Singapore's very doorstep. That violence could well foreshadow greater inter-ethnic violence in the future which could then unravel what remains of the SIJORI project. Singapore's ability to forestall that violence is limited, being reliant on the enforcement action of Indonesian authorities on Indonesia's sovereign territory. And that, of course, remains a dilemma for Singapore.

Social and National Cohesion

A small population base of only four million (of which some 20 per cent are foreign nationals) has strategic disadvantages for any country, particularly one next to other countries with population bases which are substantially larger. However, to mitigate the effects of small population size, and to project an image of a nation that is united, the Singapore Government has adopted a number of policies over the years. Unifying the ethnic Chinese population, drawn from diverse dialect groups, through the use of Mandarin Chinese has been one policy. The attempts to narrow social and income inequalities through a range of economic and educational policies has been another (although its results have been mixed, and increasing globalization has in fact resulted in reverses to those attempts). The commitment and constant promotion of multiracialism to bind potentially divisive strands in society has been a third (even if in the 1990s the Singapore Government had been placing greater stress on each ethnic community helping its own kind). All of these policies have in varying degrees succeeded in generating social and national cohesion.

The Singapore Government's concerns about ensuring a nation that is united, especially when facing potential problems on the external front, were manifested in 1997 and 1998 when Singapore and its leaders came in for heavy criticism from Malaysia over a number of issues. For instance, in 1997, Singapore Senior Minister Lee Kuan Yew was subjected to a barrage of virulent criticism from Malaysians over his comments about crime in Johor.[4] It was instructive that Singapore leaders tended to be sensitive not merely to this criticism coming out of Malaysia but also as to how Singaporeans were reacting, if at all, to the criticism. Singapore Cabinet ministers, such as Deputy Prime Minister Lee Hsien Loong and Education Minister Teo Chee Hean, were to hold dialogue sessions with groups of Singaporean professionals. The objective of those sessions was to convey the Singapore Government's point of view over the spat with Malaysia and also to gauge the level of support the Government was receiving from the ground. It appeared that in 1997, the Government may not have received as much support as it would have liked.[5] It is this kind of lack of a unified front behind the Government and its policies, especially when they relate to dealings with Singapore's neighbours, that the Government is concerned with as it could be exploited by potential adversaries, or diminish the Government's ability to speak with an authoritative voice or with moral authority.

Cultivating Southeast Asian Élites

Singapore is not noted for being generous in dispensing aid, in monetary form to other less advantaged countries. Instead, the Singapore Government has argued that the provision of technical assistance to such countries would be more beneficial to them, especially in the long run. In that regard, a range of technical assistance schemes have been put in place over the years. These schemes, principally funded by the Singapore Government, largely involve officials from a range of developing countries spending a stint in Singapore where they would be put through formalized training programmes, most of which are in the technical and managerial areas, and include attachment to both statutory boards and branches of the civil service. These schemes assist in profiling Singaporean expertise. They also generate goodwill for Singapore, especially directly with those officials who have been on the various training programmes. It is hoped that these officials would bring back to their home countries a positive image of Singapore. While these training and attachment programmes are termed "technical assistance" by the Singapore Government, many of the participants of the programmes have viewed them as simply junkets. And the extent to which goodwill is generated might be restricted to merely the participants in these programmes.

The logical extension of the technical assistance schemes has been others which target individuals who are intellectual élites in their own countries or are viewed as potential leaders. The ASEAN scholarships is one such scheme. It identifies bright youths who are given scholarships to pursue their secondary education in premier schools in Singapore. At the end of their schooling, if these individuals decide to remain in Singapore, it benefits the country as it adds to the talent pool. If, on the other hand, these youths return to their own countries, that also benefits Singapore as it is hoped that the experience they had during their formative years in Singapore would remain with them, and that they would be well disposed towards Singapore during their adult lives. Such an implicit objective is also behind the Lee Kuan Yew Fellowship scheme. This scheme identifies promising young politicians from the Asia-Pacific region, especially from ASEAN countries, who are deemed as potential leaders of their countries. Such individuals are invited to spend an all-expenses-paid week or so in Singapore where they are briefed by various government and semi-government departments as well as think tanks on a range of issues, mostly related to Singapore — how it works and how it has succeeded in tackling a range of socio-economic problems that bedevil most less developed countries. Again, generating goodwill for Singapore seems to be the underlying objective.

These various élite-level schemes (and there are others) are almost an effort at co-optation. They attempt to make friends and indeed allies of those who are or likely to be at the socio-economic or political apex of their countries: these are people who are or might eventually be in policy-making positions, and whose attitudes, actions, and predispositions could in some way or other have an effect on Singapore. The schemes are deemed a very cost-effective way of winning over élite individuals in the region to Singapore's corner. But that is also its potential pitfall. Regional observers might have already begun noting that such schemes are too élitist in nature. And that they are an inexpensive way for Singapore to win over people of a particular pedigree to its cause. Rather than such low-cost, élitist schemes, what some in Southeast Asia would like to see is Singapore being more generous with its largesse, and in a way which would effect, positively, the lives of a great many people in the region, not just the select few. The public relations mileage derived from the current schemes may therefore have begun to lose its value. Indeed, it may have already run its course.

Regional and International Diplomacy

One way in which a small country can let its voice be heard on the global stage is by channelling it through regional and international organizations, where its voice can then be magnified many times. This Singapore has done effectively through the rubric of ASEAN. The initial rationale for ASEAN and its greatest (albeit not always obvious) success has been the regulating of inter-state relations amongst its members.[6] That benign reality has been of considerable benefit to Singapore: indeed, it would not be an exaggeration to advance the view that Singapore has been the greatest beneficiary of ASEAN membership precisely because of the peaceful geopolitical environment the regional body has engendered and which has allowed Singapore to prosper. As one analyst has noted more pointedly, ASEAN has provided "an institutional framework within which Singapore can manage relations with its two Malay neighbours".[7] That was especially the case when ASEAN was an organization of just five or six countries, with the three Strait of Malacca states — Indonesia, Malaysia, and Singapore — constituting the driving force of the organization by providing intellectual and moral leadership. Those three countries were in effect the core of ASEAN.

Membership expansion, which has now fulfilled the founding fathers' vision of one Southeast Asia, has been a mixed blessing for ASEAN. On the one hand, it has removed the ideological divide separating Southeast Asia into two camps; on the other hand, it has given rise to an organization that is more unwieldy, less cozy, and, as a result, has diluted the influence or clout of the three core states.[8]

An enlarged regional entity might be useful in dealing with the external powers, which has also been one of ASEAN's strengths. However, even here, enlargement has thrown up an unexpected problem: the membership of Myanmar, whose regime is abhorred by the West, has given rise to some difficulties for ASEAN in its interactions with its Western dialogue partners, particularly the European Union. At the intra-ASEAN level, enlargement has also brought into sharp relief a number of dissimilarities between member states, in terms of their political systems, level of economic development, and threat perceptions. In other words, enlargement has led to potentially less organizational cohesion, opening the way for more disagreements between member states, even at the public level. It will take some time for ASEAN to fully digest its expansion in size to ten states, and in the meantime the road that it travels will likely be less smooth than before. And that, of course, would have obvious implications for Singapore. The Asian economic crisis had shown the strains and tensions that could emerge between ASEAN members.[9] With Indonesia — widely accepted as the unofficial leader of ASEAN — grappling with enormous domestic political, social, and economic problems,[10] ASEAN could well experience a sense of drift or at least less unity of purpose by some of its members, with possible implications for inter-state relations and security.

Other than ASEAN — which for the better part of thirty years has added to Singapore's sense of security — the Asia-Pacific Economic Cooperation (APEC), the ASEAN Regional Forum (ARF), the Asia-Europe Meeting (ASEM), the World Trade Organization (WTO), and the United Nations (UN), have been multilateral institutions in which Singapore has focused a considerable part of its diplomatic energies. This has created an international awareness of Singapore (especially when Singapore was elected to a non-permanent seat on the UN Security Council for the period 2001-2002), and has highlighted the degree to which a small nation-state — due to its intellectual and economic strengths — can have an influence disproportionate to its size. More significantly — and of particular relevance here — it also results in the international community having an interest, and indeed a stake, in Singapore's well-being, thereby providing some sense of security to the global city-state.

Establishing and Enhancing Defence Ties

"Soft-edged" aspects or approaches to directly or indirectly enhancing security, as described in the above four approaches, have their obvious limitations: for instance, they only work well when dealing with rational state actors; they have precious little application when dealing with non-state actors, like terrorist groups and organizations. Therefore, soft-edged approaches have greater utility when they are combined with more "hard-edged" approaches that provide some element of synergy or complementarity. And here we come to the various defence arrangements which Singapore has established with a number of countries.

Most of Singapore's defence ties with other countries are bilateral in nature. However, there are two examples of multilateral security arrangements. One, is the Five Power Defence Arrangements (FPDA), which groups Singapore and Malaysia with Australia, New Zealand, and the United Kingdom. The FPDA, established in 1971,[11] was revitalized in the early 1990s, an initiative largely Singapore's. The Arrangements provide for the three extra-regional powers to consult in the event of a threat to the security of Singapore and Malaysia. That, at least, is the declared policy of the FPDA; in actual terms, however, the FPDA has provided a valuable, desensitized, and multilateral forum for elements of the Singapore and Malaysian armed forces to exercise together regularly, thereby serving as a confidence-building mechanism between the two countries.[12] This reality underscores the abiding suspicions and undercurrent of tensions that continue to characterize Singapore–Malaysia relations. Apart from the FPDA, there is one other formalized multilateral security arrangement in Southeast Asia. This involves the three Strait of Malacca states, and it has a specific focus. It centres on anti-piracy operations and the maintenance of maritime safety in the Strait of Malacca. As a result of an agreement concluded in the early 1990s, the navies and coast-guards of Indonesia, Malaysia, and Singapore are allowed to engage in hot-pursuit of piratical vessels in each others' territorial waters; they can also engage in joint maritime safety and search and rescue operations in the specific confines of the Strait of Malacca.[13] This arrangement shows that multilateral defence co-operation can arise amongst Southeast Asian states but only when a potential threat is common to the interests of states involved.

Outside of the above two multilateral security arrangements, Singapore's defence ties with other countries are overwhelmingly bilateral in nature. Within ASEAN, Singapore has bilateral defence ties with a number of member states. Such defence links have included the following:

- A Singapore training battalion being deployed at Temburong in Brunei. (The Brunei armed forces appear to consider that training battalion as contributing to Brunei's security.)
- Small-scale land exercises between the Malaysian and Singapore armed forces.
- Singapore Armed Forces personnel training extensively in Thailand for jungle warfare and air force training; and the joint production by Singapore and Thailand of certain kinds of defence equipment.
- The Singapore air force using the Siabu Air Weapons Range in Pekan Baru, Central Sumatra, Indonesia. (The range was jointly constructed by the Singapore and Indonesian armed forces.)

- The Singapore defence industries supplying the Myanmar military, the Tatmadaw, with light weapons systems and other equipment.[15]
- The Singapore navy and air force conducting joint exercises with the navies and air forces of Brunei, the Philippines, Indonesia, and Thailand.

These bilateral defence links with ASEAN members are part of an overall "spider's web" of defence relationships within ASEAN. The joint exercises have the effect of inculcating in "those involved to respect each other's differences and thus avoid misunderstandings",[16] minimizing, if not eliminating friction. All this falls within the category of "defence diplomacy", which, with few exceptions, necessarily means that such defence links, largely intended to generate goodwill, *do not* have substantial operational significance.

The defence links with far more operational significance for Singapore have principally involved countries outside of Southeast Asia. They have included the significant defence relationship with Israel, which was instrumental in assisting the development of the Singapore Armed Forces during its formative years, and which has also provided a range of weapons systems to the SAF, including AMX-13 light tanks,[17] Gabriel ship-to-ship missiles, the Barak vertical-launched surface-to-air missile system, and Spike anti-tank missiles, among others. Burgeoning bilateral defence ties have also involved Australia and New Zealand, and this is quite apart from their involvement in the FPDA. Extensive training of army personnel takes place in New Zealand and Australia, with the latter also hosting significant elements (helicopter and fixed-wing aircraft) of the Singapore air force, largely because of Singapore's airspace constraints. Air force training also takes place in Bangladesh, and more recently in Cazaux, France. In the naval realm, Singapore has an important and wide-ranging relationship with Sweden, which was exemplified in the late 1990s in the purchase by Singapore of four second-hand Swedish diesel-electric submarines.[18] Other, less publicized defence links have been established with Germany (involving the supply of naval-designed systems to Singapore), India (which has included joint naval exercises), Japan, the Netherlands, Pakistan, and Turkey.[19]

Among Singapore's bilateral defence relationships, however, the one with the United States is the most significant, wide-ranging, and increasingly has the greatest effect in shoring up Singapore's sense of security. The acquisition by Singapore of vast amounts of U.S. weapon systems and equipment is one dimension — the most obvious dimension — of the myriad nature of the United States–Singapore defence relationship. Singapore has also for many years been a transit point for U.S. fleet units; U.S. naval aviation, in the form of P-3C Orion anti-submarine warfare (ASW) aircraft had also begun flying out of Singapore for ASW patrols over the Indian Ocean in the late 1970s. In August 1989, Singapore decided that it wanted to formalize its defence arrangements with the United States when it publicly declared for the first time its willingness to provide facilities for use by the U.S. Navy and air force.[20] A memorandum of understanding (MOU) was signed whereby a rotational squadron of U.S. fighter aircraft would deploy to Singapore's Paya Lebar Air Base. In 1992, another MOU was concluded which allowed a logistics unit of the U.S. Seventh Fleet to relocate to Singapore following its withdrawal from Subic Bay Naval Base in the Philippines after the Philippines Senate decided not to renew American use of Philippine bases. These gestures on the part of Singapore illustrate the extent to which the city-state views the United States as highly essential to the maintenance of stability and security in Southeast Asia and the wider Asia-Pacific region. And, indeed, of all the ASEAN states, Singapore has been the most welcoming of a U.S. regional military presence and role. As a further manifestation of that view, in January 1998, it was announced that Singapore would allow U.S. aircraft carriers to come alongside a pier being built at the new Changi naval base, operational in 2001.[21] The new pier, with its deep-water anchorage, will obviate the need for U.S. aircraft carriers to anchor offshore, at a man-of-war anchorage, thereby eliminating the need for U.S. navy personnel to be ferried from ship to shore. This new offer by Singapore is, however, unlikely to result in any significant change in U.S. Navy deployment patterns in Southeast Asian waters. This is because U.S. warship numbers continue to decline in absolute terms even if U.S. global responsibilities remain the same, if not continue increasing. At most, the new Singapore offer might encourage the U.S. Navy to extend marginally its loiter time in Southeast Asian waters, but that in itself would be viewed by Singapore as a substantial contribution to regional, and *ipso facto*, Singapore's security.

The use of military facilities in Singapore by the U.S. Navy and air force has in recent years been reciprocated by the establishment of training facilities in the United States for the Republic of Singapore Air Force (RSAF). This has been for a squadron of F-16 fighters and pilots at Luke Air Force Base in Phoenix, Arizona, and a Chinook helicopter unit at Grand Prairie, Texas.[22] In 1998, a third RSAF element, a KC-135 aerial refuelling aircraft unit, was established at McConnell Air Force Base in Kansas, further broadening the United States–Singapore defence relationship. The extent of this relationship was underscored when Singapore upgraded its military representation at the Singapore Embassy in Washington: Singapore's Washington-based defence attaché is now of one-star general, rather than colonel, rank. As it stands, although Singapore does not have a formal military alliance relationship with the United States, the extent and nature of United States–Singapore defence ties makes this particular relationship far more substantial and weighty than some of the formalized military alliances America has with other countries.[23] United States–Singapore defence ties can be expected to grow steadily in the years ahead.

Robust and Formidable Armed Forces

The Singapore Government has always worked on the basis that in the ultimate analysis, the responsibility for Singapore's defence and security will not reside with outside powers but with Singaporeans. This philosophical concept had been embraced very early on in the life of the nation as an independent state. Thus, the commitment to build up robust and formidable military forces that would deter potential adversaries went into full-swing, with the Government not sparing money and talent in this venture. The unwavering commitment to build up the Singapore Armed Forces (SAF) over the past three decades has been remarkable. At the start of the twenty-first century, Singapore has an army, air force, and navy which in combination constitutes the most powerful armed forces amongst all ten Southeast Asian states, that is, at least seen on paper. The key determinants that make the SAF so formidable relative to its Southeast Asian counterparts goes beyond its impressive order-of-battle.[24] Those determinants include:

- mobility;
- an ability to deliver an enormous volume of firepower;
- the technical skills, competence and motivation of SAF personnel;[25]
- a high level of unit operational readiness (in many instances, of up to 80 per cent), which allows for the mobilization and deployment of main force and reserve-line units at short notice;
- the adoption of combat-tested tactical warfighting techniques, like combined-arms warfare and the maritime-air operation; and
- the ability to capitalize on information warfare and other new-fangled technologies as force-multipliers, similar to Western defence establishments adopting what is known as the revolution in military affairs (RMA).

These conceptual determinants have made the SAF a significant deterrent force. And should deterrence fail, the SAF is expected to fight and prevail over any aggressor. Whether it succeeds in doing so, however, is the key question. Because of Singapore's lack of strategic depth, the SAF has to take any battle directly to the enemy and as far away from Singapore's shores. This, therefore, explains why there has been considerable stress on mobility, with a heavy emphasis on developing the air force and navy,[26] which would spearhead any attack on an aggressor, and also the development of a major rapid-reaction army unit, the Twenty-first Division. The policy then is one of "forward defence" through power projection.[27]

The six approaches to enhancing security, which Singapore has pursued, and which has been detailed above, emphasize parts of Singapore's "Total Defence" concept. Total Defence is especially needed for a small country because, in the words of the Singapore Ministry of Defence, in the event of a war:

> All areas of weakness are exploited. Pressure is exerted on the entire life of the country — the military, economic, financial and spiritual resources of the whole population.
> To meet "total attack", we must have Total Defence.[28]

There are five aspects to Total Defence: psychological defence, social defence, economic defence, civil defence, and military defence. The Total Defence concept further exemplifies the all-encompassing nature of how Singapore has attempted to ensure its security and survival in Southeast Asia. The question is whether these approaches and enormous efforts will be sufficient to ensure the nation-state's continued security in the new millennium. We now turn to the likely evolution of Singapore's threat perceptions through an examination of possible threats to the nation's security in the foreseeable future.

Contemplating the Unthinkable — A Potential Conventional Military Conflict

As intimated above, the SAF is a formidable deterrent force. But to what extent is it a viable warfighting force? The answer to this question would be purely dependent upon the kind of conflict the SAF confronts. A low-intensity conflict fought at a distance from Singapore's shores will likely to see the SAF acquit itself well, not least because the air force and navy would take the lead roles in such a military action. However, should a major conflict occur in a way that places the island in the direct line of fire, then a positive outcome is less certain. This is because in contemplating such a scenario, four major negative factors in the viable defence of Singapore come immediately to mind.

The first factor is that the SAF has no recent combat experience. The last time the SAF had combat experience was just over three decades ago when a unit of 1 SIR (Singapore Infantry Regiment) engaged in operations against Indonesian troops in the jungles of Borneo during the Indonesian confrontation. Without any recent combat experience, it is uncertain how active-duty troops and operationally-ready National Servicemen would stand up in a major combat situation right at their doorstep. What one can hazard is that Singapore is not a country that is used to taking casualties of any sort, as the national outpouring of grief over the Silk Air disaster — where an airliner of the Singapore airline, Silk Air, crashed mysteriously in the Musi River, in Sumatra, Indonesia — in December 1997 tended to highlight.

The second negative factor in the viable defence of Singapore from external attack is the extreme fragility of civilian morale, particularly when seen in the context of the SAF being an overwhelmingly citizens armed force. The history of Singapore tends to demonstrate the extent of fragile civilian morale. Unlike the peoples of China, Burma, and the Philippines, who fought heroically and gallantly against the Japanese invaders during the Second World War and even continued to harass Japanese occupying forces, the collective memory of Singaporeans of the Second World War is not one of gallantry or heroism, but of hardship, deprivation, humiliation, and total domination by the enemy. It is not entirely certain whether more than half a century later and more than three decades of nation-building has stiffened the backbone of Singaporeans. Some observers might in fact contend that Singaporeans have had the spirit wrenched out of them through years of depoliticization and paternalistic rule by a single political party. A classic example of the fragile state of civilian morale can be gauged by the fact that some Singaporeans would rush to the nearest supermarket or provision store to snap up rice, sugar, and other necessities in almost a panic-buying spree whenever there is some flap on the external front. Singaporean civilian morale is indeed very fragile; from a generally high state of civilian morale on a day-to-day basis, it would not take much for Singaporean civilian morale to nose-dive.[29]

The third negative factor in the viable defence of Singapore is that being small in size, Singapore has no strategic depth, and this can result in curiously skewed military situations. For instance, a battalion of multiple-rocket launchers, which is a tactical artillery unit, if deployed by the SAF to the northern point of the island, in Woodlands, facing Malaysia, remains a tactical unit. On the other hand, the same battalion of multiple rocket launchers deployed by the Malaysian Armed Forces to the southernmost point of peninsula Malaysia, facing Singapore, instantly transforms itself from a tactical to a strategic unit. This is because it brings the entire, heavily built-up and densely populated island of Singapore within range. A six-second barrage from such a battalion so deployed would unleash a massive volume of ordnance, inflicting thousands of casualties well before Singapore counter-batteries can even go into action. And the underlying objective of such a barrage would be to, at one stroke, shatter Singaporean civilian morale and bring about the rapid collapse of Singapore's citizens armed forces. Here, geographical asymmetry results in an extraordinary military asymmetry disadvantageous to Singapore.

The fourth negative factor, and one that is related to the third factor, is that the island of Singapore, being small in size, disposes major lucrative targets that are few in number, easily identifiable and difficult to disperse precisely because they are concentrated in a small island. An enemy might find the destruction of such targets less onerous that it might elsewhere. This partly explains why a part of the RSAF is deployed overseas (such as in Australia and the United States), largely for training purposes but also as an attempt at force preservation.

Whether the day will ever come where there will be major conflict between Singapore and one of its neighbours is another question altogether. In all likelihood, the answer to that question would be negative, although such conflict is not entirely impossible to conceive for reasons that will be discussed later. Here, one should point out that weapons systems should not be seen in purely operational terms. To see weapons systems in purely such terms tends to miss the point. Short of actually being employed in combat, weapons systems have great symbolic and psychological value, what is known as coercive power. Merely by the very existence of such weapons systems a country might achieve its objective — that is a submissive or respectful neighbour — without even having to fire a single shot.

Potential Threats to Singapore's Security in the New Millennium

Prediction is always a hazardous business, not least in the field of foreign affairs and international security. It becomes even more hazardous when regional and global trends are less than clear. This is because the phrase "post-Cold War era" suggests that the world is still in a phase of transition from the Cold War to a global paradigm that has yet to be reached or defined. In this transitional phase, a bitter contest is taking place between the forces of globalization and those of extreme nationalism. Globalization is viewed as a panacea to the ills afflicting the international state system. On the other hand, rising nationalism — anchored in ethnic, linguistic, cultural, and religious terms — is seen as a threat to that system. Violent nationalistic impulses have already been apparent in parts of Africa, Europe (principally the Balkans and the post-Soviet states), the Indian subcontinent, and Southeast Asia. As to the last, the Asian economic crisis gave rise to instability in the largest and most populous country in Southeast Asia — Indonesia —

which led to nationalistic stirrings in parts of that sprawling archipelago, from Aceh in North Sumatra, to the Maluku islands, to West Kalimantan, and to Irian Jaya. Indonesia will, therefore, be a source of concern for Singapore for some time to come.

Indonesia

The stresses and strains which the Indonesian polity has experienced since late 1997 is likely to bedevil that country for many years. Centrifugal forces, expressed in secessionist sentiment, mean a weakening of central control. The Indonesian authorities might well seek to neutralize that effect via an external dimension. An analogy with Russia might not be inapt. As the state becomes weaker, there will be a tendency for it to assert itself in the foreign policy arena for both prestige reasons and to coerce the international community to extend economic aid to the country. Russia, which since the dissolution of the Soviet Union, has seen its economic fortunes plummet, has done precisely that to indicate to the West and the rest of the world that it is not a spent force and can, if it wanted to, play a spoiler's role in global affairs. Russia has been asserting itself in the former Soviet states (its so-called "Near Abroad") and in the Balkans. Similarly, Indonesia might feel compelled to play a more assertive foreign policy role that is out-of-step with the rest of ASEAN, if only to remind the region of Indonesia's significant ability to determine the course of events in Southeast Asia. Being in such proximity to Indonesia, Singapore would be the first country to be affected by any marked change in Indonesia's foreign policy from a benign to a less benign stance. Indeed, in 1998 then Indonesian President B. J. Habibie reminded Singapore that it cannot get away from its shadow, that is Indonesia. The meaning in that less-than-subtle remark would not have been lost on policy-makers in Singapore.

An Indonesia that faces continued civil unrest, to the point of one or two provinces seceding and a few others in a state of anarchy where the writ of central authority rule no longer applies, will also prove destabilizing for Southeast Asia. Large-scale refugee outflows would be one consequence of such turmoil. And Singapore would be in the direct line of such outflows. How it might deal with this possible contingency remains to be seen.

Arms Acquisitions and Uncertainty as a Threat

A geopolitical setting that is fluid and uncertain in itself poses a threat to stability. This is because countries will then want their armed forces to be primed in such a way that prepares them for worst-case scenarios. Consequently, a military build-up would be the end result. Though the Asian economic crisis had curtailed significantly defence spending amongst most Southeast Asian states (Singapore being the major exception), the end of the crisis saw regional states go back to many of their pre-crisis defence procurement programmes. Indeed, already by the third-quarter of 1999, clear signs emerged of renewed interest by a number of ASEAN states in new weapons acquisitions. Some of these states appear interested in getting back to acquiring major weaponry if only because they do not like the idea of one state, namely Singapore, forging too far ahead in its military power. This kind of situation could well be described as a "slow-motion" arms race. In and of itself, arms racing is an interactive process of action-reaction, or what is known as escalation dominance, where one country escalates arms acquisitions to achieve some measure of dominance over an adversary or potential adversary. There has been some identifiable aspects of arms racing among ASEAN states, albeit at a low level, and most prominently between Singapore and Malaysia, and Malaysia and Thailand.

One theoretical or hypothetical example of arms acquisitions that could escalate into possible conflict involving Singapore is the acquisition of a battalion of multiple rocket launchers by Malaysia and deployed somewhere in Johor: such an action would likely be viewed very seriously by Singapore. In November 2000, Malaysia announced that it would be acquiring eighteen Brazilian-made Astros II multiple rocket launchers.[30] In such a situation, Singapore might want to counter the implicit threat posed by such a deployment. The fielding of increased numbers of counter-battery radar locked into artillery systems would be one possible counter. A military doctrine that places even greater emphasis on forward defence would be another counter. That latter counter might also entail the option of carrying out pre-emptive military strikes to take out (or neutralize) what is viewed as an identifiable threat to Singapore's security. This can essentially be likened to the "Israeli option", which involves the state reserving the right to strike at targets in neighbouring states should those targets begin to assume what is considered "threatening proportions". Such a strategy does, of course, carry significant risks of escalating into full-blown military conflict, but as the examples of Operation Desert Storm in 1991 and the war in Kosovo in 1999 tended to demonstrate, the side which initiates military action usually retains the advantage and holds it to ultimate victory. Of course, there are differences between those two conflicts and one that might involve Singapore. As already stated, a lack of strategic depth might be too much of a drawback to Singapore, not allowing it to ride out a prolonged conflict with an adversary. However, all this is hypothetical. No one can say with certainty whether any conflict would break out involving Singapore, and what might be its likely outcome.

Conclusion

From the above exposition, it is clear that the new millennium will likely throw up a host of challenges to Singapore's foreign policy that might well impact on the nation-state's security. The concept of security can never be absolute. It is relative. And it might be safe to say that relative to the 1980s and 1990s, Singapore might feel less secure in the first one or two decades of the new millennium. Changes — some of a momentous nature — are taking place to the Southeast Asian geopolitical situation. How these changes will eventually work themselves out remains to be seen. What is clear, however, is that new ways of operating in a more uncertain and complex regional environment might have to be adopted by Singapore if it wants to stay ahead of the geopolitical game. Although being small in size has its natural disadvantages for Singapore in security terms, it can also be an advantage — it allows Singapore to be nimble and fleet-footed in anticipating and responding to changes in its external environment. To that extent, Singapore can view the emerging security environment of the twenty-first century as both a challenge and an opportunity.

Notes

1. However, in a tirade against Singapore in November 2000, Indonesian President Abdurrahman Wahid did speak in pan-Malay terms (in respect of Indonesia and Malaysia) when he said: "We can do well without Singapore because basically Singapore underestimates the Malays". See, "Why Gus Dur is Not Happy with Singapore", *Straits Times*, 27 November 2000, p. A8.
2. See, "Singapore has Interest in Spratlys Peace", *Straits Times*, 27 November 1999, p. 45.
3. For various perspectives on that economic rationale see Lee Tsao Yuan, ed., *Growth Triangle: The Johor-Singapore-Riau Experience* (Singapore: Institute of Southeast Asian Studies, 1991).
4. Derek da Cunha, "Singapore in 1998: Managing Expectations, Shoring-up National Morale", in *Southeast Asian Affairs 1999* (Singapore: Institute of Southeast Asian Studies, 1999), p. 284.
5. This was because Mr Lee's comments were linked to the opposition personality, Tang Liang Hong, whom a large part of the Singapore public, especially the Chinese-speaking community, had felt was treated unduly harshly by the Government during and following the 1997 Singapore general election campaign.

6. See, "ASEAN Still a Cornerstone of Stability", *Straits Times*, 4 August 2000, p. 54.
7. Narayanan Ganesan, "Singapore: Realist Cum Trading State", in *Asian Security Practice: Material and Ideational Influences*, edited by Muthiah Alagappa (Stanford, California: Stanford University Press, 1998), p. 601.
8. See, Lee Kim Chew, "ASEAN has Grown Bigger but Not Stronger", *Straits Times*, 30 April 1999, p. 70.
9. For an elaboration of this point see Derek da Cunha, "Division and Unity: ASEAN During the Asian Crisis", in *Comprehensive Security and Multilateralism in Post-Cold War East Asia*, edited by Kwang Il Baek (Seoul: The Korean Association of International Studies, 1998), pp. 326–46.
10. See, Anthony L. Smith, "Indonesia's Role in ASEAN: The End of Leadership?", *Contemporary Southeast Asia* 21, No. 2 (August 1999): pp. 238–60.
11. The precursor to the FPDA was the Anglo-Malayan Defence Agreement (AMDA). For a scholarly account of AMDA and the defence arrangements surrounding Singapore prior to the advent of the FPDA, see Chin Kin Wah, *The Defence of Malaysia and Singapore: The Transformation of a Security System* 1957-1971 (Cambridge: Cambridge University Press, 1983).
12. See Philip Methven, *Five Power Defence Arrangements and Military Cooperation Among the* ASEAN *States: Incompatible Models for Security in Southeast Asia*?, Canberra Papers on Strategy and Defence No. 92 (Canberra: Strategic and Defence Studies Centre, 1992), p. 208.
13. See Dominic Nathan, "Singapore, Jakarta Step Up Patrols", *Straits Times*, 5 May 1999, p. 2.
14. Mickey Chiang, *Fighting Fit: The Singapore Armed Forces* (Singapore: Times Editions, 1990), p. 218.
15. Andrew Selth, "The Myanmar Army Since 1988: Acquisitions and Adjustments", *Contemporary Southeast Asia* 17, No. 3 (December 1995): 248.
16. Chiang, *Fighting Fit*, p. 218.
17. Philippe Regnier, *Singapore: City-State in Southeast Asia* (London: C. Hurst & Co., 1987), pp. 255–56.
18. Tim Huxley and Susan Willett, *Arming East Asia*, Adelphi Paper 329 (London: The International Institute for Strategic Studies, 1999), pp. 32–33.
19. Ministry of Defence (Singapore), *Defence of Singapore* 1994-95 (Singapore: Ministry of Defence, 1994), p. 11.
20. "Singapore Willing to Have Some U.S. Military Facilities", *Straits Times*, 5 August 1989, p. 1.
21. "Singapore", in *Asia Pacific Security Outlook* 1999, edited by Charles E. Morrison (Tokyo: Japan Center for International Exchange, 1999), p. 166.
22. Derek da Cunha, "A Multiplicity of Approaches to Foreign and Defence Policy", in *Singapore: The Year in Review* 1997, edited by Arun Mahizhnan (Singapore: Times Academic Press, 1998), p. 72.
23. Although in a formal alliance relationship, alliance partners are obliged to come to the assistance of a partner facing a threat, the extent of United States–

Singapore defence ties are such that there is an implicit moral obligation by one side to assist the other in some way should it face a threatening situation.

24. A fairly detailed listing of the Singapore Armed Forces' order-of-battle can be constructed from the following open sources: International Institute for Strategic Studies, *The Military Balance* 1998/99 (London: International Institute for Strategic Studies, 1999); Chiang, *Fighting Fit*; Peter H.L. Lim, *Navy: The Vital Force* (Singapore: Republic of Singapore Navy, 1992); and, Melanie Chew, *The Sky: Out Country* (Singapore: Republic of Singapore Air Force, 1993).
25. SAF personnel's motivation is largely a consequence of monetary rewards and good career prospects. See for instance, Derek da Cunha, "Sociology Aspects of the Singapore Armed Forces", *Armed Forces & Society* 25, No. 3 (Spring 1999).
26. On the mission proficiency of the Singapore navy see Derek da Cunha, "ASEAN Naval Power in the New Millennium", in *Sea Power in the New Century*, edited by Jack McCaffrie and Alan Hinge (Canberra: Australian Defence Studies Centre, 1998), p. 75.
27. Bryan Evans III, "Arms Procurement Policies in ASEAN: How Much is Enough?", *Contemporary Southeast Asia* 10, No. 3 (December 1988): 301.
28. Ministry of Defence (Singapore), *Questions and Answers on Defence Policies and Organisation* (Singapore: Ministry of Defence, n.d.), p. 6.
29. It is because of the extreme fragility of Singaporean civilian morale that a major effort has gone into stiffening the backs of Singaporeans by constantly portraying in various media the formidable fighting power and capabilities of the country's armed forces. It is hoped that through those images, Singaporeans' courage would be a bit more fortified.
30. "KL Beefs Up to Forces with Deals Worth RM16 million", *Straits Times*, 28 November 2000, p. A15.

7

EDUCATION IN THE EARLY 21ST CENTURY
Challenges and Dilemmas

Jason Tan

The turn of the millennium appears to be an exciting time for Singapore. There is constant talk of the need to re-examine old ways of thinking and doing things, and of the concomitant need for creativity and innovation. The *Singapore 21* document[1] is a key example of this government-initiated push for change. Education policy has been a prime instrument for the fostering of both economic development and social cohesion ever since the ruling People's Action Party (PAP) came to power in 1959. It is, therefore, unsurprising that education policy-makers, schools, principals, teachers, and students are being swept along in a literal tide of newly launched policy directives.

This chapter poses questions about ongoing and future challenges and dilemmas facing Singapore's education system, as it moves into the twenty-first century. It is divided into two major sections. The first section focuses on the ways in which schools are being urged to foster creativity and innovation, in order to enhance national economic competitiveness in the global economy. It examines several key policy initiatives such as "Thinking Schools, Learning Nation", the "Masterplan for Information Technology in Education", and the revised university admission criteria. It draws from relevant research literature and raises troubling and thought-provoking questions about the launching of these initiatives. It argues that attention to the technical aspects of policy implementation is insufficient to ensure successful implementation in schools. Rather, greater attention needs to be focused on the human aspects, such as teachers' beliefs about knowledge and their role as teachers. At the same time, questions are raised about the move towards the marketization of education, as manifested, for instance, in the independent schools scheme, the autonomous schools scheme, and the push for intense inter-school competition. The second section looks at social cohesion and points out the persistence of policy challenges and dilemmas with regard to language and values education, ethnic disparities in educational attainment, and social class disparities in educational attainment. The chapter concludes by summarizing several key challenges and dilemmas in education policy-making in the early years of the twenty-first century.

Challenges and Dilemmas I: Gearing the Schools for Creativity and Innovation

The growth of the global economy has added urgency to calls for upgrading education and training as prime sources of national economic competitiveness.[2] Several authors have asserted that the survival of a nation within the global economy will depend increasingly on the ability of its citizens to enhance their skills and market them in the global market.[3] In addition, having a highly skilled labour force will be crucial in order to attract international capital investment in a nation's economy.[4]

The Singapore Government can certainly be said to have taken these calls seriously. There has always been a conscious attempt on the part of policy-makers to tailor the education system to perceived economic needs. Such efforts received added impetus in the wake of the 1985–86 economic recession. An Economic Committee recommended the education of each individual to his or her maximum potential, and the development of creativity and flexible skills in order to maintain Singapore's international competitiveness in the global economy.[5] The need for creativity and innovation was repeated in a report by the Economic Planning Committee in 1991.[6] Once again, the schools have been called to play a major role in bringing about this change.[7]

A major thrust in the quest for creativity and innovation has been the growing marketization of education since the mid-1980s. The main manifestations of marketization have been increased school autonomy, as well as increased inter-school competition. The first salvo in the direction of increased school autonomy was fired by the then Deputy Prime Minister Goh Chok Tong in 1985. He spoke of the need to allow more autonomy within schools, and to grant schools the right to appoint staff, devise school curricula, and choose textbooks, while conforming to national education policies such as bilingualism and common examinations. Goh asserted that prestigious schools had lost some of their individuality and special character through centralized control.

In 1986, twelve school principals were invited to accompany the Education Minister to study the management of twenty-five "acknowledged successful schools" in the United Kingdom and the United States, and see what lessons could be learned for Singapore. The principals' report recommended greater autonomy for selected schools in order to "stimulate educational innovation" and to allow schools "to respond more promptly to the needs and aspirations of pupils and parents".[8]

Accepting the recommendations, Education Minister Tony Tan stated that several well-established schools would be allowed to become independent schools. They would be given autonomy and flexibility in staff deployment and salaries, finance, management, and the curriculum. These schools were to serve as role models for other schools in improving the quality of education. They would also help to set the market value for good principals and teachers by recruiting staff in a competitive market. Parents, teachers, and students would enjoy a wider variety of schools to choose from.

In 1987, three well-established boys' secondary schools announced their intention to go independent in 1988. Their applications for independent status were approved by the Education Ministry. They were followed a year later by two prestigious government-aided girls' secondary schools. To date, a total of eight secondary schools, all of which are well-established and prestigious, have become independent.

Right from the introduction of the independent schools scheme, there was intense public criticism over its élitist nature and the high fees charged by the schools. In the wake of the 1991 general election, which saw the governing party returned to power with a reduced parliamentary majority, the Government took steps to defuse public criticism of the scheme. One of these steps was the establishment of a new category of schools called autonomous schools. In the first three years, eighteen existing non-independent secondary schools, all of which had outstanding academic results, were designated as autonomous schools. Another two secondary schools joined the autonomous schools scheme in 2001. These schools are supposed to provide a high-quality education while charging more affordable fees than independent schools. Parents and students will thus have a wider range of choices.

Another major initiative to foster greater autonomy for all principals is the Education Endowment Scheme that was launched in 1993. The Government deposits part of its annual budgetary surpluses into an endowment fund. Part of the fund may be used to provide annual per capita grants to all schools. These grants may be used, among other purposes, to introduce enrichment programmes for students. In addition, each Singaporean between the ages of six and sixteen receives an annual grant that may be used to pay for enrichment activities and co-curricular activities organized by schools.

A second feature of the growing marketization of education is the stress on competition among schools. Besides improving the quality of education, competition is supposed to provide parents and students with a wider range of choices and to improve accountability by forcing schools to improve their programmes.[9] This competition has been fostered in various ways. For instance, all secondary schools and junior colleges have been publicly ranked on an annual basis since 1992, and the results have been published in the local newspapers. The official justification is that parents and students must be provided with better information in order to make intelligent and informed choices.[10] Secondary schools have been ranked on three main criteria. The first of these is a composite measure of students' overall results in the annual General Certificate of Education (Ordinary) Level examinations. The second measure evaluates schools' value-addedness by comparing students' examination performance with their examination scores upon entry to their respective schools. The third criterion is a weighted index that measures a school's performance in the National Physical Fitness Test, as well as the percentage of overweight students in the school.

The promotion of inter-school competition and the pressures on schools as a result of the ranking of schools have led many principals to engage in marketing activities. These include recruitment talks, the design and distribution of brochures, the screening of promotional videos, and the courting of the press in order to highlight school achievements. Even primary schools are engaging in these activities, with principals reaching out to parents of kindergarten students.

On the curricular front, three major initiatives were launched in the closing years of the twentieth century in a bid to foster greater creativity and innovation in students. Government statements have made it clear that these initiatives are necessary as part of national efforts to remain economically competitive amid the transition to a knowledge economy. The first of these, "Thinking Schools, Learning Nation", was launched by Prime Minister Goh Chok Tong in June 1997. It focuses on developing all students into active learners with critical thinking skills, and on developing a creative and critical thinking culture within schools. Its key strategies include: (1) the explicit teaching of critical and creative thinking skills; (2) the reduction of subject syllabi content; (3)

the revision of assessment modes; and (4) a greater emphasis on processes instead of on outcomes when appraising schools.[11] A start has been made in the implementation of these strategies in all schools. For instance, a new School Excellence Model was tested on a pilot basis in some schools before being launched in all schools in the year 2000. This model is meant for schools to use when conducting self-appraisal exercises.[12]

The second initiative, the "Masterplan for Information Technology in Education", was also launched in 1997. It is an ambitious attempt to incorporate information technology in teaching and learning in all schools. The Government has been generous in its pledges of support as far as physical infrastructure is concerned. Whole-school networking is to be installed in all schools. In addition, one desktop computer is to be available for every two students and one notebook computer for every two teachers. The Masterplan specifies a target of up to 30 per cent for the use of information technology in curriculum for all subjects by the year 2002.[13]

The third and most recent major initiative focuses on university admission criteria. The Committee on University Admission System recommended in its 1999 report that the admission criteria move beyond considering only the results obtained in the General Certificate of Education (Advanced) Level examination. Instead, students' scores on the Scholastic Assessment Test (SAT) (I), their grades in project work at school, and their participation in co-curricular activities will be considered as well in the case of Advanced Level applicants. Applicants who possess a polytechnic diploma will be assessed on their scores on the SAT (I), as well as their performance in co-curricular activities. The Committee hoped that the revised criteria would promote "desired" qualities such as curiosity, creativity, enterprise, and teamwork. At the same time, the revised criteria were supposed to complement the "Thinking Schools, Learning Nation" strategies being implemented in primary and secondary schools.[14]

When one considers the various strategies and initiatives that have been employed by the Education Ministry to foster creativity and innovation, one cannot but be struck by the sheer scale of these ambitious plans. All schools, principals, teachers, and students are to be included in these plans. Now that these plans have been put in place in schools, it might be worth commenting on these strategies and initiatives and raising a few thought-provoking questions. For instance, to what extent will these ambitious strategies, and initiatives result in a genuine flowering of creativity and innovation in schools and students? Are there any deep-seated dilemmas that need to be addressed?

To date, the results of increased school autonomy have been mixed. The principals of independent schools have enjoyed greater flexibility in decision-making in a few respects. Firstly, a few independent schools have recruited additional full-time administrators such as public relations officers, estate managers and bursars. Secondly, the independent schools are run by school governing boards that may determine admission policies, school fees, and major financial policies and budgets. Thirdly, all the eight independent schools have raised their fees to levels far above those charged by non-independent schools. Finally, they are able to determine their own student admission figures.

The independent schools have also exercised greater control over curriculum. For instance, several independent schools have scrapped subjects that are compulsory in non-independent schools or have made certain other subjects non-examinable. Teacher recruitment is another area in which the independent schools have taken advantage of their increased autonomy by recruiting as many teachers as their finances will allow.

However, in some other respects the degree of choice and diversity is still rather limited. The Government continues to exert a great deal of influence over all secondary schools. In particular, the imposition of national curricular requirements and the pressures imposed by common national examinations restrict the scope for curricular innovation. None of the independent schools or autonomous schools has moved away from a subject-based curriculum. In addition, the range of subjects offered in these schools is largely identical to that in non-independent, non-autonomous schools. As long as principals are held accountable for their schools' performance in national examinations, they cannot afford to stray too far from the mainstream curriculum.

The introduction of explicit measures to promote competition among schools has aroused a great deal of controversy and criticism, both within and outside the governing party. For instance, the then Senior Minister of State for Education, Tay Eng Soon, told Parliament in 1992 that public ranking of schools in terms of their academic results was "undesirable". It was "absurd" and "nonsense" to say that one school was ahead of another because of minuscule differences in their overall academic results. It would also increase tension and stress among parents while not improving education for children at all.[15] However, the results of the first annual ranking exercise were still published five months later.

It is highly contestable whether fostering competition does improve the quality of education for all students and promote greater choice and diversity for parents and students. First of all, the competition among schools does not take place on a level playing field. The terms of competition are, to a large extent, dictated by the Government. For instance, the number of independent schools and autonomous schools is determined by the Government. Next, non-independent schools enjoy less flexibility than independent schools in determining their own enrolment figures or the number of teachers that they wish to employ. Furthermore, not all secondary schools may offer certain prestigious programmes such as the Gifted Education Programme or the Art Elective Programme. The Government only conducts such programmes in selected schools, all of which are either independent or autonomous.

In other words, non-prestigious, non-academically selective schools are simply unable to compete effectively with well-established, academically selective schools. The former are caught in a vicious cycle: because they are unable to attract high academic achievers, their academic results fall far below those of the well-established schools. This, in turn, means that they remain unable to attract high academic achievers. Furthermore, the Ministry of Education offers top-scoring students in the national Primary School Leaving Examination a second opportunity to apply for admission to an independent school (with the promise of a scholarship) if they have not already made such an application in the first instance. This practice exacerbates the gulf between independent schools and their less prestigious counterparts. Analysis of the ranking results for secondary schools over the last nine years reveals that the majority of the top thirty secondary schools have remained in this category throughout the nine years. It is, therefore, questionable to what extent increased competition actually helps to improve standards in all schools.

The Government has claimed that the independent schools and autonomous schools will serve as role models for other schools in improving educational standards. This, of course, begs the question of whether what proves effective in these well-established schools can, in fact, be transplanted into other schools. The Government's reasoning also ignores the part played by a selective student intake in schools' academic success.[16] It is, therefore, not clear to what extent the experience of independent schools and autonomous schools can be valid lessons for the bulk of Singapore secondary schools struggling with less-than-ideal student ability and motivational levels.

Another criticism is that competition leads some schools to focus narrowly on those outcomes that are relevant for public ranking and that may be useful for attracting students and parents.[17] Such criticism is especially relevant in a situation such as Singapore's, where performance in competitive examinations is still a major determinant of educational and social mobility. There has been press coverage of how several reputable secondary schools have decided to make the study of English literature optional, rather than compulsory, for their graduating students. This is because English literature is perceived to be a subject in which it is difficult to do well during national examinations. These schools have been wary of the potential consequences that students' less-than-ideal performance in English literature might have on their positions in the annual ranking exercises.[18] It is particularly ironic, then, that these strategies were being employed even as the then Minister for Information and the Arts, George Yeo, was extolling the virtues of the subject to students.[19] Even physical education has not been exempt from the adverse effects of ranking exercises. Some schools have overemphasized preparation for the National Physical Fitness Test, at the expense of the acquisition of skills in sports and games.[20] The growing stress on school accountability and the use of narrowly defined, easily quantifiable, performance indicators has clearly had a detrimental impact on some schools. Far from promoting choice and diversity, heightened inter-school competition and rivalry may, in fact, work against these goals.

Even though an external review team commissioned by the Education Ministry has heavily criticized the detrimental aspects of the practice of school ranking exercises,[21] the Education Ministry has refused to consider scrapping the exercises. Its response has been, instead, to broaden the range of indicators upon which schools are to be assessed, through the use of the School Excellence Model.[22] It is arguable that the use of this model may result in some schools using more of the same covert strategies that they have been using thus far, this time in a wider spectrum of school processes and activities, in order to boost their schools' performance in as many of the aspects that are being assessed as possible.

Amid this climate of risk-averse behaviour, what then are the prospects of wide-ranging and sustained change as far as the teaching of critical and creative thinking skills, the incorporation of information technology into teaching and learning, and the promotion of project work as a form of assessment are concerned? Government leaders are united in lamenting the apparent lack of creativity and thinking skills among students and members of the workforce.[23] In a sense, it is ironic that the Government is aggressively promoting wide-ranging changes in the schools even as it touts Singapore's success in the Third International Mathematics and Science Study, a study that reportedly was "not made up of typical examination questions that our pupils are familiar with. [The test items] assessed them on creative problem-solving skills and their ability to respond to open-ended questions".[24] A cursory glance at the subject syllabuses published by the University of Cambridge Local Examinations Syndicate (the body that organizes the bulk of the secondary and pre-university examinations for Singapore students) reveals careful attention to the cultivation of higher-order thinking and analytical skills. These include selection, organization and interpretation of data, the recognition of patterns and deduction of relationships in data, critical reading, detecting logical fallacies in arguments, evaluating the reliability and accuracy of material, and applying knowledge to problems that are presented in a novel or unfamiliar manner.[25] It would appear that teachers have become rather adept in drilling and coaching their students to answer these higher-order questions very skilfully.[26]

Ever-improving examination scores in the national examinations are consequently beginning to sound less impressive.[27] In this regard, it is ironic that a few months after Prime Minister Goh Chok Tong had stressed the need to move towards critical thinking skills, a departmental head in a secondary school, when asked by a newspaper journalist about the secret behind her students' examination success, replied that it had taken months of repeated mock examination practice. As a result of at least twelve rounds of practice per subject, students were familiar not only with the examination format but, more importantly, with the examination content as well.[28]

The new moves to introduce more critical thinking skills and to introduce more project work will take place against this backdrop. The External Review Team has already pointed out that:

> [I]nstead of consistently and creatively incorporating the need for students to use thinking skills in classroom activities and daily assignments, teachers tend to resort to "over-teaching" (teaching at a greater depth than required by the syllabus for a specific level) and "over-drilling" (providing repetitive practice at answering higher-order thinking skills questions) to help students anticipate and prepare for such questions .... As such, higher-order thinking questions become predictable to a certain extent and less useful in testing the student's ability to think creatively and/or to apply skills learnt in one context to another.[29]

Policy-makers will have to realize that it is likely that new requirements, including the SAT (I), will be viewed by many teachers, parents, and students as yet more hurdles or hoops to be cleared by employing yet more of the same strategies that have worked, namely, intensive and repetitive coaching and practice. These concerns have, in fact, been raised in Parliament.[30] The intense competition among schools will see to it that a number of principals and teachers try their best, employing educationally suspect means on occasion, to ensure maximum success for their students even after the revised curricula and assessment modes have been put in place.

At a more fundamental level, much of the current effort at bringing about massive changes in teaching, learning, and assessment in all schools has tended to ignore the human factors involved in successfully bringing about large-scale change. The existing research literature is replete with cautionary advice about the difficulty in bringing about such change.[31] Morris lists several characteristics of innovations that have been found to have an influence on the success of implementation: (1) perceived relative advantage of adopting an innovation; (2) compatibility of the innovation with existing beliefs, attitudes, organization, and practices within a classroom or school; (3) complexity and comprehensibility of the innovation; (4) clear communication of features and benefits of the innovation; (5) demonstrated clarity and practicality of the innovation; and (6) demonstrated success of the innovation.[32] Numerous researchers have documented case studies where proposed innovations have either not succeeded at all or have been implemented in a piecemeal fashion instead of in the manner prescribed by reformers.[33]

A fundamental factor in bringing about teacher implementation of innovations is the changing of teachers' fundamental beliefs, values, and attitudes concerning such matters as epistemology, the roles of teachers, and the nature of teaching and learning.[34] These beliefs may have been influenced by factors such as teachers' experiences as learners.[35] These beliefs, values, and attitudes are deeply entrenched and extremely resistant to attempts at reform. Teachers are consequently often caught in a dilemma as a result of seemingly irreconcilable tensions between the push for diversity and the pull of the comfortable and familiar.[36] What often happens is that teachers appear to take innovations on board but are unable to move away from traditional didactic practice.[37] Not many teachers actually make the successful transition from initial contact with an innovation such as information technology to the final stage where they experiment with the innovation in ways that alter teaching and learning patterns and relationships in a fundamental manner.[38] Deng and Gopinathan sound a similar cautionary note in the case of information technology in Singapore schools.[39] It is also worth noting that:

> [E]ven potentially good changes do not fare well because far too many changes are in front of teachers at any one time. Regardless of the reasons, there are more changes being proposed than are humanly possible to implement — if by implementation we mean changes in behaviour and thinking.[40]

A newspaper article in Singapore echoed Fullan's concern. A school principal expressed concern that teachers were already being asked to cope with the implementation of numerous Ministry of Education initiatives and were now being asked to shoulder yet more training for a new English curriculum.[41] It is likely that not all the approximately 23,000 teachers have a clear personal understanding of such crucial terms as "critical thinking" and "use of information technology in teaching for x per cent of the time". They now have to grapple with yet another concept that was introduced in 1999: "a mass customization approach in the delivery of education".[42] Even as government leaders pronounce that all Singaporeans need to be nurtured with entrepreneurial skills and critical thinking skills, there are still unresolved issues such as whether genetic endowment is too powerful a force for environmental nurturing to undo.[43] It is crucial that all teachers who are being asked to implement crucial innovations deemed important by government leaders actually clarify their beliefs about such concepts. Research elsewhere has demonstrated that beliefs about such concepts are often diverse and may, in fact, be incompatible with the promotion of such concepts in classrooms.[44] To date, such research has not been conducted in Singapore. Instead, nearly all the available research in Singapore has focused on the more technical aspects of implementation.

What is worrying is that 31 per cent of primary school teachers are aged 50 years or above. The corresponding figure for secondary school teachers is 22.8 per cent.[45] One might argue that this considerable proportion of the teaching workforce will not find it easy to clamber aboard the wagon of change, the provision of training courses notwithstanding. Even the younger teachers are essentially charting virgin territory, without adequate role models to emulate. The challenge of sustaining these policy initiatives in a meaningful manner promises to be a continual concern to policy-makers.

Challenges and Dilemmas II: Social Cohesion

Besides its role in labour force production, education is recognized in most countries as an important vehicle for both social mobility and cultural identity. Amid calls for education to help serve the cause of enhancing national economic competitiveness, there is recognition that the benefits of globalization will not be spread equally among various countries. Even within particular nations, rewards will be distributed unequally among different groups in the population.[46] There is evidence that even in industrialized countries that have undertaken rapid educational expansion, inequalities in educational opportunity among students from different social strata have remained remarkably stable since the beginning of the present century.[47] Such intra-national inequalities could have serious implications for social cohesion.

In the Singapore case, specific government policies have been implemented since the early 1960s in an attempt to forge some kind of commonality in an education system hitherto largely segregated along ethnic, linguistic and cultural lines. For example, the Government declared its commitment to equal treatment for the four streams of education — English, Chinese, Malay, and Tamil — in 1959. The Education Ministry's Syllabuses and Textbooks Committee published common primary and secondary school subject syllabuses. In particular, a common ethics syllabus was produced for primary and secondary schools. Another measure was the concept of integrated schools, in which students using different language media for instruction were housed in common buildings under one school principal. Joint participation in sports and other extramural activities was encouraged. Common national examinations were also instituted at both primary and secondary levels. Beginning in 1966, a year after full political independence had been attained, all students were required to attend daily rituals during which they would sing the national anthem as the national flag was being raised or lowered. They had to recite a pledge of allegiance as well. More recently, the National Education initiative was launched on a massive scale in all schools in 1997. This initiative is supposed to serve several key purposes: (1) developing a sense of Singaporean national identity; (2) developing a knowledge of Singapore's recent history; (3) developing an understanding of Singapore's unique developmental challenges and vulnerabilities; and (4) instilling core national values such as the importance of meritocracy.[48]

Although these policies have been deliberately aimed at fostering social cohesion, it may be argued that certain other policies may have detracted somewhat from this aim. This section highlights the way in which education policy continues, and will continue in the early twenty-first century, to be contentious, as far as its role in fostering social cohesion is concerned. Three specific areas are discussed: language and values education policies; ethnic disparities in educational attainment; and social class disparities in educational attainment. The National Education initiative and the Singapore 21 vision will be examined critically in light of this discussion.

Language and Values Education Policies

Language and values education policies have formed a pivotal part of PAP attempts to foster social cohesion and a common national identity among a linguistically and culturally diverse population.[49] The compulsory study of two languages, one of which is the English language, has been a feature of the school system since 1960. English has been promoted as a lingua franca among people from different language groups. In addition, English is supposedly a neutral language that does not privilege any particular language group. Thirdly, English has been touted as the language that will best provide access to science and technology. At the same time, the study of one of three other languages — Mandarin, Malay, or Tamil — was promoted as a means of preserving what were termed "traditional values" and of preventing "deculturalization" amid rapid societal modernization.

At the time when the PAP Government took office in 1959, it pledged equal treatment for the four language streams of education. However, the increasing perception among parents that proficiency in English was the key to socio-economic advancement led to a rapid swing to English-medium schools in the 1960s and 1970s. In 1982, 88.5 per cent of primary school students and 83.9 per cent of secondary school students were enrolled in English-medium schools, compared with the corresponding figures of 49.1 per cent and 62.4 per cent in 1959.[50] The Government then announced in 1983 that the entire education system would become English-medium from 1987 onwards. This decision marked a major step in the move to unite the entire education system. There is also evidence that literacy in the English language is much higher among younger Singaporeans than among their older counterparts.[51] English is now the language with the highest literacy rate among the general population and is also the predominant lingua franca among younger Singaporeans, especially among those with different home languages. To the extent that the promotion of the English language through the school system has provided a common means of communication among people from different language groups, language policy may be said to have contributed towards the fostering of wider social cohesion.

However, other language policies have been criticized as being socially divisive. For example, the Ministry of Education designated nine Chinese-medium secondary schools as Special Assistance Plan (SAP) schools in 1980. These schools were intended to provide top-scoring primary school leavers with the opportunity to study both English and Mandarin to high levels of competence. Also, these schools were to preserve the character of traditional Chinese-medium secondary schools and allay fears that the Government was indifferent to Chinese language and culture amid declining enrolments in Chinese-medium schools. These schools were provided with additional government funding and resources.[52]

The establishment of SAP schools has been criticized on several grounds. First, it is not fair to non-Chinese students who do not enjoy access to these better-resourced schools. This relative lack of access has arisen because prevailing government logic since 1981 has it that students should be studying the "mother tongue" language that corresponds to their putative ethnicity. Non-Chinese students, therefore, have to request special permission from the Ministry of Education before they can study Mandarin in these schools.

Secondly, there is also concern that the students in these schools, many of whom are destined for top roles in politics, business, and the civil service, are not being provided opportunities to mingle with non-Chinese students.[53] Equally contentious is the increasing promotion since the late 1980s of Mandarin as a key economic language. This move has come amid growing economic liberalization in the People's Republic of China. In other words, Mandarin is no longer touted solely as a language for cultural transmission, but is now promoted for its economic advantage in terms of trade and investment in mainland China.[54] Since non-Chinese students are not normally allowed to study Mandarin in schools, the promotion of the language thus raises questions of inter-ethnic economic disparities. For instance, during a parliamentary session in 1993, a Member of Parliament asked the Minister for Education if non-Chinese students would be allowed to study Mandarin. The then Minister of State for Education, Ker Sin Tze, pointed out the policy dilemma involved:

> We do recognize the benefit of learning Chinese by non-Chinese pupils. But at the same time, we would like all pupils to know their mother tongue because that is the cornerstone of our bilingual policy.[55]

He said that the Ministry would make exceptions "upon presentation of very good evidence that they do need to learn Chinese in their future study or career development". He also revealed that 0.2 per cent of primary one students studying Mandarin were non-Chinese.[56] In other words, non-Chinese students are to be discouraged from studying Mandarin because that is not their "mother tongue" and, thus, would not serve the purpose of cultural transmission. At the same time, these students are being denied access to an economically useful language. It is clear too that neither Malay nor Tamil is anywhere as economically useful as Mandarin in this respect.

In early 1997, the Prime Minister attempted to allay the worries of the non-Chinese by stressing that English would remain the common working language in Singapore. He felt that this would ensure a "level playing field" for the various ethnic communities. He stressed that:

> [N]o non-Chinese will be at a disadvantage for economic or career opportunities because he does not know [the] Chinese [language], unless the company owned does business with China or Taiwan, or is a traditional Chinese owned company using the Chinese language.[57]

More than twenty years after the SAP scheme came into being, it continues to provoke public controversy.[58] The Government has now added another secondary school to the original group of nine SAP schools in a bid to encourage the nurturing of a Chinese "cultural élite". This élite is supposed to prove useful, not only for the purposes of trade with mainland China, but also to form the basis for recruitment into journalism, the arts, education, and clan leadership.[59] The SAP schools have been urged to ensure that their students socialize with their counterparts in non-SAP schools in response to public criticism over their ethnic exclusiveness. [60]It has been suggested that ethnic minorities be allowed admission into the SAP schools. Emphasis has also been laid on the fact that this Chinese élite will, in fact, be largely indistinguishable from their counterparts in non-SAP schools.[61]

This last point has become increasingly evident over the last decade, as non-SAP schools, in particular the independent schools and autonomous schools, have been allowed to offer Higher Chinese as a subject. The SAP schools have thus lost much of their previous distinctiveness *vis-à-vis* non-SAP schools. The latest government moves to expand the scope of the programme, as well as to expand the pool of secondary school students who qualify for the study of Higher Chinese, may be seen as explicit recognition that overall performance standards in the Chinese language are inadequate to sustain a high level of social interaction with trading counterparts in mainland China. It appears rather strange to be attempting to shore up the SAP scheme while claiming that students in these schools are largely indistinguishable from their non-SAP school counterparts. It remains to be seen whether the plans to shore up the SAP scheme in order to produce a Chinese "cultural élite" will, in fact, be successful.[62]

The SAP scheme may be seen as part of broader government policy to promote the status of Mandarin and to ensure high standards of proficiency in the language. However, it has been pointed out that the Speak Mandarin campaign has led to an increase in the use of Mandarin among ethnic Chinese students in schools.[63] This phenomenon, coupled with the decline in the number of students who cross ethnic boundaries for the study of another school language, may deter mixed friendship networks from developing. A 1991 report published by the Action Committee on Indian Education criticized the practice in some schools of grouping Indian and Malay students in the same classes "purely for the administrative convenience of scheduling second language periods".[64] One hopes that this practice has ceased in schools.

It should be pointed out that the link between language and cultural or values transmission is another problematic area of education policy. The use of English is sometimes vilified for its purported role in transmitting "decadent Western values". At the same time, the so-called "mother tongue" languages are supposedly indispensable for ensuring the transmission of "traditional values".

An examination of government policies in values education, however, leads one to conclude that the link between language and values is not as watertight or as simplistic as policy-makers purport it to be. For instance, between 1984 and 1989, Religious Knowledge was made a compulsory subject for all upper secondary students amid fears of a moral crisis among young people. Six options were offered: Bible Knowledge, Buddhist Studies, Confucian Ethics, Hindu Studies, Islamic Religious Knowledge, and Sikh Studies. The choice of language of instruction for the various options was revealing: English for Bible Knowledge, English and Mandarin for Buddhist Studies and Confucian Ethics, English for Hindu Studies, English and Malay for Islamic Religious Knowledge, and English for Sikh Studies. In fact, a request by the Tamil Teachers' Association for Hindu Studies to be taught in Tamil was rejected by the Government. The supposedly tight fit between language and values had clearly broken down in the case of the Religious Knowledge curriculum.

Another consequence of the Religious Knowledge subject was a segregation of students on the basis of the various options chosen. The Government had originally intended to offer a World Religions option but abandoned its plans, saying that it was too difficult to formulate a syllabus.[65] In addition, students were further segregated on the basis of the medium of instruction.

One of the main reasons why Religious Knowledge was made an optional subject in 1990, after having been compulsory for six years, was due to its role in contributing to religious revivalism and evangelistic activities among Buddhists and Christians.[66] In place of Religious Knowledge, a new compulsory Civics and Moral Education programme has been designed for all secondary school students. Curiously enough, this programme incorporates factual knowledge about the major religions in Singapore, an option that was absent from the Religious Knowledge curricula. The initial texts were published in English, thus providing a common forum for all students to be instructed in the desired knowledge and values. However, a few years later, Chinese language translations of the original texts were published as well. To date, no Malay or Tamil versions have been published. The use of English, as well as the fact that the Chinese version is a mere translation of the original English version, calls into question the assertion that English cannot effectively be used for values transmission in the same way as can the "mother tongue" languages. At the same time, one might also question the need for a separate Chinese language version of the texts that teach common national values.

Further evidence that the English language may be effective in values transmission may be found in the recent calls for National Education to be explicitly incorporated into both formal and informal school curricula. The fact that the English language is the major medium of instruction in all schools is testament to the fact that values such as community before self are actually amenable to transmission through this language.[67] Instead of viewing the language–values nexus in stark bipolar terms, it might perhaps be more fruitful for policy-makers to openly acknowledge that the situation is actually more complex and that all languages may be used for values transmission.

Ethnic Disparities in Educational Attainment

Since the early 1980s, government leaders have expressed concern over ethnic disparities in educational attainment. The results of the 1980 population census revealed that the Malays, who constituted about 14 per cent of the total population, had had the largest percentage increases over the previous decade in terms of persons with at least a secondary qualification. However, the Malays were still grossly under-represented in the professional/technical and administrative/managerial classes of the workforce, constituting 7.9 per cent and 1.8 per cent in these two categories, respectively.[68] In addition, there were only 679 Malay university graduates, making up 1.5 per cent of the 44,002 university graduates in Singapore. Likewise, Malays made up only 5.7 per cent of those with an upper secondary qualification.[69]

In August 1981, then Prime Minister Lee Kuan Yew urged Malay community leaders and educators in the government service to give top priority to upgrading the educational level and training of the large number of Malays without a secondary school qualification. This effort was part of the national drive to improve educational levels so as to keep pace with the recently launched economic restructuring programme, which involved moving away from labour-intensive industries to highly skilled ones. As a result of discussions between Malay Members of Parliament (MPs) and Malay community leaders, the Council on Education for Muslim Children (or Mendaki for short) was formed in October 1981. The formation of Mendaki was symbolic, as it marked the first major collaborative effort between the Malay MPs and non-political community leaders. Furthermore, it represented a major break from previous government policies in the 1960s and 1970s. For instance, in 1970 the Government had categorically rejected calls to establish a Malay

Secretariat that would, among other things, make recommendations to the Government on measures to narrow the socio-economic gap between the Malays and non-Malays.[70]

In his opening address at the Mendaki Congress in May 1982, Lee Kuan Yew observed that "it is in the interests of all [Singaporeans] to have Malay Singaporeans better educated and better qualified and to increase their contribution to Singapore's development".[71] This statement was a clear acknowledgement of the fact that the Malays' educational and socio-economic problems posed a threat to national integration and political stability. In addition, Lee promised government assistance for Mendaki. Lee also stressed the importance of Malays helping themselves when he said that "a government-run scheme cannot achieve a quarter of the results of this voluntary, spontaneous effort by Malays/Muslims to help themselves".[72]

Over the past two decades, Mendaki's efforts to improve Malay/Muslim educational achievement have been concentrated in three main areas: (1) running tuition classes from primary to pre-university levels, with a focus on preparing students for major public examinations; (2) providing scholarships, bursaries and study loans to students with outstanding public examination results and to those undertaking undergraduate and postgraduate studies; and (3) promoting Islamic social values that Malay leaders feel will promote family support for educational success.[73] More recently, there has been growing emphasis on the need to provide skills retraining programmes for less educated members of the workforce.

Another organization called the Association of Muslim Professionals (AMP) was launched in October 1991. This group was formed as a result of discussions at a convention of Muslim professionals in October 1990. Several professionals had felt that the credibility of Malay community organizations such as Mendaki was hampered because they were headed by Malay MPs. Like Mendaki, the AMP conducts several kinds of educational programmes such as pre-school education, family education, and skills training for adults. Like Mendaki, it receives financial and logistical assistance from the Government.

The active government support of ethnically based groups in tackling the Malays' educational problems was extended to other ethnic communities in the early 1990s. By the late 1980s, there had been growing evidence that many Indian students were faring badly in their studies. Various sections of the Indian community had called for the establishment of an organization for Indian students along the lines of Mendaki. The Government, together with community leaders, established the Singapore Indian Development Association (SINDA) in 1991 to tackle Indian educational problems.

In July 1991, Prime Minister Goh Chok Tong urged the setting up of a "Chinese Mendaki". His suggestion received new impetus when the PAP failed to capture as many votes as they had expected in the 1991 general election. The PAP saw the electoral outcome as an expression of discontent by poorer Chinese who felt neglected by the government focus on helping the Malays. Accordingly, the Chinese Development Assistance Council (CDAC) was established the following year. In October 1992, the Eurasian Association launched an endowment fund to finance education and welfare programmes for the Eurasian community. The Government pledged financial support for SINDA, the CDAC, and the Eurasian Association.

These government moves to establish more ethnically based self-help groups have raised questions about their compatibility with officially espoused multi-racial ideals. Besides fears about the heightening of ethnic differences, worries have been expressed in various quarters that the smaller organizations will simply be unable to compete with the CDAC, with its substantially larger financial resource base.[74] Also, empirical research studies conducted by Mendaki, SINDA, and the CDAC have shown that many of the problems facing educational under-achievers are often closely related to their economically disadvantaged status. Research conducted by the Government's chief statistician has demonstrated that intra-ethnic class differences have assumed greater significance, as inter-ethnic income differences have narrowed. Therefore, it has been argued that, since the problems facing under-achievers cut across ethnic lines, a more effective strategy might be to have a national body, instead of ethnically-based ones, to co-ordinate efforts to help educational under-achievers.[75]

The various criticisms levelled at the use of ethnically-based groups have so far failed to make any inroads in official policy. The government response has been threefold.[76] First, promoting these groups is not incompatible with multi-racialism as long as the groups reaffirm their commitment to multi-racialism and avoid competing against each other. To this end, the various organizations have launched several joint projects and pooled their resources on occasion. Secondly, a national body would not be sensitive enough to the special needs of each community. Lastly, and most important of all, community self-help is more effective because it draws on and mobilizes deep-seated ethnic, linguistic, and cultural loyalties. It is stressed that civil servants can never have the same degree of personal commitment as community leaders who are driven by a sense of mission.

The latest available figures show the persistence of ethnic disparities in educational attainment. For instance, ethnic Chinese are heavily over-represented in local universities and polytechnics, forming 91.4 per cent and

89.1 per cent of the respective total enrolments in 1995. Ethnic Malays (3.0 per cent and 6.9 per cent, respectively) and Indians (4.7 per cent and 3.6 per cent, respectively) are correspondingly under-represented.[77] Despite the quadrupling in the number of Malay university graduates over the period 1980 to 1995, Malays constituted only 1.6 per cent of the total population of university graduates in 1995, a mere 0.1 percentage increase over the corresponding figure fifteen years earlier.[78] Similarly, Malay and Indian students' public examination results continue to lag behind those of their Chinese counterparts. For example, 77.7 per cent of Chinese students obtained a minimum of five "Ordinary" level passes in the General Certificate of Education (Ordinary) Level examinations taken at the end of secondary school in 1997. The corresponding figures for Malays and Indians were 46.0 per cent and 59.1 percent, respectively.[79] While Malay and Indian pass rates in public examinations have improved over the past decade, so have Chinese pass rates, with the result that the former continue to fall below the latter. There is evidence that the major bottleneck for Malays and Indians is at the end of secondary school.[80] Especially troubling is the fact that this bottleneck means that the transition rates for post-secondary options for Malays and Indians (46.0 per cent and 57.3 percent, respectively, in 1997) fall far below the corresponding rate for Chinese students (85.3 percent).[81] Equally worrying is the fact that the gap between Indians and Chinese over the decade 1988–97 has remained steady, while that between Malays and Chinese has actually widened from 29.2 per cent in 1988 to 39.3 per cent in 1997.

These statistics are troubling amid the call in *Singapore* 21 to make every Singaporean matter.[82] It also has serious implications for efforts to impart key National Education messages in all students. It cannot be helpful to have ethnic minorities lagging behind in educational attainment and subsequent occupational status. At the same time, resentments about these disparities may be compounded by continuing complaints about discrimination in the job market, especially during times of economic recession.[83]

A major challenge for the Government in this decade will be the vexing question of how best to reduce these persistent disparities. The controversial nature of the whole question of ethnic disparities has been illustrated in the issue of *madrasahs* (privately-run Islamic religious schools). After a period of declining enrolments in the 1960s and 1970s, the *madrasahs* have begun enjoying increasing enrolments since the late 1980s.[84] Even though the actual percentage of Malay/Muslim children enrolled in these schools (3.5 per cent) is actually relatively low, government concern has been voiced over the possibility that students enrolled in these schools "would not be able to integrate successfully into Singapore's social and economic system, or learn to co-operate and compete as part of the Singapore team, or think critically, or be discerning about ideas and people".[85] This has led to heated debate over the existence of the *madrasahs*. Besides the question of whether schools should encourage and perpetuate ethnic segregation, there is also the question of the apparently unequal treatment of SAP schools, on the one hand, and *madrasahs* on the other. The latter receive only nominal government funding. This controversy has also touched on the right of Muslim parents to choose a more religious educational alternative for their children.[86] Clearly, questions of cultural identity, equality of treatment, and equality of outcomes cannot be easily disentangled.

Social Stratification and Education Policy

Official PAP ideology speaks of Singapore as a meritocratic society, in which socio-economic advancement is independent of one's home background and is instead dependent on one's ability and effort.[87] This is also one of the key messages within the National Education initiative. However, this ideology sits uneasily at times alongside a deeply entrenched élitist conception of how Singapore society should be structured. Lee Kuan Yew articulated this clearly in a speech to school principals in 1966,[88] when he spoke of the need for the education system to produce a "pyramidal structure" consisting of three strata: "top leaders", "good executives", and a "well-disciplined and highly civic-conscious broad mass". The "top leaders" are the "élite" who are needed to "lead and give the people the inspiration and the drive to make [society] succeed". The "middle strata" of "good executives" are to help the élite "carry out [their] ideas, thinking and planning", while the "broad mass" are to be "imbued not only with self but also social discipline, so that they can respect their community and do not spit all over the place".

Furthermore, the predominant belief of the top government leadership is that success in the education system is dependent on intelligence, which is in turn largely genetically determined. Thus, for instance, Lee Kuan Yew spoke in 1983 of the threat posed to Singapore's future if well-educated women failed to marry and to reproduce themselves adequately as compared to their less-educated counterparts. There was a brief and unsuccessful attempt in 1984 to entice married female university graduates to have more children by providing priority in school admission for their third or subsequent offspring. Despite the failure of this policy, the Ministry of Education has on several occasions in the 1980s and 1990s released data showing that the children of mothers who are university graduates outperform the children of mothers who are not university graduates.[89] As Chua points out, "'meritocratic' inequality is unapologetically accepted as a consequence of nature".[90]

The introduction of streaming in both primary and secondary schools since the early 1980s has serious implications for future social stratification. For instance, secondary school students are channelled into one of four streams upon entry to secondary school. Students in the Normal (Technical) stream, who have obtained the lowest scores in the Primary School Leaving Examination, follow a highly watered-down curriculum compared to students in the other three streams. These students formed 16.2 per cent of the total secondary one cohort in 1999.[91] Not only do they study fewer subjects, the content of each subject is considerably pared down. Thus, for example, they are merely expected to develop oral proficiency in the "mother tongue" languages, while their peers in the other three streams are expected to develop written skills as well. Consequently, mobility between this stream and the other streams is limited and becomes increasingly difficult as students progress through secondary school. Whatever the merits of streaming based on academic achievement might be, it is worth pondering about whether the children of these students will, in years to come, be disadvantaged in the academic competition against the children of better-educated parents.

The instituting of the independent schools scheme in 1988 has serious implications for class-based inequalities as well. Amid public criticism over the allegedly élitist nature of these schools, the Government has tried to dispel the notion that non-independent schools are inferior to independent schools.[92] At the same time, though, it intends to develop the independent schools into "outstanding institutions, to give the most promising and able students an education matching their promise".[93] Growing inter-school competition and the associated trend of increased selectiveness by top schools will inevitably lead to a further stratification of schools along the prestige hierarchy.[94] There is also evidence that students from wealthier family backgrounds are over-represented in the independent schools.[95]

Several observers have pointed to the growing prominence of social stratification on the Government's policy agenda, especially in the wake of the 1991 general election.[96] Whereas the issue of income stratification was largely taboo in public discussions up till 1991, there has been growing acknowledgement on the part of the Government since then of the potential impact of income disparities on social cohesion. For instance, Goh Chok Tong has acknowledged that not all Singaporeans stand to benefit equally from the global economy. He has also pointed out that highly educated Singaporeans are in a more advantageous position compared to unskilled workers and that there is a great likelihood of widening income inequalities and class stratification.[97] Goh has drawn an explicit link between income inequalities and the need to maintain social cohesion. However, Goh thinks that "we cannot narrow the [income] gap by preventing those who can fly from flying... Nor can we teach everyone to fly, because most simply do not have the aptitude or ability".[98] Instead, he has suggested a greater emphasis on worker training so as to ensure that unskilled and semi-skilled workers will not lose their jobs as a result of multinational corporations moving their labour-intensive operations to countries with abundant and relatively inexpensive labour costs. Social cohesion, Goh has pointed out, "is not just a political objective. It actually makes good business sense. Social harmony motivates people to work hard".[99] It is likely that increasing social stratification will continue to be a politically sensitive issue for the ruling party for the immediate future.[100]

Another pressing worry for the Government is how to satisfy the consumerist demands and material aspirations of the growing middle class.[101] Since the mid-1980s, access to higher education has widened tremendously. By the year 2000, more than 60 per cent of each age cohort was enrolled in local universities and polytechnics. This massive expansion of a better educated citizenry is also cause for official concern. For instance, in 1996, Lee Kuan Yew commented that:

> [T]hirty years of continuous growth and increasing stability and prosperity have produced a different generation in an English-educated middle class. They are very different from their parents. The present generation below 35 has grown up used to high economic growth year after year, and take their security and success for granted. And because they believe all is well, they are less willing to make sacrifices for the benefit of the others in society. They are more concerned about their individual and family's welfare and success, not their community or society's well being.[102]

That same year, Goh Chok Tong lamented the lack of knowledge of Singapore's recent history among many students. Goh called for National Education to be introduced to all schools in order to "engender a shared sense of nationhood, an understanding of how our past is relevant to our present and future".[103] One reads in these statements by Lee and Goh several key messages. First, there is concern that an increasingly affluent and materialistic population will be unable to satisfy their desire for car ownership and bigger housing amid rising costs of both cars and housing.[104] A second concern is whether the population will translate their dissatisfaction with unfulfilled material aspirations into votes against the PAP. Students are, therefore, to be informed through National Education about Singapore's limited land area so as to try and persuade them that it is not possible for everyone to own a car and to own landed property. Next, there is also concern that social cohesion may suffer should the economy falter and fail to sustain the high growth rates of the past few decades. Lastly, highly educated individuals are more geographically mobile and may be tempted to leave Singapore if they are dissatisfied with their living conditions.[105]

What is interesting is that different emphases in the National Education programme are being planned for students in various levels of schooling. For instance, students in Institutes of Technical Education are to "understand that they would be helping themselves, their families and Singapore by working hard, continually upgrading themselves and helping to ensure a stable social order. They must feel that every citizen has a valued place in Singapore". Polytechnic students are to be convinced that "the country's continued survival and prosperity will depend on the quality of their efforts, and that there is opportunity for all based on ability and effort". Junior college students, most of whom are bound for university, must have the sense that "they can shape their own future" and must appreciate "the demands and complexities of leadership" as future national leaders.[106] One sees in these messages clear and unmistakable signs of the stratified view of society espoused by Lee Kuan Yew more than thirty years ago. It is interesting to speculate whether there are tensions between such a stratified view on the one hand, and notions of a more participative society in *Singapore* 21, where different talents are valued and definitions of success are broadened beyond the confines of the academic domain.

Although the Government is aware of the potential impact of social stratification on social cohesion, as well as on its own political legitimacy, it shows no signs of bowing to pressure on such issues as independent schools and greater inter-school competition. This is part of its urging of all Singaporeans not to allow "our children to be softened" by the alleged denigration of academic excellence and the promotion of a "soft approach to life" by "liberals in the West".[107] It continues to insist that the education system is fair, as it is based on merit. Also, it claims that it is only right to nurture the more able students, as the whole country will ultimately benefit.[108] Equality of opportunity is what counts, not equality of outcomes.[109]

This last argument ignores the fact that school children in Singapore do not bring equal resources to school.[110] At the same time, access to primary school is not entirely meritocratic either. The difficulty in drawing up school admission criteria that fulfil policy objectives and satisfy competing demands from different sectional interests has meant that school admission criteria are highly dependent on parental background. Examples of these criteria are those relating to alumni status, parental employment in the school, voluntary service to schools, religious or clan affiliation, or community leadership. Persistent parental perceptions that not all schools offer equal life chances to their children result in more prestigious schools being over-subscribed. There were press reports in the early 1990s of parents being asked to make donations to schools in order to secure admission for their children.[111] These perceptions are not entirely unfounded, as SAP primary schools enjoy preferential funding, for instance. On a slightly different note, not all primary schools offer instruction in Tamil, thus raising questions of equality of access.[112] As long as these perceptions are present, primary school admission policy will continue to provoke considerable controversy each year over questions of fairness and social mobility.

A recurring concern for the foreseeable future will be the overlap between ethnic- and class-based disparities. The Malay and Indian minorities, especially the former, will continue to form a disproportionately large percentage of the lower income strata and correspondingly small percentage of the higher income strata. There is sufficient cause for concern that these disparities will not narrow as the effects of economic globalization make further inroads into Singapore society. For example, Malays' median individual monthly income was 0.85 times that of the corresponding Chinese figure in 1990, but this figure declined to 0.78 in 1995.[113] Once again, this phenomenon will have serious implications for the success of the National Education initiative, as well as the Singapore 21 vision. Only if and when all citizens (not just the more economically advantaged) perceive that their and their family's life chances are equal to those of other citizens can there be a genuine chance for efforts to instil a sense of equal ownership in Singapore's future to succeed. The open commitment by the Government to develop every child's full potential and to provide equal opportunities for every child to succeed in life will be severely tested in the years ahead. Another challenge will revolve around whether the dramatic upward social mobility that has been experienced by an entire generation will be repeated as the current privileged classes and élites attempt to consolidate their own position.[114] A balance will also have to be sought between entrenched views about the role of genetic endowment *vis-à-vis* environmental nurturing in students' overall personal development. If policy-makers strongly believe, for instance, that ethnic differences in educational attainment or aptitude are largely genetically determined,[115] then this belief will, in turn, have serious implications for how policy-makers think about the limits to the potential of different groups.

More recently, a new dimension has been added to the discussion about life chances and social mobility with the government advocacy of the importation of foreign talent.[116] These foreigners will be recruited not only at the level of the workforce but also at the level of the schools.[117] The growing influx of non-Singaporeans has met with resentment among some Singaporeans who perceive, correctly or otherwise, that this influx can only mean increased competition for education and other social services. In addition to managing public perceptions regarding the desirability of importing foreign talent, government policy-makers will also have to grapple with the implications of expanded immigration on the development of a national identity.[118] Schools will have to deal with the task of socializing new immigrants alongside their Singaporean counterparts. In this regard, there will be a parallel task of coping with those Singaporeans who live and work outside the country, in conjunction with the strategy of encouraging an external wing in the Singapore economy. Efforts are already being made to ensure that the children of these Singaporeans are able to re-adjust to schooling in Singapore upon their return to the country. These efforts will doubtless need to continue for the foreseeable future.

Conclusion

This chapter has reviewed several key policies and initiatives and has raised areas of concern as well. The Singapore Government continues to be ambitious in its plans to use education as a key linchpin in its efforts to promote economic development and social cohesion. Despite the often purposeful and zealous manner in which policies are pronounced, this chapter has demonstrated that it is by no means the case that policy implementation and outcomes are unproblematic and uncontroversial. Several issues will continue to bedevil policy-makers for the foreseeable future. One of these is the issue of how to bring about sustained change in such areas as curricular initiatives. No amount of government exhortation about the desirability of such innovations will succeed unless teachers are first given the opportunity to engage in reflective thinking about these innovations. Given the increasingly hectic work schedules of most teachers in schools, it will be very difficult for them to have adequate time to engage in such thinking, let alone implement the reforms in a manner true to the original intentions of the policy-framers. The last thing policy-framers desire is for teachers to go about their teaching in an unreflective, uncomprehending manner, giving the appearance of change while leaving fundamental areas of change untouched. Equally troubling would be the prospect of teachers, parents, and students merely treating the new assessment modes and subject matter as yet more hurdles to be cleared in the same way as the current hurdles have been crossed. Other dilemmas related to the tension between diversity and conformity, such as those brought about by the ranking of schools, will continue to trouble schools.

The challenges and dilemmas involved in managing a culturally diverse, and now increasingly class-stratified population, will not prove an easy task either. Language policies, and other policies that have a bearing upon individuals' life chances and social mobility, will remain contentious. Ethnic- and class-based disparities in educational attainment show no signs of diminishing in the early years of the twenty-first century and will continue to strain the ingenuity and resolve of the Government.

Notes

1. Singapore 21 Committee, *Singapore 21: Together, We Make the Difference* (Singapore: Singapore 21 Committee, 1999).
2. M. E. Porter, *The Competitive Advantage of Nations* (New York: The Free Press, 1990).
3. P. F. Drucker, *Post-Capitalist Society* (New York: Harper Business, 1993); K. Ohmae ed., *The Evolving Global Economy* (Boston: Harvard Business School Press, 1995).
4. R. Marshall and M. Tucker, *Thinking for a Living: Education and the Wealth of Nations* (New York: Basic Books, 1992); R. B. Reich, *The Work of Nations: Preparing Ourselves for 21st-Century Capitalism* (New York: Vintage Books, 1992).
5. Ministry of Trade and Industry, *Report of the Economic Committee: The Singapore Economy: New Directions* (Singapore: Ministry of Trade and Industry, 1986).
6. Ministry of Trade and Industry, *The Strategic Economic Plan: Towards a Developed Nation* (Singapore: Ministry of Trade and Industry, 1991).
7. Lee Hsien Loong, "Our future depends on creative minds", *Speeches* 20, No. 3 (1996): 34–41.
8. Ministry of Education, *Towards Excellence in Education* (Singapore: Ministry of Education, 1987), p. ix.
9. Goh Chok Tong, *National Day Rally 1992* (Singapore: Ministry of Information and the Arts, 1992).
10. Ibid.; *Parliamentary Debates Singapore: Official Report* 64 (1 March 1995), col. 27.
11. Ministry of Education, *Towards Thinking Schools* (Singapore: Ministry of Education, 1997).
12. Ministry of Education, "The School Excellence Model", which can be found at <http://intranet.moe.edu.sg/schdiv/semhome.htm>.
13. Ministry of Education, *Masterplan for IT in Education* (Singapore: Ministry of Education, 1997).
14. Committee on University Admission System, *Preparing Graduates for a Knowledge Economy: A New University Admission System for Singapore* (Singapore: Ministry of Education, 1999).

15. *Parliamentary Debates Singapore: Official Report* 59 (13 March 1992), cols. 991–92.
16. See, for instance, M. Thrupp, "The art of the possible: Organizing and managing high and low socioeconomic schools", *Journal of Education Policy* 13 (1998): 197–219.
17. See, for instance, D. Reay, "Setting the agenda: The growing impact of market forces on pupil grouping in British secondary schooling", *Journal of Curriculum Studies* 30 (1998): 545–58.
18. Mirchandani Nirmala, "Big drop in students studying O-level literature", *Straits Times*, 16 August 1997, p. 3; Mirchandani Nirmala and Braema Mathi, "Schools making Literature optional", *Straits Times*, 24 May 1995, p. 3.
19. A. de Souza, "Literature key to past, says BG Yeo", *Sunday Times*, 5 July 1998, p. 36.
20. "Physical education: Walking in thin line between fit, fat and fun", *Straits Times*, 11 April 1996, p. 40.
21. External Review Team, *Learning, Creating, and Communicating: A Curriculum Review* (Singapore: Ministry of Education, 1997).
22. Ministry of Education, "The School Excellence Model".
23. See, for instance, Goh Chok Tong, "Prepare our children for the new century: Teach them well", *Education in Singapore: A Book of Readings*, edited by Jason Tan, S. Gopinathan, and W. K. Ho (Singapore: Prentice Hall, 1997), pp. 417–25; *Parliamentary Debates Singapore: Official Report* 53 (20 March 1989), cols. 550–51; 55 (15 March 1990), cols. 310–11.
24. Chiang C. F., "Education: New Directions", in *Singapore: The Year in Review* 1998, edited by G. L. Ooi and R. S. Rajan (Singapore: Times Academic Press, 1999), pp. 65–76.
25. See, for instance, University of Cambridge Local Examinations Syndicate, *Geography examination syllabuses for* 1998 *and* 1999 (Cambridge: University of Cambridge, 1996); University of Cambridge Local Examinations Syndicate, [*Economics examination syllabuses for* 1999 (*International examinations*)] (Cambridge: University of Cambridge, 1997); University of Cambridge Local Examinations Syndicate, [*Physics examination syllabuses for* 1999 (*International examinations*)] (Cambridge: University of Cambridge, 1997).
26. See, for instance, External Review Team, *Learning, Creating, and Communicating*; *Parliamentary Debates Singapore: Official Report* 67 (30 July 1997), col. 1375; "The over-taught Singapore student", *Sunday Times*, 22 March 1998, p. 24.
27. Lee Hsien Loong, "Our future depends on creative minds", Speeches 20, No. 3 (1996); Mirchandani Nirmala, "Undergrads being taught to think and write", *Straits Times*, 2 February 1995, p. 24; Mirchandani Nirmala, "The battle for good English", *Straits Times*, 31 July 1999, p. 52; Mirchandani Nirmala and Braema Mathi, "Do more A's mean brighter students...or just students who are more exam-smart?", *Sunday Times*, 31 March 1996, p. 2.

28. Pan X. H., "*Shixing moni kaoshi xuesheng shuxi zhanchang* [Implementing mock examinations to familiarize students with the 'battlefield']" [in Chinese], *Lianhe Wanbao*, 8 August 1997, p. 6.
29. External Review Team, *Learning, Creating, and Communicating*, p. 16.
30. See, for instance, *Parliamentary Debates Singapore: Official Report* 70 (17 March 1999), cols. 1063, 1066.
31. See, for instance, L. Cuban, *How Teachers Taught: Constancy and Change in American Classrooms* 1890-1990 (New York: Teachers College Press, 1993); M. G. Fullan with S. Stiegelbauer, *The New Meaning of Educational Change*, 2nd ed. (New York: Teachers College Press, 1991).
32. P. Morris, *The Hong Kong School Curriculum: Development, Issues and Policies*, 2nd ed. (Hong Kong: Hong Kong University Press, 1996).
33. See, for instance, D. R. Carless, "Managing systemic curriculum change: A critical analysis of Hong Kong's Target-Oriented Curriculum initiative", *Curriculum and assessment for Hong Kong: Two components, one system*, edited by P. Stimpson and P. Morris (Hong Kong: Open University of Hong Kong Press, 1998), pp. 223–44; Cheah Y. M., "The examination culture and its impact on literacy innovations: The case of Singapore", *Language and Education*, Vol. 12, 1998, pp. 192–209; F. Y. F. Ng and P. Morris, "The music curriculum in Hong Kong secondary schools — intentions and constraints", *Curriculum and Assessment for Hong Kong: Two Components, One System*, edited by P. Stimpson and P. Morris (Hong Kong: Open University of Hong Kong Press, 1998), pp. 171–200.
34. S. G. Grant, P. L. Peterson, and A. Shojgreen-Downer, "Learning to teach mathematics in the context of systemic reform", *American Educational Research Journal* 33 (1996): 509–41.
35. S. G. Grant, "Locating authority over content and pedagogy: Cross-current influences on teachers' thinking and practice", *Theory and Research in Social Education* 24 (1996): 237–72.
36. A. Walker and J. Walker, "Challenging the boundaries of sameness: Leadership through valuing difference", *Journal of Educational Administration* 36 (1998): 8–28.
37. Grant, Peterson and Shojgreen-Downer, "Learning to teach mathematics"; J. P. Spillane and J. S. Zeuli, "Reform and teaching: Exploring patterns of practice in the context of national and state mathematics reforms", *Educational Evaluation and Policy Analysis* 21 (1999): 1–27.
38. J. H. Sandholtz, C. Ringstaff, and D. C. Dwyer, *Teaching with Technology: Creating Student-Centered Classrooms* (New York: Teachers College Press, 1997).
39. Deng Z. Y. and S. Gopinathan, "Integration of information technology into teaching: The complexity and challenges of implementation of curricular changes in Singapore", *Asia Pacific Journal of Teacher Education & Development* 2, No. 1 (1999): 29–39.
40. M. G. Fullan, with S. Stiegelbauer, *The New Meaning of Educational Change*, p. 130.
41. Mirchandani Nirmala, "Glad to upgrade but wary of load", *Straits Times*, 28 July 1999, p. 42.

42. Speech by Rear-Admiral (NS) Teo Chee Hean, Minister for Education and Second Minister for Defence, at the Chinese High Lecture 1999 on 16 July 1999 at The Chinese High School <http://www1.moe.edu.sg/Speeches/ sp160799.htm>.
43. See, for instance, "Entrepreneurs are born, not made", *Straits Times*, 11 July 1996, p. 25.
44. See, for instance, I. N. Diakidoy and E. Kanari, "Student teachers' beliefs about creativity", *British Educational Research Journal* 25 (1999): 225–43.
45. Ministry of Education, *Education Statistics Digest* 2000 (Singapore: Ministry of Education, 2000), p. 17.
46. P. Kennedy, *Preparing for the Twenty-First Century* (New York: Random House, 1993); R. B. Reich, *The Work of Nations*.
47. Y. Shavit and H. Blossfeld, eds., *Persistent Inequality: Changing Educational Attainment in Thirteen Countries* (Boulder, Colorado: Westview Press, 1993).
48. "Launch of National Education", Ministry of Education Press release No. 017/ 97.
49. Jason Tan, "Education and colonial transition in Singapore and Hong Kong: Comparisons and contrasts", *Comparative Education* 33 (1997): 303–12.
50. Department of Statistics, *Economic and Social Statistics Singapore* 1960-1982 (Singapore: Department of Statistics, 1983), pp. 233–34, 236–37.
51. See, for instance, Lau K. E., *Singapore Census of Population* 1990 *Statistical Release* 3: *Literacy, Languages Spoken and Education* (Singapore: Department of Statistics, 1992), pp. 31–33.
52. S. Gopinathan, "Language policy changes 1979-1997: Politics and pedagogy", in *Language, Society and Education in Singapore: Issues and Trends*, 2nd ed., edited by S. Gopinathan et al. (Singapore: Times Academic Press, 1998), pp. 19–44.
53. See, for instance, *Parliamentary Debates Singapore: Official Report* 56 (13 June 1990), cols. 189–91.
54. See, for instance, Prime Minister Goh Chok Tong in his National Day rally speech 1997: "Global city, best home" <http://www.moe.edu.sg/whats_new/ pmspeech.htm>; "Speak Mandarin drive kicks off with launch of Chinese film festival", *Sunday Times*, 22 September 1996, p. 3.
55. *Parliamentary Debates Singapore: Official Report* 61 (12 October 1993), col. 571.
56. Ibid., col. 573.
57. Goh Chok Tong, "Balancing race relations: Lessons from the general election", *Speeches* 20, No. 3 (1997): 14–18.
58. See for instance *Parliamentary Debates Singapore: Official Report* 70 (17 March 1999), cols. 1028–29.
59. Lee Hsien Long, "A cultural elite for every ethnic group", *Speeches* 23, No. 2 (1999): 44–49; *Parliamentary Debates Singapore: Official Report* 70 (18 March 1999), col. 1123.
60. Goh Chok Tong, "The key roles of schools", *Speeches* 23, No. 2 (1999): 13–21.
61. Chua Lee Hoong, "New Chinese elite will be different", *Sunday Times*, 28 March 1999, p. 1; Goh, "The key roles of schools".

62. Goh Y. S., "SAP schools can't halt decline in number of Chinese elite", *Lianhe Zaobao*, 10 April 1999, p. 21.
63. A. F. Gupta, *The Step-Tongue: Children's English in Singapore* (Clevedon: Multilingual Matters, 1994).
64. Action Committee on Indian Education, *At the Crossroads: Report of the Action Committee on Indian Education* (Singapore: Action Committee on Indian Education 1991), p. 20.
65. S. Gopinathan, "Religious education in a secular state: The Singapore experience", *Asian Journal of Political Science* 3, No. 2 (1995): 15–27.
66. E. C. Y. Kuo, J. S. T. Quah, and C. K. Tong, *Religion and Religious Revivalism in Singapore* (Singapore: Ministry of Community Development, 1988).
67. Cheah Y. M., "Acquiring English literacy in Singapore classrooms", in *Language, Society and Education in Singapore*, edited by Gopinathan et al., pp. 291–306.
68. Khoo C. K., *Census of Population 1980 Singapore Release No. 4: Economic Characteristics* (Singapore: Department of Statistics, 1981), p. 66.
69. Khoo C. K., *Census of Population 1980 Singapore Release No. 3: Literacy and Education* (Singapore: Department of Statistics, 1981), p. 15.
70. Jason Tan, "Joint government-Malay community efforts to improve Malay educational achievement in Singapore", *Comparative Education* 31 (1995): 339–53.
71. Lee Kuan Yew, "Mendaki's task is to raise education of all Malays", *Speeches* 5, No. 3 (1982): 5–25.
72. Ibid., p. 9.
73. Tan, "Joint government-Malay community efforts".
74. S. Gopinathan, "Education", in *Singapore: The Year in Review 1991*, edited by T. Y. Lee (Singapore: Times Academic Press, 1992), pp. 54–64; Lai Ah Eng, *Meanings of Multiethnicity: A Case-Study of Ethnicity and Ethnic Relations in Singapore* (Kuala Lumpur: Oxford University Press, 1995); Lily Zubaidah Rahim Ishak, "The paradox of ethnic-based self-help groups", in *Debating Singapore: Reflective Essays*, edited by Derek da Cunha (Singapore: Institute of Southeast Asian Studies, 1994), pp. 46–50; Lily Zubaidah Rahim Ishak, *The Singapore Dilemma: The Political and Educational Marginality of the Malay Community* (Kuala Lumpur: Oxford University Press, 1998); S. Tay et al., "Self-Help and National Integration", Occasional Paper Series Paper No. 3-96, Association of Muslim Professionals, 1996.
75. Tay et al., "Self-Help and National Integration".
76. See, for instance, Goh Chok Tong, "Ethnic-based self-help groups: To help, not to divide", *Speeches* 18, No. 4 (1994): 10–14.
77. Department of Statistics, *General Household Survey 1995 Release 1: Socio-Demographic and Economic Characteristics* (Singapore: Department of Statistics, 1997), pp. 67–70.
78. Ibid., p. 87.
79. Speech by Dr Aline Wong, Senior Minister of State for Health and Education, at the launch of Hindi teaching materials and Hindi Centre Day 1998 on 11 July

1998 at the World Trade Centre Auditorium <http://www1.moe.edu.sg/Speeches/110798.htm>, p. 10.

80. Department of Statistics, *General Household Survey* 1995, pp. 68–70.
81. Speech by Dr Aline Wong, p. 17.
82. Singapore 21 Committee, *Together, We Make the Difference*.
83. See, for instance, *Parliamentary Debates Singapore: Official Report* 70 (17 March 1999), cols. 1006–8.
84. Salim Osman, "Muslim schools draw small but growing number of children", *Straits Times*, 28 April 1989, p. 26; Zuraidah Ibrahim, "Singapore's Islamic schools: Slow train or higher plane?", *Sunday Times*, 1 March 1998, pp. 6, 7.
85. Leslie Koh, "Malays must tackle 4 areas to progress, says Rear-Adm Teo", *Sunday Times*, 28 December 1997, p. 23.
86. See, for instance, "Abolishing SAP schools will not lead to better unity", *Straits Times*, 8 April 1999, p. 45; Ahmad Osman, "SAP schools here to stay, says BG Yeo", *Straits Times*, 12 April 1999, p. 2; "Madrasah students face disadvantage", *Straits Times*, 17 May 1999, p. 30; "Madrasahs different from SAP schools", *Straits Times*, 17 April 1999, p. 67; "Madrasahs don't teach critical skills", *Straits Times*, 11 May 1999, p. 45; "Roots of SAP schools similar to madrasahs'", *Straits Times*, 24 April 1999, p. 61.
87. See, for instance, Chua Mui Hoong, "Merit matters most, equal chance for all", *Straits Times*, 27 May 1996, p. 1.
88. Lee Kuan Yew, *New Bearings in Our Education System* (Singapore: Ministry of Culture, 1966), pp. 10, 12, 13.
89. See, for instance, Warren Fernandez, "Latest figures show children of grads do better in exams", *Straits Times*, 3 September 1994, p. 2.
90. Chua B. H., *Communitarian Ideology and Democracy in Singapore* (London: Routledge, 1995), p. 63.
91. Ministry of Education, *Education Statistics Digest* 1999, p. 33.
92. *Parliamentary Debates Singapore: Official Report* 63 (25 August 1994), col. 398.
93. *Parliamentary Debates Singapore: Official Report* 59 (6 January 1992), col. 18.
94. Jason Tan, "The Marketisation of Education in Singapore: Policies and Implications", *International Review of Education* 44 (1998): 47–63.
95. Jason Tan, "Independent schools in Singapore: Implications for social and educational inequalities", *International Journal of Educational Development* 13 (1993): 239–51.
96. Garry Rodan, "State-society relations and political opposition in Singapore", in *Political Oppositions in Industrialising Asia*, edited by Garry Rodan (London: Routledge, 1996), pp. 95–127.
97. Goh Chok Tong, "Narrowing the income gap", *Speeches* 20, No. 3 (1996): 1–4; Goh Chok Tong, "Singapore and the East Asian 'miracle'", *Speeches* 21, No. 1 (1997): 13–9.
98. Goh Chok Tong, "Narrowing the income gap", p. 3.

99. Goh Chok Tong, "Keeping the Singapore family together", *Speeches* 20, No. 3 (1996): 17.
100. See, for instance, Derek da Cunha, *The Price of Victory: The 1997 Singapore General Election and Beyond* (Singapore: Institute of Southeast Asian Studies, 1997); Garry Rodan, "Singapore: Economic Diversification and Social Divisions", in *The Political Economy of South-East Asia: An Introduction*, edited by G. Rodan, K. Hewison, and R. Robison (Melbourne: Oxford University Press, 1997), pp. 148–78.
101. Chua B. H. and Tan J. E., "Singapore: New configuration of a socially stratified culture", Department of Sociology Working Papers No. 127, National University of Singapore, 1995.
102. Lee Kuan Yew, "Picking up the gauntlet: Will Singapore survive Lee Kuan Yew?" *Speeches* 20, No. 3 (1996): 30.
103. Goh Chok Tong, "Prepare our children", in *Education in Singapore*, p. 7.
104. Lee, "Picking up the gauntlet".
105. See, for instance, "Looking to the future", *Asiaweek*, 21 May 1999, pp. 30–34.
106. Ministry of Education, "Launch of National Education", p. 3.
107. Goh Chok Tong, *National Day Rally* 1992, pp. 32-33.
108. *Parliamentary Debates Singapore: Official Report* 59 (16 January 1992), col. 365.
109. Goh, "Singapore and the East Asian 'miracle'"; *Parliamentary Debates Singapore: Official Report* 66 (22 May 1996), cols. 331–43.
110. See, for instance, "Poor bright children will find it harder to move up in Singapore today", *Straits Times*, 1 June 1996, p. 29.
111. Sandra Davie, "Four parents call to say schools asked for money", *Straits Times*, 30 January 1992, p. 25; Sandra Davie, "Desperate parents will try all means to register a child", *Straits Times*, 30 January 1992, p. 25.
112. See, for instance, Action Committee on Indian Education, *At the Crossroads*, p. 19; Wong C. M., "Parents want Tamil in Unity Primary", *Straits Times*, 13 August 1998, p. 40.
113. Department of Statistics, *General Household Survey* 1995, p. 29.
114. Rodan, "Singapore".
115. See, for instance, M. Richardson, "US must accept racial differences in educational performance to recover", *Straits Times*, 26 June 1992, p. 3.
116. See, for instance, Goh's National Day rally speech 1997; Teo Chee Hean, "The new workforce — education and international talent", *Speeches* 21, No. 5 (1997) pp. 95–106.
117. Warren Fernandez, "1 in 5 Raffles students should be a foreigner, says SM Lee", *Sunday Times*, 5 October 1997, p. 1.
118. Yap Mui Teng, "The Singapore state's response to migration", *Sojourn* 14, No. 1 (1999): 198–211.

8

REFRAMING MODERNITY
The Challenge of Remaking Singapore

J. M. Nathan

It is notoriously difficult to grapple with a subject such as the challenge posed by modernity. It is a rather large and slippery subject, as the bewildering array of interpretations on the meaning of the terms, "modernity", "modern", and "modernization" guarantees that the battle to make sense of the conceptual map is lost before it even begins. But, as the linguist Alfred Korzybski pointed out, since the map is not the territory, I shall carve out the relevant terrain of discussion.

Broadly, the chapter begins by examining modernity and its derivatives, and then uses the insights gleaned from this examination to study the implications of "Western" modernity for non-Western societies such as Singapore. It argues that Singapore is redefining modernity in keeping with its own "historical moment" and, through the Government's present policy initiatives, is engaged in the process of negotiating with both the dilemmas of modernization and the paradoxes of post-industrial society as it moves into the new millennium. The chapter then considers a few aspects of how Singapore has thus far responded to the challenges posed by modernity in its bid to be a city of the future.

Introduction

It was Marshall McLuhan who once proclaimed, in the electric age, that we live in a shrinking world, coining that most useful, if now banal, phrase, "the global village". No doubt, at the turn of the twentieth century, our world displays a rich welter of diverse, often conflicting, strands and tendencies; yet, beneath the turbulent panorama of world wars, Cold War, regional wars, and North-South conflicts, a dominant trend or undercurrent can readily be detected: the process of globalization, the emergence of a "global city".[1] Occasionally deflected and sometimes nearly eclipsed by the din of armed struggle, this strand has the earmarkings of a relentless and near-providential force: seemingly disconnected events or episodes appear to coalesce almost mysteriously or fortuitously into a larger design.

However, although powerfully pervasive, this trend is not entirely self-propelled or akin to a natural *force majeure*: overtly or covertly, its movement is backed up by political and economic strategies as well as intellectual trajectories of long-standing. Most prominent among these strategies and directions are industrialization, market capitalism, and the ascendancy of science and technology — features pre-eminently connected with modern Western culture. To this extent, globalization can be regarded as a synonym for modernization or Westernization, that is, the dissemination of the standards of Western modernity around the globe.[2]

In its global reach, modernization is a gripping, monumental drama saturated with promises and risks. Seen from the angle of non-Western societies in particular, the drama is bound to be marked by profound ambiguity irreducible to neat formulas (of either progress or regress). On the one hand, modernization in these societies is liable to generate a new dynamism or social vigour (as in Hong Kong, Taiwan, Malaysia, or Singapore), a dynamism prone to break open congealed or ossified customs and, thus, to liberate untapped energies, especially those of previously silenced or oppressed strata of the population (as in China or the former Soviet Union, for example). Modernization in this sense can be the harbinger of social transformation and emancipation.

On the other hand, the boons of modernity come to many of these societies mainly through the vehicle of colonialism (as in Southeast Asia), or else post-colonial modes of Western (military, economic, and scientific) hegemony. Hence, unsurprisingly, modernity is also experienced as the result of foreign intervention, accompanied by the traumatic agonies of alienation, heteronomy, and Western control.

In a slight variation of the phrase coined by Horkheimer and Adorno (regarding the Enlightenment trajectory), the global drama of our age can be appropriately captured under the label of a "dialectic of modernization". Given its intrinsic ambivalence, the process is contestable and, in fact, fiercely contested on all sides. To devotees of modernity, indigenous customs or traditions in non-Western societies are liable to appear as mere obstacles or obsolete relics destined to be eradicated by the onrush of Western-style rationality and efficiency. By contrast, members of indigenous life-worlds are prone to defend these same traditions (in their original or a suitably modified form) as bulwarks of resistance against the homogenizing bent of global management. Like the role of tradition, forms of ethnic and religious distinctiveness are also intensely controverted, with charges of atavism and backwardness hurled against the catchwords of cultural autonomy and national independence.[3]

If this form of modernization is today described as "modernity" in the non-Western world, then this modern Western civilization is generally characterized by other traits as well, such as a largely secular culture, liberal democracy, individualism, rationalism, and humanism. However, whether these traits are unique in human history is controversial.

Many historical societies have had relatively free markets, have respected individuality, engaged in rational planning and rational inquiry, regarded at least part of social life as largely secular or profane, and so on. As a package, the modern Western combination of science, technology, industry, free market, liberal democracy, and so on, is certainly unique in human history, but whether each of the elements separately considered is unique is less clear. This makes the precise definition of modernity — beyond science, technology, industry, and high living standards — rather difficult.

There are also those who think that modernity is or ought to be at an end. Some call for the rejection of modernity, while others only question it, problematize it, without implying that there is any alternative. This begs the question of what modernity entails, and what it means to be "modern". However, it is possible not to speak of "the modern" or "modernism" at all, and instead look at the principles that most philosophers would regard as essential to the modern world. While there is virtue in diversity, oftentimes it may lead to confusion. Thus, some kind of clarification is in order.

Modernity refers to the new civilization that developed in Europe and North America over the last several centuries and which was fully evident by the early twentieth century. Modernity implies that this civilization is modern in the strong sense that it is unique in human history. Exactly what makes this civilization unique is to some extent uncontroversial. Few would deny that following the Enlightenment, with the exaltation of Reason in the fight against superstition and religious orthodoxy, the civilizations of Europe and

North America eventually developed a new, powerful technique for the study of nature, as well as new machine technologies and modes of industrial production that have led to an unprecedented rise in material living standards.

The positive self-image that modern Western culture has often given to itself — a picture born in the eighteenth century Enlightenment — is of a civilization founded on scientific knowledge of the world, which places the highest premium on individual human life and freedom, and believes that such freedom and rationality will lead to social progress through virtuous, self-controlled work, creating a better material, political, and intellectual life for all. Thus, in this sense, "modernity" may be said to be "the epoch in which simply being 'modern' became a decisive value in itself".[4]

This combination of science, reason, individuality, freedom, truth, and social progress, however, has been questioned and criticized by many. Some critics see modernity instead as a movement of ethnic and class domination, Western imperialism, anthropocentrism, the destruction of nature, the dissolution of community and tradition, the rise of alienation, and the death of individuality in bureaucracy.[5] More benign critics have argued sceptically that modernity cannot achieve what it hopes, i.e. that objective truth or freedom is unavailable, or that modernity's gains are balanced by losses, and that there is no alternative either to modernity or to its discontents.[6]

We have seen how it is assumed that "modern" societies are characterized by the rational use of scientific techniques, and by the application of reason to meet the common interests of all, since reason is seen as the source of progress in knowledge and society. We might go on to say that "modernization" is a theory of rational progress. But there are critics who have argued that neither common problems nor common solutions exist, and that we have already entered a world better understood by postmodernism, which may be summarized as the view that the account of the world given by modernism no longer work in the final decades of the twentieth century. So, instead of single sets of values or political loyalties, there is a wide variety of groups and classes, aims and ideologies. Such a view celebrates pluralism, and when democracy mingles effectively with pluralism, we have a situation of polyarchy, as described by the American theorist Robert Dahl. The idea is that in modern democracies, people cannot literally rule in the classical sense of democracy, but if there are free and open democratic procedures, and a variety of groups and organizations, then the many may be said to rule.

The criticisms also bring to attention how the Enlightenment ideal of progress itself depended on a concept of universal history, moving through different stages of development and culminating in a common destiny. Human history was seen as the ongoing process of emancipation, with a certain ideal of man as its axiom. However, the gap between the ideality and reality of social change in nineteenth-century Europe and beyond exposed the fundamental political and moral dilemmas of an enlightened culture: neither scientific knowledge nor rational institutional organization foreclosed on political and moral questions about how the consequences of economic growth and social progress would be experienced or should be addressed.

Further, critics point out that this emancipatory promise of modernity evaporates, in light of the fact that the end of the twentieth century — the "modern" record — has been one of world wars, the rise of totalitarian ideologies, concentration camps (in both East and West), genocide, worldwide recession, Hiroshima, Vietnam, Cambodia, the Persian Gulf, and the widening economic disparities between the rich and poor. This makes any belief in the idea of progress or faith in the future seem questionable.[7] It is possible to criticize all that modernity has engendered: the accumulated experience of Western civilization, industrialization, urbanization, advanced technology, the nation-state, life in the "fast lane", and modern priorities like career, office, liberal democracy, humanism, egalitarianism, evaluative criteria, and impersonal rules.

What is interesting here for our purposes is that many of the heated debates over these various complex, interrelated issues — and over the whole question of modernity, modernism, modernization (and even post-modernism!), and "the authority of the past" — have taken place in the West as though Asian and other non-Western traditions were neither parties to, nor affected by, the debate or its outcomes. We might ask, with J. L. Mehta:

> [I]s this "modern" period (which some date back to the end of the middle ages) a new epoch in Western history merely, or does it constitute something of a turning point in world history itself? The external facts are certainly episodes in Western history, but does not their meaning now encompass the entire world, enclosing it in a framework of ideas which it cannot escape, forming the present-day world civilization, carrying within it a whole variety of cultures, high and low, many of whom were once autonomous civilizations within their own right?[8]

The answer now seems to be "yes and no": "yes", insofar as many of the leading ideas we associate with modernity — i.e. liberal democracy, science and technology, secularism, and the rest — have challenged and informed the thinking of traditional societies throughout the world; "no", insofar as widely diverse cultures (especially in East Asia, Southeast Asia, and Africa) have refused to be "enclosed" by this framework of ideas (a framework that is itself being seriously questioned in the West today) and have, rather, struggled — with varying degrees of success — to forge creatively a new modernism appropriate to their own traditions.[9] And, as Mehta notes, the interchange has not been entirely one-sided:

> Leading Western writers have become self-conscious of their own perspective. This involves an awareness of the possible validity of other perspectives and of the need to incorporate what one can of all that was so far excluded that lay outside the field of their "single vision".

As many scholars have clearly and forcefully shown, not only are non-Western societies, such as Japan and — in time — China, potential central players on the world economic scene, they also have much to contribute, on the basis of their own experience, to the conversation concerning modernity and the authority of the past, and may yet, on the basis of their own rich resources, alter fundamentally the very meaning of modernity in the West.

Many modernization theorists did not feel the urge to validate their generalization of the Western experience because they could always fall back on a long-held tradition in Western literature which insisted that Western modernity would inevitably encompass the entire globe. The long-standing assumption that Western civilization is universal was an answer to the question of why the scholars of non-Western modernity were not confronted with the task of justifying their extrapolation from one cultural milieu to another.

The universality assumption was further reinforced in the late nineteenth and through the better part of the twentieth century when Western hegemony was expanded to Third World societies, effecting structural changes therein.

On the surface, many non-Western societies appear to have been more or less modernized. Western technologies and institutions may be traced to every corner of the globe. What is less appreciated is that below the facade of modernity lurks a great deal of discontent, resistance, and distrust. Those who fail to penetrate beneath the surface mistake the pragmatic acceptance of the forms of Western modernity by non-Westerners for a genuine commitment to its ideas and ideals, and confuse the desire to enjoy the material fruits of Western civilization with a true conviction in the validity of the project of modernity.[10]

The universality of Western experience cannot be taken as a given, i.e. as a self-evident phenomenon, for the claim of universality is not simply an assertion that Western modernity has universal implications for non-Western societies. If this was the claim, one would not think anyone could object to it, for, obviously, Western modernity has already made a profound and lasting impact on world history. The contributions of Western civilization will always be part of the evolution of human consciousness.

What is being questioned here is whether the cultural forms of Western modernity are destined to replace the traditional forms of non-Western societies, as they did with regard to Western traditional forms. What is at stake is whether non-Western societies are bound to grow in the image of the West, as many proponents of modernization contend, for many theorists believe that the modernization of non-Western societies is, in essence, a process of Westernization. Modernity enters our everyday lives through the dissemination of the products of consumer society, new technologies, and new modes of transportation and communication, and the dynamics by which it produces our present condition is described as modernization, denoting all those processes of urbanization, bureaucratization, industrialization, and so on. So we need to delineate the basic assumptions concerning the prospect for the ongoing processes of modernization of non-Western places like Singapore. We need to ask what, specifically, is the cultural import of "modernity" for Singapore.

Modern Singapore and the "Post"-Modern West

The belief that Singapore has a serious long-term commitment to the project of entering the new millennium as a modern city (or "postmodern" city) is comforting to many, challenging to some, and a source of bemusement for others. However, most of these opinions seem to have been formed by individuals who have casually and unreflectively identified "modernity" with the institutions of liberal democracy, capitalist free enterprise, and the spread of rational technologies.

No doubt these are aspects of modernity which form the heart of contemporary Singaporean interests (and anxieties) with respect to the West. The deepening crisis of "modernity" in the West, however, bespeaks a far richer, more complex, and more consequential "modern condition". It would be extremely foolish, therefore, to ignore the broader cultural accoutrements associated with and embedded in the more practical elements of the modern impulse. For some of these allied aspects carry with them such disruptive potential as to suggest that the Western cure may be more deleterious than the ailment that besets many Southeast Asian countries. In some respects, this may be one of the insights to be gleaned from Mahbubani's book, *Can Asians Think?*[11]

It may be said that the culture of the modern West is in such disarray as to be practically useless as a resource for the development of cultural accommodation models that might ease the transmission of the practical elements of modernity which some Southeast Asians nations might seek to import.

What one wishes to argue for here is that Singapore, as a case in point, is a new kind of modern society and, further, that it offers a new version of modernity, as a result of its own unique circumstances, i.e. as the result of its social ecology, which may be said to be a function of its geographical location, history, heterogeneous mix of people, and its dynamism. This claim resolves to the view that the promise of being both modern and Asian represents the Singapore of the future.

It is, thus, an argument against those who believe that Americanization or commodification or McDonald's (or some variation of all these) is seducing the world into sameness and creating a world of little Americas. Neither is this argument sympathetic to those die-hard adherents of modernization theory who believe that modernity is a single destination to which all lines of development lead and that all that matters is who gets there first and how high the price of their journey.

The assumption here is that modernity is today a global experience, and that this experience is as varied as marriage or madness, and that most societies today possess the means for the local production of modernity, and, as their members move around the world, these experiences inform and inflect one another, thus making even the paradigmatic modernity of the United States and Western Europe (itself not an unproblematic assumption) no more pristine. Singaporeans, Koreans, Turks, Indians, Chinese, Mexicans, and Mongolians now move to (and stay in) the countries of the West, not as folk ciphers waiting to be imprinted with Euro-American modernity, but equipped with their own understanding of modernity to negotiate with the ones they encounter.

Since the early days of independence, Singapore's move towards modernization has always been negotiated through an uncomfortable dilemma wherein Singapore must modernize, yet the effects of a modernization understood in terms of liberal democracy, free enterprise, and rational technologies cannot but threaten its cultural integrity and its survival as a nation-state whose viability had yet to be demonstrated. It could be said that the paternalism of the PAP Government, its stress on the solidarity of community over issues of abstract rights, and its cultivation of and response to the psychological need for dependency are all characteristics vulnerable to being effaced by the impersonality of technology, the self-interest of free enterprise, and the individualizing ideals of liberal democracy. Whatever benefits they might offer, each of these elements of modern culture leads to a bloating of the private sphere and threatens community.

Some argue that this reading of the state of affairs leads to a legitimizing of authoritarian rule, which is marked by singularism and the presence of centralized planning and control, a phenomenon whose instrumental rationality has been shown by historical events to be bankrupt, and which has, in part, been responsible for the crisis of "modernity", since it dims the emancipatory potential of reason and technology. Interestingly, this may be formulated otherwise as the Weberian paradox, according to which the more that modern society advances in the process of rationalization, the more irrational it becomes. But, of course, one person's crisis is another's long-awaited revolution. It is crucial to recognize here that the concrete activities and institutions most associated with modernization — namely, liberal individualism and the democratic institutions that uphold it, free-enterprise capitalism and the property interests that sustain it, and rational technology, which is motivated by the aim of the most efficient organization of means — originated in and, insofar as they remain intact, are sustained by the modalities of modern consciousness which are currently in crisis.

These concrete modes of modernizing praxis are intimately connected with the fragmented, crisis-ridden culture of modernity. Thus, Singapore's culture depends upon a commonality of traditions that liberal democracy renders quite fragile. The laws, rules, and values that defined the Singaporean sensibility are immanent within and relevant to the relatively specific socio-historical conditions and character of multi-ethnic Singaporeans.[12]

In more recent years, Senior Minister Lee Kuan Yew and others have noted in varying ways, that Singapore's very existence in the new millennium is not an unproblematic proposition, faced as it is with a world of increased competition, globalization of economic markets, and the advent of new technologies, a world in which information-intensive, knowledge-based economies are the *sine qua non*, making small and young nation-states even more vulnerable.

The scenario of the post-industrial society as sketched by Touraine, Bell and others, is one in which information replaces the manufacture of material goods as a central concern in the most advanced economies.[13] This "computerization of society", as Lyotard sees it, will affect the nature of our knowledge. It is not very clear how exactly our knowledge will change, but it is certain that knowledge has become "an informational commodity".[14] Such a technology that shapes the world is primarily and essentially defined by systems that collect and transmit information which, in a traditional sense, provides us with the means of "dominating" the external world. This becomes increasingly obvious as the gap between developed and underdeveloped countries is gradually revealed as a gap in the development of information technology.[15]

Scholars have noted that Singapore is becoming a post-industrial society "in which the application of knowledge and information dominates production and employment — such as in publishing, television, education, telecommunication, and data processing — and technology is primarily electronic".[16] Singapore's push for information technology in the last decade eventually culminated in the creation of the Ministry of Communications and Information Technology in July 1999. The Ministry's functions broadly include the anticipation and provision of adequate infrastructure, and the co-ordination of activities related to making the nation-state a full republic of the digital future.

Faced with the challenge of making the leap from being one of the newly industrialized countries to being a post-industrial economy, the Government has sought to manage the mechanisms and agencies of change, in an attempt to avoid the ailments and chaos that such an open society may bring. Thus, the response of the Government (which has hitherto operated on some of the assumptions of Western modernity, viz. technocratic rationality and bureaucratization) has been to gradually introduce, over the last two decades, several strategies and initiatives based on the recommendations of various committees comprising large numbers of the intelligentsia and others, as possible means of coping and preparing for an uncertain and dizzying future. This culminated in the initiative supported by various younger leaders of the PAP Government, called "Singapore 21". More of a wish-list rather than a creed, it reflects the aspirations of this younger, more vibrant and demanding generation, and what they expect to see in their society of the future.[17]

New uses of the various electronic media and the electronically-induced shrinking of the global environment (à la McLuhan) have threatened to unravel the delicate but carefully wrought web of stability of many South and Southeast Asian states. It could be said here that the founding myth of the Singapore state as a sovereign entity was based essentially on the idea of the creation and maintenance of order out of and over against the threat of chaos, in establishing its sense of beginnings.

One feature of the modern technological world that poses a direct challenge to relatively new nation-states like Singapore is the process of globalization.[18] Globalization processes have been characterized as economic, political and cultural.[19] Globalization is the extension of economic systems, but our concern here is with cultural globalization. There is a profound sense of globalization brought about by tourism, world sport, world news, McDonaldization, AIDS, and human rights.[20]

Economic liberalization — and the move towards open markets — assures the international mobility of transnational financial capital and also makes demands on an economy's political, social, and cultural structures, thus compelling the competitive state of the future to have adaptive structures and the capacity to allow for openness.

Invariably, such processes also mean the increasing penetration and growth of new technologies, due to the export and movement of communication modes, including media forms and images; the growth of transnational political and juridical groups (the European Union and its potential); the growth of international resistance and action groups (the Beijing Conference of Women); and the penetration of ideologies, producing a "world system" or Global Village.[21]

As Al-Azmeh has noted, modern history attests to the globalization of the Western order.[22] The reasons for this are, in a sense, manifest: the conditions of Western economic and political conquest and hegemony in the modern age have engendered, for good or ill, correlative conditions of equally real ideological and cultural hegemony.

This compels Asian nation-states like Singapore to navigate through the binary logic of the West — with its inherited dilemma of tradition and modernity (from that discourse) on either horn — and to arrive at a solution that is Janus-faced. To be sure, the distinction between tradition and modernity is at best misleading, for that sort of discontinuity ignores that "modern" societies also have their traditions. Thus, scholars now note that "tradition and modernity" are being amalgamated in various ways that open new directions of rationalization. The fear that compels this sort of view is, perhaps, due to the stereotyped notion that traditional societies are "anti-modern" and that, with globalization, there would be an increased tendency for fundamentalism and ethnocentrism to arise, as a way of shunning the kind of cosmopolitanism that is a main characteristic of "modern" societies. Or that, as the world begins to "shrink", the potential for conflict increases.[23]

It has been argued that one consequence of globalization is cosmopolitanism.[24] In Giddens' view, one consequence of cosmopolitanism is that all traditions are now faced with the demand that they justify themselves in dialogue with other traditions in the public space.[25] He could just as well have said this of Singapore. Faced with the reality of the multi-ethnic community it inherited, the PAP Government had opted for a policy of multiculturalism, where ethnicity tended to be treated as merely a question of culture and identity, which were thought to be easily specifiable. Given the unrests of the 1950s and 1960s, the assumption may have been that to allow and foster ethnic difference and culture was coterminous with fighting racism, with the adoption of meritocracy as a necessary prerequisite for an egalitarian society, with the insistence of English as the lingua franca, and as a means of gaining access to the resources of the rest of the world.

Despite its associated problems, one advantage of such a move is that it gives rise to what Giddens calls "detraditionalization", which combines with globalization to increase the scope and significance for individuals to become self-consciously reflective (what he terms the process of "reflexivity"), which is the continuous reordering and reconceptualizing of one's thoughts and actions as a result of an acute sense of the conditions and consequences (or "radical contingencies") present in any situation.[26]

Given a multicultural, multi-religious milieu such as Singapore's, which is said to be both modern and traditional because of its cultural inheritance, Giddens' point seems to be that conservatism, as a defence of tradition, can no longer be sustained in the face of detraditionalization and reflexivity.[27] The uncertainty in all domains of life, together with the dissolution of traditionally ascribed identities, imposes on both institutions and individuals immensely expanded opportunities and requirements for engaging in reflexive conduct.

Crudely put, the "hardware" of Chinese/Eurasian/Indian/Malay Singaporeans is modern in that they wear "Western" or "modern" dress, eat a variety of cuisine, speak English and one or two other languages/dialects, and listen to Mozart/Pavarotti/Madonna and "Canto-pop". However, their "software" is indeterminate: they conform to traditional folkways when it comes to religious practices and in marriage and funeral ceremonies, not to mention beliefs in superstitions and in "magic" and the power of amulets and charms, all of which are a mix of pre-reflective ways and folk religion. The "old ways" are gradually being eroded, with increasing awareness that — due to the processes of modernization and the interpenetration of cultural norms and practices — these are no longer necessary, useful or meaningful for social or religious identities and affiliations.

So far as individuals are concerned, the formation of self-identity is now a thoroughly open-ended "reflexive project" of self-constitution. Such an experience may capture the sense that Berman, a most enthusiastic defender of modernity, describes:

> To be modern is to find ourselves in an environment that promises us adventure, power, joy, growth, and transformation of ourselves and the world — and, at the same time, that threatens to destroy

> everything that we have, everything we know, everything we are. Modern environments and experiences cut across all boundaries of geography and ethnicity, of class and nationality, of religion and ideology: in this sense, modernity can be said to unite all mankind. But it is a paradoxical unity, a unity of disunity: it pours us all into a maelstrom of perpetual disintegration and renewal, of struggle and contradiction, of ambiguity and anguish. To be modern is to be part of a universe in which, as Marx said, "all that is solid melts into air".[28]

At the societal level, there is social reflexivity, and people are demanding access to decision-making, challenging traditional modes of authority, and coping with the effects of rapid change and chronic uncertainty. Political programmes and projects that are of relevance to the contemporary world situation must thus be founded upon a fundamental transformation in the modes of governance by which the world is organized.[29] In Berman's view, such a society must remain in a tense, often ironic, relationship with socio-economic modernization, since modernity is an irreversible condition.

This entails that any society willing to come to terms with these processes must understand that risk is fundamental to modernity. The process of modernization involves a multiplication of risk both for the individual and for social groups. Risk is always negative in one sense, because it refers to outcomes one wants to avoid; but the active acceptance of risk and risk management are at the core of the modern market economy. Risk is about the active assessment of future hazards, and it becomes more pervasive the more a society seeks to live in the future and to shape it actively.

For instance, the social and political risks to the PAP Government in fostering "critical and creative thinking", in attracting foreign talent, in gradually recognizing non-governmental organizations (NGOs), and in developing culture and the arts in general and individual creativity in particular, is that, paradoxically, these may erode what has come to be seen as the cultural and ideological hegemony by the PAP Government since independence in 1965. But such initiatives in the social and cultural domains can be seen as part of a response by a government faced with a more sophisticated electorate that is demanding a greater degree of participation and expression, and a population that seems more at ease with taking risks.[30]

In the political and social domain, for example, Singapore has seen the introduction of the Nominated Member of Parliament (NMP) scheme; the greater tolerance for publications critical of social and political policies and programmes; the flourishing of marginal groups like The Working Committee, which foster public discussion on such diverse issues as civil society; the monthly "Coffee Shop Talks" organized by the Arts Magazine; the greater recognition of civic groups like The Roundtable; and the increased representation of women in the social, political, and administrative domains.[31]

That the Government has allowed these initiatives to flourish — and, in several instances, even given its sanction — is also, in part, a response to the larger technological and economic changes taking place in the global arena, which would, as we have considered earlier, inevitably lead to a greater openness. Thus, in order for Singapore to be economically and politically viable as a nation-state in the future, it has to manage the floodgates of change, which bring with them a degree of chaos. Managing these social and cultural changes would involve giving greater participation to the populace, in order to nurture a sense of identity and commitment, which, in turn, would help to strengthen social and civic institutions and, thereby, assist in nation-building. One area that lends itself to this sort of capital is the arts, which can also be marketed for its economic potential, and, through its desirable spin-offs, help in the process of nation-building (with the attendant notions of value and identity). In an interview, Deputy Prime Minister Brigadier-General (NS) Lee Hsien Loong explained how, essentially, openness has to be balanced with control.[32]

With the use of the Internet and the revolution in telecommunications — as exemplified by the use of satellites for gaining access to various television stations throughout the world — access to information and the cultural resources of different countries is only seconds away. It is estimated that, of Singapore's approximately 4 million people, some 40 per cent enjoy direct access to the Net,[33] and that, as of September 1999, 99 per cent of all homes had access to cable television,[34] thus making Singapore close to being a "wired" society, in the manner envisaged by the cyber-cult guru, William Gibson. Despite the controlled use of channels to prevent "undesirable" values and influences from being beamed into Singaporean homes, the former Information and the Arts Minister, Brigadier-General (NS) George Yeo, reflected that these controls were merely stop-gap measures, and that it might not be possible to legislate or to control these polymorphous influences in the long run, given the speed and advance of various kinds of technology.[35] Earlier, he had also argued that:

> Countries like Singapore ... should build up their own defences against foreign influences as it is difficult to stem the inflow of information. These defence systems will give the people an ability to discriminate, to absorb what is good and reject what is bad. It

> will give them a sense of self and pride in their own cultural traditions.[36]

If openness is inevitable, then — faced with the possible onslaught of "undesirable" foreign cultural values and ideas — the only considered response would be to strengthen the social and civic institutions of society by allowing individuals to experience, build, and manage the socially negotiated emerging culture on their own. The idea seems to be that *perestroika* is necessary, since *glasnost* is the way of the future. As Prime Minister Goh Chok Tong sees it:

> We need a new vision for Singapore, an ideal, a fresh mindset. ... All Singaporeans must feel a responsibility for ... shaping their own communities.[37]

This has seen the creation and augmentation of several secular and religious self-help groups and volunteer organizations, the creation of more "personalized" neighbourhoods, and the increased participation in community service projects for the elderly, the underprivileged, and the handicapped.

At any rate, the policy of attracting foreign talent — largely in the form of professional and technical élites from all over the world, who possess the highest levels of skills and expertise — to sustain and make viable Singapore's continued economic growth, and to make the city-state "more vibrant", also, in a sense, guarantees that the cultural mindscape and landscape of Singaporeans and Singapore would be challenged, perhaps resulting in a sort of hybridization, which is a consequence of increasing cultural interpenetration — "opening up" to other cultures — and is epitomized by cosmopolitanism.[38] As the Minister of State for Home Affairs Ho Peng Kee argued:

> [W]hile foreigners who settle in Singapore bring with them their values and way of life, not all of which may be consonant with the Singaporean way of doing things ... they can enrich the Singapore social landscape and help our society leaven upwards, [...and] their presence also helps to make Singapore a more cosmopolitan city.[39]

It is, without doubt, a bold move for a nation-state that has only recently been declared a "newly industrialized" country and for whom the business of nation-building is ongoing and incomplete (and which will never be complete as the postmodernists claim). Given its multicultural heritage and a changing populace with wide exposure to studying, working, and living abroad, a truly cosmopolitan Singapore is not difficult to imagine. Indeed, cosmopolitanism is consistent with Singapore's "world city" aspirations, which it is pursuing through a social, political, and technological strategy as well, by presenting itself as an international hub for finance, arts, culture, information technology, and trade, and as a nation whose cultural organizations involve local as well as transnational relationships.[40]

As Minister Brigadier-General George Yeo envisions it,

> In the new millennium, a cultural renaissance of historic importance will accompany the dramatic economic transformation of East Asia. ... By being of continuing service to the region and the world, Singapore hopes to do for the arts what it has done for banking, finance, manufacturing and commerce, and help create new ideas, opportunities and wealth.[41]

To be sure, Singapore has enjoyed enormous success in many other industries in just this fashion, and the concerted call for commitment to fostering and developing creative ideas, in terms of establishing new infrastructure and revisioning the old, has seen the growth of new intiatives in all areas and activities, including the civil service, education, arts, and culture. An instance of this may be seen in the speech of the Deputy Prime Minister Brigadier-General Lee Hsien Loong, to the Singapore Administrative Service, in which he elaborated on the need to be relevant to the changing mores of a more educated and demanding electorate, and urged the civil service and its related bodies to "co-opt people and ideas at all levels".[42] Implicit in this call is also the idea that, in the context of an emerging pluralistic reality consequent to the creation of a dynamic and progressive environment, there is a need for institutions to harness the democratizing tendencies wrought by the processes of change.

However, implicit in the goal of becoming a "world city" or a "global city" is the worry that a balance ought to be maintained between such a goal and the reality of being a city-state.[43] It has been argued by various scholars that globalization processes threaten to make the city-state or nation-state obsolete, and this threat may give rise to ethnic or cultural parochialism, as a sort of "reactionary" response. The argument is that calls for "going global, staying local" or "glocalization"[44] are, perhaps, opposing tendencies and may even engender contradictory responses. It is true that globalization and localization go together, in that wherever there is the emergence of global consciousness, there will be a reaction that promotes an anti-global movement.

One criticism of globalization is, thus, that it is simply westernization. However, there are cultural movements coming out of Japan and other strong economies in the Asian region which are shaping the globe as well. Prime Minister Goh Chok Tong, in his 1999 National Day Rally address, drew the distinction between Singaporeans who were "cosmopolitans" and those who were "heartlanders", i.e. those who had access to global culture through travel, work, and education, as opposed to those who were still not quite in the loop, or who are "traditionalists".[45]

The distinction was made to point to the dangers of a clash as a result of a widening gap or rift between the two world-views, and the need of a government to be mindful of diverse groups when formulating policy. The Prime Minister also voiced the hope that the gap would close and for those who had the access to help those who did not. In this regard, organizations like the Singapore International Foundation — set up initially with the purpose of providing Singaporeans who are resident overseas with a means of keeping in touch with local happenings, as well as to provide opportunities for Singaporeans to become volunteers in other nations as a sort of cultural exchange — could be harnessed to provide programmes and avenues for realizing the aspirations of "global citizens" and a true cosmopolitanism.

Prime Minister Goh has also spoken on the sensitive but tangled issue of how ethnic minorities, in particular the Malay-Muslim community, must press on and keep pace with modernity, with the promise that the Government would render any assistance that might be necessary in ensuring that its members are well-prepared for the information-intensive, knowledge-based economy of the future.[46] But, as Berman notes, the modern situation requires individuals and larger aggregates to make sense, on their own terms, of the seeming contradictions and demands that pull them in opposite directions.[47] This presumes that individuals, both individually and collectively, have the necessary resources to draw from in negotiating their response to what they may perceive as "undesirable" or "good".

In this instance, the traditionalist's solution is that the cultural resources would be traditional customs and beliefs, which are often essentially religious, offering a stability of world-views and, in some instances, a *weltanschaaung*. As always and in most places, they are constantly negotiated on both individual and societal levels, subject to the forces of industrialization, technology, and the media. However, what makes religious faith or religious commitment problematic in a globalized modern society is that everyday life has become part of a global system of exchange of commodities which are not easily influenced by political leaders, intellectuals, or religious leaders. The corruption of pristine faith, so to speak, is going to be brought about by MTV, Madonna, and Coca-Cola, and not by rational argument. What many scholars fail to emphasize is that the Ford motor car did more damage to Christianity than any type of argumentation.

Thus, in the presence of new technologies that might have "negative" consequences, such a mix of total openness and technological savvy could be seen as inimical to Singapore's continued growth and flourishing. Some may view these initiatives as the actions of the Sorcerer's Apprentice who set in motion forces he could no longer control, but, for all the rhetorical cries in the media for information technology, the PAP ideologues are not blind to the radical and possibly subversive effects such technologies may have. In fact, the new wave of the knowledge economy has been likened by Minister Brigadier-General George Yeo to the European Renaissance, which was a period of high information and knowledge intensity. The idea here is that if Singapore is to become a city of the new millennium, its people will have to cope with information that is produced and exchanged at exponential rates. In turn, this requires that its citizenry has a broad-based education system, to adapt and make itself relevant to this new order by having a grasp of different subjects, different languages, and different cultures. In short, such an information-intensive, knowledge-based economy requires Singapore to be "open" because the flow of information and cultural resources cannot be policed or regulated closely or for very long.

The worry is that, in such an environment, Singapore would be unable to cope with "perpetual disintegration and renewal", as Berman puts it, and would be faced with the spectre of social anomie, unrest and, eventually, the breakdown of social structures. To live in such a pluralistic world means to experience freedom as a continual oscillation between belonging and disorientation. As the Minister for Information and the Arts, Brigadier-General George Yeo, observed, "without a clear moral sense, the age of new knowledge will also be an age of intellectual and moral confusion, because information by itself can be a force for good or ill".[48] In that same speech, the Minister also alluded to Rome and its decline due to a corruption of the cultural ideals and values that had been responsible for its flourishing, and he emphasized how necessary it was to have cultural "balance". Such balance is often explained with reference to the Chinese symbol of *yin* and *yang*. Though the economic imperative of optimizing human resources to position Singapore as a hub for commerce, finance, culture, communication, and transportation is presented at the level of official discourse, the reference to the essential nature of the necessary cultural "grounding" is almost always to be found scattered among official speeches as well. This kind of constant oscillation between a sense of certainty and experimentation, and the tension that ensues, also echoes Berman's sense of modernity, where identities are never static and experiences are in constant flux, which is sure to bring about a marked level of unease with individuals and collectivities who do not cope well with the problems of change.

In fact, the sense of rapid change may be too overwhelming for some, who may seek relief or respite through beliefs in animistic superstition, talismans, cult groups, and so on.[49] Instances of Japanese religion, variations of mystical and occult teachings of Eastern religions and even heterodox versions of traditional religions persist in present-day modern Singapore: that is both refreshing for the anthropologist and despairing for the modernist.

A sense of the exasperation, despair, and confusion (due to the influx of foreign talent, and globalization, and the need to press on with building the new infrastructure necessary for the new millennium) may be evident in two letters published in *The Straits Times*, in which one author claimed that, while he could understand the need for foreign talent to help Singapore compete globally, he was perplexed at the need for such talent to represent Singapore in sports competitions. The other argued that there should be a renewal and revival of the uniqueness of ethnicity, culture, and heritage, since "the biggest losers will be those who have lost their sense of identity by being irreversibly separated from their cultural heritage" as a result of globalization and the information age.[50]

At one level, it may be said that such responses are instances of a struggle to come to terms with the apparent conflicts arising from certain notions of identity and difference. This struggle also constitutes the experience of modernity. But the response could also lead to the parochialism we considered earlier, in the fashion of the second writer's response. On another level, such responses bring to the fore certain misconceptions and demonstrate the confusion that may arise in formulating problems, which eventually become self-defeating paradoxes.

For instance, the first letter fails to consider that Singapore's identity and culture are themselves the result of immigrant settlers, and that the early migrants' struggle with loyalties and identities is also part of Singapore's cultural and political inheritance, relevant to the ever-receding goal of nation-building and the need for National Education; and that, just as the early settlers eventually found Singapore to be a welcome and safe haven for their ways of life and productive interests (enough for it to become their home and then its "citizens"), the situation for these potential settlers would not be very different. As Ho Peng Kee, a Minister of State, explains:

> Without immigrants, we would not have had many of the members of the first generation leadership. ... Of course, our forefathers were here first. But should we keep out later-day migrants wishing to join us? This cannot be.[51]

The writer's concerns also express the apparent underlying problems inherent in the tension in the call for attracting foreign talent, "going global" and "staying local", since the questions that arise in this connection revolve around the important but difficult issues of citizenship and national identity, since the ideal of citizenship carries with it, in the Western tradition, rights and duties. This is a question that occupies sociologists Kwok Kian Woon and Mariam Ali,[52] and prefigured in some ways by Chan Heng Chee in 1975:

> Just what does it mean to be a citizen in a country like Singapore, when there are those who are, in a matter of speaking, "sojourner-citizens", "employee citizens", and "non-citizens"?

But these challenges to the notions of citizenship, identity, and nationhood — as the earlier section of this chapter indicates — are to be construed as part of the challenge of modernity brought about by post-industrial change, and, as Gellner notes, "Social change forces us to rethink what we take for granted".[53] And the Western nations are no exception to this, in the sense that they are not immune from its associated problems, as the very large literature on the subject demonstrates. One need not even consider the idea of dual-citizenship (which is antithetical to the values of many "newly" constituted nation-states), since the privileges of citizenship are marginal in countries like Singapore (which only allows government-subsidized housing for citizens), compared with the more developed nations where citizenship often entails free medical benefits and a host of other provisions. Further, offspring of naturalized citizens would still undergo national service, and being a permanent resident alone allows almost as much access as a person who is a citizen from birth.[54] What is true is that the emerging ideas on what it means to be a "citizen" would turn on redefining the very structures that lend the notion its validity, and this promises to be an exciting challenge as essential to the notion of citizenship as political mobilization and conflict.[55]

On the other hand, the second writer yearns for a return to "parochial ethnicity", which is in a sense nostalgic.[56] Much has been written of nostalgia as an expected response to this condition,[57] but what is interesting is the notion that culture, identity, and ethnicity are "natural", "invariant", and universally valid categories of thought. Essentially, the *reductio* is of the form: that, unless we are willing to see tradition, history, culture or ethnicty as something fixed, unchanging, "objective", and which may be "accessed" much like a computer hard disk that stores "everything and for all time" so that "it" is recoverable, then we must accept that such a view evaporates in the face of the fact that there is no "objective history", tradition or culture, since these are not entities, but processes and the result of our shared intersubjective understandings.

Tradition is not to be identified with a stock of accumulated beliefs, customs, and ways of doing things, but, rather, with an ongoing process of intergenerational transmission. Understood in this way, tradition is not simply a replicative process but also a process of change. Sure, it is possible and perhaps even necessary, to take pride and have a sense of one's cultural tradition (as Brigadier-General Yeo indicates), but to have a sense of tradition that is immutable and impervious to Singaporeans' interpretation or experience of it is problematic. To gain a sense of the notion of culture that this chapter implies requires an explication of the differing and sometimes conflicting views of culture present in Singaporean discourse.

The Notion of Culture

The term "culture" is, conceptually, an unwieldy and difficult one. Use of the term varies according to historical periods and the particular theoretical or ideological agenda of their proponents.[58] Use of the term in official speeches, in the media in Singapore, and among the intelligentsia in the last two decades does not lend itself to a clear application of the concept. This chapter suggests that the notion and ideological flavour of the concept of "culture" in official discourse has changed, from being a sort of hypostasized "entity", to a more pluralistic and process-oriented notion of culture as communicative practice.[59] However, the older representation of culture as an entity, despite all attempts against reification, is to be found even among political and sociological analysis.[60] The idea found in political rhetoric that Singaporean culture should be free of "social pollutants" to "keep it intact" is an illustration of this view which had currency at that time.[61] This sense is different from Brigadier-General Yeo's use of the notion of "undesirable influences" we saw earlier, which contains some irony. But it does not mean that hypostasized notions are no longer to be found. There are such notions still in circulation,[62] and tensions and contradictions in the use of the term are present in official and popular discourse. What is certain is that this "progressive" view of culture has taken root,[63] and it is to be expected that, given the dynamics of rapid social and cultural change in the context of Singapore, it would become the tacitly accepted view.

In a theoretical sense, the hypostasized view is ironically closer to a Marxian model. According to the Marxian model, culture is determined by or dependent on the economic base or infrastructure. Each type of economic structure — "mode of production" — has a corresponding superstructure which includes social, political, legal and cultural institutions, and customs. Culture is not simply an epiphenomenon but is produced by and integral to a particular type of economic system and dependent upon the type of technology which prevails. This elementary Marxist model of culture may seem rather abstract, although it does encompass the idea of culture as something "lived" and "produced" in the course of social and economic activity. However, on the basis of this model, it is difficult to see how culture and ideology are anything but reflections of class relations, with the content entirely determined by the ideas and beliefs of those with power. The implication is that culture is monolithic and homogeneous and cannot in itself produce effects.

An intermediate notion of culture as a set of practices emerges in Althusser's re-reading of Marx. This model allows for ideology to be a level or system of reality in its own right: it is a structure of thought and consciousness in which we all think, act, and experience the world and ourselves. Thus "ideological state apparatuses" — such as the culture industries, including religion, education, the family and mass media — develop and reproduce the values, beliefs and ideas which form Singaporean culture.

Finally, the view that Singapore does, indeed, have a national culture requires a notion of culture as a living, active, productive process — it can be developed only from within, it cannot be imposed from without or above. The theoretical focus and analytical object shifts, from representation, to everyday cultural activity and artistic practices. There is a realization that the cultural landscape is always difficult territory for those who wish to control it (whether for economic, ideological, or disciplinary reasons). And for a knowledge-based, information economy, this is crucial. For the economic needs of the industries can be met only if the people can turn cultural commodities to their own interests and create their own meanings out of their social identities and social relations, as adequate resources for cultural capital. This notion suggests that, while cultural commodities are distributed by a profit-motivated culture industry that follows its own economic interests,[64] the commodities also bear the interests of those who produce it. The point seems to be that culture, however industrialized, cannot be adequately described in terms of the buying and selling of commodities.[65]

The assumption is that culture does not constitute a "thing", but a relational continuum in and through time, so that culture is both a product of the past and a creator of the future. Socialization, or the interactive social process in which agents receive from and add to their distinctive cultural heritage, and tradition (as we considered earlier) entail culture as both a product and an emergent force at any given time, insofar as socialization leads to shared patterns or forms of life that have become "patterns" by virtue of a greater or lesser degree of institutionalization through tradition. According to this view, tradition and progress are not polarities; they do not embody two opposed tendencies but, rather, a single continuum. Progress — or more precisely, change — becomes a built-in characteristic of tradition, and development is seen, therefore, as both a part of a given cultural continuum and the instrument for cultural transformation. To be sure, the merging of the old and the new involves in its operation both affirmative and negative properties, and change is not tantamount to a smooth advance or progress.[66] Such a view is also optimistic in that it rejects notions that people are easily manipulated, incapable of discrimination and, thus, at the economic, cultural, and political mercy of the barons of the culture industry. It also dispenses with the notion that there could be "decultured" individuals.[67] Every discovery and innovation in the arts and sciences knits a new pattern of society.

In a way, this view of culture as process is also an empowering and democratizing one, since it implies that agents, individually and collectively, can and do contribute to the making of their own history. And, when properly understood, such a view could result in a fundamental change in the nature of social and political life. This is so, since the government and the governed will come to rely on the shared intersubjective norms that allow for an expression of their own distinct subjectivities and their shared concerns and antagonisms, within the larger framework of a state which respects the limits in which minds meet. This process would, in time, dialectically, achieve a society with a more pluralist orientation. To see just what such an orientation entails would require a brief digression.

The burden on the pluralist is to devise a judicious blending of social and political institutions that will accommodate such diversity. The pluralist, on this score, is usually regarded as a liberal since he has the desire to accommodate such diversities. However, even a conservative can be a pluralist. In fact, it may be argued that a conservative who preaches non-interference in the rights of others to pursue their own good is better equipped to be a pluralist. He would demand that the state be, as far as possible, neutral towards questions of personal morality, common conceptions of the good, and the aims of life. Besides, the state should provide a framework of law and other institutions — a framework within which individuals and communities would pursue their own goals. Pluralism stipulates that we do not need substantive moral agreement, except only for the basic agreement about the indispensability of mutual tolerance.

There are many for whom the social/political/cultural changes in Singapore bespeak or betray a social disintegration currently taking place. Thus, inevitable social change turns into social decay. This disintegration thesis is a powerful challenge to our convictions, but such a view is mistaken. Social, cultural, and political conflicts are indeed prevalent, but they betoken change, not disintegration. We are witnessing the birth and struggle of the new, not the death throes of the old. Singapore society is changing in deep ways: alongside discontinuity, there is substantial continuity. The disintegration thesis is not mistaken about the facts but about the interpretation of the facts. What defenders of it observe is certainly there, but it is not as they interpret it.

The deep social/political/cultural changes do indicate that something is disintegrating; it is, however, not Singapore society, but merely a particular conception of it. The reason why the disintegration thesis misinterprets the present social/political/cultural situation is that it mistakenly identifies Singapore society with this conception, and it mistakenly supposes that, as this conception becomes untenable, thus Singapore society itself is threatened. The disintegration thesis recognizes only two alternatives — the acceptance or rejection of a particular conception of society — and it falsely supposes that Singapore culture itself stands or falls with the fortunes of that conception. Such a view could also be in the grip of a "static" and hypostasized notion of culture and tradition, as discussed earlier.

Consider, for instance, how the introduction of new initiatives in the development of culture and the arts would also engender and encourage a plurality of competing visions of society. In part, this call is also a response to the changing times, as well as an anticipation of the changes that increased globalization and "the information society" brings with it. It could be argued that they are strategies to (i) make space for individual demands and to counter any ill effects of an affluent society, and (ii) to strengthen the social and civil institutions of the nation.

As more opportunities for artists and performers are created in Singapore and their endeavours encouraged and given due credit, it is inevitable that there would be a greater sense of ownership and identity among those who are involved in the arts industry in one way or another. While a causal nexus cannot be established, it is to be expected — as greater numbers participate in the cultural and artistic process of creating cultural products, building infrastructural support, curating artists' works, staging plays, and being supportive audiences — that a deeper appreciation of cultural traditions and values would result. This alone goes a long way in the effort towards nation-building, since cultural participation cannot take place without an element of commitment to the community (however antagonistic or contradictory to the dominant political culture) that makes such creation and participation possible.

Initiatives by the PAP Government to correct the perceptions of over-dominance and to deliver on its promise of a more consensual style of politics have also been felt in the areas of building civil society — a gradual easing of the grip in the economic and financial sectors, and, most importantly, incremental but significant steps to allow for, and encourage, greater participation and autonomy in the areas of culture and the arts.

The promotion of culture and the arts has thus taken on a renewed importance in terms of changes in the culture industry's infrastructure reflecting a qualified liberalization, if not a re-interpretation, of the rules governing censorship in the arts,[68] which were a frequent complaint a decade ago.[69] While these changes may not in themselves be reflective of an obvious difference in the political sphere,[70] the subtle and subterranean raids that go on in the domain of popular culture may be seen to have a slow but incremental effect on the social fabric as a whole, and so the question of control and "acceptability" is only a function of time. Any change that takes place in the realm of the "popular" would have a multiplier effect overall.[71]

Yet it should be said that this emergent popular or public culture is not the same as a Singaporean national culture, for national culture itself is a contested mode — embattled, on the one hand, by transnational cultural messages and forces (which sometimes threaten the nation-state) and, on the other hand, by indigenous critiques from various sectors, which continuously threaten the cultural hegemony of the nation-state. National culture in countries like Singapore is the site of an uneasy collaboration between the cultural agencies of the nation-state and the private, largely commercial, agencies that dominate certain kinds of cultural production. Today, in Singapore, the control of cultural production is shared in a fragile and variable way between the state and private enterprise, depending on the kind of cultural product that is involved.

Public culture in Singapore in the late twentieth century is thus a contested terrain, and perhaps this would be true even of the early twenty-first century. The actors and interests in the contest are a variety of producers of culture and their audiences; the materials in the contest are the many cultural modalities — sport, television, cinema, travel, radio, and the arts; and the methods, increasingly shared by all parties, involve the mass media and related mechanical modes of reproduction. What is at stake in the contest, of course, is no less than the consciousness of the emergent Singaporean public. The messages of public culture are, therefore, directed to audiences, without regard to the limits of family, locality or social category. This does not mean that the new images are directed to a homogeneous and universal Singaporean, but that they are designed to appeal to a consciously diverse audience. The irony here, of course, is the content of the ethnic programmes scripted and aired over television, which tend to reflect values and styles of life that are inimical to the "officially received" view. For instance, it is not uncommon to find Chinese serials or dramas depicting both father and son "hanging out" at nightclubs or lounges with the father's "mistress" present, or else the hostesses who entertain them. Moreover, instances of young women drinking alcohol and pubbing in these programmes are a ready sight. In the Tamil dramas, for instance, one can easily discern the anti-modern values depicted: the central place of patriarchy and the importance of preserving the family, even in abusive relationships. One response to these criticisms may be that the content depicts a realist sense; others may say that they should all espouse values consistent with modernity. To be fair, there is a good deal of content that is moralistic as well, but that is also another instance of the contradictions of a society in a vortex of influences.

The embattled arena of public culture has behind it particular social, political, and economic forces and interests. Of these, the hardest to pin down is the burgeoning middle class which, as always, is vigorously pursued by market research firms employed by entrepreneurial interests. In addition to the middle class, another key interest group in the shaping of public culture is the variety of entrepreneurs and commercial institutions that constitute what have been referred to elsewhere as the "culture industries". Included here would be all those who have floated new magazines; the entire entertainment industry, with all its technical adjuncts; the tourist industry; and, cutting across all of these, the burgeoning advertising industry.

The media boom in contemporary Singapore is part of a worldwide explosion whose cultural contours are barely understood. Critical to this boom are the older cinematic and print forms and the newer electronic and digital recording technologies. In the case of print media, the most notable recent development is the enormous increase in the number of electronic news stations. This boom creates and feeds an extraordinary hunger for a variety of information, opinion, and news directed towards the interests of different audiences. Competition in this business is intense. The central thrust of these news stations appears to be the bringing together of gossip, politics, cinema, sport, and investigative journalism within the same purview — not aimed directly at Singapore politics, yet adventurous enough in pursuing some social issues and policies. At the same time, there is a multiplication of specialized magazines directed at particular tastes, interests, and fashions. It is in and through the pages of these magazines that Singaporeans of various social categories are learning where and how they can gain access to knowledge of the emergent lifestyles.

Equally important, print and electronic media both support and extend the empire of advertising. As in other parts of the world, advertising links media to changes in the market place and acts as a crucial vehicle for shaping public taste in general and traditional cultural forms in particular.

For an example of how social change occurs and what becomes acceptable generally, consider the Anchor beer advertisement shown in Singapore cinemas over the last decade. In earlier days, the woman in the advertisement merely sits next to the man who is holding the beer; but, a few years later she is pouring the beer into the glass for him. In the following year, she is seen holding the glass herself, and, finally, in the last two years, actually drinking the alcoholic beverage. These subtle guerrilla raids on the dominant values may be a useful analogy to explain the way in which social change occurs, and instances where what might otherwise be censored is not. There are also examples from theatrical plays staged with great success, which carry themes of transvestitism, homosexuality, and single-parenthood — plays which tend to be critical of the "moral majority". More recently, there have been books written by citizens critical of the Establishment — its political values and social culture — but who did not receive any censure or a rap on the proverbial knuckles. These include the opposition party member and former university lecturer, Chee Soon Juan, and political researcher and ex-student activist, James Gomez, both of whom have written and published books sold in Singapore.

Despite opinions that government strictures are still very real in curtailing freedom of artistic and political expression, this argument is perhaps best seen as part of the larger question of the gradual evolution of social and political freedoms within Singapore. To be sure, the state plays a key role in making and sustaining public culture. The state is an active competitor in the market place of cultural images and productions — for example, in important aspects of the travel industry, in the radio entertainment industry, and, most of all, in its growing organization of cultural centres, spectacles, and publications. The state is also a crucial gatekeeper and referee in the contest of private cultural entrepreneurs, through its powers of licensing and censorship, and through its control of various regulations involving public morality and order, although these have been less high-handed in recent years.

These examples of initiatives in the social, cultural, and artistic spheres are but some instances of the fundamental change occurring in the landscape of Singapore, and the attendant and incremental changes in the mindscape of Singaporeans. But these changes are not apparent immediately because of the deep nature of the social, economic, and structural changes that would be required. The implementation of a new vision, accompanied by shifts in policy direction, cannot occur before its time. Social and cultural changes follow a diachronic pattern of dialectical exchange, and the results are not always predictable.

Conclusion

This chapter has suggested that the concept of "modernity" evokes an incoherent cluster of significances occasioned by and reflected in the actual disarray of modern Anglo-European culture and, thus, that there appears to be no viable context of modern cultural values to export to non-Western countries along with the concrete elements of modernizing programmes and projects. On reflection, this situation turns out to be beneficial to Singapore, since the values underlying the critique of modernity resonate more profoundly with the dominant cultural interests of Singaporeans than with the interests and values of the modern West.

The various initiatives towards liberalizing control and direction in the economy, the encouragement of individual initiative in business, education, the arts, and culture — juxtaposed with the bilingual language policy, the Desired Outcomes of Education manifesto, national education, and national service — compels the notion that traditional forms would not be eradicated completely, but would instead combine with other modalities, thus providing new hybridized idioms for the evolving political, social, and cultural tapestry, which would be, collectively, the ongoing response of Singapore to the challenge of modernity.

Notes

1. Regarding globalization, see Mike Featherstone, ed., *Global Culture: Nationalism, Globalization and Modernity; A Theory, Culture and Society Special Issue* (London: Sage Publications Ltd, 1990); Roland Robertson, *Globalization: Social Theory and Global Culture* (London: Sage Publications Ltd, 1992); Martin J. Gannon, *Understanding Global Cultures: Metaphorical Journeys Through 17 Countries* (Newbury Park: Sage Publications Inc., 1994).
2. As Lucian W. Pye wrote, in a display of rare candour: The process of modernization "might also be called Westernization, or simply advancement and progress; it might, however, be more accurately termed the diffusion of a world culture — a world culture based on advanced technology and the spirit of science, on a rational view of life, a secular approach to social relations .... At an ever-accelerating rate, the direction and the volume of cross-cultural influence has become nearly a uniform pattern of the Western industrial world imposing its practices, standards, techniques, and values upon the non-Western world". See his *Aspects of Political Development* (Boston: Little Brown, 1966), pp. 8–9, 44–45.

3. Compare Mark Juergensmeyer, *The New Cold War? Religious Nationalism Confronts the Secular State* (Berkeley: University of California Press, 1993); and Frank Wilmer, *The Indigenous Voice in World Politics: Since Time Immemorial* (Newbury Park: Sage Publications Inc., 1993).
4. Gianni Vattimo, *The Transparent Society* (Baltimore: Johns Hopkins Press, 1992).
5. J. Tomlinson, *Cultural Imperialism* (Baltimore: Johns Hopkins Press, 1991).
6. We cannot digress here to debate the relative truth of each of these claims; nevertheless, it can at least be said that, while there is some truth in each of them, the whole truth is more complex.
7. See Howard Melzer, *History and the Idea of Progress* (Harvard: Harvard University Press, 1996).
8. J. L. Mehta, *Philosophy and Religion: Essays in Interpretation* (New Delhi: Indian Council of Philosophical Research, 1990), p. 229.
9. The continuity of culture is generally related to traditions which, in turn, are made up of cultural forms. Tradition is often defined as the handing down of knowledge or the passing on of a doctrine or a technique. What is crucial here is to ask what goes into the making of a tradition as well as that which is interpreted by historians as tradition. We often assume that a form is handed down in an unchanging fashion and that what comes to us is in its pristine form. However, the sheer act of handing on a tradition introduces change, and not every tradition is meticulously bonded by mnemonic or other devices to prevent interpolations or change. A tradition, therefore, has to be seen in its various phases.
10. Edward Said, *Orientalism* (London: Routledge, 1979); Bryan S. Turner, *Marx and the End of Orientalism* (London: George Allen and Unwin, 1978).
11. Kishore Mahbubani, *Can Asians Think?* (Singapore: Times, 1998). See, also, the interesting interview with Mahbubani at the Eighth International Conference on Thinking, "Asian thinking doesn't need Western help", in *Edmonton Journal*, 8 July 1999.
12. For a brief historical background in establishing the multi-racial policy, see "Shaping Singapore: Building a multi-racial polity in the Republic", *Sunday Times*, 11 July 1999, pp. 32–33, based on the book, *Lee's Lieutenants*, edited by Kevin Tan and Lam Peng Er (London: Allen and Unwin, 1998).
13. A. Touraine, *The Voice and the Eye* (Cambridge: Cambridge University Press, 1981); Daniel Bell, *The Coming of Post-Industrial Society* (New York: Basic Books, 1973).
14. Jean F. Lyotard, *The Postmodern Condition: A Report on Knowledge* (Minneapolis: University of Minnesota Press, 1984).
15. Vattimo, *The Transparent Society*.
16. See Chew and Chew, *op. cit.*, p. 17, 1992.
17. A suggestion recently by Brigadier-General Lee Hsien Loong to civil servants to co-opt ideas from all levels, could be seen as part of this spirit of Singapore 21.
18. L. Morriss, "Globalization, Migration and the Nation-State", *British Journal of Sociology* 48, No.2 (1997): 192–209.
19. Featherstone, ed., *Global Culture*.

20. This sense of globalism has encountered its contest as regards the issue of human rights, which many in the non-Western nations do not accept, though often for arguments that are less than logically or philosophically compelling. See, for instance, the argument in, "Where are the arguments for Asian values?", a review of the book by Joanne R. Bauer and Daniel Bell, *The East Asian Challenge for Human Rights* (Cambridge: Cambridge University Press, 1999), where the writer conflates the question of cultural relativism with ethical relativism, and dissipates the grave issues on the grounds of incommensurability.
21. Immanuel Wallerstein, *The Modern World System II: Mercantilism and the Consolidation of the World Economy 1650-1750* (New York: Academic Press, 1980); "Culture as the Ideological Background of the Modern World System", in Featherstone, ed., *Global Culture* pp.31–56. See also Marshall McLuhan, *Understanding Media* (London: Routledge, 1975).
22. Aziz Al-Azmeh, "The Discourse of Cultural Authencity: Islamist Revivalism and Enlightenment Universalism", in *East-West Philosophic Perspectives* (Hawaii: University of Hawaii Press, 1991).
23. A. Ahmed, *Postmodernism and Islam* (London: Routledge, 1992).
24. See Stephen Toulmin, *Cosmopolis: The Hidden Agenda of Modernity* (New York: Free Press, 1990).
25. Anthony Giddens, *Modernity and Self-Identity: Self and Society in late Modern Age* (Cambridge: Polity, 1991).
26. As the term is used here, reflexivity, has two senses, one very general and the other more directly relevant to modern social life. All human beings are reflective in the sense that thinking about what one does is part of doing it, whether consciously or on the level of practical consciousness. Social reflexivity refers to a world increasingly constituted by information rather than pre-given modes of conduct. It is how we live after the retreat of tradition and nature, because of having to take so many forward-oriented decisions. In that sense, we live in a much more reflexive way than previous generations have done.
27. C. Campbell, "Detraditionalisation, Character and the Limits of Agency", in *Detraditionalisation*, edited by P. Heelas, S. Lash, and P. Morris (Oxford: Blackwell, 1996).
28. Marshall Berman, *All That Is Solid Melts Into Air: The Experience of Modernity* (New York: Simon and Schuster, 1982).
29. L. Back, *New Ethnicities and Urban Culture* (London: UCL Press, 1996).
30. We live in a "risk culture", which is to be explained by the radicalizing and generalizing of modernity. Various changes are leading or forcing us to think more and more in terms of risk. One is the dwindling hold of tradition. The more social activities are structured by what has been done in the past, the more people tend to think in terms of fate. The more we take active decisions about future events, the more we think in terms of risk, whether we are aware of it or not. See, also, U. Beck, *Risk Society* (London: Sage, 1992).

31. The number of women in Parliament has seen a steady increase in the last five years, but this has also been felt in the higher echelons of the administrative service where, in the last year, the first woman deputy secretary of a ministry was appointed. This is to be considered a milestone in Singapore's civil service, no doubt also as the result of the sterling performance of women such as Professor Chan Heng Chee, appointed as the republic's first woman ambassador several years ago.
32. See the interview in July 1999 with *Time* magazine. This was also the subject of an interview that he gave with *Business Week* in April 1999.
33. This percentage promises to increase exponentially with the offer by one Internet service provider to allow free access to the Web in Singapore. See *Straits Times*, 4 December 1999.
34. *Straits Times*, 21 August 1999.
35. *Speeches*, 6 August 1994.
36. *Straits Times*, 27 July 1994. The Minister's remarks bring to the fore the tension inherent in the need to have a sense of tradition and culture and, yet, to realize the distinctness of being Singaporean, as opposed to being Chinese or Indian or Malay, in which case the loyalty would then be to the motherland. See, also, Brigadier-General Yeo's comments on the Suzhou problem as well as Chinatown in *Straits Times*, 20 June 1999, p. 24.
37. *Singapore Parliamentary Reports*, 5 June 1997: 401.
38. See "Increasing the Talent Pool: Attracting Foreign Professionals to Singapore", a talk by Ho Peng Kee, the Minister of State for Home Affairs, reproduced in *Commentary*, 1997. See, also, J. Friedman, "Global Crises, the Struggle for Cultural Identity and Intellectual Porkbarrelling: Cosmopolitans versus Locals, Ethnics and Nationals in an Era of De-Hegemonisation", in *Debating Cultural Hybridity*, edited by P. Werbner and T. Modood (London: Pluto, 1997), pp. 70–90. See, also, U. Hannerz, *Cultural Complexity: Studies in the Social Organisation of Meaning* (New York: Columbia University Press, 1992).
39. See, also, Senior Minister Lee Kuan Yew's remarks in "Foreign talent key to Singapore's future", *Straits Times*, 15 August 1999. See, also, Joel Kotkin, *Tribes: How Race, Religion and Identity Determine Success in the New Global Economy* (New York: Random House, 1992).
40. See U. Hannerz, "The Creation of World Cities", in *Humanising the City?*, edited by Anthony P. Cohen and K. Fukui (Edinburgh: Edinburgh University Press, 1993).
41. Quoted in *Destination Singapore: The Arts Experience*, undated industry document jointly published by the Singapore Tourism Board and the Ministry of Information and the Arts.
42. See "Co-opt people, ideas at all levels, urges BG Lee", *Straits Times*, 30 March, 1998.
43. See the chapter by Linda Low published in this volume.

44. See R. Robertson, "Globalisation: Time-Space and Homogeneity-Heterogeneity", in *Global Modernities*, edited by M. Featherstone, S. Lash, and R. Robertson (London: Sage, 1995).
45. *Straits Times*, 10 August 1999.
46. *Straits Times*, 3 December 1999.This is not to draw any particular attention to the lack thereof in the Malay-Muslim community; it is often a reminder that the needs of that community are sometimes more pressing, given that, among the other ethnic groups, the Malay community was perhaps slow to enter mainstream English-language schools. It should also be said that, while religion is no barrier to modernization, there may often be some scepticism among adherents of a faith about the desirability or validity of the values espoused by technological rationality, or, given the close kinship between westernization and modernization, they may be wary of the latter because of the former. Hence, there needs to be sufficient effort to dispel the notion that the two are synonymous; here, that powerful agent of socialization, the school, should be called into task. But in the presence of Muslim schools, this becomes a tricky task. This is particularly interesting because, while multiculturalism is officially enshrined, there remains the tension between what is seen as being the desiderata at the national level, and what is beneficial to particular indigenous communities. For other problems relating to this community at the educational level, see Jason Tan's analysis in this volume.
47. See how this question of the conflicts between loyalties to one's ethnic group or culture as a result of language policies (that could easily degenerate to a parochialism) is handled in "Views from the periphery" by Quah Sy Ren, *Straits Times*, 3 July 1999, p. 39. The writer's concerns here is with the Chinese language and the emergence of a Chinese élite, and how this squares with the idea of modernity.
48. *Straits Times*, 18 May 1997.
49. See Shirley Yee, "Material Interests and Morality in the Trade of Thai Talismans", *Southeast Asian Journal of Social Science* 24, No. 2, 1996.
50. See *Straits Times* forum page, 21 August 1999, "Why foreign talent for games" and "Beware of diluting sense of ethnic pride". See, also, the very interesting comment earlier on 18 July 1999 where the *Straits Times* commented that "Singaporeans have yet to come to terms with foreign talent, judging from the debate at a feedback meeting", in "Foreign talent still hot topic", p. 30.
51. See the speech by Ho Peng Kee, in *Commentary*, 1997.
52. "Cultivating Citizenship and Cultural Identity", in *Singapore: Re-Engineering Success*, edited by Arun Mahizhnan and Lee Tsao Yuan (Singapore: Institute of Policy Studies and Oxford University Press, 1998). See, also, "Singapore in the International Economy: Going Global, Staying Singaporean" by Tan Kong Yam, in the same volume.
53. See Ernest Gellner, *Nations and Nationalism* (London: Allen and Unwin, 1964).

54. I do not mean to offer this as an oblique argument for "foreign professionals", but it is worthwhile to note that for a foreigner (if he is from the developed Western nations) to become a citizen of Singapore would sometimes mean considerable long-term sacrifices, when just having permanent residency status would suffice for most purposes. It is thus not an easy task to attract and keep such highly mobile individuals for more than their work contracts or their working life.
55. See Maurice Roche, *Rethinking Citizenship: Welfare, Ideology and Change in Modern Society* (Cambridge: Polity Press, 1992, p. 244).
56. See Benjamin R. Barber, *Jihad vs McWorld: How Globalism and Tribalism are Reshaping the World* (New York: Ballantine Books, 1995).
57. See Jean Baudrillard, "Modernity", *Canadian Journal of Political and Social Theory* 11, No. 3 (1987): 63–72.
58. See R. Scruton, *Notes on the Idea of Culture* (Oxford: Oxford University Press, 1997).
59. See, also, the speeches by Minister George Yeo, "Managing Singapore's Cultural Diversity", 15 January 1994; and "The Paradox of Multi-Racialism", 1 March 1997.
60. A less culpable view (though interesting in that it constitutes a search for an alternative way of looking at things), is to be found in Philip Jeyaratnam's, "What sort of culture should Singapore have?", in *Debating Singapore: Reflective Essays*, edited by Derek da Cunha (Singapore: Institute of Southeast Asian Studies, 1994).
61. For an elaboration, see Geoffrey Benjamin's, "The Cultural Logic of Singapore's Multiculturalism', in *Singapore: Society in Transition*, edited by Riaz Hassan (Kuala Lumpur, 1976).
62. Sometimes it finds its way into the speeches of those who push for the organic view. See Minister George Yeo's speech to the students of Hwa Chong Junior College on 6 August 1994.
63. For example, see Minister George Yeo, "A Total Culture is Needed to Stay Ahead", *Straits Times*, 18 September 1993. He had also argued previously about how it is "not possible to graft 'pieces' of culture from the outside onto Singapore culture, like it was a thing".
64. The term here is used loosely to refer to government and pro-government agencies, including the media, whose work has a bearing on culture. It is not to be conflated with the Frankfurt School's use of the term.
65. See Stella Kon's "The Arts and the Market", in *Debating Singapore*, edited by da Cunha; *cf.* Sanjay Krishnan's "The West, popular culture, and Singapore", in the same volume.
66. Such a view of culture is to be found scattered in the works of several German philosophers, including Herder, Vico, Wittgenstein, Gadamer and others. See, also, Philip Bagby, *Culture and History* (Los Angeles, 1959); F. M. Barnard, "Culture and Political Development", *American Political Science Review* 63 (1969): 379–97, and Raymond Williams, *Culture and Society*: 1780-1950 (London: Penguin Books, 1958).
67. See John Clammer, *Singapore: Ideology, Society and Culture* (Singapore: Chopmen Publishers, 1985); and "National Ideology and the Question of Race: Reflections

on the dynamics of Ethnicity in contemporary Singapore", in *Thinking About Democracy*, edited by Cedric Pan (Singapore: NUS Political Association, 1989).

68. In many ways, the formation of the National Arts Council may be said to be a gradual departure from centralized control by the Government.
69. From this perspective, it is easier to understand the nature of a view such as Gopal Baratham's "Censorship and Me", reproduced in *Commentary* 10 (December 1992).
70. For instance, performing arts groups still need a licence for public performances, and this is granted by the Ministry of Home Affairs; and the Ministry of Information and the Arts still has jurisdiction over the distribution of books and movies.
71. In the past fifteen years, the term "popular culture" has undergone a complicated set of shifts, expansions, critiques that start with the straightforward use of the term among European social historians to refer to the history of the inarticulate. There is now much greater self-consciousness about the politics of the term "popular culture". The study of the popular by historians is now linked to the problematics of the public sphere, of community politics, of class, and of conflict. Particularly among historians of culture, there is growing awareness of the political trajectory that unites subaltern consciousness, the transformation of leisure and work, communitarian politics, and the dynamics of decolonization.

9

NATIONAL IDENTITY, THE ARTS, AND THE GLOBAL CITY

C.J.W.-L. Wee

Introduction

The 19 July 1999 issue of *Time* magazine had this blurb on its cover: "Singapore Swings: Can Asia's Nanny State Give Up its Authoritarian Ways?". The magazine said, "Culturally, Singapore is permitting artists to stage a range of socially and politically controversial performances".[1] The major moment of change, it argued, came with the 1990 naming of Goh Chok Tong as the politician who would replace Lee Kuan Yew as Prime Minister, and this led to a formulation of cultural policy by the People's Action Party (PAP) Government. The National Arts Council was set up in 1991 and the Ministry of Information and the Arts created. This ministry had — as *Time* put it, in its inimically over-wrought literary style — "PAP intellectual-in-waiting [George] Yeo in charge". It said: "The new minister enthused about fostering a global renaissance city, about making Singaporeans more creative, about forging a civic society — the buzzwords flew like hornets among government departments."[2]

While it may be argued that *Time* exaggerates the extent to which the Singapore state has changed in its attitude towards high culture and its relation to civil society at large — articulated as "civic society" by Minister Yeo[3] — there is no doubt that, first, there has been a burst of high cultural energy since the 1980s and that, second, the state now has a discernible cultural policy in place — a key feature of which is a desire for Singapore to become a

"Global City for the Arts" — in sharp contrast to the utilitarian and instrumental-rationalist 1960s and 1970s.

This chapter examines some of the developments that have occurred in the arts since the 1980s, along with the rapid attempts by the state to exploit the commercial potential of such developments, and considers how the arts have to a fair degree been concerned with issues of identity, multiculturalism, cultural heritage, and history as a reaction to the Singapore state's top-down approach to economic orientation, along with an intensive modernization of society that allowed little space for cultural issues. Understanding how and why the arts have focused on such thematics will provide a better grasp of the distance that still needs to be traversed before the arts can flourish and be an effective part of the symbolic life of the city-state, a realm that should not be wholly commercialized. Consequently, the chapter will also look at some of the considerations put forth by the Government for a "Global City for the Arts" and examine whether the wish to maximize immediately the potential of the arts is conducive or detrimental to the autonomy necessary for local arts development.[4]

As it is impossible to examine arts development *in toto*, even for a small city-state, the chapter will concentrate on Singapore theatre — especially English-language theatre — which has been one of the most dynamic areas of cultural ferment since the 1980s. It will also consider related developments outside and reflect upon the potential progress and nurture of this cultural arena.

English-Language Theatre and the Cultural Identity Question

In 1986, Singapore Cultural Medallion winner Max Le Blond wrote that there was a need to address the "urgent business ... [of] the creation of a truly Singaporean theatre, a theatre by Singaporeans, about Singaporeans, for Singaporeans". His experience directing Robert Yeo's play, *One Year Back Home*, in 1980 — where the actors struggled with local versus "proper" accents, including the artificialities of the "lahs" and the "mans" interspersed in the dialogue — indicated to Le Blond that "we are not yet at home on stage; at home, that is to say, with ourselves as Singaporeans".[5]

A Singaporean theatre had developed far enough that the "Septfest '98" conference at the Substation arts centre was entitled "Looking Back at Singapore Theatre".[6] The conference afforded a chance to assess how much Singaporeans are now at home "with ourselves as Singaporeans", and to see how theatre developments form part of the ongoing debate over what Singapore's national identity should, might, or can be. This has been a persistent issue and difficulty since Singapore's independence in 1965. The intense pace of state-driven modernization, combined with Singapore's inherited multilingual plural society — created in a colonial context, and compounded by the history of the left-wing in the nation — set the historical framework for these cultural identity concerns.[7]

Kuo Pao Kun, one of Singapore's major theatre figures and a significant humanistic intellectual, gave the keynote address at the conference on 18 September 1998. Among other things, he spoke of how the "fragmented history of Singapore theatre talks to us of Singapore itself". The ethnic groups that came to colonial Singapore did not conceive of themselves having a "Singaporean" identity until quite recently. How could they, when they were still overseas Indians or Chinese?

Having said this, Kuo — proceeding from his assumption that Singaporeans have a fractured collective memory — recalled that Chinese theatre played a part in the rising political consciousness which led towards independence. In the turbulent post-war years of the anti-colonial struggle, cultural vigour manifested itself in the modern Chinese-language theatre that drew inspiration from China's May 4th Movement, which had tried to rework China's culture as part of the modern world. There was also a dynamic mass base to this theatre, a fact which may surprise those who think that theatre is a middle-class institution. The historical dynamism of Singapore's Chinese world was noted in Mr Lee Kuan Yew's commentary in *The Battle for Merger*, broadcast over Radio Singapore in 1961: "[T]he Chinese-educated world [was] a world teeming with vitality, dynamism and revolution ... in which the Communists had been working ... with considerable success."[8]

By the 1980s, however, following the state's crackdown on Chinese theatre in the mid-1970s, and aided by the emphasis on English as the major medium of school instruction, English-language theatre began its rapid ascent. Kuo remarked that people in Chinese theatre felt there was a "kind of arrogance" in the claim that English could be the language of a national theatre. However, the declining number of well-educated Chinese high schoolers and the political shadow of communism (which gave an unfortunate taint to Chinese life), meant that any renewal of Chinese theatre would be difficult.

The "arrogance" imputed to English-language theatre arose partly from the legacy of the English language in ethnically diverse Singapore. English, as the English-educated politicians have argued, was not a "communal" but a neutral language which could help foster a unity based on pragmatic economic considerations. Despite the less pragmatic orientation of cultural practitioners, English-language theatre had absorbed aspects of this thinking in investigating the "Who are Singaporeans?" question.[9]

The situation, however, is certainly not as simple as that. One must recall Kuo's own multilingual *Mama Looking for Her Cat* (1988), which was restaged in 1998 by the bilingual Toy Factory Ensemble as part of a growing local repertoire of works deemed worthy of restaging. This play helped redefine the contours of single-language theatre. It was a study of who "we" are, cast in terms of a broader humanity instead of the racial terms carried in the official and currently predominant "Chinese, Malay, Indian, Other" (CMIO) categorizations of identity. *Mama* was a significant event, given what many acknowledge as theatre's general historical tendency to be a monolingual and monocultural enterprise. The 1980s, Kuo contended, saw the rise of a Singaporean theatre which "recognizes the local conditions".

Later sessions recalled the experiences of Malay, Tamil, English, and Chinese theatre in Singapore. Regarding Chinese-language theatre, Tan Beng Lan of the Practice Performing Arts School argued that, historically, the school was the first to "localize" its plays. In the 1930s, leftist theatre wanted to unite people by turning out plays which tried to reflect people's Malayan lifestyle. In the 1970s, she said, this engagement with the local led to an attempt to depict the realities of labour displacement brought on by rapid industrialization.

Tan's larger emphasis, however, was not to elevate the social progressiveness of Chinese theatre over other theatre groups, but to try to discern and recognize what had been the *common* concerns among theatres in the different languages (including English) and to see the overall process of the localization — and, thus, Singaporeanization — of drama. Tan's presentation was important for recognizing what constituted overlapping and, thus, "common" elements among these groups, for such an understanding has ramifications for our present investigation of common identity.

The final session was on "Singapore Theatre Today", which featured, among others, TheatreWork's Ong Keng Sen and The Necessary Stage's Alvin Tan, two Singaporean theatre practitioners. Both Ong and Tan embody the present cultural probing of the "who are we" question, but do so in different ways by indicating divergent, if linked, theatre ideals. Ong said that TheatreWorks began in 1985 to attempt "Singaporean theatre". His question now is: "Who is the Singaporean in relation to the *rest of the world*?" That is, national identity issues need not be the primary targets of artistic investigation. Instead, what Ong called "inter-culturalism" represents his new way. Ong's Asian *Lear* project was thus situated at the cultural border — juxtaposing six Asian performers from different ethnic backgrounds — but, in consequence, no one in Singapore wanted to "own" it. Instead, the Japan Foundation's Asia Center had to support the production financially. It premiered in Tokyo in 1997, finally appearing in

Singapore only in January 1999. *Lear*, Ong argued, is still Singaporean because *he* [Ong] is Singaporean. By this he meant that, as a Singaporean, he is familiar with cultural juxtapositions, this being the daily reality in Singapore. More than merely juxtaposing Asian performances, however, he said he also wants to renegotiate the very terrain of multiculturalism, as Singaporeans understand it.

Towards the end of 1998, TheatreWorks hosted their second "Flying Circus Project", an ambitious research and performance programme which brought together fifty Asian artists in theatre, dance, and music, in workshops and classes that encouraged creative strategies, in order to regenerate traditional arts in contemporary performances. Ong wants Asian artists to be able to "enter" other Asian cultures and develop a vision for a wider Asian (and not just Singaporean) arts. Ong feels that the national framework of local theatre is currently inadequate and perhaps even parochial. If the Singaporean state and Singaporean theatre-goers are too cautious in envisioning what a society could be (responding only to that which is directly Singaporean), then Singapore will not become the "Global City for the Arts" that the Government desires.

In contrast to Ong, Alvin Tan sees his work as being *intra-* and not *inter-*cultural. Thus, Tan wishes to remain within Singapore's multi-ethnic context and to ask the "who are we" question as it has been evolving. The different contemporary forms of hybrid "Singlish" found here — for example, Indian Singlish and Malay Singlish — constitute a rich linguistic source he draws on to show that our uses of English do not indicate the lack of a distinctive Singaporean-Asian identity.

What we can see, even from the limited discussion thus far, is that theatre development from the 1980s is conscious of and engages with the plethora of issues that define Singapore as a nation. Many of these issues remain sensitive: inter-ethnic relations, communism's supposed links with sections of Chinese life, the social problems as well as the benefits of Singapore's rapid economic growth, and Singapore's relationship to the rest of the world, in terms of the world as both its economic hinterland and its export market.

These issues have historical origins, and "History" — with all the sensitive spots — has emerged as a key area in Singapore theatre's confrontation with the "Who we are" question. Many theatre productions have tried to "remember", even if many of the physical historical markers of Singapore's cityscape no longer exist.[10]

For example, the Toy Factory Theatre Ensemble's multilingual *Titoudao* (1994) recalls a now-fading *wayang* culture, and TheatreWork's production of Leow Puay Tin's *The Yang Family* (1996) offers a fictional multi-generational perspective of a Chinese family in Chinatown. These are artistic attempts to allow the disparate voices from Singapore's fractured past to speak, at a point in Singapore's national development when it seems far enough removed from sensitive events — such as the 1964 racial riots and the separation from Malaysia — to be able to reflect publicly upon them. This ability has been evident in the Government's ongoing formulation on the direction of the National Education programme.[11]

Naturally, there has been disagreement as to what constitutes the key elements of Singapore's past — such dissonance in relation to official views is inevitable and occurs everywhere, and Singapore should not be considered an exception. Dissonance was evident in 1999 when the Singapore Heritage Society and members of the public showed their discomfort regarding the Singapore Tourism Board's proposals to "theme park" Chinatown's history. A passionate letter from an overseas reader of the *Straits Times* directly linked the Chinatown matter to the question of memory and identity.[12] Kelvin Wang wrote, "in connection with the continuing discussions on what makes Singapore 'home' and not just a hotel and the debate over turning Chinatown into a 'theme park' (it is already one, doesn't anyone realise that?), surely one important criterion must be the presence of collective memory, touch points for all Singaporeans?" He added that government agencies' plans for conservation "do not always reflect public feelings ... adequately".[13] The Substation's retrospective on theatre, along with the discussion of "where" theatre is now, indicates that theatre is integral to the debates on the sort of culture Singaporeans want.

Other areas in the arts reflect similar concerns with identity and memory in the context of rapid modernization and multiculturalism. One visual arts event often cited as a "break" in the local arts world was the collaborative "Trimurti" exhibition by S. Chandrasekaran, Goh Ee Choo, and Salleh Japar at the Goethe-Institut in 1988, the same year in which Kuo's multilingual and, thus, multicultural *Mama* was staged. Through installation sculpture, performances, and individual works that drew upon Hindu, Islamic, and Taoist elements, the artists attempted to show a larger universe that transcended their individual traditions. In their own words:

> It is true that each artist has his own culture and religious background. ... These are but very small parts manifested in the universe, each interrelated to the whole structure. Expressing this unity, each artist shows one aspect of this universal manifestation.[14]

Behind this general, almost mystical, pronouncement, lie artistic actions "challenging the [multiracial] streams structure, ... forging a rapprochement between streams"[15] which were worked out at a moment when the state itself, in the 1980s, became aware of the "sense of cultural void amidst the successful creation of an efficient yet 'decultured' working force". According to museum curator Ahmad Mashadi, the three artists' work fitted into an emerging political vision in which "the arts were seen as able to encourage appreciation and respect for the cultural and social values of the different races and, according to the report submitted by the [Government's] Committee of the Visual Arts, 'provide the gel for social integration of our nation and form the basis to build the spirit of the nation'".[16]

Ahmad's point is a contentious one, for it suggests that the artists' departure from official multiculturalism — with its current tendency to separate the ethnic groups into "hyphenated" identities (e.g., Chinese-Singaporean, etc.) that can be encouraged to function as cultural ballast for nation-building — is not as radical as it appears. Be that as it may, his argument indicates the deep connection between the arts and the ongoing formation and formulation of a national cultural identity that can withstand capitalist modernity's destabilizations, particularly the cultural dislocations that are of pertinent concern to Singaporeans.

While the Substation conference had a specific emphasis on Singapore identity, we have seen that Ong Keng Sen tried to expand the discussion. For his part, Kuo Pao Kun too has suggested that Singaporeans should start asking whether they can produce theatre that reaches beyond Singapore's shores, theatre that can address the general human condition. He recently argued that: "History has proved that there is no way [Singaporeans] could reconnect to their parent cultures *per se*. However, having lost their own — cut loose and therefore set free — they have thus become natural heirs to all the cultures of the world."[17] In certain respects, these arguments agree with the Government's plan for a global renaissance city.

Given that the Government wants Singapore to be a hub for science, information technology, and the arts, sociologist Kwok Kian Woon enunciated a cautionary note at the conference that this hub not be simply an empty space without "content", as it were, where things move through. This danger is not inevitable, as Singapore is a society rich in culture and history, if it can be recovered and preserved — presumably, it can then be a "specific" hub in which genuine intercultural transactions may transpire.

There is a general convergence between Kuo, Kwok, and Ong. As an artistic embodiment of the argument, Ong's work is at its best when he has a script with a strong historical consciousness, such as the English version of Kuo's

Descendants of the Eunuch Admiral (1995), which allowed Ong to evoke in a contemporary setting the relevance for us today of a cosmopolitan traveller like Cheng Ho, who ventured not only into Southeast Asia but also Africa. *Eunuch* draws its power from a definite historical dimension. This, then, may be the sort of "content" that Kwok speaks of. The attempt by these three cultural thinkers to move towards envisioning Singapore's diverse cultures within a global culture — towards what may be called a "rooted cosmopolitanism", abstract and contradictory as that sounds — may eventually help to encourage a rethinking of CMIO multiculturalism and, thus, of the Singaporean identity question itself. In this respect, both Ong and Kuo come close to what literary-cultural critic Bruce Robbins has spoken of as the need for a scaled-down and less-privileged version of cosmopolitanism, in which there is location and embodiment, as "a reality of (re)attachment, multiple attachment, or attachment at a distance".[18] What is harder to ascertain is how this works out in terms of access to and having possession of the Asian and Western high cultures that Singapore now only very inadequately possessed.[19]

One should not forget that the local dilemmas of Singaporean identity, while now more directly addressed by artists and the man-in-the-street alike, still require ongoing attention. Singapore needs a stronger and *critical* historical discourse so that Singaporeans can have a deeper understanding of history, as the past is the foundation of individual and collective identity. Given capitalism's amazing capacity to commodify, a rigorous approach will help pre-empt the potential danger of theatre either catering merely to nostalgic impulses or falling prey to easy notions of "global culture", as exemplified by the multicultural emptiness of Benetton advertisements. The arts can and should contribute towards a larger socio-cultural consciousness, but arts practitioners should be cautious in presenting indisputable "authentic" truths in their narratives. As has been seen, "authenticity" is the *very problem* that besets Singaporeans.

How Singaporeans see their own artistic development reaching outwards when it remains uncertain as to how it is anchored — in literary and artistic traditions of both once-migrant and indigenous cultures, and also in the Anglo-American West that resides in Singapore's midst — is an issue that still must be addressed. Do Singaporeans reach out because they cannot have their own mainstream — because Singapore is too small a place? Or is it that Singapore's geographical location as an island in the near centre of the Malay Archipelago causes Singaporeans to look outwards? These remain issues to be grappled with.

The late Cambridge Professor of Drama, Raymond Williams, wrote in the late 1950s that: "The making of a society is the finding of common meanings and directions, and its growth is an active debate and amendment under the pressures of experience, contact, and discovery, writing themselves into the land."[20] This point seems of special relevance to a city-state so much a part of the ebb and flow of global capitalism. In the present context of change and mutability, Singaporeans need to ensure that the local is culturally rooted, even as it seeks the global.

The Ongoing Development of the Arts

While the development of the arts in Singapore in the new millennium depends primarily on the artists themselves and on the artistic processes that are constantly evolving, the supporting environment set up by the state is also important. Within the ambit of what is called "globalization", cultural policy worldwide increasingly recognizes the economic importance of the creative arts such as film, video, new media, broadcasting, and so on. The PAP Government, too, has noticed these trends. Given the present changes, it is possible to see aesthetic values being replaced by the commercial values of the market place — but it is also possible to see the new media as offering an expansion of creative possibilities. For these possibilities to be realized, however, it is imperative that a fundamental point be recognized: *that the arts lie at the core of the cultural sector, and creativity as a process is at the core of the arts.*

While more funding is now available for the arts, and the Government makes major public proclamations on the subject (for example: "MITA [Ministry of Information and the Arts] will develop Singapore as a vibrant global city for information and the arts, while enhancing our Singaporean identity and multi-cultural heritage"[21]), there needs to be more of a marked shift in thinking from the entrenched disciplinary, economics-oriented and instrumental-rationalist approach towards socio-cultural development, if Singapore is to achieve deep and significant artistic movement.

It is notoriously hard to predict what will happen in the arts — or even, as we have seen from the previous section, to fully comprehend present developments. Genuine creativity is unpredictable; who could have predicted in the late 1980s what the Internet would become? A number of artists emphasize the importance of being open to the rest of the world, to be able to benefit from outside resources and, also, to speak to the global without jettisoning the national. But, the thing is that artistic and cultural development should not be *confined* to the national. The fact that much of Singapore's history has already been cut away by the state's intense modernizing efforts over the past decades only accentuates both the limitations and needs of the present cultural situation. One way of recasting the direction for development is to recognize the need for the local to be conjoined with the global, to have — as one buzzword has it — "glocality". The present commitment to a free-trade regime, reinforced by the IMF's bailout packages in Southeast Asia in the wake of the 1997 Asian economic crisis, *forcibly* ensures the ongoing importance of globalization to the city-state's — indeed, the region's — creative life.

In the end, however, the encouragement of cultural dynamism and of the artistic process itself is more important than opinions on how the arts "should" develop. The relevant factor simply may be: *more autonomy*.

Kuo Pao Kun has written forcefully on this topic, and his thoughts summarize the current impasse in arts developments. The 1990s, he says, has been good for the arts in Singapore — new artists and creative groups; more commercial galleries; more festivals; and, importantly, more young people "plunged into the arts profession". However, he notes:

> [O]ne crucial impeding factor remains: state domination. To date, the control system put in place by the state is almost comprehensive. Directly and indirectly, the state and its numerous agencies control the bulk of the public funding for the arts, all the major performing and exhibition venues and their year round schedule ... as well as the underpinning power to censor all public shows. ... As the country enters a new millennium with a resolution to become an international arts centre, not to mention its ambition to be part of the Asian Renaissance, this arts regime ... appears totally out of date. ... The apologists of this regime claim that this mighty machinery is primarily conducive to arts development. While it is true that such infrastructures can and do provide opportunities, state management has been generally suffocating in spirit and political in orientation because their allegiance requires them to be subservient to government politics. Instead, the arts, as a dimension functionally distinct from politics and economics, deserves its own autonomous space above institutional politics because original and creative expressions always shoot up from the ground and are inclined to evoke longer philosophic vision, larger intellectual perspectives and more radical aesthetics venturing beyond the status quo.[22]

Kuo also refers to the 1993 controversy over Performance Art and Forum Theatre, which are effectively banned because state agencies will not fund such art forms. How is it, he asks, that entire art forms can be "outlawed", since this risks "condemning all potential creations in that form before they were even attempted?" (p. 21).[23] The fundamental problem, he observes, may be that the Government is interested mainly in nurturing an arts market or industry rather than the arts *per se*. If this is true, he adds, then

> Singapore is short-changing itself. Controlled innovation programmes and managed innovative arts industries are useful additions to its economy.... But Singaporeans deserve the full flowering of the arts, as they deserve the full spectrum of creative thinking. Not to do so is to under-rate the people's intellectual and intuitive potentials, to deny them the opportunity to make primary contributions. Primary and Original — these are key concepts in the world of Art and Creativity (p. 22).

In fact, one might add, it may stanch the creativity necessary for the knowledge-based and cultural industries we want for our post-industrial economic future. (Later discussion will return to this point.) To reiterate a key point: it is important to recognize that the arts lie at the core of the cultural sector, and creativity as a process is at the core of the arts.

In many ways, what Kuo enunciates chimes with the findings of the Singapore 21 Committee, as published by the Government in *Singapore 21: Together, We Make the Difference*. In the chapter "Active Citizens: Making a Difference to Society", it was noted that a 1998 survey "found only 15 per cent of Singaporeans willing to contribute to their community". Three recurring themes helped explain this lack: first, no sense of ownership over the issues facing the citizenry; second, no sense of respect accorded to the citizenry; and third, no trust in the citizenry: Singaporeans "feel that trust on a level that can enable the Government to explain issues freely to the people, and the people to respond freely with their views, has yet to be reached".[24] The artistic sections of Singapore's national community, thus, constitute a representative sociological sample of opinion. In terms of an emerging and active civil society — the "people sector", as Education Minister Teo Chee Hean prefers to call it[25] — it can be said that artists are willing to make their citizenship count through their participation in making (in Kuo's phrase) "primary contributions" to their society.

The solution advanced by *Singapore* 21 is "active citizenship", an idea "as old as the idea of democracy itself" (p. 51). The document states: "We will benefit from greater responsiveness, more consultation and a wider range of views and ideas. The crux is how to do so without losing the efficiency, decisiveness and collective [meaning, more accurately, government] action that has enabled Singaporeans to thrive" (p. 50). Therein, perhaps, lies the rub — and it is as one might expect. It returns us to Kuo's observation that, while the arts (in Singapore at least) represent a realm "functionally distinct from politics and economics", they *will*, nevertheless, evoke "perspectives ... venturing beyond the status quo".

J. M. Nathan has written of the future of the arts in Singapore that burgeoning artistic works and processes will lead to

> a deeper appreciation of cultural traditions and values.... This alone goes a long way as an effort towards nation-building, since cultural participation cannot take place without an element of commitment, *however antagonistic or contradictory to the dominant political culture*, to the community that makes such creation and participation possible [emphasis mine].[26]

That is to say, you cannot make an omelette without breaking eggs — it is just not possible. For the arts to not be — as Nathan puts it — on the "fringe" of society, changes in Singaporean life must continue and a greater level of autonomy accorded to the arts. Apart from enhancing the sense of place and belonging, a greater "legitimation of the arts industry" — recognized by the state "at first, ironically, for its subversive and economic potential" — also may have "the effect of deepening democracy because of the plurality of competing visions for social change that might result".[27]

Nathan's argument is in line with the *Singapore* 21 view that "active citizenship" is an idea "as old as the idea of democracy itself" and should be encouraged in the world of the arts. In the long term, it would be best *not* to see more "active citizenship" — and the role played in it by the arts and artists — as the loss of efficiency, decisiveness, and strong government action, but as the *means* by which the city-state will be able both to survive and to thrive in an era of globalization.

The Global City for the Arts

As mentioned earlier, many of those involved in formulating cultural policy around the world have become increasingly aware of the economic potential of cultural industries. The same realization has also emerged among some key leaders within the Singapore Establishment. The danger, however, of substituting aesthetic and cultural values with commercial values subject to the market place is real, especially so in a society in which these values are still very little understood. That said, globalization and the ever-increasing reach of capitalism into arts markets do offer arts practitioners expanded creative possibilities. The stimuli of new modes of communication and aesthetic discourses can be invaluable. Policy-makers can also take the opportunity to reflect upon, and gain a larger perspective of, the role of culture in the economy.

At the same time, one needs to be more conscious of the limitations which beset cultural production. We have seen that present state policy holds up the arts as a realm that can provide cultural ballast to the nation. This, indeed, is a sea change in official thinking since the 1970s. The arts now have a place within official nationalism, as one way of anchoring national identity while the state voluntarily subjects its people to further globalization. The high speed by which the arts have been incorporated into and made visible through an official notion of the "national", and included in the ongoing discourse of developmentalism (compared to the arts' general absence in the 1970s), is indicative of the tremendous flexibility of Singapore's idea of the "pragmatic".[28]

However, the changes may not spur the arts on as effectively as they might, for — apart from the politically related reasons already discussed — Singaporeans' general mindset is still too mired in older forms of instrumental-rationalist thinking. The effects of Singapore's history of national identity formation via intensive economic development are still very much present,[29] and this must be addressed in a more thoroughgoing way before more trenchant forms of cultural policy thinking and implementation can result.

To begin with, one can look at the Economic Development Board (EDB, the national body that has contributed so much to the city-state's capitalist industrial success) and MITA's document, *Singapore — Global City for the Arts*, published in 1992, as a representative instance of pragmatism's limitations. The document announced the impending arrival of a number of distinct national cultural institutions — mainly to potential overseas investors — such as the Singapore Art Museum, the Asian Civilizations Museum, and the Singapore History Museum. They are to function in a heritage district: "[The Museum Precinct's] importance is underscored by its site in the heart of the Civic District, an area rich in history. Five museums will be housed in this precinct, linked by commercial complexes and surface and underground passages."[30] The creation of such institutions may result in a cultural scope that could encompass the region as well: "It is our hope that Singapore will be a centre of culture in East Asia" (p. 3). This hope sounds grandiose, though commendable.[31]

It is when one looks carefully at the "Overview", however, that a number of concerns can be raised. The opening paragraph states that "Singapore, who draws her energies from the dynamics of her multicultural population, is plugged into the network of cultural capitals. She aims to be a global city for the arts by 1999" (p. 3). Apart from the fact that 1999 has passed, the text erroneously suggests that "high culture" can be managed and produced from a complex "multicultural population", in the same way as can a printed circuit board, and according to a timetable. What sort of *qualitative* performance indicators would one use, in any case, to measure the arrival of Singapore as the New York City or London of Southeast Asia, save pure facts on how many art auctions were held here (considering that Singapore has become a regional centre for art auctions, fairs, and exhibitions)?

The "Overview" then proceeds to enunciate the economic assumptions behind the document: "Economic opportunities in the area of the arts are virtually unlimited. Where the Republic once forged a reputation in trade, manufacturing, financial and service industries, she is now setting the stage for an arts industry to thrive" (p. 3). Singapore's history of statist social engineering, forming the basis for nation-building, is present here: we have the technology, we have the means, this history says. EDB Chairman Philip Yeo is quoted as saying: "There is now in Singapore a major opportunity to develop the arts, not only for cultural enrichment, but in the interest of economic growth" (p. 3). No one can take issue with that; but it leaps too hastily from "cultural enrichment" to "economic growth".

The section on "Arts Training" does announce the "software" (p. 21) that relevant state agencies are to put in place to support this new enterprise. This "software" includes formal arts training, informal arts training, grants, and scholarships. The current availability of such supporting mechanisms represents a clear improvement from the past. The sticking point here, however, is not only a lack of will to advance beyond a certain point, but also the actual difficulty in moving away from older notions of economic instrumentalism, in relation to culture's role in enriching Singaporeans' lives.

For instance, the document says that part of "Future Developments" will be a Singapore Arts Centre (now called "Esplanade — Theatres on the Bay") with five auditoria — a 2,000-seat concert hall, a 2,200-seat lyric theatre, a 200-seat black box, and two halls with 400 and 800 seats — apart from rehearsal facilities and outdoor performance areas. Obviously, most local theatre groups are unlikely at this juncture in their development to be able to fill the lyric theatre — thus, the need for the smaller-capacity halls.

We have learnt in the press — not officially, but from a letter to the *Straits Times* — that the smaller halls had been abandoned. Roger Jenkins of the group Dramaplus Arts related this situation to the way that opinions of expert members of the arts and other relevant communities were ignored in setting up the Esplanade:

> While it is true that many people sat on committees to formulate the Esplanade ... it is highly debatable how much of our input was actually taken into consideration.... Ask almost any member of the Singapore theatre community to choose between the 1,800-seat Lyric under construction and the three smaller theatres ..., which the advisory committees spent so long considering before they were scrapped in 1993....[32]

The response from the public relations manager of the Esplanade was to say that local needs were being met by converting "two of our rehearsal rooms into fully-equipped performing studios ... cater[ing] to audiences of up to 250 people".[33]

The point here is not to vilify the Esplanade staff for apparently being evasive and placatory, or to highlight the fact that Jenkins' letter implicitly questions the depth of the Singapore 21 spirit behind the Esplanade's actions. Rather, it is to recognize that this situation indicates the distance Singaporeans must still travel to make effective cultural policy that could, indeed, lead to "the stage for an arts industry to thrive". High-quality arts must be nurtured by giving them not only money, but space, time, facilities, and more autonomy; and the arts should be allowed the integrity to confront important cultural issues such as cultural and social heritage and identity before it can be shared in an effective commercial way with the world.

As already noted, while it is foolish to contend that the arts occupy a space free from the processes of commodification (as one Japanese specialist has noted: "Since the arts and media make up a major part of the [Japanese] media programme, media policy will feature prominently in cultural policy development. The notion of cultural development for the sake of culture is increasingly difficult to maintain"[34]), it would be a *misconception* to think that the arts can flourish if commercial utility were to be the only driving force, without affording it at least some protected space where it can develop and mature. While such an argument in Singapore — or anywhere else — is hardly a new one, it is particularly relevant to the city-state's stated goal of becoming a cultural hub. It could become that — but, as noted, it may simply serve as an empty hub for other peoples' high or popular/mass culture to pass through. Such a "hub" would not serve Prime Minister Goh's goal of making Singapore a "world-class home" in which the arts help "Singaporeans [to] want to stay", rather than to emigrate.[35]

The above reflection does not mean that Singapore need retreat into making only protective *intra*-national cultural policies; in any case, given the reality of the Internet and other new technologies of communication, this would be impossible. Considering that globalization advances in the context of an asymmetrical interdependence of the world system, it is also necessary — in the words of one academic analyst — that "the peripheral countries [or semi-peripheral, in Singapore's case] need to try cultural policies that allow them to exploit their capacities and at the same time place themselves in a less disadvantageous position in relation to the central countries".[36] But even before fully considering how such a policy position applies to a small city-state, one needs to ask to what level Singapore's "capacities" have been developed.

The major stumbling block for Singapore is its own history of pragmatic economic developmentalism. As a result of this history, Singapore's post-independence cultural development has varied from the experience not only of Western European countries, but also of many post-colonial Latin American, African, and Asian countries. States have generally taken on the responsibility for maintaining their material and non-material historical heritage and, in the process, they differentiated themselves from other nations. In many of the plural societies which the colonial powers constructed (Singapore is but one example of that particular legacy of empire), a "national" heritage was built up on a foundation of élite culture, which was sometimes of European origin. Modern institutions, such as museums and university departments engaged in the study of the new nation's culture, were developed and historical sites maintained in order to strengthen national identity. Supporting ethnic arts and crafts was also part of these strategies (for, while national identity needed to be valorized, the provincial or the regional could not be eradicated in the process, but instead had to be assimilated as a subsection of the national), as was support for the modern arts (literature, music, the plastic arts) and the mass media. There naturally arose questions of and debates over how the centre and the periphery, the modern and the traditional, were to be reconciled in such multi-level support of a national identity. But whatever differences were expressed, the idea of the "national" dominated, and the state played a leading role.

Nation-building in Singapore, and the PAP Government's way of dealing with ethnic fissures in society, took a very different route from the more dominant means of creating the "national", which incorporated cultural policy. "Culture", in the many senses of that term, was in fact played down. The meritocratic Singaporean way was the way to go in the late 1960s and the 1970s. Only since the 1980s, with the "hyphenated" Singaporean policy, has there been a re-emergence of the "ethnic mosaic" model of ethnic management from the period before the 1965 separation from Malaysia,[37] and with that, an increasing emphasis on the importance of culture and cultural values. But these changes from the 1980s do not in themselves signify a fundamental shift in the underpinning instrumental-rationalist mentality of nation-building. Nor can one realistically expect economically pragmatic ways of thinking to disappear overnight; they have too long been an intrinsic part of Singapore's way of national being. The pressing issue, though, is that we must more and more come to terms with this politico-cultural legacy and its consequences — and not expect a quick fix.

Conclusion

This chapter has looked at some of the key issues related to arts development within the larger framework of cultural identity issues in Singapore. It offers no direct prescription but an analysis of some of the difficulties that need to be directly confronted if cultural progress is to be achieved. It has been argued here that Singapore's still dominant instrumental-rationalist attitudes need to be reassessed, if there is to be not only a "Global City", but also a "Global City for the Arts". While there is a desire for the transcultural exchange that could result (and could further lead to a dynamic creativity in a global society), current intra-national cultural policy should be reviewed to determine whether it is conducive to such developments. Creative arts industries will not arise if there is no maturing national arts scene in the first place.

The state's presence (conceived of as a democratic and plural space) and effective support are necessary if cultural production in Singapore is not to be reduced to the level of simple manufactures, since cultural production and the symbolic values they stand for are part of the larger symbolic life of the city-state itself that cannot be commercialized. In this regard, arts development in terms of museums and art schools, among other institutions subsidized by the state, represents a good start — but it is just that, a start. More public–private initiatives (with cultural and other civil society organizations, and more artists allowed actual capacities to help make changes) are necessary to protect the interests of Singaporeans in terms of the information, cultural experimentation, and recreation that form part of their daily lives.

Acknowledgements

Thanks to Charlene Rajendran and Lee Weng Choy for reading versions of this essay under much duress, and to Kwok Kian Woon for ongoing discussions.

Notes

1. Terry McCarthy with Eric Ellis, "Singapore Lightens Up", *Time*, 19 July 1999, p. 17.
2. Ibid., p. 19.
3. Regarding the complications between the two terms, Koh Tai Ann indicates that "Civil society with contesting interests and adversarial stance towards … the state is … de-politicized and re-conceptualized into a 'civic society' where … 'good sons and daughters are prepared to dedicate themselves to help others' " (author's manuscript, "Civil or Civic Society?: The Singapore Idea[l]", p. 1). Sociologist Chua Beng Huat puts this distinction slightly differently: "There are … at least two different parts to civil society in Singapore. One is directly wooed with financial and administrative resources.… Politically, they are reformist in character. … The other [part] embraces independent viewpoints that contest those of relevant government agencies, and resist incorporation but are often at pains to present themselves as politically non-threatening to the ruling party. … It is a moot point which set … is better for the nation's interests as a whole. But what is less in dispute is that the alienation of the second group may lead to increasing privatization of interests by the individuals involved. It becomes a matter of concern if it eventually reduces the social capital and resources for the society as a whole" ("The Two Versions of Civil Society", *Straits Times Interactive* <http: //www.straitstimes.asia1.com/pages/cpel_0611.html>).
4. "Globalization" has become an intrinsic part of the reminders issued by the Government's leadership as to how Singapore must go, in order to survive. As journalist Chua Lee Hoong commented on Prime Minister Goh Chok Tong's 1999 National Day Rally speech: "Globalization, entrepreneurship, innovation, competitiveness, foreign talent. The old faithfuls of National Day Rally speeches were all there, reminders to Singaporeans of the constant need to hold on to its glorious place in the sun" ("Moulding a System That will Help Singapore Endure", *Straits Times Interactive*, 23 August 1999 <http://straitstimes.asia1.com.sg/sin/sin20_0823.html>).
5. Max Le Blond, "Drama in Singapore: Towards an English Language Theatre", in *Discharging the Canon: Cross-Cultural Readings in Literature*, edited by Peter Hyland (Singapore: Singapore University Press, 1986), pp. 114 and 117. For a broad background of English-language theatre, see David Birch, "Singapore English Drama: A Historical Overview 1958-1985", in *Nine Lives: 10 Years of Singapore Theatre 1987-1997*, edited by Sanjay Krishnan (Singapore: The Necessary Stage, 1997).
6. The following discussion is drawn from the notes that I made during the conference.
7. For a larger assessment of the context of "tradition", the "modern" and their relationship to identity issues, see Kwok Kian Woon, "The Problem of 'Tradition' in Contemporary Singapore", in *Heritage and Contemporary Values*, edited by Arun Mahizhnan (Singapore: Times Academic Press, 1993). For an assessment of the left wing in Singapore, and their presumed connection with the Malayan

Communist Party, see T. N. Harper, "Lim Chin Siong and the 'Singapore Story'", in *Comet in Our Sky: Lim Chin Siong in History*, edited by Tan Jing Quee and Jomo K. S. (Kuala Lumpur: Insan, 2001).

8. Lee Kuan Yew, *The Battle for Merger* (Singapore: Government Printing Office, n.d.), p. 16.
9. Cf. Ong Keng Sen: "In the 'eighties, the concern for identity was not confined to a small core of individuals. Many theatre companies had as their mission statement the promotion of Singaporean expression through our own plays. ... The fervour in the theatre coincided with a nationalistic fervour in the late eighties. Singaporeans were beginning to develop a national pride, which was harnessed further by the ruling government" ("The Practice of English Language Theatre in Singapore", in *Prize Winning Plays: Volume V 1991*, edited by Thiru Kandiah (Singapore: UniPress, 1991), p. 185.
10. Cf. Ong: "The power of memory and nostalgia is demonstrated in ... [plays] by Practice [Ensemble, now the Theatre Practice, Kuo's company] and TheatreWorks ... which affected audiences and brought them into contact with the very soul and heart of the Singaporean experience: modernity and sophistication which is skin-deep, a subconscious desire for the past and memory and tradition to be anchors in a changing environment as Singapore is reinvented" ("Practice of English Language Theatre", p. 187). The question of statist modernization and urbanization is also part of the heart of the identity question; see K. K. Seet, "Implications of Urban Development on Singapore Creative Writing: The Case of Singapore English Drama", in *Malaysia and Singapore: Experiences in Industrialization and Urban Development*, edited by Lee Boon Hiok and K. S. Susan Oorjitham (Kuala Lumpur: University of Malaya, 1993).
11. In September 1996, during the Teachers' Day Rally, Prime Minister Goh spoke of the need of a National Education school programme. A newspaper survey indicated that the younger citizenry's consciousness of Singapore's post-war tribulations was weak. Mr Goh argued that the "basic facts" of nationhood, and the principles of meritocracy and multiracialism have to be rediscovered and a national symbology firmly foregrounded (Goh Chok Tong, "Prepare Our Children Well for the New Century", *Contact*, September 1996, p. 2). Issues of ethnicity, history, and meritocracy now became removed from the realm of Asian regional identity and re-inserted into the realm of the national. Of course, there was no discussion of the state's socio-cultural engineering role in the national amnesia. The National Education Plan launch transpired in May 1997. Deputy Prime Minister Lee Hsien Loong told teachers that "Amnesia is not an option" (Lee Hsien Loong, "National Education", Ministry of Education [Singapore] website, 17 May 1997 <http://www1.moe.edu.sg/speeches/170597.htm>) in relation to thorny, past inter-racial relations. In general, the plan is "to equip ... [the young] with the basic attitudes, values and instincts which make them Singaporeans". This "common culture" is the "DNA to be passed from one generation to the

next". The concept of "common culture" — with its organicist implications — is jarringly used for a rationalist commitment to cultural identity formation. However, the PAP's established ideology of economic survival also remains at the core of National Education.

12. For comprehensive documentation of the debate over Chinatown, see the documents lodged on the Knowledge Net website, <http://www.knowledgenet.com.sg/singapore/SHF/forum/articles/articles.html> and *Rethinking Chinatown and Heritage Conservation in Singapore*, edited by Kwok Kian Woon, C.J.W.-L. Wee, and Karen Chia (Singapore: Singapore Heritage Society, 2000).
13. *Straits Times*, 8 December 1998.
14. S. Chandrasekaran, Goh Ee Choo and Salleh Japar, "Trimurti, 1988 Statements and Documentation", in *Trimurti and Ten Years After*, edited by T. K. Sabapathy (Singapore: Singapore Art Museum, 1998), p. 11.
15. T. K. Sabapathy, "Trimurti: Thoughts on Context", in *Trimurti and Ten Years After*, edited by Sabapathy, p. 25.
16. Ahmad Mashadi, " 'Different Things': Trimurti and Multicultural Assertions", in *Trimurti and Ten Years After*, edited by Sabapathy, pp. 37, 40.
17. Kuo Pao Kun, "Contemplating an Open Culture: Transcending Multiracialism", in *Singapore: Re-Engineering Success*, edited by Arun Mahizhnan and Lee Tsao Yuan (Singapore: Institute of Policy Studies and Oxford University Press, 1998), p. 61.
18. Bruce Robbins, "Introduction Part 1: Actually Existing Cosmopolitanism", in *Cosmopolitics: Thinking and Feeling Beyond the Nation State*, edited by Pheng Cheah and Bruce Robbins (Minneapolis: University of Minnesota Press, 1998), p. 3.
19. Or, as Malaysian arts practitioner and critic Charlene Rajendran observed: "But to be 'set free' and to have cut loose is perhaps as mythical as being rooted" (e-mail communication to the author).
20. Raymond Williams, "Culture is Ordinary", in *Studying Culture: An Introductory Reader*, edited by Ann Gray and Jim McGuigan (London: Edward Arnold, 1993), p. 5.
21. "Building a Vibrant, Global City. Ministry of Information and the Arts: Mr Lee Yock Suan", *Straits Times Interactive*, 8 October 1999 <http://straitstimes.asia1.com.sg/sin/sin22_1008.html>.
22. Kuo Pao Kun, "Re-Positioning the Arts", *The Arts Magazine*, November/December 1999, pp. 19–20. All other page citations will be given in the main text.
23. For further discussion, documentation and assessment of the events Kuo refers to, see the articles and papers in the "Arts" section of *Looking at Culture*, edited Sanjay Krishnan, Sharaad Kuttan, Lee Weng Choy, Leon Perera, and Jimmy Yap (Singapore: Artres Design and Communications, 1996).
24. Singapore 21 Committee, *Singapore 21: Together, We Make the Difference* (Singapore: Singapore 21 Committee, 1999), p. 49. All other page citations will be given in the main text.
25. "RAdm Teo for People Sector", *Strait Times Interactive*, 21 June 1998 <http://www.straitstimes.asia1.com/pages/sin6_0621. html>.

26. J. M. Nathan, "The Culture Industry and the Future of the Arts in Singapore", in *Southeast Asian Affairs* 1999 (Singapore: Institute of Southeast Asian Studies, 1999), p. 300.
27. Ibid., p. 301.
28. Cf. National Arts Council Executive Director Choo Thiam Siew: "The arts has never been Singapore's number one priority. There was a lack of push. But now, the Prime Minister has himself made it a necessity" (quoted in Kelvin Tong, "Show Me the Money: Renaissance City", *Straits Times Interactive*, 29 August 1999 <http://straitstimes.asia1.com.sg/lif/life1_0829.html>); Tong himself adds, "If MONEY flows as freely in the name of art here as it did during the Renaissance, many arts groups feel that Singapore will take a quantum leap forward. Not only will culture be resuscitated, the country will also be able to reap the [economic and technological] benefits of some of its virtues that parallel those enjoyed by yesterday's Florence and Venice."
29. In the National Day celebrations on 3 June 1961, marking the self-rule gained in 1959, then Prime Minister Lee Kuan Yew told the people that a country-wide capitalist modernity could be our new identity: "We are hoping to build a modern society in which everybody will have a better life because we will have factories to make more and more of the things which make life easier.... Recitation of poetry and writing of essays are important things in a civilized society. But important also is the turning of screws and lathes. They make our modern world hum" (cited in Alex Josey, *Lee Kuan Yew* [Singapore: Donald Moore Press, 1968], pp. 172, 173). Older Malayans "were brought up in a different world", in "a backward community" of small-holding farmers, rubber tappers and tin miners; in this world there was no "tolerance and respect for each other" (p. 172). Economic success could also function to hold the various ethnic groups together. While there have been changes in the way ethnicity has been managed (see C.J.W.-L. Wee, "Capitalism and Ethnicity: 'Local' Culture in Singapore", *Inter-Asia Cultural Studies* 1, No. 1 (April 2000): 129–43), there is a clear continuity from 1961 to the present.
30. *Singapore — Global City for the Arts* (Singapore: Economic Development Board and Ministry of Information and the Arts, 1992), p. 11. All other page citations will be given in the main text.
31. In any case, such statements need to be phrased very carefully if they are not to be misunderstood — as such statements often are — as indicating cultural imperialist intentions. Given regional sensitivities, we need to be mindful of this.
32. Roger Jenkins, "How About Local Theatre Needs?", *Straits Times Interactive*, 4 September 1999 <http://straitstimes.asia1.com.sg/for/for7_0904.html>.
33. Seet Tze Ching, "Give Esplanade a Chance to Work", *Straits Times Interactive*, 10 September 1999 <http://straitstimes.asia1.com.sg/archive/st/5/ for/for4_0910.html>.
34. Michihiro Watanabe, "Cultural Policies in Japan", in *Culture, Creativity and Markets: World Culture Report* 1998 (Paris: UNESCO, 1998), p. 174.

35. Zuraidah Ibrahim, "Singapore's New Goal: Be a World-Class Home: Besides Building First-Class Economy, Excellence in Education, Arts, Sports and Culture is Also Important", *Straits Times Interactive*, 23 August 1999 <http://straitstimes.asia1.com.sg/one1/one1.html>.
36. Néstor Garcia Canclini, "Cultural Policy Options in the Context of Globalization", in *Culture, Creativity and Markets*, pp. 169–70.
37. See Geoffrey Benjamin, "The Cultural Logic of Singapore's 'Multiracialism'", in *Singapore: Society in Transition*, edited by Riaz Hassan (Kuala Lumpur: Oxford University Press, 1976); David Brown, *The State and Ethnic Politics in Southeast Asia* (London: Routledge, 1994); Eddie C. Y. Kuo, "Confucianism as Political Discourse in Singapore: The Case of an Incomplete Revitalization Movement", in *Confucian Traditions in East Asian Modernity: Moral Education and Economic Culture in Japan and the Four Mini-Dragons*, edited by Tu Wei-ming (Cambridge: Harvard University Press, 1996); and Wee, "Capitalism and Ethnicity".

10

THE MEDIA AND THE FLOW OF INFORMATION

Ang Peng Hwa

Introduction

If there is one image that captures and explains the impact of the West on the media, it is the printing press. Although the first presses were invented in China and Korea, it was the Europeans who exploited it for mass consumption. Accompanying the technology are the values of the country of its origin; in the case of Singapore, the source was Britain. Singapore's early newspapers, as well as its first radio station, were started by Britons under colonial British media laws. From the British, Singapore derived the more universally accepted restrictions of defamation and copyright (once, the right given by the monarch to make copies), as well as the Official Secrets Act, the Internal Security Act, and the much-amended Newspaper and Printing Presses Act.[1]

The modern image that captures and explains the impact of America on the media in Singapore and around the world is a computer wired to the Internet. The key components that make up the Internet — a computer chip running on software and connected to other units by a telephone system — were invented in the United States. Already, American values are being passed along through the adoption of the Internet.

For the foreseeable future, the influences on the media will likely come from the United States. This chapter argues that even if controls on the media could be said to have worked in the 1970s and 1980s, and perhaps even in the 1990s, they are unlikely to work in the foreseeable future. Because of technology and other reasons, Singapore's media laws and regulations will need to be revisited to realize her ambition to become a major world city. Just as the traditional mass media have developed differently in Singapore compared with Great Britain, so the use of the Internet is likely to develop differently in Singapore compared with the United States. This means the laws and controls on the media will not mirror that of the United States.

Colonial Legacy

The history of press regulation by the British Government has not been linear. In 1835, the British Government abolished a law that required newspapers to submit pre-publication copies of the paper to the colonial governor for vetting. In celebration, the *Singapore Free Press* was started that year.[2]

In 1920, the British Government introduced the Printing Presses Act that required all printing presses and publishers to apply for an annual licence.[3] In practice, control was lax. A journalist recollected being called in by the spokesman for the colonial government, George Thomson, in the late 1950s and being a little "nervous" of the "very influential man". Thomson told the journalist: "I am not asking you to make the correction. I just wanted to show you the facts." Apart from his own embarrassment at a professional failing, that journalist suffered no other consequence.[4]

Whatever controls had been in place were increased by the newly-elected Singapore Government after independence. The rationale for controls was understandable. In 1950, riots broke out in Singapore over the publication of an unretouched photograph of a Dutch girl brought up as a Muslim by a Malay family, being forced to take up the Christian religion. Riots in 1964 have also been blamed on uninhibited reporting.[5] Also, upon independence, the Singapore and Malaysian Governments agreed not to circulate their respective newspapers, an agreement still in force at the time of writing.[6] This means that it is possible for the average Singaporean to buy French, German, and Japanese newspapers at the news-stands but difficult to find Malaysian newspapers (you have to go to the Malaysian High Commission).

History is also useful for understanding the *animus* of the Government towards the press. In 1959, the *Straits Times* moved its headquarters from Singapore to Kuala Lumpur, Malaysia, a move that appeared to signal a lack of confidence in the People's Action Party (PAP) Government when it came into power. There were sound economic reasons: Kuala Lumpur was better located to serve the peninsula, and circulation was higher in Malaysia. But there was also fear that the PAP would censor the press.[7] Commenting on the move, the secretary-general of the party, Lee Kuan Yew, wrote in a letter to the *Straits Times*:

> We of the PAP believe just as zealously in the freedom of the Press. If locally owned newspapers criticize us we know that their criticism, however wrong or right, is *bona fide* criticism because they must stay and take the consequences of any foolish policies or causes they may have advocated. Not so the birds of passage who run the *Straits Times*.
>
> ... The folly of allowing newspapers to be owned by people who are not citizens or nationals of the country, is that their sense of responsibility is blunted by the knowledge that if the worst came to the worst, they could always buzz off to some other place.[8]

This notion that the Singapore press had to be Singaporean-owned is one theme that the Lee government has maintained. Thus, the *Eastern Sun* and *Singapore Herald*, both started in the late 1960s, were closed down in the early 1970s on charges that they were backed by foreign businesses.[9] The law was changed then by overhauling the Newspaper and Printing Presses Act so that, among other things, ownership of a newspaper would not be with one person. The current shape of the media laws can be traced to this period.

Local newspapers were made to go public. This meant that daily and weekly newspapers had to be owned by a minimum of fifty shareholders (an implication of being a public company). Each shareholder could not own more than 3 per cent of the company.[10] Further, there were to be created a special category of management shares where 1 per cent of the company was to be held by persons approved by the Government. This 1 per cent commanded 200 times the voting power of an ordinary share.

In the mid-1980s, the rules were amended to regulate the distribution of foreign news publications that sold more than 300 copies weekly or more frequently. Those that were deemed to be "interfering in domestic politics" were pronounced to be "declared publications" in the *Government Gazette* and had their circulation restricted. Thus far, several major English-language weekly news magazines have been deemed to be "interfering" and have been, in local parlance, gazetted: *Time*, *Far Eastern Economic Review*, *Asiaweek*, *Economist*, *Asian Wall Street Journal*.[11] Because these publications have high credibility, restricting their circulation does not win points in any press freedom ranking.

In its 1999 ranking, Freedom House placed Singapore in the "not free" category of press restriction, with a score of 66 out of 100 (least free)[12] — identical with Malaysia's 66 and less free than Indonesia's 51. This score was based on four criteria:

- laws and regulations that influence media content (on which Singapore scored 13 out of 15 for print and broadcast media each);
- political pressures and controls on media content (on which Singapore scored 8 for broadcast and 10 for print out of a maximum of 15 each);
- economic influences over media content (on which Singapore scored 7 for broadcast and 15 for print out of a maximum of 15 each); and
- repressive actions (on which Singapore scored zero out of 5 for each of the two media).

The method used to derive the scores above can always be nit-picked. But it is instructive to see that the scoring considers the broadcast media to be less regulated: this is in spite of the fact that the Government holds the broadcast media more directly than the newspapers, which are owned by a listed company. In other words, the Government can own the medium and yet, contrary to conventional wisdom, exercise less control.

The broadcast industry has been moving towards greater autonomy in the face of increasing competition. In 1980, Radio and Television Singapore, a department under the Ministry of Culture responsible of all broadcasting, was transformed into the Singapore Broadcasting Corporation (SBC) through an Act of Parliament. Although it was still wholly-owned by the Government, being a corporation and not a department gave it greater autonomy and flexibility in personnel, financial, and production matters. The period marked the beginning of more locally produced programmes. In 1984, SBC started Channel 12 to provide an extra dimension in the form of documentaries, cultural performances and works, drama, art-house movies, educational programmes, and sports.[13]

In 1994, in a major exercise to restructure the broadcast industry to face a more competitive environment, SBC was corporatized and became the Singapore International Media (SIM). In 1999, the name was changed to Media Corporation of Singapore (MediaCorp).[14] This company holds all the broadcasting enterprises in Singapore, including the Television Corporation Singapore (TCS), Singapore Television 12 (STV12), and Radio Corporation of Singapore (RCS). Currently, TCS operates Channel 5 (an all-English language channel) and Channel 8 (an all-Chinese language channel). TCS plays the role of the national station. Together, the two channels captured about 80 per cent of the market share, but this has begun to decline with the introduction of the 50-channel-capable cable television service in 1995.[15]

More recently, in June 2000, the Singapore Government introduced "controlled competition" into the media industry. Singapore Press Holdings (SPH), which until then published all the daily newspapers in Singapore, was licensed to operate up to two free-to-air television channels and run one or two radio stations. The hitherto-national station, MediaCorp, obtained a newspaper licence.[16]

Singapore Press Holdings started two newspapers. In August, it rolled out *Project Eyeball*, a newspaper for the "hip and opinionated" working crowd aged 20 to 40.[17] In September 2000, it launched *Streats*, a free morning tabloid for commuters.[18]

Meanwhile, MediaCorp published its free morning tabloid, *Today*, distributed at MRT stations and bus interchanges. Its joint venture partners are the government-owned rail transport company, SMRT, bus operator Delgro Corp, and Singtel Yellow Pages Pte Ltd.[19]

Noticeably absent from the competition are foreign companies. Minister for Information and the Arts, Mr Lee Yock Suan said: "Much as we welcome foreign talent to work in Singapore — and many international media are already operating here — the regular reporting on Singaporean affairs for the Singapore audience has to be done by Singaporean media."[20]

The Government is concerned that its message may be lost if the media are not Singapore-controlled. This loss of "mindshare", where the majority of the public turns to non-government-dominated media for information, is inevitable and most evident on the Internet. Singapore was the second country in Southeast Asia, after Malaysia, to offer public Internet access in July 1994. In typical Singaporean style, however, once the decision to get wired was made, the various agencies moved to ensure the Internet diffused very quickly. In March 1995, Singapore became the first country in the world to set up a national Internet Website, *Singapore InfoMap* <http://www.sg/>. However, also in typical Singaporean style, there was concern that Internet content could be destructive to the values that Singapore wants to uphold. So, in July 1996, the Singapore Broadcasting Authority announced new rules and the Class Licensing Scheme to censor the Internet. The new Internet regulations stirred a major controversy and received wide publicity all over the world. It portrayed Singapore as a country attempting to regulate what many described as impossible to regulate. To date, however, no one has been charged with violating those rules.[21] Further, in 1999, the rules for entry as an Internet service provider (ISP) were relaxed to allow total foreign ownership.[22]

Rationale for Censorship[23]

The underlying paradigm for the regulations is the "powerful effects" model of the media. That is, the media are seen as exerting a powerful influence on a "weak" and "passive" audience.[24] Advertising executives adopt the paradigm when they argue that advertisements will cause the audience to buy the advertised product or service. In public debates, such a paradigm suggests that where the matter is of greater national interest, such as in politics, it is all-important to ensure that the media disseminate the right information.

The powerful effects paradigm is common in many parts of the world. In Singapore, as well as a number of other countries, political communication is heavily regulated during general elections. In Singapore, there are rules on how much advertising is allowed, defamation laws are not lifted during electioneering and political parties cannot make films.[25] The elections, after all, are extremely important to the national well-being. Such an approach contrasts sharply with the free speech approach in the United States where the argument is that there should be greater debate precisely because the matter is of national importance. There, plenty of airtime and newspaper space are given over to political debate during electioneering, which can begin a year or more before the date of the election.

The powerful effects paradigm has been disproven in communication research, which has shown that media effects at best are "powerful but limited". That is, the effects, even if powerful, are limited to the time and situation.[26] In the case of Singapore, Kuo et al., in their study of the media in the 1991 Singapore general election found a correlation between what was *not* reported in the media and what was going through the minds of Singaporean voters.[27] This finding is the opposite to that of in the West where newspapers apparently do set the agenda for public thinking.

But the Government is taking no chances. In 1995, the execution of a Filipina domestic helper sparked off anti-Singapore sentiments in the Philippines, which were, on hindsight, fanned by the Filipino media.[28] From the Singapore perspective, the lesson was that uninhibited, as well as erroneous, reports can cause demonstrations and protests. News reports like these are, therefore, seen as justifying the need for the controls on the media, as the unimpeded flow of ideas — instead of leading to enlightenment — can sometimes have negative consequences. The Singaporean populace generally supports such controls on the media. Surveys conducted by or familiar to the author have found the average Singaporean supportive of the current regime of censorship.[29] Control of the media in Singapore is, therefore, justified on historical as well as socio-political grounds, favouring caution and prevention over liberalism. This position has been systematically articulated by the Government and accepted by the populace as one of the boundaries within which Singapore society must function.

But Singapore is also pragmatic. Information is certainly important to its well-being, and so it has been willing to loosen its rules when the rules conflict with sound economic sense.[30] For example, when the Gulf War broke out in 1991, financial institutions in Singapore learned of it 30 seconds later than other international markets — the time difference between the CNN news announcement and the wire service stories. This delay was not acceptable to the financial community and the Government subsequently allowed financial institutions to use satellite dishes.[31]

An analysis of the censorship rules used to guide the Ministry of Information and the Arts demonstrates how Singapore attempts to balance the conflicting possibilities of free information flows. First, materials going into the home are more heavily censored than those going into the corporate world. Information for the home is seen to be of a less critical nature, so censorship of such information is regarded to not have as deleterious an effect. Thus, for example, businesses can have unfiltered access to the Internet.[32] Second, materials for the young are more heavily censored than those for adults. Third, materials for public consumption are more heavily censored than those for private consumption. This is a corollary of the second principle as it is assumed that the public includes those who are "weaker". It should be noted that those found in private possession of certain categories of banned or uncensored materials may be convicted in court. Finally, materials deemed to have artistic and educational merit are less heavily censored. This is a recently articulated principle and has been applied to movies, which now have an R(A), for Restricted (Artistic), rating.

In sum, censorship in Singapore has an element of differentiation: home versus business, children versus adults, public versus private consumption.[33] Further, materials that can be shown to have some tangible and wider benefit — such as for business, art, and education — are censored in a more light-handed manner. On the other hand, materials deemed to have less tangible benefit — such as "pure entertainment" — are more heavily censored. It may seem strange, but the transparency of these rules has enabled Singapore to be a regional hub for companies broadcasting programmes to the region. Several huge international media giants, such as Home Box Office (HBO), music channel MTV and U.S. sports network ESPN have set up regional centres in Singapore in spite of its tough censorship regulations.[34] Some of these companies boast that the programmes have been "censored to Singapore standards" and, therefore, should be "safe" for the target country.[35]

Free Speech and the U.N. Declaration

Singapore is not alone in regulating the media; there are internationally-accepted areas of control. At the international level, free expression reached its pinnacle in Article 19 of the United Nations' Declaration of Human Rights in 1948. It could be argued that Singapore was not then a member of the United Nations; indeed, it was not even a country. But this is being pedantic: human rights should be universal rights. The problem with the Declaration is that it is unrealistic. Article 19 (a free speech group has even been named after it) states: "Everyone has the right to freedom of opinion and expression; this right includes freedom to hold opinions without interference and to seek, receive and impart information and ideas through any media and regardless of frontiers." The sweeping Article ignores such universal concerns as defamation, obscenity,[36] and national security. That is, under Article 19, anyone could defame anyone else; similarly, anyone could engage in espionage without consequence. It may be a cynical view, but perhaps the drafters were able to be so expansive of the right because they did not have to enforce it. Not surprisingly, the 1966 U.N. International Covenant on Civil and Political Rights[37] interpreted Article 19 of the 1948 Charter more narrowly and realistically. It noted that:

> [T]he exercise of (freedom of expression) carries with it special duties and responsibilities. It may therefore be subject to certain restrictions ...
>
> - For respect of the rights or reputations of others
> - For the protection of national security, or of public order, or of public health or morals.

Perhaps a more realistic but somewhat quirky clause dealing with free expression may be found in Article 10 of the 1950 European Convention on Human Rights. The Article allows controls to be placed on, among other things, television broadcasting, which is a culturally sensitive matter in Europe. The Article states:

> 1. Everyone has the right to freedom of expression. This right shall include freedom to hold opinions and to receive and impart information and ideas without interference by public authority and regardless of frontiers. This Article shall not prevent States from requiring the licensing of broadcasting, television or cinema enterprises.
> 2. The exercise of these freedoms, since it carries with it duties and responsibilities, may be subject to such formalities,

> conditions, restrictions or penalties as are prescribed by law and are necessary in a democratic society, in the interests of national security, territorial integrity or public safety, for the prevention of disorder or crime, for the protection of public health or morals, for the protection of the reputation or rights of others, for preventing the disclosure of information received in confidence, or for maintaining the authority and impartiality of the judiciary.

In the author's view, because the Article had to be enforced by the European Court of Justice, it was, therefore, drafted more realistically in recognizing the limits to free expression. However, of the three articles above, it is also the most restrictive.

Singapore's equivalent, Article 14 of the Constitution, may have swung too far in the direction of realism. The Article reads:

> Article 14 Freedom of Speech, Assembly, and Association
>
> (1) Subject to clauses (2) . . .
>
> (a) every citizen of Singapore has the right to freedom of speech and expression ...
>
> (2) Parliament may by law impose
>
> (a) on the rights conferred by clause (1)(a), such restrictions as it considers necessary or expedient in the interest of the security of Singapore or any part thereof, friendly relations with other countries, public order or morality and restrictions designed to protect the privileges of Parliament or to provide against contempt of court, defamation or incitement to any offence;
>
> (b) on the right conferred by clause (1)(b), such restrictions as it considers necessary or expedient in the interest of the security of Singapore or any part thereof or public order; and,
>
> (c) on the right conferred by clause (1)(c), such restrictions as it considers necessary or expedient in the interest of the security of Singapore or any part thereof, public order or morality.

The clause has been interpreted to include freedom of the media. Here, the right begins with the exception. In legalese, the right is qualified from the start; in contrast, the rights in the other articles are unqualified. In lay terms, this is analogous to someone greeting a visitor with: "Except for my bedroom and study, welcome to my house." This means that freedom of the media is subject to other laws, such as, for example, defamation (J.B. Jeyaretnam vs Lee Kuan Yew [1992] 2 SLR 310). To date, no law has been found to be in breach of this Article of the Constitution.

Societal and Political Implications

A major implication of the various media rules is that barriers of entry into the newspaper business are very high. Further, mergers have created monopolies in the local news markets for newspapers[38] and television. It may be argued, of course, that there is no monopoly in the newspaper market because news is available from diverse sources. But the numbers suggest otherwise. Well-managed newspapers in a competitive environment typically have a 15 per cent profit margin. As the market decreases in competition and becomes more monopolistic, the margin increases to 25 per cent. Margins above that tend to invite competition, if new entrants are allowed. In the case of Singapore Press Holdings, the margin is 40 to 50 per cent.[39]

Television and radio stations are run by government-linked entities. It took competition from an Indonesian radio station based in Batam in 1988 to shake up the radio scene. Using the American format for radio, the Filipino disc-jockeys at Batam called their station "Zoo", gave themselves animal names, kept chatter to a minimum, and played music most of the time.[40] When the Singapore companies were allowed to enter the fray, the Batam station was vanquished. The Batam radio station also faced two hurdles. First, although the numbers were extremely appealing to advertisers, many were wary of advertising on the station. They feared being associated with a station that could fail.[41] Further, they feared being perceived as disloyal to the Singapore radio station. Typically, these advertisers were based in Singapore but marketed their products regionally. Second, under Indonesian law then, all radio stations had to relay the same Indonesian news, which came from Jakarta, every hour on the hour. The news was in Bahasa Indonesia and disrupted the English-language American format. The disruption made the Batam station vulnerable because it meant that listeners could change stations every hour on the hour. Despite the Indonesian news, the Batam radio station captured, at its height, 14 per cent of the daily Singapore radio audience[42] and a peak listenership of as high as 70 per cent.

Starting from about a half-dozen radio stations in the mid-1980s, the market expanded to fourteen stations under the dominant RCS alone, plus two each under the Singapore Armed Forces Reservist Association (SAFRA) and the National Trades Union Congress (NTUC).

Just how uncompetitive and complacent the radio market before Batam had become may be gauged by the fact that, when NTUC radio was given a licence, it became profitable in the first year — even paying a bonus. The station introduced innovations such as satellite broadcasting, whereby disc jockeys worked in glass-enclosed booths at shopping centres. Listeners flocked to the booths to meet the personalities behind the voices or simply wave to them. NTUC Radio was to the Chinese-language radio programme what Batam was to the English. Just as the incumbent could shake off the threat from Batam, so it managed to shake off the competition in the Chinese radio market. More accurately, the Chinese radio station self-destructed economically. Instead of keeping to its profitable formula, the station changed its focus away from entertainment towards providing more informational content for its listeners. There is little doubt that the approach is the death-knell for profits. To its credit, the NTUC had decided that its mission was not profits but education.

The developments in the radio industry are worth noting for several reasons. First, the success of the industry (advertising expenditure has grown in both absolute numbers and in percentage of the advertising pie) caught even media professionals by surprise. In the mid-1980s, advertising executives thought the local radio market could double to a maximum of twelve radio channels. In economic terms, the lack of competition, if not outright monopoly, in radio had stunted the growth of the market.

Second, the government-run Singapore Broadcasting Corporation had been shown to be mainly reactive and not innovative, let alone proactive.[43] However, once the resources are mobilized, like a behemoth set on the right course, it can marshal its resources and shake up the industry. The radio stations under the relabelled Radio Corporation of Singapore have never been more profitable, competition notwithstanding.

Third, the developments in radio are instructive of the dominance of the American approach to media. The British (and former SBC) approach of having one radio station catering to the entire spectrum of the audience has been shown to be less economically viable. The British format, with rock music for an hour, a cookery class in the next, encouraged listeners to switch. In contrast, the American format has a commercial logic: it encourages the same type of listener to stay with the station. The question for the other media is to what extent these foreign formats, refined by competition, will be allowed to flourish in Singapore. The answer does not lie purely in economics. Because media have an impact on the social, cultural, and political life of a country, many countries have regulations that affect and sometimes even stifle the economic logic. For example, many European countries treat media products as cultural products and place them outside the ambit of free trade rules. Could a similar threat from competition apply in the television industry?

Sometime after the radio wars, there was an exploration into the possibility of a television station in Batam broadcasting to Singapore. A Hong Kong television station was to be hired as consultant for the Batam station. The Singapore Government said it would be prepared to meet the competition. However, Jakarta denied the permit and the threat of television competition from Batam did not emerge.

Currently, the competitive threat to local television is from satellite direct broadcast. As dishes get smaller, it would conceivably be possible to have a smuggled receiver surreptitiously receiving television signals in some backyards. The introduction of cable television is intended to forestall such a threat, since it is more convenient to subscribe to cable than to use an illegal dish: with a dish, it is still necessary to pay for the more interesting programmes, anyway.

Impact of New Technologies

The satellite dish is just one example of the threat to information control that new technologies will pose to Singapore. Most, not all, commentators are of the view that new technologies will force Singapore to relax the rules on censorship for all media. Political scientist and Singapore-watcher Garry Rodan quotes Rupert Murdoch as saying that "[a]dvances in the technology of telecommunications have proved an unambiguous threat to totalitarian regimes everywhere" and "[s]ome even see the Internet 'allowing democracy of a more participatory nature than at any time since the ancient Greeks'".[44] Rodan himself, however, holds the view that the Internet is not necessarily a force for democracy and sees the Singapore model as having potential application outside of Singapore.[45] Similarly, Staksrud wonders if, "in certain social and political settings, the Internet has the potential to assist authorities in identifying government critics".[46]

On a related and more technologically deterministic note, it has been suggested that "technology can only amplify the process of surveillance and hegemonic domination".[47] The more common view, however, is that technology will change Singapore. It is a conclusion this author agrees with, but for reasons different from that usually given. In essence, the dominant argument runs thus: it is technically impossible to censor the new media where uncountable pages of content are created daily. Also, the new technologies have economic benefits and control could, as in the case of satellite television, have a backlash. For that reason, and to maintain the consistency of censorship rules across media, the rules should be relaxed. In a recent survey, Stephen Yeo and Arun Mahizhnan made a strong case that censorship rules must be relaxed if the new information technology is to take off in Singapore.[48] Certainly, the case cannot be lightly dismissed — Yeo was Chief Executive Officer of the National Computer Board, the agency tasked with the promotion of information technology and the IT2000 plan in Singapore.

This author takes a slightly different position. On the one hand, it is clear that many governments are backpedalling from their original statements of intention to control the Internet. Vietnam, for example, once said it would not even allow the Internet. Less than six months later, it organized an Internet day.[49] On the other hand, many countries in the West are enforcing laws that appear difficult to enforce. For example, at the time of writing, the United States, for all the advocacy of free speech on the Internet, had convicted more people for offences regarding Internet content than the rest of the world combined.[50] Over a more than two-year period, the U.S. Federal Bureau of Investigation had arrested 700 people on charges of "trafficking in child pornography or luring minors across state lines for sexual encounters with child pornographers".[51] More recently, the U.S. Department of Justice, the European Union, and the Australian Government organized a high-level conference bringing together 250 representatives from law enforcement, industry and users from Europe, North America, and Asia to discuss ways to combat child pornography.[52] The conference ended with some strong recommendations for, among other things, greater international co-operation among law enforcement officers of different countries and the setting up of hotlines to report offending sites.[53] Usually, international conferences of such a do-good nature dissolve into "whereas's" and recommendations that are difficult, if not impossible, to implement. But in this conference, there was, first, broad agreement on a number of steps to be taken. What really surprised this author was, second, the determination of the law enforcement and judiciary officers to tackle the problem in the face of the usual statement that "the Internet cannot be policed".

In sum, the evidence seems to suggest that the Internet can be policed, within limits, if the police are determined enough. Given the international character of the Internet, it clearly helps if there is co-operation from other police agencies. It is here that the author suggests that Singapore censorship rules will have to change with the Internet.

On the Internet, it is not impossible to censor content: it is impossible to censor content that are deemed to be harmful to Singapore standards, and only Singapore standards. This means that censorship of nudity, violence, and sex — content that many countries in the West do not censor — would be increasingly difficult to enforce; pornography is not illegal in many countries. Even Singapore's proxy server filtering of 100 sites can be bypassed by choosing another public proxy server.[54] However, where there is consensus on materials deemed to be illegal and harmful, there is likely to be greater consensus and, therefore, greater control. Child pornography is the most obvious example of where there is consensus. Another area with almost as wide agreement is gambling. More peculiar to the Internet is the concern over personal data privacy. This means that on the Internet, the standards for what are acceptable would have to track international norms. It is unlikely that Singapore will be able to filter out all adult pornography and political dissent sites. In such instances, it is possible that the divide between the media could persist. Thus, it is very possible that censorship of the traditional media would be subject to a higher standard than that of the Internet, concerns about inconsistency notwithstanding.

The Next Ten to Fifteen Years

It is very likely that Singapore's current censorship and media rules will be changed over the next ten to fifteen years. The changes, however, should be made gradually. Otherwise, because of the lack of rules, the sudden lifting of censorship could very well result in a backlash, as evidenced by the introduction of restricted (R) movies. History has shown that such sudden moves create a legal vacuum.[55]

The rules regarding media control also need easing. Overall, the current rules clearly benefit the incumbent.[56] The current position assumes that competition can be kept at bay, an assumption likely to be challenged by the continuing development of technology. Just as the rules regarding banking are being relaxed to let local banks face international competition, it would make sense — if the local media were to thrive in the long term — to open them up to competition. The monopolistic situation of the main media creates an environment that does not reward the best performers. If they do not fit the corporate culture, where can they go but out of Singapore?

There is also — perhaps looking at it with a jaundiced eye — the School of Communication Studies, of which the author is a faculty member. Communication studies at the tertiary level in both the polytechnic and the university attract very highly qualified and talented students. Students entering the Nanyang Technological University for communication have entry points second only to medicine. It is hard to imagine how such cream of the Singapore education crop will not change the local media scene over time.

What Will Freer Speech Depend On

The pace of the change will depend on several factors. It is beyond the scope of this chapter to dwell on them at length, so they are discussed briefly below.

Demands of an Increasingly Educated Population

Unlike the American Generation-X, the younger generation in Singapore is probably better described as the Competent Generation — the generation that wants to be seen, heard, and valued.[57] In contrast, the Singapore Government feels strongly and has acted strongly when it has felt that there were information leaks.[58] This notion of "control" appears to have inadvertent spillover effects in that Singapore may well be one of the few countries, if not the only country, where the statutes have a copyright. In other countries, copies may be made freely. There seems to be some recognition by the Government of the wants of the newer generation. Sometime in March 1999, several Acts were made freely available over the Internet.[59] And in May 1999, when the censors changed "shag" in the title of the James Bond spoof movie, *Austin Powers: The Spy Who Shagged Me*, the appeals board overruled them, saying that today's educated Singaporeans were well able to cope with sexual humour.[60]

Degree of Government Tolerance of Errors

This point may seem like a tautology, but the notion is that the Government should allow the press some room to make mistakes. Prime Minister Goh Chok Tong has said that the Singapore press should not adopt an adversarial role just because news organizations in other countries have done so. However, he added that "this doesn't mean that I want the Singapore press to be a government mouthpiece". He concluded that Singapore's media model is a "responsible press freedom".[61] But what is a responsible press? National Trades Union Congress Secretary-General and Minister Without Portfolio Lim Boon Heng was reported as saying that the media had not done enough to project the right image of the labour movement.[62] Logically, this would mean that the media should also project the right image of various government bodies. If it were then the media's task to project an image (presumably "right" would be defined by those bodies), how different would that be from being a government mouthpiece? To be fair, the same report quoted Minister Lim as saying, "Overall, I would say the media have reported us fairly. In some cases, they have taken the trouble to explain complicated issues to their readers in simple language. I appreciate their efforts." But there had also been instances where "serious errors" were not corrected by the media.[63]

More recently, the tabloid *New Paper* published a lead story quoting the Minister of Home Affairs being unhappy with the *Straits Times* over a report that "stood out with its prominent headline 'CJ raps police for 12-year lapse'". The Minister was quoted as saying: "Although the police were not the only party 'rapped' by the CJ, readers of headlines would have thought that it was the case".[64] The *Straits Times* reported the Minister as saying:

> The report sent an "unmistakable signal" that the newspaper was crusading on Soh's behalf by asking whether her basic rights had been violated by the police. ... It would seem to be an insidious report to mobilize public opinion and to conscribe the powers of the police. It is not the business of newspapers to do that...[65]

The Government believes that it should not be "challenged", especially by the media, because the Government's views are carefully considered, but journalists, as Senior Minister Lee Kuan Yew has said, "just go to the computer and type away. They can write another, and a different, story the following week".[66] The Senior Minister was talking about out-of-bounds markers that should not be crossed by the press. These markers, however, are not defined but appear after the fact — as in the case above regarding the police, where the press was said to have indulged in "crusading" journalism.[67] But even if these out-of-bounds markers are cast in stone, as long as newspapers are produced by human hands and human minds, there will always be errors. Who should correct these errors if the media refuse to do so? A press council is probably a good answer. It gives the average citizen recourse and it also lifts the heavy hand of government.

Sensitivity of Neighbours

A constraint that is recognized in the Singapore Constitution and that is unlikely to go away, has to do with the possible consequence of news reports on neighbouring countries. For example, the movie *The Year of Living Dangerously* was banned in deference to Indonesia.[68] News reports in Singapore call the smoke from the forest fires in Indonesia "haze",[69] while similar reports in journals from the West call them smog.[70] Even with a competitive media system, it is likely that the media would not feel themselves totally free to report on the neighbours. No editor wants to be blamed for offending Malaysia and being the person who caused the drinking-water taps to run dry.

Sensitivity of Populace (and Government) to Criticism

The issue of sensitivity to criticism also applies to the public. Libel suits in Singapore show that the brand of American journalism, in which public figures are fair game for even unfair accusations, is not permitted in Singapore. As one observer has pointed out, the Singapore system defends political reputations.[71] The rationale is that it is hard enough to motivate good and capable people to serve politically. Having a freewheeling press that is able to pin unfair charges with impunity not only wastes time in having to reply to ward off such attacks but also discourages capable people.

The fallout from this, however, is that there are also cases in which the public at large has had to apologize for apparently trivial remarks. In May 1999, a woman who sent a defamatory e-mail had to pay $50,000 in damages and legal costs, and she also made a public apology in the *Straits Times* and *Lianhe Zaobao* to the National Kidney Foundation (NKF).[72] The report said the e-mail went to forty-eight other persons, some of whom, according to the Foundation, may be "the subject of legal action". There are several oddities in the law as practised. First, in the case involving the NKF, the apology actually repeats the libel. It is frequently argued by lawyers that apologies never fully redress the hurt because some of the mud always stick. Well, if there was harm done by the libellous statement, it should certainly not be repeated to a million readers. It should be sufficient for an apology via the same medium used by the original libellous statement.

A precedent may have been set in 1996 in a case involving former Deputy Prime Minister Toh Chin Chye and one of the papers in the Singapore Press Holdings group, the *New Paper*. Despite a recall of 80 per cent of the copies in circulation and the fact that it caused no real harm to reputation (since no one seemed to have believed the report),[73] the company apologized on the front pages of all its papers. Second, as in the above case, the law currently uses an objective measure of harm; if the statement appears to cause harm and is indeed false, damages are due. The law should be changed to recognize actual, not imputed, harm. In the case involving Dr Toh Chin Chye, his reputation was intact. Even without damages, the black eye belonged to the *New Paper*. In the case of the NKF, it is hard to see the damage from e-mail. Third, the more sophisticated view surely is to note that winning a libel suit is not necessarily winning public opinion. Hence in the NKF case, anecdotal evidence suggests that the public sympathy was more with the female offender, who appeared to have written the e-mail while in a state of mental distress.

What is the Government's position? In a Parliamentary debate, MP Davinder Singh said:

> Singaporeans have had to sacrifice some of their individual rights for the larger interests of the community. For example, we do not make disparaging remarks about race, language, religion and culture. The result is stability. ... We do not defame without basis. As a consequence, reputations which are painstakingly built up are protected. ... The model that we seek to construct cannot ignore these core values.[74]

The position seems to be that protecting reputations is a core value. By and large, however, reputations are individual. It is possible to sue as a group under a class action, but such suits are rare. Further, relaxing some of the rules for libel would allow the media to have some leeway to make mistakes. As the press will always make the occasional mistake, it has been suggested that perhaps libel should be considered a form of malpractice.[75] In short, there are some community gains from *not* protecting reputations as strictly as is done now. Singapore is sailing against the wind here, because many countries around the world, in fact, take the opposite view — that individuals have to sacrifice their reputations for the greater interests of the community so that the possibility of wrongdoing may be investigated.

A final point to note on the issue of sensitivity to criticism is that the press should also be able to handle criticism of it. A necessary component of freedom of the press is the freedom to criticize the press. For example, the *Straits Times* has been said to be reluctant to correct errors.[76] A self-critical press, where one newspaper can criticize another and where one television or radio station can criticize the other, allows errors of excess to be corrected as well as divergent views to emerge. This self-critical press will take time to develop as the current structure alone militates against it.[77]

Economic Demands

Singapore's hopes to be a financial centre demands a freer flow of information, particularly in the business arena. This means that more foreign business journalists must be allowed in. This is already happening. Newspapers from far-flung places are basing their correspondents in Singapore, high cost notwithstanding, because of the excellent "hard infrastructure" in transport and communication. But these journalists cannot be expected to cover only business information or news about the region. Eventually, they will turn around to cover Singapore.

Impact of Censorship

Must Singapore really change? Many of the arguments for a more relaxed censorship regime are grounded in technology and business concerns. In the author's view, the arguments are not wholly satisfactory. Singapore's censorship rules *are* already shaped with those concerns in mind — materials touching on technology and business are lightly censored, if at all. But there are no qualms about censoring other areas, such as art. In the author's view, the major objection of censorship is that it is a bundled package — several matters spring out from it. Censorship strives for consistency of norms across media. Its impact, therefore, cannot be isolated. And because the ultimate goal of censorship is to turn both producers and audience into self-censors, it means self-censorship in all areas.

Censorship, therefore, creates blind spots in the mind.[78] The author has seen it even in academics. One professor in Singapore expressed amazement at seeing a first-year political science examination question asking why the political opposition member Dr Chee Soon Juan had chosen to go to jail. He said, "You ask such questions?". Staksrud wrote that Singapore scholars sometimes gave answers that were out of context. When one was asked if the lack of media freedom bothered him or the average Singaporean, the scholar chose to talk about housing policy.[79] Staksrud[80] and Paul[81] have found that Singaporeans were afraid of being quoted. Staksrud surmised that it was out of the fear of sanctions for speaking too much or for getting it wrong compared with the official version.

The media's credibility has also been found wanting in those areas most controlled by the Government: one survey discovered that the public found the press generally credible except when it covered domestic politics and government affairs.[82]

It is understandable if throughout the various chapters in this book there is a call for a change of "mindset". A mind that is set is difficult, if not impossible, to change. More importantly, mindsets are by-products, not products. In other words, it is likely to be more fruitful to change the conditions leading to the mindset than even attempting to change the mindset itself. In the case of censorship, it is a by-product of the legacy of control.

Conclusion

There is a price that the Singapore Government pays for the current structure of the media. Conceptually, the Government exerts great control over the press.

In practice, however, as any local journalist can attest, there is no direct daily government intervention. The fact that ministers have to "rap" the press now and then indicates as much. The "raps", however, rein in the press and, therefore, are an indirect means of control. Not surprisingly, headlines, news reports, and even the layout of articles are treated as official positions.

As related earlier, Prime Minister Goh Chok Tong has said that he does not want the media to be a government mouthpiece.[83] According to Prime Minister Goh, when Mr S. R. Nathan (currently the President of Singapore) was invited in 1982 to be the executive chairman of the newspaper, then Prime Minister Lee Kuan Yew told him that the *Straits Times* was like a china bowl. "You break it, I can piece it together, but it will never be the same." Mr Lee added: "Try not to".[84]

Still, as long as the structure is in place for government control, even if there is no direct intervention, this perception of the media being the official mouthpiece will persist. Bill Gates, head of Microsoft Corporation, has been quoted as saying that he found Singapore leaders "surprisingly enlightened" about regulating the Internet.[85] Mr Gates need not have been so surprised; Singapore ranks flatteringly high on a number of indicators by international bodies and there are few, if any, unenlightened number ones.

But, for Singapore to continue to develop, the rules regarding media must be relaxed. The relaxation, however, should be gradual to avoid a legal vacuum that triggers a chain reaction leading to a backlash. The "R" movie case in Singapore is instructive. Because the rules regarding taste have been shaped by the Government and not by industry, when "R" movies were allowed, taste went out the window. In the West, many of the rules regarding content, such as taste, are set by industry. As a result, the media are sensitized. For example, when the Ken Starr report on the Monica Lewinsky and Bill Clinton case was published in the United States, a number of the newspapers ran the report with a warning that the report was graphic. In Singapore, the *Straits Times* ran the report without any such warning. There was no indication of the sensitivity of the editors.

The spirit of the times is that of liberalization. *Time* magazine wrote a piece about "funky" Singapore.[86] Even the report of a censorship review has been taken as a positive development[87] when, in fact, a review is conducted every ten years.[88] In short, it would appear that any move by the Government to look into the area is viewed favourably as a relaxation of some sort. Brigadier-General George Yeo, the immediate past Minister for Information and the Arts, warned of possible disappointments. So the Government is aware that it has to manage those expectations.[89]

Singapore's move towards greater media freedom will happen, but it is unlikely to follow the Western, particularly the U.S., model. The principle of censoring pornography, religious, and political materials is likely to continue, Internet notwithstanding. But the standards by which these materials are censored will change.

Bill Gates is reported to have observed that Singapore wants to have its cake and eat it too.[90] But that is what the debate over free speech and free expression is all about — not compromising or surrendering but having everything one wants: being able to say anything one wishes and yet, somehow, not bringing down the roof. It is not censorship that will make Singapore great in the new economy — that will allow it to "punch above its weight" — but, rather, the approach of trying to have its cake and eat it too, as the country wrestles with the issue.[91]

Notes

1. Ang Peng Hwa and Yeo Tiong Min, *Mass Media Laws and Regulations in Singapore* (Singapore: AMIC, 1998).
2. Tan Y. S. and Soh Y.P., *The Development of Singapore's Modern Media Industry* (Singapore: Times Academic Press, 1994), p. 2.
3. Ibid., p. 36.
4. Telephone interview with Kah Chong Chin, Publisher, *Pananews*, on 15 October 1999.
5. Ang Peng Hwa and Berlinda Nadarajan, "Censorship and the Internet: A Singapore Perspective", *Communications of the* ACM 39, No. 6 (June 1996): 72–78.
6. Ho K. T., "S'pore, M'sia Can Team Up To Boost Region's Influence", *Business Times*, 18 January 1995. p. 3.
7. C. M. Turnbull, who was hired by the *Straits Times* to write its history on its 150th anniversary, wrote that, in its reports on the electioneering, the paper "left no doubts about a PAP victory". *Dateline Singapore: 150 Years of The Straits Times* (Singapore: Singapore Press Holdings, 1995), p. 215.
8. Ibid., p. 217, citing *Singapore Standard*, 20 May 1959.
9. Tan and Soh, *Singapore's Modern Media Industry*, pp. 5–6.
10. To remove some uncertainty, the Singapore Government said that it would amend the law to limit fund managers to 3 per cent as well. In Teh Hooi Ling, "Newspaper stake limit law to be amended by Q1: No entity to be allowed to hold more than 3 per cent of voting shares", *Business Times*, 22 October 1999.
11. G. Pierre Goad, "Singapore Imposes Circulation Curbs on the Economist", *The Wall Street Journal*, 3 August 1993, p. A11.
12. In the ranking, countries scoring 0 to 30 are regarded as having a free press; 31 to 60, a partly-free press; 61 to 100 a not-free press. In L. R. Sussman, *Press Freedom 1999: News of the Century* (New York: The Freedom House, 1999).

13. Eddie Kuo and Ang Peng Hwa, "Singapore", in *The Media in Asia*, edited by Shelton Gunaratne (New Delhi: Sage, forthcoming).
14. Teo Pau Lin, "SIMple Change of Name for Media Group", *Straits Times*, 16 June 1999. L3.
15. Kuo and Ang, "Singapore".
16. "Liberalisation of Media Industry", *Singapore Bulletin* 28, no. 7/8 (2000), Ministry of Information and the Arts. <http://www.sg/flavour/092000/bb-arts.html>.
17. *Project Eyeball* folded ten months later, a victim of the slowing economy, high cover price (80 cents vs 60 cents for the visibly thicker *Straits Times*) and weak distribution ("Media war and pricing hurt Eyeball", *Straits Times*, 3 July 2001).
18. *Singapore Bulletin* 2000, *op. cit.*
19. Ibid.
20. Ibid
21. Kuo and Ang, "Singapore".
22. Tammy Tan, "TAS Lifts Cap on Foreign Equity for Net Providers", *Straits Times*, 14 September 1999, p. 55.
23. This section draws heavily on Ang and Nadarajan, "Censorship and the Internet".
24. A popular textbook covering this area is *Milestones in Mass Communication Research*, by Shearon Lowery and Melvin De Fleur (New York: Longman, 1995).
25. "BG Yeo Explains Ban on Party Political Films", *Straits Times*, 28 February 1998.
26. This notion of a limited media effect is hard to kill. In a paper, Edwin Tan (1996), intending to show the powerful effects of the movies, said *Sleepless in Seattle* "launched a national craving for the hitherto humble and relatively unknown Italian dessert *tiramisu*". Even if true, from a scientific point of view, not all movies with desserts launch similar cravings for those desserts. So, if the effect of showing a dessert in *Sleepless* was powerful, it was limited to that movie.
27. Eddie C.Y. Kuo, Duncan Holaday, and Eugenia Peck, *Mirror on the Wall: Media in a Singapore Election* (Singapore: AMIC, 1993).
28. See, for example, Antonio C. Campo, "Piece of Cake: Boycott Singapore", *Filipino Reporter*, 30 March 1995. p.18.
29. Albert C. Gunther and Ang Peng Hwa, "Public Perceptions of Television Influence and Opinions About Censorship in Singapore", *International Journal of Public Opinion Research* 18, No. 3 (1996): 248–65.
30. "Fullest Access to News Vital for Success", *Straits Times*, 2 March 1999, p. 24.
31. Mark Hukill, "Structures of television in Singapore", in *Contemporary Television: Eastern Perspectives*, edited by D. French and M. Richards (New Delhi: Sage, 1996).
32. Singapore Broadcasting Authority website: <http://www.sba.gov.sg/>. Accessed 15 October 1999.
33. This is mirrored by a 1999 Freedom Forum study, which found that "Americans feel the more accessible the medium is, the less permissible sexually explicit content should be". The following shows the various media represented in the survey and the percentages of those who strongly or mildly agreed they should be able to carry sexually explicit material:

- Video stores: 63 per cent
- Premium cable: 59 per cent
- Magazines: 45 per cent
- Basic cable: 26 per cent
- Internet: 24 per cent

Source: Paul McMasters, "Analysis" in State of the First Amendment: A survey of public attitudes, First Amendment Center, Nashville, Tennessee, Vanderbilt University, <http://www.freedomforum.org/first/sofa/1999/analysis.asp>. (Accessed 21 October 1999.)

34. P. Meinert, "Despite censorship, international media giants set up in Singapore", *Deutsche Presse Agentur*, 4 October 1995.
35. Ang and Nadarajan, "Censorship and the Internet".
36. The U.S. First Amendment distinguishes between indecent "communication," which is tolerated, and obscene communication, which is not protected under the Constitution.
37. At the time of writing, Singapore was not a signatory to the Convention.
38. The last independent paper, the *Tamil Murasu*, was bought out by Singapore Press Holdings in 1995. (M. Nirmala, "Singapore Press Holdings buys Tamil Murasu for $500,000", *Straits Times*, 3 November 1995.)
39. Singapore Press Holdings, *Annual Report*, various years.
40. Cherian George, "SBC Radio: Sounds Successful", *Straits Times*, 17 October 1992, p. 32, and D. Birch, "Media Practices: The Singapore Press", in *Singapore Media: Communication Strategies & Practices* (Melbourne: Longman Cheshire, 1993), p.30.
41. Singapore readers would be able to identify this as yet another manifestation of the *kiasu* syndrome. Literally translated from the Hokkien dialect, the fear of losing out.
42. George, "SBC Radio: Sounds Successful", p. 32.
43. Reminiscent of this, the newspaper monopoly Singapore Press Holdings started planning in earnest for two papers after the Swedish Modern Times group began its plans for a paper to be distributed through the subway stations. In Jann Perng Chee, "SPH to launch two new papers", *Straits Times*, 7 October 1999, p. 2.
44. Garry Rodan, "The Internet and Political Control in Singapore", *Political Science Quarterly* 113 (Spring 1998): 63–64.
45. E-mail correspondence from Garry Rodan, on 25 October 1999.
46. In a meeting during a conference at Munich (1999), Elizabeth Staksrud said the thesis was for something "between a bachelor's and a master's degree". Staksrud, *Ideology of Survival: Freedom of Expression, Internet Regulation and Political Legitimization in Singapore* (Norway: University of Oslo, 1999), p. 5.
47. Haymalatha Suppiah, "The Intelligent(Ce) Island: Surveillance and Social Control in Singapore" (Masters thesis, Queen's University At Kingston, Canada, 1996).
48. Stephen Yeo and Arun Mahizhnan , "Developing an Intelligent Island: Dilemmas of Censorship", in *Singapore: Re-Engineering Success*, edited by Arun Mahizhnan and Lee Tsao Yuan (Singapore: Institute of Policy Studies and Oxford University Press, 1998), pp.138–49.

49. Ang Peng Hwa, "How Countries are Regulating Internet Content", paper presented at the Internet Society Annual Conference, Kuala Lumpur, Malaysia. June 1997. Available at <http://www.isoc.org/isoc/whatis/conferences/inet/97/proceedings/B1/B1 3.HTM> (accessed 15 October 1999).
50. Ibid.
51. Courtney Macavinta, "FBI Net Porn Stings Contested", available at: <http://news.cnet.com/news/0-1005200-122241.html> (accessed 18 October 1999).
52. David McGuire, "Combating Online Child Porn." *Newsbytes*. 2 October 1999, available at: <http://www.currents.net/newstoday/99/10/02/news5.html> (accessed 18 October 1999).
53. <http://www.stop-childpornog.at/conc.asp> (accessed 18 October 1999).
54. It should be noted that it is getting more difficult to use the public proxy servers. When it became known to some that this author was gathering all the addresses of the public proxy servers for purposes of research, an e-mail arrived saying in essence that the addresses should not be made widely available. Indeed, recently some of these public proxy servers have suffered abuse and increasingly they require registration by users. Another way of looking at this is that the Net is seeing more rules and, arguably, less freedom.
55. In essence, the media regulate their conduct based on rules. Without rules, they do not feel the need to restrain themselves. An alternative to government rules is to use industry codes of conduct, where media police themselves. In such instances, the industry becomes more aware of the need for ethical behaviour, which increases the credibility of the medium.
56. On occasion, the newspaper monopoly creates awkward situations. The author once wrote a piece arguing why the Official Secrets Act should not be used in prosecuting the *Business Times* journalist. The piece was not run. Regarding another case involving the alleged libel of former Deputy Prime Minister Toh Chin Chye by the *New Paper*, this author wrote a piece explaining why the actions of the Singapore Press Holdings group (a recall of the paper, a public apology on *all* its papers, and an undisclosed settlement) was overkill. The piece was not run because, so it was explained, it would make the paper appear less than contrite. (The *Straits Times* offered to run the article as a letter to the editor. Not wanting to set a precedent — where commentaries are run under the letters page, the author declined. This article is available at <http://www.medialaw.com.sg/tohchinchye.htm>.)
57. Credit goes to John Ryan, Assistant General Counsel of America Online, Inc., for the characterization made during his presentation at the International Conference on Combating Child Pornography on the Internet, Vienna, October 1999.
58. Ian Stewart, "PM defends raid on paper in Singapore", *South China Morning Post*, 9 September 1992, p. 14.
59. <http://www.lawnet.com.sg/freeaccess/>.
60. "On the loose in Singapore", *The Economist* (U.S. Edition), 29 May 1999, p. 7.

61. "Singapore's Media Model", *Straits Times*, 12 November 1995, p. 6.
62. "NTUC Chief's Examples of When Media Fell Short", *Straits Times*, 3 March 1998, p. 35.
63. Ibid.
64. "Minister Says: These Reports are Damaging", *New Paper*, 22 October 1999.
65. "Kan Seng Singles out ST for Criticism", *Straits Times*, 23 October 1999.
66. Irene Ng and Lydia Lim, "SM: Danger In Challenging System", *Straits Times*, 9 September 1999, p.2.
67. Ibid.
68. Parvathi Nayar, "Still Relevant after 15 Years", *Business Times*, 23 April 1999, p. EL4.
69. Dominic Nathan, "Haze Talks with Owners of Plantations Shelved", *Straits Times*, 28 September 1999, p. 37.
70. "Pollution. An Asian pea-souper", *The Economist* (U.S. Edition), 27 September 1997, p.7; Asia's Choking Haze", *Maclean's*, 6 October 1997, p. 59.
71. Koh Buck Song, "Tang Case Shows System Upholds Political Reputations", *Straits Times*, 11 May 1997.
72. Samantha Santa Maria, "NKF Acts against E-Defamation", *Straits Times*, 5 May 1999, p. 3.
73. The report alleged a hit-and-run case. The common reaction, which the reporters and editors appeared to have overlooked, was: "What's a 70-year-old man doing, driving a goods van at 2 a.m.?"
74. Quoted in "Davinder Opens Debate with Posers", *Straits Times*, 12 October 1999, p. 30.
75. Todd Simon, "Libel as Malpractice: News Media Ethics and the Standard of Care", *Fordham Law Review* 449 (1984): 53.
76. "NTUC Chief's Examples", 3 March 1998.
77. At the time of going to press, the dominant media companies were allowed to cross-own media. So Media Corporation of Singapore was allowed to run a newspaper and Singapore Press Holdings to run a television station.
78. By definition, the author has to declare that he is not exempt either. In fact, he may be picking up sawdust from the eyes of others while missing the entire log in his own eye.
79. Elizabeth Staksrud, *Ideology of Survival: Freedom of Expression, Internet Regulation and Political Legitimization in Singapore* (Norway: University of Oslo, 1999), p.17.
80. Ibid., p. 20.
81. Eric C. Paul, "Prospects of Liberalization in Singapore", *Journal of Contemporary Asia* 23, No. 3 (1993): 296.
82. Xiaoming Hao, "The Press and Public Trust: The Case of Singapore", *Asian Journal of Communication* (1996): 111–23.
83. Warren Fernandez, "Develop Our Own Brand of Journalism — Call by PM", *Straits Times*, 16 July 1995.

84. "How the Press Can Best Serve Singapore — Be Fair, Be Truthful, Be Part of a Virtuous Cycle: Develop Our Own Brand of Journalism — Call by PM", *Straits Times*, 16 July 1995, p.4.
85. Chua Mui Hoong, "Internet Data Cannot be Filtered Totally: Bill Gates", *Straits Times*, 7 February 1996.
86. Terry McCarthy and Eric Ellis, "Singapore Lightens up", *Time* (Asian edition), 19 July 1999.
87. Michelle Levander, "Singapore to Relax Censorship Laws as it Seeks to Expand Internet Access", *Wall Street Journal*, 1 September 1999, p. A18.
88. Ang and Nadarajan, "Censorship and the Internet.
89. Catherine Ong, "BG Yeo Uneasy with S'pore's Funky Image: He Urges the Media not to Exaggerate Changes, Risk Disappointment", *Business Times*, 21 October 1999.
90. Chua Mui Hoong, "Internet Data Cannot be Filtered Totally".
91. Ng Wei Joo and Eliza Teoh, "Singapore 'Can Keep Punching Above Its Weight'", *Straits Times*, 16 January 1997.

11

CONCLUSION

Derek da Cunha

The world of the new millennium is a very different place from that which Singapore found itself in during its first three decades as an independent nation-state. Singapore's socioeconomic development made impressive gains during the 1970s, 1980s, and 1990s. A confluence of factors were responsible for that salubrious state of affairs. Internal stability, engendered by the dominance of a single political party with generally authoritarian ways, ensured a peaceful and harmonious domestic socio-political environment. Externally, the regional environment was also stable. This was due, in the first instance, to the to the stand-off between the superpowers — the United States and the Soviet Union — during the Cold War years, which paradoxically provided some semblance of constancy and stability in the Southeast Asian geopolitical construct. Subsequently, in the wake of the end of the Cold War, the steady eradication of the ideological divide in Southeast Asia was to see the expansion of the Association of Southeast Asian Nations (ASEAN) to encompass eventually the whole of Southeast Asia. Singapore had positioned itself well during those two phases.

Smallness in size has been an advantage to Singapore, simply because the city-state has been able to react far quicker to international developments than could other larger countries. The lengthy tenure in power of the People's Action Party (PAP) also meant that while the country could quickly adapt itself to any rapidly evolving geopolitical or geoeconomic situation, it still had a long-range vision of itself. Long-term plans and programmes could be formulated without any fear of a change in government, which could otherwise derail such plans and programmes. Additionally, the PAP Government's traits of consistency, predictability, and relative incorruptibility have been the sorts of credentials that have made Singapore a highly attractive location for foreign direct investment. This has been particularly apparent in contrast to much of the rest of Southeast Asia, where governments have been known to be far less consistent, predictable, and incorruptible. The Asian economic crisis of 1997–98 showed the extent to which Singapore was different from other affected countries in Southeast Asia. This was largely seen in the generally calm and considered way the Singapore Government reacted to the crisis — an approach which resulted in Singapore coming out of the crisis far better than other regional states.

A world where globalization is the watchword of the times has also seen Singapore attempt to embrace this concept wholeheartedly. This has been manifested not merely in Singapore's drive to be a financial centre of not just regional, but international standing, but also in the extent to which information technology has been adopted to a highly remarkable degree to turn the country into an "intelligent island". To that extent, the pursuit of a knowledge-based economy (KBE) is viewed by the Government as one way to ensure Singapore's economic survival in an increasingly competitive global environment. Another aspect of globalization that can be observed in concrete terms was the Singapore Government's decision in the late 1990s to throw the country's doors wide open to large numbers of foreign talent. Singapore has always been receptive to foreign talent. However, in the past this was largely restricted to foreigners at managerial or senior levels who earned lavish expatriate salaries. Now, foreigners with the requisite skills are being recruited at all levels and not just from the top tier, and are hired on local salary packages. The Government has periodically produced statistics to show the extent to which foreign talent has contributed to the development of the city-state. It can be argued that foreign talent is now one of the pillars of the Singapore economy.

Economic development has inevitably produced a people who are increasingly more educated, sophisticated, and who demand greater choices for themselves. This will be one of the major challenges the Government will have to contend with in the years ahead. But the Government's ability to meet such a challenge is generally not in doubt, judging by its enviable track record of rising to a variety of challenges thrown up over the years. Singapore's tranquility and relative prosperity in a region where people of neighbouring countries have experienced strife and hardship, make Singaporeans generally satisfied with their lot, even though many might resent the PAP Government's overbearing nature and paternalism.

Some foreign observers have commented that since the late 1990s, the Singapore Government has actually been less austere on the political front. That is, the Government has provided more space for Singaporeans to express dissenting views and to portray different realities of life in the city-state from that articulated by the authorities. Examples of such "opening up" include the Government's tolerance of civil society activists organizing themselves, almost as pressure groups, so as to attempt to influence policy-makers, albeit indirectly. Then there was the establishment in August 2000 of a "free-speech" venue, Speakers' Corner, to allow citizens to say their piece (although restrictions, such as not touching on religious, racial, and linguistic sensitivities, and the laws of defamation, still apply). The arts community has also been provided with greater space to stage plays and other forms of the performing arts that are either politically satirical in content or which reflect alternative lifestyles that would otherwise not sit well in Singapore's generally conservative society. These aspects of opening up have been applauded by some observers who give the Government credit for its apparently new-found and enlightened tolerance. However, a more in-depth examination would reveal that the supposed opening up is in fact so stage-managed that it is not very meaningful. Indeed, it can be argued that the Government has in fact clamped down far more politically than it has actually opened up since the late 1990s, but for various reasons — which will be dealt with below — this has not always been noticed even by what would normally be astute observers.

The first point to appreciate about aspects of the apparent political opening up in Singapore is that it came just after the 1997 general election. That election saw the PAP Government adopt generally heavy-handed tactics to defeat the challenge mounted by the political opposition, with the result that the already paltry opposition parliamentary presence was reduced, from four to just two members (this did not include an opposition Non-Constituency Member of Parliament, a position given to the opposition by the "good grace" of the Government). The result of the 1997 general election — in terms of the division of parliamentary seats — belied the extent of the actual opposition to PAP rule on the ground. The fact of the matter is that just slightly over a third of the popular vote in contested constituencies went to the opposition. Therefore, at the grassroots level there was little doubt that there existed a significant reservoir of anti-PAP sentiment.

Historically, the PAP Government has generally adopted the tactic that if something negative is not visibly manifested then it can usually be ignored, and the Government can pretend that such negativity does not exist. This might well be explained in terms of the apt cliché, "out of sight, out of mind". In that regard, the key determinant of democracy in Singapore is the number of parliamentary seats the PAP secures relative to the rest of the combined opposition. With the PAP's parliamentary presence so overwhelming and, inversely, the political opposition hardly in evidence, the Government can assume, and indeed has assumed, a stance that gives the impression that there is similarly overwhelming support for its rule at the popular level. To that extent, the PAP Government's dominance, particularly after the 1997 general election, has meant that it has been relatively secure. The Government has, therefore, been willing to allow some room for dissent. But the point is that such dissent, and whatever other aspects of apparent opening up there has been, have occurred purely on the Government's terms. The Government has defined the parameters of any slackening of the leash on which it has kept Singaporeans politically tethered. This reflects the fact that while Singaporeans are economically empowered, they largely lack political empowerment, with the key exception of going to the polling booth every four or five years to exercise their democratic rights. But even that procedural aspect of democracy has begun to lose significance, as will be elaborated below.

The Government has used its overwhelming parliamentary majority to make changes to the Constitution that modify the electoral structure in such a way that is to its advantage, entrenching the ruling party even further in the body politic. The modifications largely revolve around Group Representation Constituencies (GRCs), first introduced at the 1988 general election ostensibly to ensure adequate ethnic minority representation in Parliament. Contests in GRCs must involve a group of candidates, with at least one being an ethnic minority. In 1988, each GRC comprised three members, and not all constituencies were converted to GRCs as a significant number of single-member constituencies (40) were retained. In the 1991 general election, the GRCs were enlarged in size to four team members each and the number of single-member constitiencies were reduced by half (to 20).

At the 1997 general election, the nature of GRCs was modified again. This time they did not have a fixed size, but rather ranged from four-member GRCs to six-member GRCs. The net effect was a further enlargement of GRCs and consequently another reduction in the number of single-member constituencies; reduced to just nine. Not satisfied with the extent to which the electoral system was so heavily skewed in its favour, just before the 2001 general election, the PAP Government modified the nature of the GRCs yet again. This time it scrapped the four-member GRCs. The smallest size GRC would now comprise five team members.

GRCs and their increased size assist the ruling party in several ways. One is the fact that opposition parties find it difficult to put up a full slate of candidates, including a suitable ethnic minority candidate, to contest such enlarged electoral divisions. (Under the law, most — that is, 9 out of 15 — GRCs must have at least one Malay candidate each to broadly reflect the demographic profile of the constituency, while in the other GRCs the requirement is for an Indian or Eurasian candidate.) Because it is largely accepted that the PAP will win the overall popular vote nation-wide, the larger the size of a GRC, the more it begins to reflect the size of that vote. That is to say, GRCs do not generally allow for localized factors to come into play during elections. This is a reason why opposition parties have felt that it is only in single-member constituencies that they stand any chance against the ruling party. And that appears to be the reason why the PAP Government has progressively reduced the number of single-member wards. In single-member constituencies, a voter has a sense of empowerment, knowing that his/her vote does count. However, a voter in a GRC does not have that same sense of empowerment, since the reality is that his/her vote is just one out of maybe over 100,000. Thus, it is arguable that Singaporeans may have felt more politically empowered in the 1980s and early 1990s than they do today.

The modification of the electoral boundaries, including GRCs, and the lack of lead time given between that modification and the calling of the 3 November 2001 general election unsurprisingly led to the PAP overwhelming the opposition parties, which had put up candidates to contest in only 29 of 84 parliamentary seats. Other factors, such as fears related to prospects of a prolonged economic recession (particularly in the wake of the 11 September 2001 terrorist attacks in the United States) and the need for national unity in such a difficult time, also assisted the PAP in the 2001 general election, where its overall vote surged by 10 percentage points to 75 per cent from the level attained in 1997. Even the two sitting opposition Members of Parliament — although retaining their seats — saw their vote decrease.

Publicly, PAP leaders expressed deep satisfaction that the electorate had given the ruling party a ringing endorsement at the 2001 general election. Few objective analysts, however, would ascribe much significance to the results of that election. They would find it difficult to argue that it was a fair contest. It may have been a free election, but the entire electoral process was stacked against the opposition. If there was an event which highlighted graphically just how naïve those who felt that there had been a liberalization of the political atmosphere in Singapore since 1997, then it was the process leading up to, and culmination of, the 2001 general election.

Paradoxically, the PAP can claim, and justifiably so, that the 2001 election met all the procedural aspects of democracy, and that if the election was unfair, as the opposition had claimed, why then did the opposition contest the election? This indeed is the paradox: by contesting the 2001 general election, the opposition parties merely gave respectability, credibility, and legitimacy to the entire electoral process. All that would have been withheld had the opposition parties refused to play by the rules established by the PAP through refraining from contesting in the GRCs, and just restricting themselves to the nine single-member constituencies. It can, therefore, be said that the opposition had inadvertently endorsed the 2001 electoral process, giving the PAP moral authority to govern Singapore in whatever way it deems fit. This is the reality, and it is a reason why the PAP can feel secure, and can easily brush aside criticism — whether from foreign or domestic sources — of how politics is played out in the city-state.

Politics is, therefore, not going to be a challenge for Singapore and its ruling party in the years ahead. Keeping Singapore economically competitive, however, is. With Singapore's economy now at a mature stage, attempting to chalk up even moderate rates of economic growth will be a key challenge. That challenge is compounded by the fact that the Southeast Asian regional locale will continue to witness political volatility that would impact adversely on Singapore's economic prospects, not least because a significant number of foreign investors would be disinclined to channel investment funds into a region with a high political risk variable. The lure of the China market, particularly after that country's accession to the World Trade Organization (WTO) in late 2001, will also impact negatively on Singapore and the rest of Southeast Asia over the medium term, since the flow of foreign direct investment (FDI) into China is expected to accelerate markedly, and *ipso facto* divert some part of FDI flows away from Southeast Asia. The geoeconomic terrain will, therefore, be more difficult for Singapore to navigate.

Equally, in security terms, Singapore will also find new challenges in the years ahead. The Southeast Asian geopolitical environment is less predictable and stable than it was during the 1990s. The region's largest state, Indonesia, is expected to continue to be afflicted by the twin problems of secessionist sentiment in some parts of its sprawling archipelago and by political in-fighting in Jakarta. If these developments take a turn for the worse, just by sheer geographical proximity Singapore would be affected negatively, not least by the possibility of refugee outflows from Indonesia. More generally, the 11 September 2001 terrorist attacks in the United States has also highlighted the fact that Singapore is vulnerable to similar attacks. The attacks underscore the fact that security will now be defined in a way that takes on new parameters and dimensions, and these might not be so easy to grapple with. The 11 September attacks would have had a salutary effect on the political leadership in Singapore. That leadership together with the people of Singapore may have convinced themselves that the combination of great economic success and being conventionally armed to the teeth provide for security. But in the wake of the attacks in the United States they would have been jolted to a new reality. Economic well-being and robust conventional military forces provide for security only up to a point. And those aspects work well when one is dealing with governments which operate rationally. Not all governments are rational state actors. And non-governmental groups or organizations might operate even less rationally. At the same time, while most governments themselves might be rational, they are held hostage to the irrationality of their civilian populations.

Where the notion of security needs to be redefined, and which has significant implications for Singapore, is in terms of giving greater weight to diplomacy in the service of shaping regional and global perceptions of a nation-state, that is, its image in the eyes of the rest of the world. Diplomacy and national image — in enhancing security — needs to be front and centre, it cannot be considered just a subsidiary or adjunct to other things, such as economic strength and military power, which for long have underpinned Singapore's security. And if the past is any guide, Singapore would have to make renewed efforts in improving its diplomacy — and by that fact, its image — in Southeast Asia, if its sense of security is to be shored up. That will be a challenge for Singapore. But it is a challenge well within Singapore's ability as it navigates a future that provides both the promise of better things to come and the surprise of unexpected developments which will test the resolve and mettle of both the government and people of this unique city-state in Southeast Asia.

INDEX